# The Nature of Prosocial Development

Interdisciplinary Theories and Strategies

# DEVELOPMENTAL PSYCHOLOGY SERIES

SERIES EDITOR
Harry Beilin

Developmental Psychology Program
City University of New York Graduate School
New York, New York

*In Preparation*

DAVID MAGNUSSON AND VERNON L. ALLEN. (Editors). *Human Development: An Interactional Perspective*

EUGENE S. GOLLIN. (Editor). *Malformations of Development: Biological and Psychological Sources and Consequences*

ALLEN W. GOTTFRIED. (Editor). *Home Environment and Early Cognitive Development: Longitudinal Research*

*Published*

DIANE L. BRIDGEMAN. (Editor). *The Nature of Prosocial Development: Interdisciplinary Theories and Strategies*

ROBERT L. LEAHY. (Editor). *The Child's Construction of Social Inequality*

RICHARD LESH and MARSHA LANDAU. (Editors). *Acquisition of Mathematics Concepts and Processes*

MARSHA B. LISS. (Editor). *Social and Cognitive Skills: Sex Roles and Children's Play*

DAVID F. LANCY. *Cross-Cultural Studies in Cognition and Mathematics*

HERBERT P. GINSBURG. (Editor). *The Development of Mathematical Thinking*

MICHAEL POTEGAL. (Editor). *Spatial Abilities: Development and Physiological Foundations*

NANCY EISENBERG. (Editor). *The Development of Prosocial Behavior*

WILLIAM J. FRIEDMAN. (Editor). *The Developmental Psychology of Time*

SIDNEY STRAUSS. (Editor). *U-Shaped Behavioral Growth*

*The list of titles in this series continues on the last page of this volume.*

# The Nature of
# Prosocial Development

## Interdisciplinary Theories and Strategies

EDITED BY

## Diane L. Bridgeman

*Psychology Board of Studies*
*University of California, Santa Cruz*
*Santa Cruz, California*

**ACADEMIC PRESS**  **1983**

*A Subsidiary of Harcourt Brace Jovanovich, Publishers*

New York     London
Paris   San Diego   San Francisco   São Paulo   Sydney   Tokyo   Toronto

ACADEMIC PRESS, INC.
111 Fifth Avenue, New York, New York 10003


*United Kingdom Edition published by*
ACADEMIC PRESS, INC. (LONDON) LTD.
24/28 Oval Road, London NW1 7DX


Library of Congress Cataloging in Publication Data
Main entry under title:

The Nature of prosocial development.

   (Developmental psychology series)
   Includes bibliographical references and index.
   1. Social psychology--Addresses, essays, lectures.
2. Human behavior--Addresses, essays, lectures.
3. Altruism--Addresses, essays, lectures. 4. Life
cycle, Human--Addresses, essays, lectures. I. Bridgeman, Diane. II. Series.
HM251.N354   1983      302           83-7065
ISBN 0-12-133980-7


PRINTED IN THE UNITED STATES OF AMERICA

83 84 85 86    9 8 7 6 5 4 3 2 1

To Natalie and Tess
and especially to Bruce

# Contents

## Introduction

PAUL MUSSEN

chapter **1**

## The Two Distinct Routes beyond Kin Selection to Ultrasociality: Implications for the Humanities and Social Sciences *11*

DONALD T. CAMPBELL

chapter **2**

# The Evolution of Cooperation                                                  43

**ROBERT TRIVERS**

# Commentary and Critique:
# Sociobiological Approaches to Prosocial Development                            61

**DENNIS KREBS**

part **II**

# PSYCHOLOGICAL AND PHILOSOPHICAL APPROACHES
# TO PROSOCIAL DEVELOPMENT

chapter **3**

# The Early Appearance of Some Valued Social Behaviors                          73

**DALE F. HAY and HARRIET L. RHEINGOLD**

chapter **8**

# Altruism and Moral Development                                                  *185*

**BILL PUKA**

# Commentary and Critique: Psychological and Philosophical Approaches to Prosocial Development    *205*

**DENNIS KREBS**

part **III**

# CROSS-CULTURAL APPROACHES TO PROSOCIAL DEVELOPMENT

chapter **9**

# The Genesis of Prosocial Behavior                                              *221*

**BEATRICE BLYTH WHITING**

# Commentary and Critique:
# Applied Approaches to Prosocial Development                               *341*

**DENNIS KREBS**


# Afterword                                                                 *347*

**DENNIS KREBS**


*Subject Index*                                                             *351*

# Contributors

*Numbers in parentheses indicate the pages on which the authors' contributions begin.*

JANE M. BLACKWELL (113), Department of Psychology, Washington State University, Pullman, Washington 99163

DIANE L. BRIDGEMAN (95, 163), Psychology Board of Studies, University of California, Santa Cruz, Santa Cruz, California 95064

DYKE BROWN (273), Wm. and Flora Hewlett Foundation, 525 Middlefield Road, Menlo Park, California 94025

DONALD T. CAMPBELL (11), Department of Social Relations, Lehigh University, Bethlehem, Pennsylvania 18015

NANCY B. GRAVES (243), Anthropology Board of Studies, University of California, Santa Cruz, Santa Cruz, California 95064

THEODORE D. GRAVES (243), Anthropology Board of Studies, University of California, Santa Cruz, Santa Cruz, California 95064

DALE F. HAY (73), Department of Psychology, State University of New York at Stony Brook, Stony Brook, New York 11794

DENNIS KREBS (61, 205, 265, 341, 347), Department of Psychology, Simon Fraser University, Burnaby, British Columbia, Canada V5A 1S6

MARY DRIVER LEINBACH (113), Department of Psychology, University of Oregon, Eugene, Oregon 97403

PAUL MUSSEN (1), Department of Psychology and Institute of Human Development, University of California, Berkeley, Berkeley, California 94720

**BILL PUKA** (185), Department of Philosophy, Rensselaer Polytechnic Institute, Troy, New York 12101

**HARRIET L. RHEINGOLD** (73), Department of Psychology, University of North Carolina at Chapel Hill, Chapel Hill, North Carolina 27514

**AMY E. SIBULKIN** (139), Department of Psychology, Carnegie-Mellon University, Pittsburgh, Pennsylvania 15213

**JUDITH G. SMETANA** (163), Graduate School of Education and Human Development, University of Rochester, Rochester, New York 14627

**CATHLEEN L. SMITH** (113, 309), Department of Psychology, Portland State University, Portland, Oregon 97207

**DANIEL SOLOMON** (273), Child Development Project, San Ramon, California 94583

**BARBARA J. STEWART** (113, 309), School of Nursing, Oregon Health Sciences University, Portland, Oregon 97201

**ROBERT TRIVERS** (43), Biology Board of Studies, University of California, Santa Cruz, Santa Cruz, California 95064

**ELLIOT TURIEL** (163), School of Education and Institute of Human Development, University of California, Berkeley, Berkeley, California 94720

**BEATRICE BLYTH WHITING** (221), Graduate School of Education and Anthropology, Harvard University, Cambridge, Massachusetts 02138

# Preface

How aptly does the definition "the reasonable animal" describe our species, *Homo sapiens?* What is an accurate assessment of the social nature of human beings? To appreciate the complexity of this simply stated inquiry, we need to consider research findings from several disciplines.

Most of our behavior is *prosocial;* but our more dramatic, negative behaviors, although less frequent, claim more scholarly and social attention. The consequences of antisocial behavior are indeed serious and deserving of our concern, but examining positive forms of behavior is not antithetical and is in fact necessary for a fuller understanding of antisocial behavior. More important, the intellectual and social needs for understanding and enhancing prosocial development have never been more urgent, given the promise and peril embodied in our current social system.

Researchers across the disciplines are deeply puzzled by the role of intent and the antecedents to prosocial development. Scholars from diverse areas, using differing methods, levels of analysis, and orientations are linked by their common concern for a better understanding of how prosocial development unfolds. The uniqueness of each approach, however, often makes integration problematic. In this volume we attempt to show that, taken together, these approaches can provide a more comprehensive way of viewing and appreciating positive development.

It has become commonplace for researchers to acknowledge that attention to prosocial issues has been long overdue. The field is now well established as a legitimate area of study. Both psychologists and biologists, for example, with varying levels of acceptance, have asserted the necessity of prosocial behavior in structuring societies. Because an enormous amount of work has accumulated in the prosocial literature, we are now ready for a decisive confrontation between the established concepts and new insights. What rings true? Which constructs need to be reconsidered, perhaps through a different lens? What novel areas need to be examined, and how much closer are we to a comprehensive explanation of how prosocial behavior develops when all of this knowledge is brought together?

Like many significant areas of inquiry, a deeper understanding is achieved through a systematic consideration of interdisciplinary studies and varied methodological approaches. Within the disciplines, advances in theory and strategy have paralleled work across age levels. This volume attempts to integrate isolated efforts from pertinent disciplines, illuminating areas of convergent thinking as well as gaps in our knowledge. It does so by emphasizing original research and providing reviews by both leading authorities and new scholars. The contributors bring to bear a refreshing variety of theoretical constructs and empirical strategies from the disciplines of psychology (with several orientations represented), philosophy, sociobiology, anthropology, and education. Consequently the book will be of interest to students and researchers from all of these fields.

Most work on prosocial issues has focused on adult behavior and to a lesser extent on middle childhood. This volume emphasizes origins and extends to prosocial behavior by the elderly in an attempt to appreciate and better explain positive behavior across the life span.

An introductory chapter provides a thorough and thoughtful preview and serves as an organizing framework for the unfolding of subsequent chapters.

Part I begins with a primary and promising area, examining whether there are prosocial behaviors that have altruistic motivations. Using differing sociobiological frameworks, the first two chapters seem to arrive at similar conclusions.

Part II (Chapters 3–8) considers psychological and philosophical issues. It begins with a thorough questioning of origins and antecedents and a healthy skepticism toward the conventional tenets regarding the processes through which prosocial behavior develops. The role of salience to prosocial opportunities is also considered, as is an examination of mediating variables (such as pros and cons of the role of perspective-taking in positive development). Other concepts explored include the influence of situational factors, children's preferences for considerate behavior, a social cognitive approach to differentiation of domains of moral thought, and a look at morality from a logical and moral philosophical position.

Part III presents a range of concerns, bringing together two cross-cultural chapters (9 and 10) by anthropologists. The section begins with an exploration of often underemphasized cultural influences and extends to gender findings that, though sometimes conflicting, in these studies are remarkably consistent.

Finally, two unique considerations of applied prosocial development are set forth in Part IV. Chapter 11 is a promising and integrative in-progress model for enhancing prosocial development in educational settings, and the last chapter (12) takes an original and much needed look at positive development among the elderly.

The four parts are united by the conviction that an understanding of the nature of prosocial behavior must involve descriptive inquiries, and must also extend beyond to incorporate methods that focus on the roles of intentionality and social interaction.

An important feature of this volume is its integration by insightful chapter commentaries on each of the four parts. These commentaries critically analyze the various approaches and locate them within the state of the art. This ambitious effort provides an active way for the reader to consider the virtue of each orientation on its own merit as well as on its ability to contribute to a global view of prosocial development, thus forging a fuller synthesis than has previously been attempted.

I hope the result will excite and encourage students and researchers from across the disciplines to continue their dialogues and to build on this effort, so that a better understanding of prosocial development is achieved. Perhaps this knowledge will then lead to strengthening a prosocial world.

# Acknowledgments

I am indebted to the following people who allowed me opportunities to develop my positive thoughts and behaviors, and specifically to my parents, mentors, colleagues, and friends, among them Bruce Bridgeman, Elliot Turiel, Elliot Aronson, M. Brewster Smith, Steve Lynch, Thomas Krauss, Michael Cunningham, Lee Treichler, Karl Pribram, Larry Stark, Netta Grandstaff, Richard A. Smith, and Morris Silverman.

All of the contributors to this volume undertook this endeavor in a scholarly and creative manner. It was a rich experience and a pleasure to work with such talented individuals.

I am also grateful to the staff of Academic Press for their guidance, patience and support.

The following people at the University of California, Santa Cruz were particularly helpful: Janet Burton for excellent editorial support; and Pat Sanders, Melessa Hemler, and Judy Burton for valuable and thoughtful secretarial help.

This effort was partially supported by a faculty research grant from the Academic Senate Committee on Research, University of California, Santa Cruz.

*"A person's highest happiness is shared happiness."*

—Anonymous

# Introduction

**PAUL MUSSEN**

Viewing the terrifying state of contemporary human society—the increasing quantity and viciousness of crime, intergroup and international conflicts, the real possibility of nuclear holocaust and destruction of life on the planet—the sensitive person asks the social scientist a naive but pointed question: "Why have social scientists not provided more solid information that could be applied in overcoming these deplorable conditions and in raising the levels of compassion, kindness, and concern for the welfare of others?" The question seems to be highly appropriate, for social science seems to have contributed little that is useful for improving the moral quality of modern life.

There are many possible answers to the question. For one thing, actions that are immediately threatening to society—violence, intergroup tensions, delinquency—have a more salient, urgent quality. These seem to demand immediate attention, as though certain conditions have to be alleviated before we can turn our attention to the study of positive or prosocial behavior, such as kindness, consideration, and charity. Therefore, antisocial and problem behaviors seem to have higher priority and have been more thoroughly researched. Furthermore, because of the enormous methodological difficulties involved in the study of prosocial phenomena, important early studies, such as Hartshorne and May's Character Education Inquiry (in the late 1920s) yielded few findings that were of theoretical or practical significance. The failure of these studies discouraged social scientists from further research on critical, but complex, social and moral issues.

This volume indicates, however, that the current state of affairs in this area is far better than the questioner thinks. As you will see, research in prosocial behavior and

1

moral thinking has increased greatly in scope, quality, and vigor in the last 15 years. More problems and more profound theoretical issues are being investigated, newer and better research methods have been designed, theoretical approaches have been expanded and refined, and many significant empirical facts have been established. Some research findings appear to be applicable in interventions designed to raise the level of prosocial behavior and moral thinking. Consequently, a more just assessment of the field may be that we have a good, but modest, start—although only a start—in understanding the origins and development of prosocial behavior and moral judgment.

The phenomena with which this book is concerned are inherently complex; there are always multiple determinants of moral thoughts, prosocial acts, and altruism. Full understanding of the many facets of moral thinking and prosocial behavior—and the personality, social, cultural, cognitive, and motivational antecedents of these cognitions and responses—depends on conceptual analyses and empirical data from the fields of psychology, philosophy, sociology, anthropology, and biology. Hence the multidisciplinary approach of this volume makes it a particularly valuable and timely contribution. As is the case in all areas of social science, every new finding or theoretical advance in the area of prosocial behavior reveals gaps in our understanding and thus becomes a source of more ideas for further research and analysis. As data accumulate, we become increasingly aware of the complexity of the issues and the limitations of our present knowledge. This awareness in turn leads to new and more adequate conceptualizations, as well as to more refined and differentiated definitions of concepts. Then researchers formulate hypotheses that can be tested empirically, frequently inventing more comprehensive and appropriate methods, or improving on available techniques, for this purpose.

This introduction is essentially a preview of the subsequent chapters, but it has several other aims. The first is to sketch in broad strokes the state of the art as reflected in this volume, demonstrating that some significant data have been accumulated and that some of these data are potentially applicable in efforts to improve the quality of life. Another goal is to sensitize the reader to both the strengths and limitations of available theory and empirical data. Finally, some urgent needs for further research and conceptual clarification will be delineated.

We begin Part II with the finding that the human potential for prosocial behavior is a strong and enduring one; it is apparent at very early ages and persists into the years of later maturity. The third chapter, by Hay and Rheingold, documents the prevalence of friendliness, cooperation, sharing, caregiving, comforting persons in distress, and helping others in the behavior of most infants. Friendliness seems to appear as early as 6 months, and the other characteristics are first manifested at approximately 10–18 months. Significantly, field observations in everyday settings such as parks and stores confirm laboratory findings, thus challenging the widely held notion, marked in Piaget's theory, that young children are egocentric in their thinking and behavior. Moreover, the data suggest that prosocial behavior in infancy extends beyond attachments to caregivers. Hay and Rheingold reach the happy conclusion that "the very early appearance of valued social behavior supports an optimistic view of human potentiality, informed efforts to realize it, and provides the conviction that it can be realized."

As the work of Stewart and Smith (Chapter 12) shows, the prosocial responses studied in children—helping, sharing, teaching, comforting—have counterparts in the social interactions of older adults. In their survey, most persons 65 and older reported that they are helpful to others, especially their children and grandchildren. High levels of prosocial behavior among the elderly are associated with other positive outcomes, such as higher morale, better self-concepts, and perceived good health. Some theoretical interpretations of these relationships are proposed, but the authors underscore the need for more systematic investigation of the antecedents and consequences of prosocial actions among older people.

Gender and cultural differences in prosocial acts, particularly nurturance, are noted in a number of studies, including the study of the elderly. In all 12 societies studied by Whiting (Chapter 9)—many of them "in parts of the world that are not dominated by cultural beliefs, values, and social standards of the Western world"— girls over the age of toddlerhood exhibited more nurturance than boys of comparable ages. Data reported by Nancy and Theodore Graves (Chapter 10) support this finding. In the small modernizing island society they studied, girls had far more practice than boys in performing useful chores around the home and in meeting adult needs. This was particularly true in extended families in rural settings where girls displayed most of the altruistic behavior, and there were sharp contrasts between boys and girls. In general they found that "more technologically complex, industrialized, mass market societies stress individualistic competitive tendencies . . . while simpler, subsistence level economies with kin-based social organization are more apt to emphasize group oriented, cooperative behavior."

Other important antecedents of the early development of prosocial behavior are also explored in this volume. Situational factors play a critical role in influencing prosocial responses. Thus, according to naturalistic observations of parent–child interactions (Chapter 4), preschool children are most likely to exhibit prosocial behavior, especially nurturance and helping, when in the presence of both parents, less when only with their mothers, and least when only with their fathers. A child's sharing was significantly correlated with the mother's tendency to share.

Smith, Leinbach, Stewart, and Blackwell (Chapter 5) demonstrated that exhortations by adults, another external or situational factor, may promote prosocial behavior. In their experiment, 4- and 5-year-olds who had heard either power-assertive or inductive preaching, manifested more helping and sharing behavior than a control group. As a consequence, the investigators are convinced that "adults can enhance the helping, sharing, teaching, and comforting behaviors of preschool children by furnishing them with exhortations to behave prosocially and opportunities to rehearse or practice behavior." Although a number of theorists postulate that perspective- or role-taking are among the principal antecedents of prosocial behavior, these investigators found no relationship between a measure of affective perspective-taking and comforting responses among 3- to 7-year-old children. In view of the methodological limitations of the study, however, the relationship cannot be considered disconfirmed.

Two chapters (6 and 7) deal explicitly with cognitive aspects of morality. Prosocial behavior cannot be understood without investigating its meaning and importance for children. Silbukin (Chapter 6) shows that children generally place a high value on positive social behavior (specifically, consideration, kindness, nurturance, helpfulness, enhancing the well-being of others); they prefer to act considerately rather than in other attractive and socially acceptable ways. This preference is somewhat related to children's sensitivity to others' distress, measured by projective techniques, but not to measures of peer or teacher reputation for considerateness. Although the findings must be considered suggestive because only a limited range of values was measured, the problem is important, and the investigator's approach, expanded and refined, may be a fruitful one.

Smetana, Bridgeman, and Turiel (Chapter 7) make the point that an exclusive concern with prosocial behavior may miss important distinctions in motivations and evaluations of such behavior. The authors point to distinctions among three domains: the moral, the social-conventional, and the personal. They report persuasive evidence that children apply different criteria to the three domains, evaluating social-conventional events as relative to the social context and contingent upon the presence of formulated rules, whereas moral events are not. From an early age children regard moral rules as more compelling and moral transgressions as more serious offenses than social-conventional transgressions. In judging the rightness or wrongness of events, young people between ages 10 and 20 are more likely to give moral justifications (justifications based on welfare, justice, and fair distribution of resources) for their "most right" (or "most wrong") judgments than for rankings of "less right" (or "less wrong").

Although Brown and Solomon (Chapter 11) offer no new data, they present a well-balanced and succinct summary of research on the factors that foster the development of high levels of prosocial behavior (e.g., empathy, imitation of prosocial models, role-taking, moral lectures, assignment of responsibility, rewards for cooperation and sharing, participating in activities that help others, optimism, confidence, and positive self-esteem). On the basis of their thorough examination of the literature, they conclude that "we do not know as much as we would like to know about prosocial development, but we know a great deal more than we take advantage of in our current practices." This chapter presents a persuasive demonstration of a route from research to application. Building on accumulated knowledge and wisdom about prosocial development, Brown, Solomon, and their associates designed a comprehensive school intervention program intending to raise the level of children's prosocial thinking and behavior. Details of this excellent experiment are given in Chapter 11.

This concentration on the empirical data and findings should not be taken to imply that conceptual and theoretical issues are neglected in this volume. On the contrary, a very high proportion of the book is devoted to discussion of these issues.

Three of the chapters, by Puka (Chapter 8), by Campbell (Chapter 1), and by Trivers (Chapter 2), are centered primarily on conceptual issues. Noting that Kohlberg's assessments of moral development may be too narrow and may over-emphasize criteria of justice, Puka analyzes the basic components or dimensions of moral judgment and the concept of altruism from the points of view of logic and moral philosophy. He believes that moral levels should be evaluated on grounds that take into account altruism, love, and kindness, as well as the qualities of the individual's interests, values, intentions, and ideals of character development, life-style, and social progress. The ideas presented, although not sufficiently precise or systematized to be of great value in research, are intriguing and provocative and are especially useful in sensitizing us to the diversity of qualities, motivations, and activities that must be considered in any comprehensive definition of moral stages.

Campbell (Chapter 1) argues that, although the principle of kin selection is a prominent "ultimate cause" in sociobiological theory, it is inadequate to explain what he calls "ultrasociality," a highly social form of animal organization that includes "effective information sharing on sources of food and danger, self-sacrificial action including collective defense, and other forms of absolute or hard-core altruism." The chapter deals directly with the age-old nature–nurture problem—the relative contributions of biological makeup and experience—in the acquisition of altruism. Drawing on concepts from game theory, Campbell emphasizes the interplay of biological and cultural evolution through which human ultrasociality develops, "mutual monitoring forcing altruism on fellow group members who cannot survive without cooperative membership and the social evolution of norms and beliefs, at least partially inhibiting a biological residual of tendencies toward self-serving and nepotistic behavior." Currently this argument attempts to explain a characteristic of the *species;* perhaps with further refinement it can be extended to the problem of understanding the development of individual differences in human proclivities to prosocial behavior.

Trivers (Chapter 2) hypothesizes that, during the course of evolution, strong selection factors have produced phenomena of reciprocal altruism and cooperation. It is advantageous for individuals in species such as baboons to cooperate in defending the group from predators. Detailed observational data focused on cooperation in baboons, neighboring in birds, and the helping behavior of hunting dogs, dolphins, and whales support the hypothesis. The facilitating conditions include long life span, low dispersal rates, degree of mutual dependence of members of the species, and stable groupings; kinship is *not* a necessary condition. In addition, a number of emotions motivate altruistic behavior: friendship, moralistic aggression, gratitude, sympathy, guilt, and a sense of justice. As might be expected, those who give aid frequently receive aid most frequently. Increases in mutual dependency may contribute significantly to the evolution of higher-order intelligence in dolphins and humans by producing strong selection pressures for individuals to practice reciprocal altruism with greater sophistication.

Discussions of many other concepts and theoretical issues, too many and too complex to be summarized here, are interwoven in the texts of other chapters. For example, as noted earlier, the chapter by Smetana, Bridgeman, and Turiel (Chapter 7) confronts the problem of specifying the basic components of morality, the issue of how to categorize and evaluate differentiated domains of moral judgment.

Several other authors posit broad, general explanatory theoretical models and hypotheses about the genesis and development of prosocial behavior. Thus, Hay and Rheingold (Chapter 3) see the course of this development as fundamentally a differentiation from general responsiveness (especially to others' emotional reactions) to more specific social responses involving greater intentionality and goal directedness. This is said to be the result, not of "direct tutelage," but of "everyday social interaction." However, the nature of such interactions, the processes or mechanisms by which they help shape prosocial behavior, is not delineated.

The critical role of cognitive factors in the development of prosocial behavior is acknowledged in all theoretical discussions, including those by investigators concerned with situational determinants. Thus, in explaining the effects of exhortation on children's comforting behavior, Smith *et al.* (Chapter 5) note that prosocial actions "stem from the constructive interplay of environmental events and cognitive activity by which each person construes information and generates potential behaviors."

Like other theorists, Whiting (Chapter 9) believes that the growth of propensities toward prosocial behavior is related to increasing cognitive and linguistic skills, better understanding, and greater capacities for empathy and role- or perspective-taking, but she does not deal with these variables specifically. In her model socialization training is regarded as the most powerful determinant of prosocial behavior, and the importance of the environmental and cultural contexts of parent–child interactions is stressed. Furthermore, she postulates that certain kinds of parental orientations as well as children's wants and desires are universal; these govern all social practices all over the world. In essence, Whiting's is a modern social learning theory that incorporates cognitive components.

No one has yet formulated a theory that is sufficiently comprehensive to encompass all the situational, motivational, cognitive, and socialization influences on the development of prosocial behavior. The theory we need—the ideal theory—must be able to integrate and explain all accumulated findings, such as those reported in this volume. It must do this while preserving in its structure the natural complexity of prosocial development. The implication is that an adequate, comprehensive theory would have to specify the *nature* of the interactions among the various categories of influence (e.g., biological, cognitive, social, cultural, personality), that is, the mechanisms and processes involved in these interactions. Obviously this is a large order. No one has yet filled it.

The major contributions of this volume stem from its richness as a source of hypotheses to be tested empirically and its suggestions for more satisfactory conceptualizations and models. Reviewing the contents we learn a great deal about major gaps in our knowledge of prosocial development. How are general advances in cognitive abilities transmuted into higher levels of moral thinking and prosocial action? Although interaction effects are frequently the topics of speculation, very few systematic explorations of these effects exist. For example, we know virtually nothing about how situational variables such as presence (or absence) of parents or peers interact with personality characteristics or predispositions to mold children's tendencies to share prizes they have won. How is a youngster's general level of cognitive ability reflected in her or his *interpretations* of a peer's distress, thus affecting the tendency to help? Under what conditions will a high level of moral maturity be translated into significant prosocial actions and under what conditions are levels of moral reasoning and judgment relatively independent of overt behavior?

Many studies explore the socialization of prosocial behavior, but we need much more information than we have about the influences of extrafamilial agents—peers, teachers, the mass media. The motivations underlying children's prosocial actions have not been adequately explored; in research studies children are seldom asked, directly or indirectly, to explain why they perform or fail to perform prosocial acts. Finally, there is the problem of *individual differences* in personality, motivation, cognitive ability, and styles as determinants of predispositions to behave prosocially. Broad and general as this list is, it represents only a sampling of the many kinds of issues and questions that have not yet been resolved by systematic empirical research.

As the histories of several social sciences attest, better research, practically and theoretically, depends first on the improvement and expansion of methods in current use and second on creative design and invention of new methods. A number of the studies reported in this volume show that there has been marked progress in research methodology in the area of prosocial behavior. For example, Turiel's methods, reminiscent of Piaget's *methode clinique,* used in the Smetana *et al.* study (Chapter 7), suggest excellent ways of tapping the ideas, thoughts, feelings, motivations, and interpretations of situations that influence overt behavior.

To be applicable, research findings must have ecological validity; hence children must be observed in natural settings. Contrived situations used in laboratory studies are useful in exploring the fundamental processes underlying prosocial responses, but we cannot be certain that experimental results can be generalized unless we test them directly in other settings. In addition, close observation of prosocial acts in everyday situations is more likely to yield information about interaction effects than experimental manipulations can. It is therefore gratifying to find that a number of studies reported in this volume are focused on behavior in the "real" world. It is to be hoped that other researchers, learning that such studies have indeed proven fruitful, will conduct more naturalistic studies.

The route from research findings to practical applications is long and hazardous, but happily some investigators are willing to try to follow it (see Brown and Solomon, Chapter 11). How wonderful it would be to find that their work is effective, that research results can indeed be used to design interventions that raise levels of moral thinking and prosocial actions!

# SOCIOBIOLOGICAL APPROACHES TO PROSOCIAL DEVELOPMENT

# The Two Distinct Routes beyond Kin Selection to Ultrasociality: Implications for the Humanities and Social Sciences[1]

## DONALD T. CAMPBELL

The theory of kin selection is successfully providing a unifying core to a wide range of sociobiological studies. Its relevance to humans may be even greater than for other animals because of the human capacity for reckoning kin beyond the associative contiguity of mother and sibling. In the enthusiasm engendered by this success, anthropologists, sociologists, and biologists doing human sociobiology are apt to claim too much, are apt to claim that kin selection can explain all the basic forms of social behavior, and are apt to end up with the conclusion that ultra-sociality, the division-of-labor social systems found only in the social insects and urban humankind, are in both instances to be explained by the same evolutionary mechanism, namely, kin selection. Instead, neither kin selection nor structured demes theory can explain degrees of sociality beyond the semisocial wasps and baboons. Additional mechanisms are required to explain the ultrasocial forms. We already know enough about the routes to the ants and the termites to know that the human route was quite different. When these two different routes to ultrasociality are explored, the portrait of human nature provided is much more compatible with that found in the humanities and social sciences than is the current oversimplified

[1]The preparation of this chapter has been supported, in part, by NSF Grant BNS 792-5577, by the New York State Board of Regents Albert Schweitzer Chair at the Maxwell School, Syracuse University, and by Lehigh University through a university professorship. I am greatly indebted to Patrick D. Hahn for help in the final revisions. Earlier versions have been used for presentations at the American Sociological Association, August 1980, and at the American Anthropological Association, December 1980.

THE NATURE OF PROSOCIAL DEVELOPMENT

sociobiological model. This more complex theory of human nature comes from paying *closer* attention to the details of biological evolutionary theory rather than denying its relevance for human social behavior.

## SOME ESSENTIAL CONCEPTS OF EVOLUTIONARY BIOLOGY

I believe that social scientists interested in sociobiology will be more likely to take my argument seriously if they attend to the evolution of the social insects. For this reason, and to include in my audience those not yet into sociobiology, I will review briefly some of the central concepts, in particular: individual selection, group selection, inclusive fitness, kin selection, second-choice strategies (facultative polymorphism), structured demes, and trait groups.

Mathematical models combining Mendelian genetics and Darwinian theory emerged in the 1920s and 1930s. In one of the three founding books, J. B. S. Haldane (1932) called attention in a special appendix to the apparent impossibility of natural selection of traits that were adaptive for the group or species but costly to the chances for life and procreation for the individual showing the trait. (Restriction of own fertility to avoid resource exhaustion and bravery in group defense can be taken as examples.) He introduced the term *altruistic* for such genes. (Connotations of self-conscious altruistic motivation are not necessarily implied, not indeed ruled out, in this usage.) Haldane's position epitomizes the *individual selectionist* position generally dominant in evolutionary biology today. An effective, self-sacrificial altruistic trait benefits the whole group, including group members lacking the trait. For individuals manifesting the trait, the net gain is reduced by the risks run. However, fellow group members lacking the trait reap the benefits without these risk costs. Thus the net gain in procreational opportunities is greater for the nonaltruists, and their numbers will increase more rapidly in future generations.

This technical argument, made most explicit in the mathematical model, was largely neglected in subsequent nonmathematical discussions of biological evolution and naturalistic descriptions of animal social behavior. The issue was focused in recent times by Wynne-Edwards (1962) in his major presentation of the *group selectionist* point of view. He argued that the individual selection processes described by Haldane could be overcome by the selection of whole groups in competition with other groups. Against this possibility Williams (1966) raises two arguments:

1. The only way in which sizable groups can become different in the frequency of a given gene is through individual selection within the group, which rules out a prevalence of an altruistic trait in any group if the trait reduces the bearer's procreational opportunities relative to the nonaltruist's.
2. Even if once established by extreme group selection of very small groups differing by chance in frequency of the altruistic gene (as Sewall Wright,

another of the three founders, suggested perhaps as early as 1938), intragroup individual selection would soon erode it.

The point at issue in the Haldane and Williams analyses has its parallels in the prisoner's dilemma of game theory and in the economist's discussions of the ''free-rider'' problem, collective goods, and externalities (Olson, 1968). The restraints under which this limitation may be overcome are quite different in biological evolution than in collective human social interaction.

Although the currently developing consensus is between the two extremes epitomized by Wynne-Edwards and Williams, the counteraltruistic effects of *genetic competition among the cooperators* remains a very important reality in all models, and one that I will stress.

The issue of *group* versus *individual* selection is central to this chapter, as to much of the intellectual ferment in current sociobiology. The connotations of *group selection* vary. For this chapter, the emphasis is on directly interacting individuals. For the social insects, *nest selection* or *colony selection* (E. O. Wilson, 1971) are more appropriate. For social man, some phrase like *functioning social unit* or *band* or *city* would avoid some inappropriate connotations of *group selection* as that phrase is used in population genetics. But the central issues are intertwined among all such concepts.

The traits at issue are only those few for which group selection and intragroup individual-versus-individual selection are opposed. Probably for most traits they are coaligned rather than in opposition. In what follows, where I invoke group selection at the biological level this should be read as *net* group selection achieved by curbing intra-cooperating-group individual selection that would otherwise have undermined the effects of group selection. Similarly, where I invoke a nonbiological group selection of beliefs and customs in social evolution, this should be read as a *net group selection* of beliefs that would tend to be undermined by an individual-versus-individual selection and transmission of beliefs.

Although the unit of selection is usually the individual, the unit of retention is the gene. An individual's *inclusive fitness* is the frequency of its genes in the future generations of its breeding group. Such inclusive fitness can be increased by the effective fertility of near relatives, since they share many of the same genes. If a self-sacrificial altruistic act increases the progeny of near relatives greatly, this contribution to the inclusive fitness of the altruist may overcome the costs to its inclusive fitness coming from the risks and outright costs of the altruistic act. This is a crude verbal summary of Hamilton's (1964/1971) theory of *kin selection*. Elaborations and applications of this theory are currently the main activity of theoretical sociobiology, in studies and mathematical models ranging from the social insects to complex human societal systems. The fact that knowledge of kinship is generally not innate but has to be inferred by proximity and similarity (both of which are faked by the cuckoo and cowbird) add rich complexities as well as limitations to the theory. In Hamilton's (1964/1971) presentation, this source of familial altruism is balanced by noting the parallel source of intrafamilial competition:

> To express the matter more vividly, in the world of our model organisms, whose behavior is determined strictly by genotype we expect to find that no one is prepared to sacrifice his life for any single person but that everyone will sacrifice it when he can thereby save more than two brothers or four half-brothers or eight first cousins [p. 42].

> In the model world of genetically controlled behavior we expect to find that sibs deprive one another of reproductive prerequisites provided they can themselves make use of at least one half of what they take; . . . and so on. Clearly from a gene's point of view it is worthwhile to deprive a large number of distant relatives in order to extract a small reproductive advantage [p. 43].

Trivers (1974) has elaborated on competition between parents and offspring, finding the inclusive fitness of the offspring plays a role in curbing parental optimization even when the offspring are sterile workers of social insect colonies (Trivers & Hare, 1976). More generally, Hamilton notes that the more prevalent the altruisitc genes, the greater the selective advantage of a selfish or spiteful alternative. Contrariwise, the more prevalent selfish genes, the greater the selective advantage of kin altruism.

Kin-selection advantages play a role in many *second-choice strategies*. Again and again one finds that evolution has produced alternative behavioral dispositions in animals, a dominant one, which is optimal for inclusive fitness in normal environments, and one or more alternatives, which represent second- or third-choice optima under abnormal or nonoptimal environments. (See West-Eberhard, 1979, pp. 229–231, for a review of such "facultative polymorphism.") Thus for a rabbit threatened by a wolf, silent hiding or escape is normally optimal, but once in the wolf's jaws, terrified squealing produces little or no increase in individual jeopardy and a great advantage to the chances for life and progeny of those kin who are thereby warned of the predator's presence. The rabbit's first-choice strategy is selfish silence. When that has failed, the warning squeal contributes more long-term net inclusive fitness via kin advantage than would continued silence. Temporary acceptance of subordinate roles in dominance hierarchies also exemplify second-choice strategies, supported both by optimizing long-term individual genetic advantage as well as through contributing to inclusive fitness via kin selection. Genetic preparation for environmentally triggered second-choice strategies can go so far that in certain species of fish, males losing out in male–male combat metamorphize into females. Particularly relevant for this chapter is the forgoing or postponement of the individual's own fertility to assist in parental or sibling brood care when nesting sites or food resources are scarce, a facultative option found in a wide variety of animals: minimally social wasps, Florida scrub jays, and African wild dogs.

Finally, we need the concepts going under the terms *structured demes* and *trait groups*. Here I depend on D. S. Wilson (1980), *The Natural Selection of Populations and Communities*. He calls attention to the hidden implications of a seemingly innocent simplification in the mathematical models from Haldane on, the assumption of random associations within the breeding population or *deme*. This homogeneity assumption makes it inevitable that selection theory focus on *relative* rather than absolute fitness. Thus even if a spiteful trait is harmful in reducing the fitness of the carrier, in homogeneity models that trait will still be selected if it reduces the fitness of noncarriers still more. If an altruistic trait benefits its carriers but benefits noncarriers still more, it will be eliminated through natural selection. These conclusions from the mathematical models have seemed incorrect to most naturalists studying social behavior and its evolution, including E. O. Wilson (1975).

D. S. Wilson shows that these particular conclusions disappear if a heterogeneity assumption is substituted for the homogeneity assumption with regard to the interindividual interactions producing altruistic or spiteful effects on other individuals, providing that the associations in breeding include a larger and more nearly random pattern of association. If the deme is spatially extended and if trait-relevant interaction is concentrated in local areas, then even a random initial assortment of individuals into the local interacting regions (trait groups) will produce varying local proportions of altruists. Local areas high in altruists will be more productive because of the advantageous local environments produced by the altruists. They are also higher in altruistic genes, relative to those other trait groups characterized by few or no altruists. If at a later breeding stage there is a mixing of progeny from many of these local trait groups, the more numerous progeny from the high-altruist trait groups leads to an increase in the frequency of the altruistic gene in the total deme.

At this point, D. S. Wilson (1980, p. 29) introduces a formal distinction between "weak altruism" and "strong altruism" (corresponding to E. O. Wilson's [1978, pp. 155–159] "soft-core altruism" and "hard-core altruism"). In weak altruism, the altruistic trait benefits the carrier but benefits the nonaltruists still more. The trait contributes positively to absolute fitness but negatively to relative fitness. D. S. Wilson (1980) shows by algebraic models and computer simulations that, where the mutual effects of a trait are distributed more locally than the maximum mixing population of breeding or other dispersal stages, such weak altruism will be selected. Such traits will be focused on conspecifics but not restricted to kin or presumptive kin. Kin selection considerations may speed up the process but do not change the asymptotic balance under a stable repetition of generational patterns in a stable environment. Strong altruism, reducing the altruist's inclusive fitness in absolute as well as relative terms, is very unlikely in any of D. S. Wilson's models. (Suicidal acts by fertile individuals beneficial to other group members, or acts producing own sterility, represent extremes of strong altruism.)

D. S. Wilson also convincingly presents the route to altruistic social behavior that comes from group members forcing altruism on others. Innate tendencies of this type do not bear the self-sacrificial costs of own tendencies to perform altruistic acts voluntarily. This class of considerations had been earlier raised by Trivers (1971) in his concept of "moralistic aggression." D. S. Wilson (1980, pp. 50, 53–84) elaborates this class of considerations under the concepts of "exploitation" and "interference." "Non-selective interference," in which the behavior forced on others neither favors nor disfavors the genes of the interferer relative to other group members, seems to be the most likely. Those "interfered" with are forced into altruistic roles by being excluded from their first-choice strategies, accepting second-choice strategies either as prudent deferral of their first-choice route (explainable on individual selection grounds) or, via kin selection, as contributions to inclusive fitness.

Although selective and too brief to explain or convince, I hope the preceding paragraphs have conveyed some of the conceptual resources and complexities available in the consideration of what kinds of social behavioral tendencies biological evolution might have produced in a single species such as humankind. With regard to the special theme of genetic competition among the cooperators, some recapitulation may be helpful: Strong altruism is ruled out under most conceivable circumstances. Absolute or relative costs in fitness to the altruist always impede the evolution of such behaviors. Even if absolute self-sacrificial altruism could be selected in nature, it would not be observed if there existed a more selfish route to the same group benefit, such as interference may provide (D. S. Wilson, 1980, pp. 46–47).

## ULTRASOCIALITY

By *ultrasociality* I refer to that high level of sociality in which full-time division of labor occurs, with specialized roles whose occupants do no food gathering and are fed by others. Usually there are stored foodstuffs. A soldier role may have evolved to protect such granaries. Often there are compact apartment-house-like residential arrangements. Always there is extreme effectiveness in communicating relevant information. Complex multi-individual cooperative acts are achieved. Self-sacrificial, even suicidal, bravery in collective defense occurs. (This literature is reviewed in Campbell, 1965.)

Such ultrasociality is found in the social insects (termites, ants, bees, and some wasps) and in urban humankind. It is absent in all vertebrates except humans. Baboons, chimpanzees, wolves, marmots, scrub jays, jackdaws, etc., achieve at best a lower level of sociality. With the exception of E. O. Wilson's (1975) *Sociobiology* (and two protosociobiology books, Ghiselin, 1974; Williams, 1966), many works on sociobiology omit reference to the social insects or deliberately deny their relevance (Count, 1958, 1973; Goldschmidt, 1976). Although fully displayed in E. O. Wilson's (1971) *The Insect Societies,* the superior sociality of the social insects is overshadowed in *Sociobiology* (1975) by the mixing of vertebrate and insect examples on various topics and by insistence on the sociableness of the most social vertebrates. Yet, if one reads *Sociobiology* carefully, on each topic the social insects are much more social than the most social vertebrate examples. E. O. Wilson's films of weaver ants constructing a new nest by sewing together leaves will convince the viewer that nothing in the primates short of communal barn raising by Mennonite farmers can approach it for flexible, "intelligent," cooperative effectiveness, extemporaneously fitting together the available materials in their unique spatial arrangements. The nonhuman primates at their best correspond to the semisocial wasps, (i.e., to predecessor forms far less social than the social insects or urban humankind).

To achieve ultrasociality, a stronger form of social unit selection is required than is provided by kin selection or structured demes. In D. S. Wilson's (1980, p. 29) terms, "strong altruism" is required. This is obviously so for the self-sacrificial acts of soldiers, but I suspect is also required for extreme degrees of honesty of communication, sharing of information about food sources, and cooperative activities producing group products. We know enough already of how this was achieved in the evolution of the social insects to know that the human route had to be entirely different. We know this on biological evolutionary grounds.

## THE SOCIAL INSECT ROUTE TO ULTRASOCIALITY

An excursion into the evolution of the social insects will provide a background against which to contrast the human case. The obstacle setting the limit on sociality as achieved by kin selection and structured demes is, as we have said, the remaining *genetic competition among the cooperators*. The social insects have gotten past this restriction by eliminating such competition and by relegating the extreme cooperative activities to sterile castes of varying degrees of specialization. This sterility is only 99% complete, not 100%. Not only are some ant workers capable of becoming fertile if the queen is removed, some also bootleg unfertilized haploid eggs capable of producing males even while a reigning queen is present. Similar rare exceptions occur among the termites. These exceptions are enough to make clear that there would be a reversion to worker fertility if some continual inhibition did not enforce it. Yet the late nineteenth century insight linking caste sterility and insect ultrasociality surely retains its validity in light of the modern analyses showing the limitations on altruism that genetic competition among the cooperators produces. In the evolution of the social insects, the first stage was the inhibition of fertility in sets of offspring making up a helping caste sharing brood care with the queen, but morphologically undifferentiated from the queen except for their undeveloped gonads. Preserving this worker caste sterility, the extremes of behavioral and anatomical specialization evolved subsequently. The sterility of the cooperators is almost certainly a prerequisite of this later evolution of strong altruism, making possible a strong social-unit selection, insofar as the group of cooperators is concerned.

My emphasis on caste sterility as a major mechanism making possible the evolution of ultrasociality is somewhat out of line with modern discussions on the evolution of insect sociality and is more akin to older turn-of-the-century formulations. My fellow social scientists are hereby warned of a possible bias in this presentation. It may be no more than a difference of focus. It is related to the differing connotations of *ultrasociality* as I use it, and *eusociality,* the common term among biologists referring to the extremely social insects. E. O. Wilson (Oster & Wilson, 1978, p. 322; E. O. Wilson, 1971, p. 464; 1975, p. 584) identifies *eusocial* as referring to a syndrome including all three of the following: (*a*) "cooperation in caring for the young;" (*b*) "reproductive division of labor, with more or less sterile individuals working on behalf of individuals engaged in reproduction;" and (*c*) "overlap of at least two generations of life stages capable of contributing to colony labor." The food gathering and mutual defense aspect of division of labor, the extremes of complex social coordination, the communication effectiveness, and the self-sacrifical altruism, which I emphasize as being shared by ultrasocial urban humans and social insects, are omitted from the definition, although not for reason of their absence among the eusocial insects. Instead, aspects of the insect syndrome are emphasized, which I interpret as evolutionary prerequisites of the social insect route to ultrasociality: Generational overlap is usually a prerequisite to cooperative brood care; worker sterility must be added to cooperative brood care as a prerequisite to ultrasociality by the social insect route; and cooperative brood care and generational overlap are shared as sexual and generational divisions of labor and as a facultative second-choice strategy by many insect and vertebrate forms that are only semi-social, for example, Florida scrub jays (Woolfenden, 1981) and Australian babblers (Brown, Brown, Brown & Dow, 1982).

They, of course, also characterize the ultrasocial insects but are not distinctive. The sterility of castes is distinctive, as too are the features I have identified as ultrasocial. There is no real disagreement here. Oster and Wilson (1978, p. 3) state "Caste and division of labor are at the heart of colonial organization. . . . Division of labor is the single trait essential to advanced modes of colonial existance."

Whereas caste sterility is in Wilson's list of requirements, his wording, "more or less sterile" (E. O. Wilson, 1971, p. 464) stands in great contrast with my "99%." In some species all castes are completely sterile, and the colony dies with the queen. In others all castes are sterile except that a few pupae or larva that might have become workers can become fertile on the death of the queen. In still others some adult workers can become fertile on the death of the queen. In still others some female workers regularly lay haploid eggs, some of which the nest mates may allow to mature into fertile males. (This is probably an evolutionary development subsequent to an earlier stage of more complete caste sterility.) In most species, the number of these exceptions are very rare as a percentage of the total nest population. (The 99% is a metaphoric expression, not an authoritative figure.) It is my prediction that the emphasis upon sterility among the cooperators as a prerequisite to further evolution of social interdependence will soon return in the technical literature (Hahn & Campbell, in preparation), as modern analyses make it clear that net selection by cooperating unit is required, that kin selection and structured demes are not enough to explain the highest elaborations of the social insects. Sterility of the castes means that selection is focused on queens and nests (i.e., on the overall effectiveness of the cooperating group) without this selection being undermined by the differential survival of the cooperating individuals that constitute it.

The preconditions to entering the stage of sterile castes are under active discussion in the technical literature (e.g. Bartz, 1979; Charnov, 1978a, 1978b; Hamilton, 1964, 1972; Lacy, 1980; Wade, 1978;), but enough can be stated about it to dramatize the contrast with the human case. Social cooperation limited to the offspring of a single pair of parents is an initial prerequisite for origin, if not always for maintenance (Bartz, 1979; Wade, 1978). Very high degrees of genetic similarity among siblings is required so that the inclusive fitness strategy of helping with the broods of a parent exceeds or is trivially different from investing in own offspring. In the ants and bees, the fact that the males have only one set of chromosomes and genes, rather than two, creates settings in which a female is more closely related to a sister than to a daughter, which can promote sterile sibling helping as a stable strategy across generations if the sex ratio favors females (Charnov, 1978b; Trivers & Hare, 1976; Wade, 1978). In the case of termites, extreme degrees of inbreeding alternated with wide dispersal for nest founders may produce settings in which siblings are more genetically similar to each other than to their own offspring (Bartz, 1979). Among the termites male heterozygosity for reciprocal translocations among the chromosomes can produce assymetrical coefficients of relatedness, with same sex siblings being more closely related than parent to offspring (Lacy, 1980). (Note that sterile termite workers and soldiers are both male and female.) Even if the genetic similarity to siblings does not exceed similarity to offspring but merely becomes equal or approximately so, mechanisms implementing parental interest in sterile offspring helpers can evolve, either by parent selection for genes producing sterility when appearing in the offspring (Charnov, 1978a) or through pheromones inhibiting sexual maturity in offspring. These mechanisms require that the queen's fertile life be many times longer than the maturational time of the sterile offspring, otherwise it is the comparison of the inclusive fitness routes through nieces and nephews versus own offspring that becomes crucial. (Reviews of the extensive literature are to be found in Alexander & Borgia, 1978; Crozier, 1979; Oster & Wilson, 1978; Starr, 1979.)

West-Eberhard's (1979, 1981) recent work on a Panamanian semisocial wasp may be used to illustrate a first step of one route by which this threshold into sterile cooperators may have been crossed. In the absence of adequate nesting sites, these wasps will forego their own nest building and egg laying in favor of helping feed or protect a sister's offspring. This is a second-choice strategy explainable by kin selection. The invoking of such an option is made more likely by high degrees of genetic similarity, which reduces the difference in contribution to inclusive fitness between sister's offspring and own offspring. (Mother helping rather than sister helping would make this first stage still more likely.)

If in such a local ecology, multiple adult brood care were to become prevalent, the competitive situation might make it essential, with unassisted brood care losing its viability in competition with the multiple caretaker nests. At this stage there would be genetic selection for making the second-choice strategy more readily triggered. At a later stage, the competition between nests might have made it optimal to have *several* sterile auxiliary helpers for each nest. (Brown et al. [1982] have experimentally demonstrated that the Australian gray babbler is at a stage where one helper is not enough, in a study dramatically confirming the advantage provided by multiple helpers.) Once such a stage developed, the effective second-choice strategy of each auxiliary helper would expand to include trying to prevent co-auxiliaries from defecting to set up their own independent nests. Such a disposition would be supported not only because such defectors would be direct genetic competitors reducing the likelihood of own eventual fertility, but also because such defection jeopardizes the payoff of the cooperative kin-caring, second-choice strategy.

In such a selective setting, were a fertility-inhibiting pheromone to become available, a rigid caste sterility might evolve. Such pheromones emanating from ant queens have been demonstrated. The present analysis (and the technical details of genetic competition between parents and offspring, as in Trivers, 1974; Trivers & Hare, 1976) would lead one to expect, in addition, mutual sterility-enforcing behaviors among the workers. This includes distributing the queen-produced sterility pheromone. Feeding the eggs produced by fellow workers to the queen and to the larvae have been observed. Worker-produced sterility pheromones might also occur. The self-sterilizing side effects are less costly of inclusive fitness than the gain from sterilizing coworkers, as in D. S. Wilson's (1980, p. 65) nonselective interference.

It follows from kin selection theory that the sterile workers have inclusive fitness interests in spite of their sterility. These interests are to some extent at least in conflict with the queen's, as is stressed in parental-exploitation theories of the origin of eusociality (Charnov, 1978a), by Trivers and Hare (1976), and by Oster and Wilson (1978, pp. 88–97). What needs to be stressed also is the sense in which the sterile workers' interests differ from each other. For each worker the first-choice strategy is for it to be fertile in the production of haploid males while all of the other workers remain sterile so that the productive cooperative be maintained. But the maintenance of cooperation is so important that if keeping the other workers sterile requires accepting sterility oneself, this is a better fall-back position than having the colony fail to function. Each worker's inclusive fitness interest is clearly in keeping the other workers sterile, not in volunteering own sterility. It is only after the individual interests have been expressed in mutual sterilization that one can regard the inclusive fitness interests of worker and co-workers as collectively identical. It must be emphasized that for these routes to work individuals must not be able to escape the sterility enforcement coming from parents or sibling co-workers. For the termites this may have been augmented by their dependence on anal feeding from other termites for the renewal of the intestinal protozoans required for digesting wood after each molt.

Once helper sterility be established, then selection would be at the level of nest and queen. Selection by functioning group would have been implemented without the competing erosion from individual selection. The development of group-advantageous self-sacrificial altruism on the part of the specialized castes could no longer be inhibited by genetic competition among the cooperators. At this initial sterile worker state, ultrasociality has not yet been achieved. The queen still gathers food, defends the nest, and is only reproductively differentiated in structure and behavior.

Later to come is worker feeding of the queen and the development of soldiers and other castes fed by the workers.

The use of the term *group selection* for this process has led to confusion. Clearly there is selection by functioning social unit. Clearly the erosion of self-sacrificially altruistic behavior tendencies due to genetic competition among the cooperators, so well described by Haldane (1932) and Williams (1966) has been almost entirely eliminated. However, as the mathematical models for group selection are taken as applying only to groups of *fertile* organisms, it may be denied that *group selection* as used in population genetics is at work for the social insects. But certainly no selection for groups of queens and nests is implied when E. O. Wilson (1968, p. 41) says, "In fact, colony selection in the social insects does appear to be the one example of group selection that can be accepted unequivocally." Boorman and Levitt (1980) explicitly define group selection so as to exclude the social insects: "Mating does not normally take place between reproductives produced by the same social insect colony. Insect colonies are therefore not reproductively closed populations and accordingly cannot be treated as demes for the purposes of group selection. In turn, this means that group selection is largely ruled out as an explanation of most cases of insect sociality [pp. 13–14]." However, they do not mean to rule out selection by cooperating social unit. In fact they (Boorman & Levitt, 1980) also say "If selection is mostly at the colony level, workers can be altruistic to the remainder of the colony [p. 41]." While they do not explicitly mention that net "selection primarily at the colony level" can only take place when selection at the individual worker level has been eliminated, it is probable that they would agree.

J. B. S. Haldane, the most explicit founder of the individual-selectionist emphasis, was clear on the special case of the social insects in his founding book (1932): "In general, qualities which are valuable to society but usually shorten the lives of their individual possessors tend to be extinguished by natural selection in large societies unless these possess the type of reproductive specialization found in social insects. This goes a long way to account for the much completer subordination of the individual to society which characterizes insects as compared to mammalian communities [p. 130]."

## A TANGENT ON THE THEORY OF GAMES IN BIOLOGICAL EVOLUTION, SOCIAL EVOLUTION, TRIAL-AND-ERROR LEARNING, OR COOPERATIVE INTELLECTUAL PROBLEM SOLVING

This tangent is inserted for my psychology and social science colleagues who prefer to avoid positing biological bases for behavior, or biological or social evolutionary sources of behavioral dispositions. Although there will be a stress in the following argument on social evolutionary sources of individual behavioral dispositions, the argument inevitably falls within the more general encompassing "theory of games'' which is being employed and developed in economics, political science, social psychology, and evolutionary biology. Each focuses on problems of competition and cooperation, indirect cooperation as a by-product of competition, coalition formation and preservation, collective goods and the obstacles to achieving them, as exemplified in the ''the prisoner's dilemma,'' etc. I can claim no special competence in this general theory, being largely ignorant of the vast experimental literature in social psychology derived from the inspiration of the prisoner's dilemma problem, and lacking detailed mastery of the elaborations of the theory in economics or political science. Nonetheless, I have no hesitation in acknowledging that there is emerging here an elaborate unifying theory of detailed relevance to all of our fields.

A problem setting is assumed in which there are great payoffs from collaborative action and in which such payoffs are often not obtained because of individual efforts to optimize one's own well-being in competition with one's fellows. It is assumed that most collaborative payoffs (collective goods) are of net benefit to the individual even though often precluded if each individual acts with rational self-interest (the ''free-rider'' problem in economics). However, the route to optimizing collective goods usually or often creates a collective entity whose survival and optimization becomes a goal potentially achieved at the cost of a reduced net benefit to some individuals and perhaps even to the average individual.

These problems and possibilities can be explored in a number of ways, foremost as a purely normative rational model that makes no pretense of describing how actual decision makers (individual and collective) behave but that provides advice to them as to how they should behave so as to optimize certain goals in certain settings. The *Theory of Games* of Von Neumann and Morgenstern (1944) is just this normative theory of rational behavior: not psychology, not sociology, not biology, not descriptive economics, but instead a form of logic. If these problems, possible solutions, minimax strategies, saddle points, nonoptimal hill peaks, etc., do get reflected in human social behavior, this can be through a number of routes:

1. The current social actors, as rational human problem solvers, may have logically analyzed their situation and have consciously agreed upon rational solutions including appropriate contract-enforcement mechanisms (*individual rationality*).

2. The current social actors may have had explained to them by mentor generations their game-theoretic predicament and the accumulated rational analysis of optimal behavior (*individual rationality augmented by social evolution.*)

3. A trial-and-error learning process (involving uninsightful floundering among the current social actors as to personal behavior, personal beliefs, and cooperative action) may have discovered both the rationally optimal solution (or a satisficing [Simon, 1957, p. 204] improvement) and rational and irrational beliefs that would support the social maintenance of the theory-of-games rational behavior (*individual trial-and-error learning*).

4. The current social actors may have learned from their elders recipes achieved in previous generations by the uninsightful exploration of alternative beliefs and

behavior tendencies (*social evolution based upon accumulating individual trial-and-error learning*).

5. Whereas, in the four previous alternatives, the problem-solving unit was an individual mind or, if collective, still a trial-and-error exploration taking place within individual lifetimes (several iterations per generation), so that the contrasts between alternatives could be experienced by individuals, in this fifth alternative there is a form of social evolution in which the organized group and its belief system is the unit of variation and selection. With wide variations among intercommunicating groups, with marked variations in modes of organization and communally shared beliefs and customs, with some groups conspicuously flourishing more than others, these successful groups hanging onto their ways or enforcing their ways on others through conquest or having their customs, organizational forms, and beliefs more imitated by neighboring independent social groups—with all this—an uninsightful trial and error at the group level might hit upon beliefs and behaviors implementing theory-of-games rational behavior, perhaps under supernatural or transcendent rationalizations (*social evolution at the group-attribute selection level*).

6. Biological evolution of neural pathways and neurotropic hormone systems may have explored social behavioral possibility space by blind mutational substitution of one DNA molecule for another and thus uninsightfully hit upon theory-of-games optima. The possibilities along this line have been reviewed in the preceding sections on biological evolution along with the tendency for individual selection to undermine or preclude this route to preserving collective goods (*biological evolution*).

The abstract, logical, normative theory of games is not yet completed. Analysis at any one of these levels may contribute to the general theory of what is optimal, the possible routes to getting there, and modes of retaining such a solution. Evolutionary biology, for example, is expanding the general theory as represented in economics (Hirshleifer, 1977, 1978). We may expect contributions like those of D. S. Wilson (1980) to inspire additions to formal economic theory and vice versa (Samuelson, 1983). Trivers' (1971) concepts of reciprocal altruism and moralistic aggression, although proposed in a biological context, may actually be more appropriate at other levels. However, the more important point may be not which level implements which possibility, but rather that all operate in parallel under the constraint of a common problem set and common formal theory. Because of this, the reader is invited to read with a double agenda—attending separately to the plausibility of the argument at the level of optimal social behavior on the one hand, and on the other hand, to the question of the proper explanation of the presence or absence of such behavior, in terms of the rational–irrational, individual–group, biological–social alternatives. Thus as Brewer (1981) has argued, Trivers' (1971) analysis of reciprocal altruism is worthy of elaboration and application even by those who would avoid hypotheses of biological dispositions in human social behavior.

This chapter, however, is less noncommital and will freely and tentatively speculate on rational versus blind discovery and upon social versus biological routes. All this is particularly relevant to the social insect–human contrast on which this chapter centers. These speculations are intended as an invitation to careful criticism and much more detailed elaboration. In its present state, my discussion of the human route to ultrasociality is unsatisfactory even to me—a collage of unintegrated apercus (some of them no doubt wrong). The political danger of plausible but wrong analyses offered to the public as "scientific" truths is immense, given public faith in science, a faith that is not yet justified in this area. For example, I am sympathetic to the criticism that at present the theory of games supports conservative or reactionary political systems by its focus on individual-versus-individual competition to the exclusion of other human values. However, through the prisoner's dilemma example, its influence on economics has been to increase attention to the problem of collective goods and social externalities and the way in which these are undermined by individual selfishness and distrust. The theory of games is open as to which of the many human "utilities" humans choose to optimize. It is my conjecture that when the problem of collective goods and the problem of how to curb the self-serving and nepotistic biases of those given administrative power are solved, the more mature theory of games will support a form of popular participatory, decentralized socialism making use of primary group means of social control (Campbell, 1982). The metaproblem of collective goods—how to avoid solutions that make the survival of the nation an overriding goal undermining, rather than increasing, individual welfare—and the related problem of international warfare, will have to be a part of that more mature theory of games. Even here, however, theory of games limited to individual goals and values (as opposed to optimizing the nation as an end in itself) already asserts the stupidity of war.

The six ways in which theory-of-games rationality might be discovered have, of course, been presented with exaggerated discreteness. Biological evolution makes possible individual learning and, augmented by cultural evolution, rational thought. Cultural evolution itself is in these and other ways made possible by biological evolution. Rational analysis of human problems has no doubt often been inspired by the conceptual rationalizing of wise behavior tendencies originally hit upon by noninsightful learning, etc. These interroute dependencies work downward through the list as well as upward. Individual trial-and-error learning will be, in fact, blind only insofar as the rational thought of the individuals involved has not provided intelligent trials. Social inheritance of individually acquired wisdom will mix Modes 1 and 3 or 2 and 4. The group-to-group differences that provide the new variations for group selection to operate on in mode 5 will in part be prewinnowed for wisdom by Modes 1 and 3, (as Boehm, 1978, emphasizes.)

Discoveries initially made by learning and social evolution can also become embodied in biological structures, as noted in the theories of Baldwin (1902), and of Waddington (1957) in his concept of genetic assimilation. Normally, the achievements of biological evolution are restricted to those that can be reached by intermediate stages, every one of which is an improvement even without the final stage. However, the capacity to learn may relax this restriction. Thus an animal can move into a new ecological niche that it initially adapts to by vision and learning. Once this adaptation becomes common and routinized, then any biological mutation that predisposes or accelerates this learning will be adaptive and selected. Around the template thus provided by the recurrent learned habit, there can be assembled, in any order, a set of mutations that can eventually turn the recurrent habit into an instinctive behavior repertory, even though in the absence of the habit these individual mutation elements would have been useless or worse. So too, recurrently adaptive discoveries made by Modes 1–5 may acquire innate biological predispositional support through the fact that any mutation facilitating their learning or transmission tends to be selected and retained.

Waddington (1960) and others have posited biologically based tendencies and capacities for the prepubescent to be an avid tradition absorber, favoring Modes 2, 4, and possibly 5. An innate openness to awe, a sense of the numinous, or superstitious belief, would facilitate Mode 5. Such innate predilections could conceivably also be accumulated around more specific adaptive discoveries, in logical or superstitious form. Thus reifications of collective purposes useful in solving the problem of collective goods, superstitiously embodied in belief about powerful, transcendent gods or in an individual afterlife of rewards and punishments, if recurrently adaptive, might further the selection of biological predispositions to such religious emotions and beliefs.

We materialists or physicalists often tend to reject any speculation about innate ideas. Behaviorist psychologists are particularly prone to do so. Where this comes from an emphasis upon the power of learning, perception, and thinking to solve our problems, or from a culturalogical–environmental explanation of ethnic differences, I endorse this tendency wholeheartedly, but it may often be due to a residual mentalism. Innate ideas obviously have to be embodied in flesh, blood, neurones, hormones, intraneuronal molecular structures affecting electrical transmission harmonics, chemical transmitters, and the like. However, it is often implicitly assumed that new thoughts and the products of learning lack such embodiment. A consistent physicalism or materialism recognizes instead that each different thought is differentially embodied in neurophysiology. (Note, however, that modern functionalist physicalist philosophers such as Dennett [1978] are careful to specify that these embodiments need not be in structural detail exactly parallel in any two persons having the "same" idea, any more than two chess-playing computer programs embodied in two computers of the same model, making the same move at the same point in the same game, would be expected to have the same exact internal structure of routing links and magnetic core polarizations.) The great adaptive value of flexible circuitry, of learning rather than rigid hardware wiring, all supports an expectation of learned adaptations over innate ones. Feasible computers, however, still have a great deal of fixed circuitry, and recent small high capacity models may have relatively more than the big time-sharing monsters. The continued dependence on external programming and the great time costs of "learning programs" that invent their own detailed programs may provide an analogy favoring innateness for recurrently adaptive ideas.

## THE HUMAN ROUTE TO ULTRASOCIALITY

### Biological Evolution of Individual Human Social and Altruistic Behavior Tendencies

Elaborating the role of kin selection for human social behavior is the major activity of human sociobiology. (For samples and reviews, see Alexander, 1979; Alexander & Tinkle, 1981; Chagnon & Irons, 1979; E. O. Wilson, 1979.) The appropriateness and success of this effort is applauded rather than challenged here. My emphasis that it does not suffice to explain ant or human ultrasociality should not be read as denying its relevance to human social behavior, not only as an evolutionary precursor to ultrasociality, but also as a continued presence in urban, division-of-labor society. Indeed, its explanatory force may be greater for humans than for other animals due to the learned component in kin recognition, and the human ability to reckon more remote degrees of kinship than can animals who are limited to associations based upon proximity at birth. Holmes and Sherman (1983) review a number of studies demonstrating a genetic component in kin recognition. These studies affirm the importance of learning as well. Indeed, in Holmes and Sherman's own experiments with ground squirrels, rearing together is a much stronger determinant of territorial acceptance than biological sibship. Human preoccupation with reckoning more remote degrees of kinship is very likely explainable through the kin-selection advantages of solidarity with cousins, etc. (e.g. Alexander, 1979), despite the frequent independence of socially designated kin and biological kinship to which Sahlins (1976) has called attention. In comparing differing kinship systems, inclusive fitness considerations may indeed explain why patrilineal societies are more concerned with female chastity than are matrilineal ones (Alexander, 1979; Green, 1978) and why the greater the material benefits a father can pass on to a son, the more extreme is the concern with female chastity and the more elaborate its institutional forms (Dickemann, 1981). Note that Dickemann's study comes from a complex urban division-of-labor society. Even though kin loyalty often may operate more often as an obstacle to than as a facilitator of societal complexity, its effects no doubt remain.

We may expect to see very soon a similar application of D. S. Wilson's (1980) structured deme theory to the evolution of human social behavior. In the development of primate sociality, achieving cooperating groups of more than one family was no doubt a major hurdle, hindered rather than helped by kin selection. Structured deme theory does not require that the beneficial interaction be among kin and achieves the same eventual degree of altruism whether kin selection accompanies it or not, although kin selection may speed up the process. The relative self-sacrificial altruism that it selects is not specific to kin but is expressed toward all neighbors. The widespread human traditions of exogamy favor the processes Wilson describes, in providing a greater dispersal in breeding than in the mutually efficatious social interactions. This furtherance of innate social solidarity behavior may be fully as important as the avoidance of recessive genes in explaining the prevalence of exogamy. The prevalence in human societies of patrilocal or matrilocal residence and loyalty obligations (as opposed to ambilocal residence and bilateral kin loyalty) also facilitate structured deme conditions. (The effect of matri- versus patrilocality on sex differences in altruism and nonselective interference warrants careful analysis.)

D. S. Wilson's (1980) concept of nonselective interference becomes particularly important at that stage of protohuman development when humans become dependent on membership in a multifamily or multifertile male group for survival, that is, where a single male and consort or harem cannot survive alone. At this stage, protohumans became trapped in group membership and thus susceptible to the pressures of other group members for prosocial behavior. Trivers's (1971) concept of *moralistic aggression* expresses such a possible development. Parallel to the scenario described earlier for the social insects, in which the inclusive fitness interests of the sterile workers come to include keeping the other workers sterile, even at the costs of own sterility, so too, in more limited degree, once multimale social groups became essential, these primate groups forced mutual restraint, cooperation, and risk-taking for collective benefit upon each other. As noted earlier, D. S. Wilson emphasizes, however, that the continued presence of genetic competition between these cooperating males sets limits on such altruism. My own emphasis is that the social insects, due to caste sterility, have been able to evade these limits. The Russells have made this contrast vividly:

> In principle, the whole system of ant aggression is clearly designed to ensure complete peace within the nest and merciless hostility to all potential rivals of the community as a whole. There could not be a more complete contrast with monkey bands, more prone to internal dissension than war, or human communities, oscillating between civil and foreign conflict, and requiring every encouragement of mass redirection to make them engage in warfare [Russell & Russell, 1968, p. 263].

We need a speculative and critical elaboration of the possible stages of innate social dispositions in protohumans. Kummer (1971, 1980), Goodall (1976, 1982), and Boehm (1982) provide the beginnings of such, although this brief scenario is more dogmatic than they would support. (I have also profited from discussion with William J. Hamilton, III, and Donald S. Sade.) The multimale social groupings of rhesus monkeys, macaques, and baboons (trapped into group life for mutual defense and intraspecific group versus group competition) have evolved very strong, clear-cut, facultative polymorphisms of dominance and submission. Although the dominance is less than that of a single-male harem territorial species (such as the proverbial elephant seal), it is still so strong as to preclude food sharing because the dominant animal hogs it all and therefore, in W. J. Hamilton's opinion, prevents the big game hunting of which his chacma baboons would otherwise be capable. (Menzel and Halperin [1975] found less following of one experimentally informed "leader," presumably because that leader was overly dominant and failed to share food.) This dominance–submission polarity had to be substantially reduced in the route of human evolution while maintaining and increasing multifamilial social solidarity. Chimpanzees share information about food location (Menzel, 1971; Menzel & Halperin, 1975) and food, with enough peer equality and recognition of private property so that the dominant male will beg meat from a subordinate who happens to be in possession of it (Goodall, as cited by Gruter, 1982). The proto-human route may well have expanded the social coordinative facultative polymorphisms in the direction of eliminating complete dominance hierarchies in which every male or female in the group has a clear-cut rank with dominance over lower ranks and submission to higher ones (insofar as such are ever found [Bernstein, 1981]), in favor of a readiness to accept either leadership or followership roles, with an unranked followership and a sense of justice favoring equality. Boehm (1982) notes the universal presence of an ideology (if not practice) of equality in hunter–gatherer societies.

Along with diminished strength dominance–submission relationships would go a facultative polymorphism for cooperation or spite vis-à-vis single other equal status conspecifics. This has been called the "tit-for-tat" strategy in recurrent-play prisoner's dilemma games (Rapoport & Chammah, 1965). In a brilliant integration of this literature with that of mathematical models of evolutionary theory, Axelrod and Hamilton (1981) have shown that this rule of cooperating until cheated, then retaliating, and of returning to cooperation after the other player changes to cooperative choices is one of two "evolutionarily stable strategies" for a long-continued two-person game. The other stable strategy is continuous defection. In extending the model to multiactor groups, clusters of tit-for-tat cooperators cannot be eroded by continuous defection strategists and thus dominate. Required for this solution is the ability to recognize individuals, good memory, and ecologies that enforce continued interaction with the same persons (a requirement seemingly greatly reduced in modern, high-mobility, multiurban society).

Given these requirements Alker and Tanaka (1981) have called attention to the fact that, even in an asymmetrical payoff, repeated-play prisoner's dilemma game, within the tit-for-tat strategy, the low-payoff person often achieves near equality in payoff by occasional defections, which the high-payoff person tolerates as an equalizing ritual, without which the low-payoff person would defect continually, to the disadvantage of both. They fail to note, however, that to use this subordinate sabotage power, the low-payoff member must be able to do without the game or to survive on the lowest, often negative, double-defection payoff. In multiplayer games, such forced equalization of cumulative payoffs probably comes from coalitions of the weaker. Nonetheless, we see here hints as to how an evolving proto-human species could have moved in the direction of equalizing actual payoffs and, even more clearly, into an individual goal of equal payoffs as a facultative polymorphic alternative to getting a monopoly share for oneself and preferable to passively accepting one's lower role in the hierarchy and hence getting a still smaller share or none at all (Campbell, 1979b).

In accordance with modern cognitive psychology's recognition of the purposefulness (intentionality) of animal and human behavior (even animal recognition of purposefulness in a fellow animal's behavior [Premack & Woodruff, 1978]), the behavioral tendencies we have been describing would be accompanied by what can be called *criterion images* or their equivalent in various cognitive and cybernetic behavior theories (e.g., "templates for object-consistent responses" [Campbell, 1963, 1966]). Criterion images and purposefulness are involved for instinctive as well as learned response tendencies, insofar as flexible actions fitted to variable circumstances are involved. Thus protohuman "moralistic aggression" à la Trivers (1971) must be triggered by some kind of matching of current perceptual input with a criterion image for this antisocial behavior. Thus the tendency (reviewed by Boehm, 1982) for a dominant primate male to stop overt conflict between pairs of unrelated subordinates, adults or juveniles, must be triggered by aversive reaction to the perception of such conflicts.

The criterion images for prosocial and antisocial behavior will be most fundamentally focused on the behavior of fellow group members, only secondarily (as described later) on own behavior. This follows from the primate predicament of genetic competition among the cooperators, which produces, in multifamily social groups, behavioral temptations for self-and-progeny serving cheating on the social contract. Any "innate ethical sense" (Lorenz, 1973, 1975) will be motivated primarily by preferences as to others' behavior, not one's own. The monitoring of social behavior will be basically mutual monitoring, not self-monitoring. The invoking of implicit norms, as for example in moralistic aggression, will be primarily in response to others' violations. The individual's own self- and progeny-serving violations, if undetected by others, will tend to go unnoticed. Reports of such self-serving biases in the implementation of social coordination are noted in most primate studies of dominance and submission relationships, as where the submissive member of the dyad stealthily usurps the dominant member's prerogatives when this can be done undetected.

In accordance with my outline for this chapter, we are still in the section dealing with biologically based behavioral dispositions and with social group processes at the nonhuman primate level, with speculative extention to protohuman stages of biological evolution not currently exemplified in any primate. The topic of self-monitoring criterion images which I come to next is also, I believe, appropriate to this protohuman, biologically based level, but, in this brief and exploratory exposition, I do not find it possible to adhere to this orderly limitation and will mix in illustrations from well-acculturated, modern humans as well, without being meticulous as to whether the behavioral dispositions involved are carried by means of genes or cultural indoctrination.

While I am out of line with mainstream sociobiology in positing a conflict between the behavioral norm exhortations of culture and the inclusive fitness interests of the single individual, and in invoking a group selection of ideologies to account for this conflict (see the following) we have no real disagreement as to the innate biological dispositions produced where there exists both genetic competition among the cooperators and great payoffs for cooperation. Trivers (1972) and Alexander (1975, 1979) point out that, in such an ecology there will be selection pressure for hypocrisy, that is, for the evasion of mutual enforcement by the appearance of prosocial behavior while disguised dereliction from prosocial duty takes place. This, in turn, will be accompanied by the evolution of skill at detecting hypocrisy. They also speculate about optimal strategies of contrition and repentance if found out. Alexander (1975, 1979) also suggests that self-deception as to dereliction will emerge, and that "sincere" hypocrisy, with repressed awareness of own guilt will optimize individual inclusive fitness. The inclusive fitness advantages of self-deception over self-conscious deception of fellows is hard to make explicit, but expanding the criterion-image model to include effective self-monitoring for prosocial behavior helps.

The social grouping must be effective for the selection pressure for mutual monitoring activities and for staying in the group to be maintained. This implies that despite dereliction and deceit the social sanctions are predominately effective and violations of the shared criterion images for antisocial behavior are detected and punished (and probably too that exceptionally vivid individual examples of prosocial behavior are rewarded by the group). As a result it becomes advantageous to monitor one's own behavior with prosocial and antisocial criterion images so as to avoid punishment and to maximize rewards. It is perhaps obvious that one's perspective on one's own behavior is different from one's perspective on the behavior of fellows. Detailing this difference emerges as a major and ubiquitious finding in current social psychology's attribution theory (e.g., Jones & Nisbett, 1971). This perspective difference means that the criterion images for monitoring one's own pro- and antisocial behavior will have to be separate from those used in monitoring others.

It is characteristic of the phenomenology of threshold monitoring organs that, in addition to the situation-specific thresholds that can be observed in overt behavior, there are separate thresholds for all-or-none or categorical experience. Take the continuum for temperature, for example: In a controlled experimental environment, one can establish the metric temperature at which an iron handle generates the subjective experience "cold" and a separate threshold temperature for "hot," in between which the handle is experienced as neutral, or not noticed, or perhaps warm. There are separate sense receptors in the skin for cold and for heat (as for touch, pressure, and pain). That these sense receptors are subject to adaptation and hence the thresholds subject to systematic relativistic change, and that extremes of hot and cold also activate pain receptors, add further complexities . These cold and hot experience thresholds will usually be separate from the hand-withdrawal thresholds, which will depend further on motivational and informational context. Thus whereas sociologists of group life, sociobiologists, and behavioristic psychologists may all emphasize the role of the overt behavior, there is a related, but not identical, phenomenology for which continuous dimensions are typically turned into experiential absolutes—all-or-none categories. This point has been further elaborated in the concept of *phenomenal absolutism* (Campbell, 1969; Segall, Campbell, & Herskovits, 1966), emphasizing the suppression from awareness of the relativity of judgments and the similar effect of culturally induced categories.

If we posit such a phenomenology for the criterion images for prosocial and antisocial behavior, the model becomes complex enough to encompass instances such as in mutual monitoring where noticed derelictions of others go unheralded and, for self-monitoring, in which one is aware of one's own norm violation and thus knowingly sins. One route to get to Alexander's thesis about self-deception is to further posit that the criterion image for one's own behavior is in general more lenient than the criterion image for others' behavior (that it takes a greater degree of selfishness to be experienced as SELFISH, a lesser degree of bravery to be HEROIC, for self than for other). If so, then there will occur frequent instances where others see one as guilty but one's self-perception is of innocence.

When the inclusive fitness or immediate lifetime reward for self and other criterion threshold settings are examined closely, a self-leniency bias is not a foregone conclusion, although it may accord with common observation. I do not have a thorough analysis to offer, although here are some of the ingredients that such an analysis must eventually contain: Lifetime self-interest and inclusive fitness implications of genetic competition among the cooperators would press for a self-leniency bias were there not punishment for infraction to be considered. Holding punishment severity constant, the greater the uncertainty of detection and the greater the uncertainty of punishment if detected, the greater the self-lenient bias. (Both these uncertainties reduce the net expected costs of violating the norms represented by the others' criterion image for other group members.) However, the punishment for detected-and-enforced violations can conceivably be made severe enough to reduce the self-leniency bias or even to reverse the direction of discrepancy so that the criterion image for own behavior might be set more stringently than that for others' behavior. Costs to the tattler in detecting others' violations and cost to the enforcers (if different) complicate both sides of the process. Fellow group members are a needed resource if cooperative action is to pay off, and too severe sanction enforcement may alienate the offender to another group or to solitary life. The value of fellow members will fluctuate with the presence of competitive and hostile outgroups, as will the opportunities and rewards of defection. Degree of punishment (or reward) may vary as a function of degree of violation or frequency of violation. The excess rewards produced by selfishness (if they do not destroy cooperative group effort entirely) are made up from the sum of small losses to others so that individual motivations to detect and punish are assymetrical with individual motivations to cheat. For this reason it is probably necessary to distinguish between unfair-share derelictions and group-function-threatening derelictions. There are no doubt still other relevant own-lifetime and inclusive-fitness payoff considerations.

Without being able to compute net expectations for criterion images, I am willing to guess that the net discrepancy is in the direction of a self-leniency bias. If so, this produces a weak version of Alexander's self-deceived cheating on the social contract, but I do not believe this fully explains the phenomenon to which he points. To do so seems to me to require a further sociobiological analysis of honesty and cheating, of the sorts of self-monitoring that produce autonomic reactions for lying as opposed to truth telling, of the ways in which liars signal their dishonesty in facial expression and gesture (Ekman, 1981). One of the most obvious gains of social life is in the "economy of cognition," in sharing knowledge of routes to food, etc. (Campbell, 1965, pp. 44–45). Honesty and trust of fellows is essential for this, but the inclusive fitness analysis of this where genetic competition among the cooperators exists is yet to be adequately done.

These complexities are some of the inevitable consequences of inclusive fitness theory when the advantages of complex social coordination are achieved concomitantly with genetic competition among the cooperators. In the social insect route, they are avoided. Except for mutual monitoring of fertility, the ants, bees, and termites probably do no mutual monitoring for antisocial behavior, nor mutual reward and punishment for violation. Criterion images for own prosocial behavior probably suffice. Although narcissism and selfishness rather than the death instinct best epitomize what Freud (1930) observed, the contrast he noted seems correct:

> The natural instinct of aggressiveness in man, the hostility of each one against all and of all against each one, opposes this programme of civilization. . . . Why do the animals, kin to ourselves, not manifest any such cultural struggle? Oh, we don't know. Very probably certain of them, bees, ants, and termites, had to survive for thousands of centuries before they found the way to those state institutions, that division of functions, those restrictions upon individuals, which we admire them for today. It is characteristic of our present state that we know by our own feelings that we should not think ourselves happy in any of these communities of the animal· world, or in any of the roles they delegate to individuals [pp. 35–36].

I hope these paragraphs begin the task of convincingly illustrating how attention to the two distinct routes can provide an evolutionarily authentic portrait of social man essentially consistent with that found in great literature, old religions, and sociology. As an exemplar, may I call attention to the Summer, 1979, issue of *Daedalus* on the topic of "Hypocrisy, Illusion, and Evasion," to the editorial preface by Stephen Graubard, and to the contents of the essays, flagged by such titles as "Shakespeare's Hypocrites" (Brian Vickers), "A Study of Themes of Hypocrisy and Pessimism in Iranian Culture" (Mary Catherine Bateson), and "Hypocrisy and the Spanish Inquisition" (Stephen Gilman).

## Cultural Evolution

Cultural evolution contrasts with biological evolution in that the storage of the behavioral dispositions is dependent on nongenetic means associated with group life. Individual capacity to learn is centrally involved but does not become cultural evolution until there is transgenerational transmission. If the learned habits of adults become a part of the environment to be learned by the juveniles in such a way that the adult ways of behaving are maintained by the juveniles when they become adults, then a cultural evolutionary process is present. Cultural evolution in nonhuman primates goes beyond this minimum, in that specific teaching by adults is present, as well as innate tendencies to imitate (Bonner, 1980). In addition to individual brains and memories, social organizations with role replacement and artifacts such as the bow and arrow, which provide in themselves a learning environment in which the apprentice relearns the adult skill, provide social evolutionary storage mechanisms. Such storage mechanisms make possible an adaptive variation-and-selective-retention process, analogous to biological evolution in this general algorithm but deviating in other details, one of the most important of which is the possibility of cross-lineage transmission. Campbell (1965) reviews the earlier presentations of this insight. Lumsden and Wilson (1981) present a quite complete bibliography. If such social evolutionary capacity furthers inclusive fitness, as it no doubt does in fluctuating ecologies at least, then one would expect innate mechanisms furthering social evolution. Furthermore, many of the mechanisms of mutual monitoring, as previously described, and other aspects of social behavior may require transgenerational social memory for their efficacy. One example follows.

In Trivers' (1972) seminal article on reciprocal altruism he calls attention to the possibility of an innate tendency to be predisposed to the creation of reciprocal altruism contracts with other individuals, an innate tendency for what I have called "clique selfishness" (Campbell, 1975, 1979a). The moralistic aggression, already mentioned, supports contractual fidelity in the form of murderous rage toward contract breakers. Such contracts would be fragile in negotiation and too dyadic to accommodate group social coordination. The concepts become more realistically applied to protohuman and human conditions by noting that these weaknesses would be avoided if individuals were to socially inherit membership in a reciprocal altruist clique (Brewer, 1981), with innate tendencies for moralistic aggression against traitors. Trivers' two concepts thus merge with traditional concepts of ethnocentrism and in-group versus out-group polarization (LeVine & Campbell, 1972; Sumner, 1906). An analysis of the problem of collective goods, free-riders, etc., would probably show that a reciprocal altruist pact would probably be advantageous even if every human in the world were included, but the mechanism for enforcing it would be difficult to achieve or maintain. Certainly in early protohuman stages, the selective advantage of clique selfishness would have been greater if there were nonclique members to exploit. The sharing of food no doubt required limitations on the number sharing and hence explicit group membership recognition. Even before protohumans, at the level of the multifamily social grouping of macaques and baboons, the threat of other groups of conspecifics became a major pressure for in-group solidarity. Clique selfishness, fully as much as individual selfishness, undermines the rational implementation of the collective good of larger social organizations.

Before shifting fully to social evolution, a review of the probable biological supports for social evolution may be in order. These include, of course, the capacities for imitation, language, and memory, long childhood with parental tutelage, innate longing for group membership, fear of social ostracism, and conformity tendencies (Campbell, 1961). Waddington (1960) has posited an innate preadolescent period of readiness for the reverent learning of cultural traditions. Whether age-specific or not, human credulity for group-shared beliefs of a supernatural kind must be counted as a universal aspect of genetically based human nature. Festinger's (1950) classic article notes in addition to conformity tendencies, a motivation to address persuasive communications to in-group members expressing deviant beliefs, up to the point where they cease to be defined as members of the group (Festinger, Gerard, Hymovitch, Kelley, & Raven, 1952). This mutual monitoring for belief uniformity may be posited as a further part of our innate equipment favoring social evolution.

This speculative reconstruction of the human route to this point has taken us up to the level of human "primary groups" or "face-to-face groups," as designated in the older sociological literature. This is somewhat short of ultrasociality in which full-time division of labor has extended to the presence of specialties that gather no food. The size of the coordinated social primary group is 100 rather that 1000 or 10,000. Even at this stage social evolution is essential. Even at this stage human capacity for gullible acceptance of traditional beliefs plays an important role. As I have often spelled out in more detail (e.g., Campbell, 1965, 1974a), all systems capable of increasing adaptive fit or knowledge require mechanisms for variation, selection, and retention. Essential in this process is a mechanism for rigid, loyal retention. At the level of the gene, this is achieved in the precise gene replication mechanisms of meiotic and mitotic cell division. For our human group, there are, of course, winnowing processes at the level of individual learning, with perceptual criteria employed for selection, but we must, I believe, allow for a social cumulation of adaptive recipes for behavior that go beyond those achievable by individual learning and physical-object-based thought, achieved instead by an uninsightful *blind* variation and selective retention of beliefs. (This, of course, does not exclude the occurrence of "intelligent" variation [Boehm, 1978], involving creative thought and individual learning, these too ultimately interpreted as vicarious blind-variation and selective-retention devices [Campbell, 1974b].) Human capacity for credulous belief in shared superstitions plays this blind retention role. Analogously to the loyal replication of neutral and dysfunctional genes along with adaptive ones in meiotic cell division, so too tribal memory must transmit all beliefs not yet winnowed out, including ones that will be later weeded out. The retention process cannot be clairvoyant. The selection process is inevitably stochastic, full of error and made up in part of transient features too unstable to support adaptive convergence. Only thus can superstitious tribes acquire beliefs that—at the functional level—are wiser than the individuals transmitting them. This at least has been my perspective previously (Campbell, 1965, 1975).

To get to the stage of self-sacrificial heroism in warfare or to procreational abstinance on the part of custodians of the tribal wisdom and to get into full-time

division-of-labor societies made up of numerous primary groups, some of the beliefs transmitted to enculturated individuals must predispose behavior that is counter
to any single individual's inclusive fitness (even though increasing the group's
collective or average inclusive fitness). At this point the new model of social
evolution of Boyd and Richerson (1982) becomes of particular value. It attributes a
variation-generating function to the human capacity for belief conformity and to the
human tendencies to force belief conformity on in-group fellows (Festinger, 1950).

Boyd and Richerson (1982) start with the mathematical models of biological
evolution. A first modification is to permit multiple parents and cross-familial
parenting in the transmission of beliefs, customs, skills, etc., to a younger generation. In the linear version of this model, in the absence of selection, the proportion
of offspring carrying the trait is the same as the parent generation in the local
communicating group. Selection imposed upon this model favors individual advantage under most circumstances and precludes the selection of beliefs, behavioral
tendencies, and customs favoring group effectiveness at the expense of the individual carrying the belief. Such a belief transmission system would fail to select
beliefs inhibiting the erosion of collective advantage by individual opportunism in
the interests of individual inclusive fitness. Under such a model, the moral preachments to offspring would be of this nature: "Get others to cooperate, but be a free ri-
der yourself." "Don't be a sucker." "Better a procreating coward than a dead hero."
No doubt self-serving preachings such as these often go on in the privacy of homes
directly or indirectly, consciously or unconsciously. We can envisage on an individual selection basis a double standard of preaching, an altruistic morality for
exhortation to others, a self-serving one for own offspring. I anticipate that in the
long run such a system would *not* work to produce complex social coordination,
even though it would end up with the altruistic preachings heard by the offspring
generation being many times more numerous than the selfish ones.

In Boyd's and Richerson's nonlinear version of social transmission, the offspring
are influenced to adopt the majority position of the parent generation. Under these
conditions, groups move rapidly toward internal uniformity in the social transmission. With small groups, chance pluralities would occur in different directions from
group to group, and thus the model predicts both internal homogeneity within
groups and large group-to-group differences. This is the condition that permits
group selection to be effective and, thus, the selection of beliefs and culturally
induced behavioral tendencies that are beneficial to the group but costly to the
individual. Such group selection at the cultural evolutionary level is, of course, a
matter of the selective propagation of belief systems, as by the recruitment of new
members to apparently successful groups or by the influence of group success on
diffusion (i.e., the adoption by other groups of a successful group's beliefs and
customs) or by the imposition of beliefs upon conquered peoples. (The biological
extinction of whole groups, which is probably very rare, would only incidentally
contribute to this process.) In addition, their model predicts the existence of dramatic group-to-group differences on socially transmitted traits that are neutral or only

slightly beneficial or harmful, thus obviating the need felt by earlier social evolu-
tionists to try to explain all such difference as adaptations by unique ecological
circumstances.

## IMPLICATIONS

This model of social evolution, along with the biological model of human social
behavioral evolution, makes more explicit, and, I hope more plausible, the point of
view I have presented (Campbell, 1972, 1975) on the social functional origin of the
counterhedonic components in cultural beliefs dealing with moral behavior: the
commandments not to covet, the deadly sins of greed and sloth. For optimal communication to the mainstream of sociobiologists interested in both social and biological evolution (e.g., Alexander, 1979; Cavalli-Svorza & Feldman, 1981; Durham,
1979; Lumsden & Wilson, 1981; Pulliam & Dunford, 1980), I should not have used
the flamboyant title "On the Conflict[s] between Biological and Social Evolution"
(Campbell, 1975), because this is most easily read as implying too great an independence for social evolution from biological inclusive fitness considerations. Instead,
social evolution, where functional, has furthered *average* individual inclusive fitness through representing the inclusive fitness interests of all of the other group
members, countering the selfish inclusive fitness interests of the individual and,
thus, generating socially and culturally behavioral tendencies toward absolute altruism, which biological evolution alone could not have produced under conditions of
genetic competition among the cooperators.

On the other hand, the notion that cultural evolution in the area of self-sacrifical
altruism is producing behavioral dispositions that run counter to individual selfish
and nepotistic behavioral dispositions remains valid. This was better indicated in the
phrasing of my 1972 title "The Counter Hedonic Components of Human Culture"
and in the earlier presented concept of a self-serving double standard for judging
selfishness in self and others.

The overall view of human nature resulting from this scenario of the human route
to ultrasociality is, I believe, much more compatible with that found in the humanities and social sciences than is the simpler view of human social nature being
presented by much of current sociobiology. There is not space in this chapter to
elaborate further. I have called attention to the themes of betrayal and hypocrisy.
The theme of guilt-ridden ambivalence and vacillation between animal lust and
social duty found in Augustine and Tolstoy also fit with it. The grounds have been
laid for an explanation of the human predilection for an ideology of equality (Campbell, 1979b) as well as the liberty and fraternity that standard sociobiology may also
explain. (The notion of an innate human eagerness for submission to authoritarian
tyranny has found no support.) The theory converges on our understanding of
ethnocentric dynamics and the role of out-group hostility in furthering in-group
cooperation. In a previous article (Campbell, 1975), this orientation has been used
to explain the specific content of moral preachments, commandments, and lists of

deadly sins. Light has been thrown on the functional role in implementing collective purposes of beliefs in ultimate purposes and values transcending individual human life, beliefs in reincarnation and/or a rewarding afterlife, and upon the role that economically wasteful regal burial practices may have in adding credence to such beliefs. Waiting for further elaboration is the way in which this view helps us understand the inevitable tendencies toward self-serving and nepotistic distortions of bureaucratic rationality on the part of administrators. Why legal efforts at social control fail unless supported by primary group mutual monitoring or superstitiously internalized self-monitoring also becomes understandable (Campbell, 1982).

## SUMMARY

Ultrasociality refers to the most social of animal organizations, with full-time division of labor, specialists who gather no food being fed by others, effective information sharing on sources of food and danger, self-sacrificial action in collective defense, and other forms of absolute or hard-core altruism. This level has been achieved by ants, termites, and humans in several scattered archaic city states. The currently standard concepts of evolutionary theory used in sociobiology, such as kin selection and structured deme theory, adequately explain only moderately social forms such as semisocial wasps and baboons. In the social insects, the further route to ultrasociality has been made possible by caste sterility, which almost entirely removes genetic competition among the cooperators. This route has *not* been available for human urban societies. Instead, the development has been through mutual monitoring, forcing altruism on fellow group members who cannot survive without cooperative group membership, and a cultural evolution of norms and beliefs at least partially inhibiting a biological residual of tendencies toward self-serving and nepotistic behavior. Attending to the details of these two distinct routes to ultrasociality provides a portrait of human nature compatible with traditional religious, literary, sociological and psychological views of human nature. Light is thrown on human ambivalence, honesty, deceit, bravery, and cowardice; the specific contents of lists of sins and commandments; human intuitions of justice, equity, and equality; the dynamics of ethnocentrism; and self-seeking and nepotistic distortions of collective bureaucratic rationality.

## REFERENCES

Alexander, R. D. The search for a general theory of behavior. *Behavioral Science,* 1975, *20,* 77–100.
Alexander, R. D. *Darwinism and human affairs.* Seattle: University of Washington Press, 1979.
Alexander, R. D., & Borgia, G. Group selection, altruism, and the levels of organization of life. *Annual Review of Ecology and Systematics,* 1978, *9,* 449–474.
Alexander, R. D., & Tinkle, D. W. *Natural selection and social behavior.* New York: Chiron Press, 1981.
Alker, H. R., & Tanaka, A. Resolution possibilities in ''historical'' prisoner's dilemmas. Project

working paper, Center for International Studies, Massachusetts Institute of Technology, March 1981.

Axelrod, R., & Hamilton, W. D. The evolution of cooperation. *Science*, 1981, *211*, 1390–1396.

Baldwin, J. M. *Development and evolution.* New York: Macmillan, 1902.

Bartz, S. H. Evolution of eusociality in termites. *Proceedings of the National Academy of Sciences, U. S. A.*, 1979, *76*, 5764–5768. (Corrections, 1980, *77*, 3070.)

Bernstein, I. S. Dominance: The baby and the bathwater. *The Behavioral and Brain Sciences*, 1981, *4*, 419–429.

Bonner, J. T. *The evolution of culture in animals.* Princeton, N. J.: Princeton University Press, 1980.

Boehm, C. Rational preselection from Hamodryas to Homo sapiens: The place of decisions in adaptive process. *American Anthropologist*, 1978, *80*, 265–296.

Boehm, C. The evolutionary development of morality as an effect of dominance behavior and conflict interference. *Journal of Social and Biological Structures*, 1982, *5*, 413–421.

Boorman, S. A., & Levitt, P. R. *The genetics of altruism.* New York: Academic Press, 1980.

Boyd, R., & Richerson, P. J. Cultural transmission and the evolution of cooperative behavior. *Human Ecology*, 1982, *10*, 325–351.

Brewer, M. B. Ethnocentrism and its role in interpersonal trust. In M. B. Brewer & B. E. Collins (Eds.), *Scientific inquiry and the social sciences.* San Francisco: Jossey–Bass, 1981, 345–360.

Brown, J. L., Brown, E. R., Brown, S. D., & Dow, D. D. Helpers: Effects of experimental removal on reproductive success. *Science*, 1982, *215*, 421–422.

Campbell, D. T. Conformity in psychology's theories of acquired behavioral dispositions. In I. A. Berg & B. M. Bass (Eds.), *Conformity and deviation.* New York: Harper & Row, 1961.

Campbell, D. T. Social attitudes and other acquired behavioral dispositions. In S. Koch (Ed.), *Psychology: A study of a science* (Vol. 6). *Investigations of man as socius.* New York: McGraw–Hill, 1963.

Campbell, D. T. Variation and selective retention in socio-cultural evolution. In II. R. Barringer, G. I Blanksten, & R. W. Mack (Eds.), *Social change in developing areas: A reinterpretation of evolutionary theory.* Cambridge, Mass.: Schenkman, 1965.

Campbell, D. T. Pattern matching as an essential in distal knowing. In K. R. Hammond (Ed.), *The psychology of Egon Brunswik.* New York: Holt Rinehart & Winston, 1966.

Campbell, D. T. A phenomenology of the other one: Corrigible, hypothetical and critical. In T. Mischel (Ed.), *Human action: Conceptual and empirical issues.* New York: Academic Press, 1969.

Campbell, D. T. On the genetics of altruism and the counter-hedonic components in human culture. *Journal of Social Issues*, 1972, *28*, 21–37.

Campbell, D. T. "Downward causation" in hierarchically organized biological systems. In F. J. Ayala & T. Dobzhansky (Eds.), *Studies in the philosophy of biology.* London: Macmillan, 1974. (a)

Campbell, D. T. Evolutionary epistemology. In P. A. Schilpp (Ed.), *The Philosophy of Karl R. Popper.* LaSalle, Ill.: Open Court, 1974. (b)

Campbell, D. T. On the conflicts between biological and social evolution and between psychology and moral tradition. *American Psychologist*, 1975, *30*, 1103–1126.

Campbell, D. T. Comments on the sociobiology of ethics and moralizing. *Behavioral Science*, 1979, *24*, 37–45. (a)

Campbell, D. T. The origins of the ideological preference for equality in the genetic competition among the cooperators. Unpublished presentation at the second annual meeting of the International Society of Political Psychology, Washington, D. C., May 1979. (b)

Campbell, D. T. Legal and primary-group social controls. *Journal of Social and Biological Structures*, 1982, *5*, 431–438.

Cavalli-Sforza, L. L., & Feldman, M. W. *Cultural transmission and evolution: A quantitative approach.* Princeton, N. J.: Princeton University Press, 1981.

Chagnon, N., & Irons, W. *Evolutionary biology and human social behavior: An anthropological perspective.* North Scituate, Mass.: Duxbury, 1979.

Charnov, E. L. Evolution of eusocial behavior: Offspring choice or parental parasitism? *Journal of Theoretical Biology*, 1978, *75*, 451–465. (a)

Charnov, E. L. Sex-ratio selection in eusocial hymenoptera. *American Naturalist*, 1978, *112*, 317–326. (b)

Count, E. W. The biological basis of human sexuality. *American Anthropologist*, 1958, 60, 1049–1085.

Count, E. W. *Being and becoming human: Essays on the biogram.* New York: Van Nostrand–Reinhold, 1973.

Crozier, R. H. Genetics of sociality. In H. R. Hermann (Ed.), *Social insects* (Vol. 1). New York: Academic Press, 1979.

*Daedalus: Journal of the American Academy of Arts and Sciences* (Vol. 108), Hypocrisy, illusion, and evasion. Boston: American Academy of Arts and Sciences, 1979.

Dennett, D. C. *Brainstorms: Philosophical essays on mind and psychology.* Montgomery, Vt.: Bradford, 1978.

Dickemann, M. Paternal competence and dowry competition: A biocultural analysis of purdah. In R. D. Alexander & D. W. Twinkle (Eds.), *Natural selection and social behavior.* New York: Chiron Press, 1981.

Durham, W. H. Toward a coevolutionary theory of human biology and culture. In N. A. Chagnon & W. Irons (Eds.), *Evolutionary biology and human social behavior.* North Scituate, Mass.: Duxbury, 1979.

Ekman, P. Mistakes when deceiving. *Annals of the New York Academy of Sciences*, 1981, *364*, 269–278.

Festinger, L. Informal social communication. *Psychological Review,* 1950, *57*, 271–282.

Festinger, L., Gerard, H., Hymovitch, B., Kelley, H., & Raven, B. H. The influence process in the presence of extreme deviates. *Human Relations*, 1952, *5*, 327–346.

Freud, S. *Civilization and its discontents.* London: Hogarth, 1930.

Ghiselin, M. T. *The economy of nature and the evolution of sex.* Berkeley: University of California Press, 1974.

Ghiselin, M. T. (Comment). *American Psychologist*, 1976, *31*, 358–359.

Goldschmidt, W. Comment: Biological versus social evolution. *American Psychologist*, 1976, *31*, 5, 355–357.

Goodall, J. Continuities betweeh chimpanzee and human behavior. In G. L. Isaac & E. R. McCown (Eds.), *Human origins: Louis Leakey and the East African evidence.* Menlo Park, Calif.: Benjamin Cummings, 1976.

Goodall, J. Order without law. *Journal of Social and Biological Structures*, 1982, *5*, 353–360.

Greene, P. J. Promiscuity, paternity, and culture. *American Ethnologist*, 1978, *5*, 151–159.

Gruter, M. Biologically based behavioral research and the facts of law. *Journal of Social and Biological Structures,* 1982, *5*, 315–323.

Hahn, Patrick D. & Campbell, Donald T. Beyond kin selection: The role of caste sterility in the evolution of extreme eusociality. Manuscript in preparation, Lehigh University, 1983.

Haldane, J. B. S. *The causes of evolution.* London: Longmans Green, 1932.

Hamilton, W. D. The genetical evolution of social behavior, I & II. *Journal of Theoretical Biology,* 1964, *7*, 1–52. (Reprinted in G. C. Williams [Ed.], *Group selection.* Chicago: Aldine–Atherton, 1971. Pp. 23–87, with addendum pp. 87–89.)

Hamilton, W. D. Altruism and related phenomena. *Annual Review of Ecology and Systematics*, 1972, *3*, 193–222.

Hirshleifer, J. Natural economy versus political economy. *Social Biological Structures*, 1978, *1*, 319–337.

Hirshleifer, J. Economics from a biological viewpoint. *The Journal of Law and Economics*, 1977, *20*, 1–52.

Holmes, W. G., & Sherman, P. W. Kin recognition in animals. *American Scientist*, 1983, *7*, 46–55.

Jones, E. E., & Nisbett, R. E. The actor and the observer: Divergent perceptions of the causes of behavior. In E. E. Jones (Eds.), *Attribution: Perceiving the causes of behavior.* Morristown, N. J.: General Learning Press, 1971.

Kummer, H. *Primate societies: Group techniques of ecological adaptation.* Chicago: Aldine, 1971.

Kummer, H. Analogs of morality among nonhuman primates. In G. S. Stent (Ed.), *Morality as a biological phenomenon.* Berkeley: University of California Press, 1980.

Lacy, R. C. The evolution of eusociality in termites: a haplodiploid analogy. *American Naturalist*, 1980, *116*, 449–451.

LeVine, R. A., & Campbell, D. T. *Ethnocentrism: Theories of conflict, ethnic attitudes and group behavior*. New York: Wiley, 1972.

Lorenz, K. A. *Civilized man's eight deadly sins*. New York: Harcourt Brace Jovanovich, 1973.

Lorenz, K. A. Konrad Lorenz responds. In R. I. Evans (Ed.), *Konrad Lorenz: The man and his ideas*. New York: Harcourt Brace Jovanovich, 1975.

Lumsden, C. J., & Wilson, E. O. *Genes, mind, and culture: The coevolutionary process*. Cambridge, Mass.: Harvard University Press, 1981.

Masters, R. D. Evolutionary biology, political theory and the state. *Journal of Social and Biological Structures*, 1982, *5*, 439–450.

Menzel, E. W. Communication about the environment in a group of young chimpanzees. *Folia Primatologica*, 1971, *15*, 220–232.

Menzel, E. W., & Halperin, S. Purposive behavior as a basis for objective communication between chimpanzees. *Science*, 1975, *189*, 652–654.

Olson, M. *The logic of collective action*. New York: Schocken, 1968.

Oster, G. F., & Wilson, E. O. *Caste and ecology in the social insects*. Princeton, N. J.: Princeton University Press, 1978.

Premack, D., & Woodruff, G. Does the chimpanzee have a theory of mind? *The Behavioral and Brain Sciences*, 1978, *4*, 515–526.

Pulliam, H. R., & Dunford, C. *Programmed to learn: An essay on the evolution of culture*. New York: Columbia University Press, 1980.

Rapoport, A., & Chammah, A. M. *Prisoner's dilemma: A study in conflict and cooperation*. Ann Arbor: University of Michigan Press, 1965.

Russell, C., & Russell, W. M. S. *Violence, monkeys, and man*. London: Macmillan, 1968.

Sahlins, M. *The use and abuse of biology: An anthropological critique of sociobiology*. Ann Arbor: University of Michigan Press, 1976.

Samuelson, Paul A. Complete genetic models for altruism, kin selection and like-gene selection. *Journal of Social Biological Structures*, 1983, *6*, 3–15.

Segall, M. H., Campbell, D. T., & Herskovits, M. J. *The influence of culture on visual perception*. Indianapolis, Ind.: Bobbs–Merrill, 1966.

Simon, H. A. *Models of man*. New York: Wiley, 1957.

Starr, C. K. Origin and evolution of insect sociality: A review of modern theory. In H. B. Hermann (Ed.), *Social insects* (Vol. 1). New York: Academic Press, 1979.

Sumner, W. G. *Folkways*. Boston: Ginn, 1906.

Trivers, R. L. The evolution of reciprocal altruism. *The Quarterly Review of Biology*, 1971, *46*(4), 35–57.

Trivers, R. L. Parental investment and sexual selection. In B. Campbell (Ed.), *Sexual selection and the descent of man*. Chicago: Aldine, 1972.

Trivers, R. L. Parental–offspring conflict. *American Zoologist*, 1974, *14*, 249–264.

Trivers, R. L., & Hare, H. Haplodiploidy and the evolution of social insects. *Science*, 1976, *191*, 249–263.

Von Neumann, J., & Morgenstern, O. *Theory of games and economic behavior*. New York: Wiley, 1944.

Waddington, C. H. *Strategy of the genes*. New York: Macmillan, 1957.

Waddington, C. H. *The ethical animal*. London: Allen & Unwin, 1960.

Wade, M. J. Kin selection: A classical approach and a general solution. *Proceedings of the National Academy of Sciences, U. S. A.*, 1978, *75*, 6154–6158.

West-Eberhard, M. J. Sexual selection, social competition, and evolution. 1979, *123*, 222–234.

West-Eberhard, M. J. Intragroup selection and the evolution of insect societies. In R. D. Alexander & D. W. Tinkle (Eds.), *Natural selection and social behavior*. New York: Chiron Press, 1981.

Williams, G. C. *Adaptation and natural selection*. Princeton, N. J.: Princeton University Press, 1966.

Wilson, E. O. The ergonomics of caste in the social insects. *American Naturalist,* 1968, *102,* 41–66.

Wilson, D. S. *The selection of populations and communities.* Menlo Park, Calif.: Benjamin Cummings, 1980.

Wilson, E. O. *The insect societies.* Cambridge, Mass.: Harvard University Press, 1971.

Wilson, E. O. *Sociobiology: The new synthesis.* Cambridge, Mass.: Belknap Press, 1975.

Wilson, E. O. *On human nature.* Cambridge, Mass.: Harvard University Press, 1978.

Wilson, E. O. The evolution of caste systems in social insects. *Proceedings of the American Philosophical Society.* 1979, *129*(4).

Woolfenden, G. E. Selfish behavior by Florida scrub jay helpers. In R. D. Alexander & D. W. Tinkle (Eds.), *Natural selection and social behavior.* New York: Chiron Press, 1981.

Wynne-Edwards, V. C. *Animal dispersion in relation to social behavior.* Edinburgh: Oliver & Boyd, 1962.

# The Evolution of Cooperation[1]

## ROBERT TRIVERS

Altruistic acts are defined as ones in which an actor confers a benefit on some other individual at a cost to the actor, where cost and benefit are measured in terms of reproductive success (numbers of surviving offspring). Thus, an altruistic act appears to decrease the number of surviving offspring produced by the altruist and is, thus, opposed by the action of natural selection. Two mechanisms may permit the selection of altruistic behavior. First, the actor and the recipient may be related. In this case, the gene or genes leading to altruism may enjoy a net benefit since they are also located in the recipient with some probability, called $r$ or degree of relatedness (Hamilton, 1964). Second, the altruistic act may lead to some return benefit to the altruist larger than the initial cost suffered by the altruist. The most important kind of return benefit occurs when the recipient reciprocates the altruism at some future time. This requires that the roles of donor and recipient frequently reverse themselves (Trivers, 1971).

In kin-directed altruism, the main problem for the altruist is to ensure that the degree of relatedness to the recipient times the cost–benefit ratio of the act is larger than 1. In studying such altruism, we look for positive associations in nature between degree of relatedness and frequency of altruism. In reciprocal altruism, the main problem for the altruist is to ensure that the frequency of future interaction between the two will be sufficiently high that enough altruism will reach the actor, in return, to compensate for instances of nonreciprocation. In searching for evidence of reciprocal altruism in nature, we look for evidence ($a$) that individuals tend

---

[1]From R. L. Trivers, *Principles of Social Evolution* (Addison–Wesley), in preparation.

THE NATURE OF PROSOCIAL DEVELOPMENT

to direct altruism toward those that direct altruism toward them; and (b) that individuals discriminate against nonreciprocators by failing to extend to them additional altruism. The frequency of interaction between individuals is critical because when this is low individuals who extend altruism will have insufficient opportunities to direct this beneficence only to others who tend to reciprocate, so that losses from nonreciprocators may outweigh the occasional gains.

We can also look at the two kinds of altruism from the standpoint of the nonaltruist. In systems of kin-directed altruism, these individuals risk a lower inclusive fitness by failing to see that significant parts of themselves are located in other individuals and thus failing to benefit this extended self. In systems of reciprocal altruism, the nonaltruist risks a failure to receive additional altruism from those whose initial altruism it has failed to reciprocate.

Several factors are expected to increase the chance that two individuals will repeatedly interact in such a way as to be able to share the benefits of reciprocal altruism. For example, both a long life span and a low dispersal rate will tend to maximize the chances that two individuals will interact repeatedly. The same is true for the degree of mutual dependence. Interdependence of numbers of a species (to avoid predators, for example) will tend to keep individuals near each other and increase the chance that they will encounter altruistic situations together. Parental care and kin-directed altruism more generally are relationships that will tend to bind individuals together so as to encourage reciprocity between them. Of course, any asymmetries among the individuals in their ability to affect each other will decrease the possibilities for altruistic exchanges. A strong dominance hierarchy usually means that those on the upper end are able to seize benefits from those lower down without any need to reciprocate, but even in such species, individuals low in the hierarchy may be able to trade many small altruistic acts for occasional large benefits in return. Thus, a subordinate may groom a more dominant individual and gain some protection in return.

## RECIPROCAL ALTRUISM IN HUMAN EVOLUTION

Based on the importance of reciprocal interactions in all human cultures today and on the strong emotional system that underlies our relationships with friends, colleagues, and acquaintances, it seems likely that, during our recent evolutionary history (at least the last 5 million years), there has been strong selection on our ancestors to develop a variety of reciprocally altruistic actions. Humans routinely help each other in times of danger (for example, accidents, predation, attacks from other human beings, and so on). We routinely share food, we help the sick, the wounded, and the very young. We routinely share our tools, and we share our knowledge in a very complex way. Often these forms of behavior meet the criterion of small cost to the giver and great benefit to the recipient. Although kinship often mediates many of these acts, it never appears to be a prerequisite. Such aid is often extended in full knowledge that the recipient is only distantly related.

During the Pleistocene, and, probably before, a hominid species would have met the preconditions for the evolution of reciprocal altruism: for example, long life span; low dispersal rate; life in small, mutually dependent, stable social groups; and a long period of parental care leading to extensive contacts with close relatives for many years. Likewise, it seems likely that dominance relations were very complicated, with many opportunities for reversal depending on aid from others and preferential access to weapons. Aid in intraspecific combat, particularly by kin, almost certainly reduced the linearity of the dominance order in early humans. Studies of fights in living hunter–gatherers, such as the San of the Kalahari Desert, show that, in almost all fights that are initially between two individuals, others soon join in. Mortality, for example, often strikes the secondaries rather than the principals. Tool use has also probably had an equalizing effect on human dominance relations, and the San have a saying that nicely illustrates this. As a dispute reaches the stage where deadly weapons may be employed, an individual will often declare: "We are none of us big and others small; we are all men and we can fight; I am going to get my arrows."

Before turning to the emotional system underlying human reciprocal altruism, it is useful to distinguish between two kinds of cheating. In *gross* cheating the cheater fails to reciprocate at all, and the altruist suffers the cost of whatever altruism has been dispensed without compensating benefits. More broadly, gross cheating may be defined as reciprocating so little, if at all, that the altruist receives less benefit from the gross cheater than the cost of the altruist's acts of altruism to the cheater. Clearly, selection will strongly favor prompt discrimination against the gross cheater. *Subtle* cheating, by contrast, involves reciprocating, but always attempting to give less than one was given, or more precisely, to give less than the partner would give if the situation were reversed. In this situation, the altruist still benefits from the relationship but not as much as if the relationship were completely equitable, whereas the subtle cheater benefits more than if the relationship were equitable. Because human altruism may span long periods of time and because thousands of exchanges may take place involving many different goods and with many different cost–benefit ratios, the problem of computing the relevant totals, detecting imbalances, and deciding whether they are due to chance or to small-scale cheating is an extremely difficult one. Even then, the altruist is in an awkward position, symbolized by the folk saying "half a loaf is better than none." For if attempts to make the relationship equitable lead to the rupture of the relationship, the altruist may suffer the loss of the substandard altruism of the subtle cheater.

The importance of this last fact depends on the degree to which relationships are mutually exclusive. To some degree, they inevitably are, as altruistic acts exchanged between two individuals could be directed elsewhere. An individual who feels that another individual is subtly cheating on their relationship has the option of attempting to restore the relationship to equity or attempting to pair with another individual, thereby decreasing the possible exchanges between the altruist and the subtle cheater and replacing these with exchanges between reciprocal individuals. In short, he or she can switch friends.

The human altruistic system is a sensitive, unstable one. Often it will pay to cheat: namely, when the partner will not find out; when the partner will not discontinue his or her altruism even if he or she does find out; or when the partner is unlikely to survive long enough to reciprocate adequately. Also the perception of subtle cheating may be very difficult. Given the unstable character of the system, where a degree of cheating is adaptive, natural selection will rapidly favor a complex psychological system in which individuals regulate both their own altruistic and cheating tendencies and their responses to these tendencies in others. The system that results should allow individuals to reap the benefits of altruistic exchanges, protect themselves from gross and subtle forms of cheating, and practice those forms of cheating that local conditions make adaptive. Individuals will differ not in being altruists or cheaters but in the degree of altruism they show and in the conditions under which they will cheat.

## Friendship

The tendency to like other individuals who are not necessarily closely related, to form friendships, and to act altruistically toward friends and toward those one likes provides the immediate emotional rewards to motivate altruistic behavior and the formation of altruistic partnerships. We know from the work of social psychology that the relationship between altruism and liking is a two-way street: One is more altruistic toward those one likes, and one tends to like those who are most altruistic (reviewed in Trivers, 1971).

## Moralistic Aggression

Once strong, positive emotions have evolved to motivate altruistic behavior, the altruist is in a vulnerable position, because cheaters will be selected to take advantage of these positive emotions. This, in turn, sets up a selection pressure for a protective mechanism. I believe that a sense of fairness has evolved in human beings as the standard against which to measure the behavior of other people, so as to guard against cheating in reciprocal relationships. In turn, this sense of fairness is coupled with moralistic aggressiveness when cheating tendencies are discovered in a friend. A common feature of this aggression is that it often seems out of proportion to the offense that is committed. Friends are even killed over apparently trivial disputes, but since small inequities repeated many times over a lifetime may exact a heavy toll in inclusive fitness, selection may favor a strong show of aggression when the cheating tendency is discovered.

## Gratitude and Sympathy

If the cost–benefit ratio is an important factor in determining the adaptiveness of altruistic behavior, then humans should be selected to be sensitive to the cost and benefit of an altruistic act, both in deciding whether to perform one and in deciding how much to reciprocate. I think the emotion of gratitude has been selected to regulate human responses to altruistic acts and that the emotion is sensitive to the cost–benefit ratio of such acts. I believe the emotion of sympathy has been selected to motivate altruistic behavior as a function of the plight of the recipient of the behavior. Crudely put, the greater the potential benefit to the recipient, the greater the sympathy, and the more likely the altruistic gesture, even to strange or disliked individuals. Of course, this feature of sympathy applies to kin-directed altruism as well as reciprocal altruism, whereas gratitude only seems to apply to reciprocal relationships. Psychologists have shown that human beings reciprocate more when the original act was expensive for the benefactor, even though the benefit given is the same (Trivers, 1971).

## Guilt and Reparative Altruism

If an individual has cheated on a reciprocal relationship and this fact has been found out, or may shortly be found out, and if the partner responds by cutting off all future acts of aid, then the cheater will have paid dearly for the misdeed. It will be to his or her advantage to avoid this, and it may be to the partner's benefit to avoid this, since in cutting off future acts of aid, the partner sacrifices the benefits of future reciprocal help. If so, the cheater should be selected to make up for the misdeed and to show convincing evidence that future cheating is not planned; in short, a reparative gesture is called for. It seems plausible that the emotion of guilt has been selected for in humans partly in order to motivate the cheater to compensate for misdeeds and to behave reciprocally in the future, thus preventing the rupture of reciprocal relationships. The key is that one's cheating tendencies have been discovered. Social psychologists have produced a variety of evidence that publicly harming another individual leads to reparative altruistic behavior, but only when this harm is known to others (Trivers, 1971).

## Sense of Justice

As we have already noted, in complex systems of reciprocal altruism, individuals need a standard against which to judge the behavior of others. This will be especially true in species such as our own in which a system of multiparty altruism may operate in which an individual does not necessarily receive reciprocal benefits from the individual aided but may receive the return from third parties. This sense of justice involves two components: (a) that individuals share a common standard or sense of fairness; and (b) that infractions of this standard are associated with strong emotional reactions and aggressive impulses. Moral philosophers contend that a social arrangement is judged as fair when an individual endorses it without knowledge of which position in the arrangement the individual will occupy. In other words, a fair social arrangement must appear so, equally for each individual involved in the arrangement.

## COALITIONS IN BABOONS

Irven DeVore discovered 20 years ago in Kenya that there were two kinds of dominance hierarchies in free-ranging troops of baboons. On the one hand there was the usual, linear dominance hierarchy in which an individual was dominant to everyone below itself in the hierarchy and subordinant to everyone above. For example, in a troop of baboons in Gilgil, Kenya, in 1972, the five most dominant individuals were all adult males and were arrayed in decreasing order of dominance as follows: Arthur, Carl, Sumner, Rad, and Big Sam. This dominance hierarchy was ascertained by noticing which animal dominated the other in pairwise interactions in which other baboons were not taking part. So if Arthur and Carl were fighting over a piece of food apart from other baboons, Arthur would dominate Carl, and likewise everyone whom Carl dominated, Arthur also dominated.

In some situations, however, especially in male–male competition over access to estrous females, we may see expressed what has been called a central hierarchy. Individuals may support each other in fight in such a way as to reverse some of the usual dominance rankings. For example, in this particular troop, Carl was the centrally most dominant male. In fights with Arthur over access to a female named Anne, he was supported by Sumner, Rad, or Big Sam.

Irven DeVore and I watched some fascinating interactions for several days at Gilgil in 1972. Events revolved around Anne, who was exceedingly attractive to both Carl and Arthur. What happened was that Carl would spend the night with Anne; we would arrive in the morning and find them going off to feed. Arthur would stay close to Carl and Anne while pretending disinterest: not looking at Anne, not looking at Carl, but always moving off in the same direction they did. DeVore soon noticed that Anne was playing her own game in this relationship; namely, she was leading Carl away from other troop members. Once DeVore pointed this out, it seemed very obvious. It appeared that Anne wanted to get Carl away from his supporters in order to see a one-on-one confrontation between Arthur and Carl. So she wandered through quite a bit of the troop's range that day, and we saw three separate occasions on which a member of the central hierarchy intervened to try to prevent Arthur from interrupting Carl and Anne's mating. Carl would mount Anne and start thrusting, at which point Arthur would rush in to try to break up the copulation. One of the males—Sumner, Rad, or Big Sam—would respond to this scene by interposing himself between Carl and the onrushing Arthur. If this was successful, then Carl and Anne would be able to complete their copulation, and the two males would join together and chase Arthur off.

Arthur had joined the troop 6 months earlier. He was not only not related to any of these males (so far as we knew), but he also had not had much time to establish friendly relationships with them. By contrast, Carl and the other central males had been in the same troop for some time. Studies of many baboon troops show that males do not stay in the troops they are born in but disperse as young adults to new troops, and they appear to disperse independently of each other, so that two brothers growing up in the same troop are not likely to end up as adults in the same troop.

This alone suggests that these coalitions are based on mutual support more than on kinship.

A student of monkey behavior, Craig Packer, published in 1977 an analysis of baboon coalitions he observed at the Gombe Stream Preserve in Tanzania. He watched 18 adult males in three troops. He was interested in whether individuals who supported others in fights got support in return and, in particular, whether they got support from the same individuals they helped. (A baboon solicits help in several ways, primarily by repeatedly and rapidly turning its head from the solicited individual toward the third individual—the opponent—while continuously threatening the third.)

Packer saw 140 solicitations of which 97 resulted in support. This, in itself, is a strong tendency for individuals to act altruistically among themselves. Of these solicitations, 20 involved conflict over a female in estrous, in which the attacker solicited aid from another male. These solicitations over an estrual female were supported significantly more frequently than solicitations over other matters. In 6 of the 20 cases, the female was lost by the defender to the two attackers. In all 6 of these cases, the female then went into consort with the male who solicited the help. Note that this would give the supporter only the pleasure of his support, which may have occurred at some real risk. (Adult male baboons are armed with dagger-like canines and the supporting musculature to use them, and fights sometimes result in substantial injury.) If this behavior were to make sense, we would expect the altruist to receive some return support in the future.

Since central males do not travel around together in a clump, solicitations are vital in order to elicit the central hierarchy. Encounters between coalitions and single individuals do not seem to affect subsequent pairwise encounters between a coalition member and the same opponent. Coalitions at Gombe were generally formed by one male enlisting another male to fight against a third. The partner was not directly involved in the interaction before he was enlisted.

Packer found 13 different pairs of males who reciprocated in joining coalitions at each other's request. In 6 of these pairs, each pair member enlisted the other against the same opponent. Individual males who most frequently gave aid were those which most frequently received aid. Likewise, each male tended to request aid from an individual who, in turn, requested aid from him. Ten males solicited other males on 4 or more occasions. For 9 of these 10, the partner that was solicited most often (the solicitee), in turn, solicited the other male (the solicitor) more often than the average number of occasions on which the solicitee solicited all other adult males in the troop.

These correlations could result entirely from effects of kinship. If you and I are blood brothers, related by $\frac{1}{2}$, then, on the basis of kinship, I will act altruistically more often toward you than toward others, and, on the basis of the same kinship, you will act altruistically toward me more often than toward others. So we will appear to reciprocate each other's altruism, when, in fact, we are each basing it on the common kinship. We need information other than these correlations to rule out kinship.

Packer has additional information for 4 of the 13 reciprocating pairs, and our knowledge of other baboon troops suggests that Packer would find similar results for his other 9 pairs if he had the right information. Namely, both individuals of these 4 reciprocating pairs were first seen as young adults in different troops, before they had apparently dispersed. They did not end up residing in the same troop until at least 5 years had passed. It was when these males were residing in the same troop that the reciprocating relationships were formed. This suggests that kinship is not mediating these four relationships, and, by extension, does not have much to do with central hierarchies in baboon troops.

One last fact from Packer's study: Adult males were sometimes solicited by adult females and by juveniles of both sexes, but they responded to such solicitations less frequently than to those of other adult males. This also suggests reciprocity in interactions between adult males because adult females and juveniles cannot, in fact, return the favor very effectively. Their support is of very little value in a fight with another adult male (and their support is unnecessary in other fights). In fact, adult males only solicit each other.

DeVore and I witnessed, in the interaction between Carl and Arthur over Anne, one particularly unique behavior, namely, a double message. Arthur decided to have a discussion with Rad, who had been aiding Carl against Arthur. The form of the discussion was to threaten Rad from extremely close quarters, and in such a way that it made the hair on Rad's body bristle. Arthur would circle Rad, and then he would show his canines and flash his pad; then he would get down and then come up and flash them again. The double message was this: While displaying his canines at Rad, Arthur also turned his rear end toward Rad. In baboon society, presenting your rear end is a friendly, affiliative gesture, with a slightly subordinate flavor, whereas threatening with your canines is decidedly hostile. The threats seemed to say, ''You better think this thing through carefully. You do this again, and I am going to eat you alive,'' but the affiliative gesture seemed to say, ''There is potential for a new central hierarchy in the Gilgil troop, and, if you play your cards right, there could be a special place in it for you.''

I cannot tell you the excitement that went through me watching all this. First of all, Arthur was a superb male in his young prime. Carl was a middle-aged male who had seen better times but had the right connections. This, in fact, mimicked exactly, from my standpoint, my relationship with Professor DeVore, and, sure enough, he found himself identifying with Carl, whereas I was completely with Arthur. In fact, I was certain, based on my general knowledge of animal behavior and my strong identification with Arthur, that in a matter of days this thing would be wrapped up. Carl's body would be found cast aside somewhere in the undergrowth, and Arthur would be treated with the respect that was his due, but DeVore was saying, ''You don't understand social change. You don't understand the power of the establishment. No dramatic change is going to take place. The system is stronger than you think.'' DeVore was right: No dramatic change did occur. Arthur got his one night with Anne, and she got her night with him, but the next morning she was back with Carl. There were other females who came into estrus during the next several months, but Anne was not one of them, and the competition between the males was much less intense. Then Arthur was shot to death one day for raiding someone's fruit trees, so we never found out if he was able to establish a new central hierarchy under his benevolent leadership.

I think one of the reasons a baboon solicits another male by looking at him is to make sure the eyes meet each other. Then he knows that the other male sees his need, and he knows that, if the male does not respond, it is because he is choosing not to. The importance of eye contact is suggested by an observation we made at the Mara-Maasai Game Preserve in Kenya. Tourist food was dropped in the garbage dump around 2:30 every afternoon, and about 15 species of animals, including a baboon troop, were onto this fact and started congregating from about 1:30 P.M. to get the fresh food. When the food was dumped, the hyenas chased out the other species; then the baboons came in and chased out the hyenas, and then the most dominant baboon chased out all the other baboons, so he ate alone a few minutes while all the other baboons were ringing the garbage pit and looking on. Then an adult female with a very young infant came down, joined the most dominant male, sat very close to him, and started feeding. Presumably he permitted her there because of the young infant, and one is tempted to believe that he may have been the father or may have supposed himself the father. In any case, the sight of this female, who was much less dominant than the second-most dominant male, enraged the second-most dominant male. But he could not attack the female while she was sitting next to the most dominant male, so he threatened her. She was just like Carl when Arthur was threatening Rad; she always positioned herself so as not to see the threat. He would stand right on the edge of the garbage pit and threaten her directly, while she would turn her back to him. He would then run around the garbage pit until he was facing her and would threaten her, but always by the time he had gotten there, she had shifted her position again. The significance of this seemed to be, ''If I threaten you, you see it, and you still sit there, then later when I catch you alone, there is going to be a very unpleasant interaction; but if you can arrange not to see the threat, then it is as if there is no moral obligation to respond to it.'' This seemed true even though it was obvious that she was going out of her way to avoid seeing it, which means she was aware of it.

Baboons are monkeys that took to the ground some 10–30 million years ago and faced intense predator pressure. It was advantageous for adult males to cooperate in defending the group from predators. Presumably this is the primary selection pressure that molded the social group and molded male–male relationships so as to permit the further evolution of reciprocity between the males in interactions with each other.

## NEIGHBORING

Any relationship with a neighbor is a partly hostile, partly cooperative interaction. Imagine two neighboring male birds, setting up their breeding territories. They share a common boundary, and initially they argue over exactly where the boundary should be. They could argue with each other for months over exactly where the boundary should be, and, at the end of all that arguing, the boundary would probably not be much different than it is after the first week of settling in. On the other hand, they have wasted time and energy in constant bickering. They have made themselves more available to predators and more vulnerable to male interlopers while they are busy fighting each other. So there should exist in nature a strong selection pressure to settle down and say, in effect, "That is my neighbor. As long as he is in his territory, he is all right with me. I will not waste energy in foolishness."

This has been verified experimentally by using playbacks of male song. Males sing in the morning to advertise territory to other males and to females. You can record these songs and then play these tape recordings back so as to run experiments on how intense the reaction is of the bird hearing the playback. What you find is that after the birds have settled into adjacent territories, if you play an individual's song from inside his territory, you get a mild aggressive response from his neighbor. If you tape record the song of a bird hundreds of meters away and play the tape as if coming from the neighbor's territory, it elicits an intense aggressive response. So males clearly discriminate between familiar neighbors and unfamiliar birds, the less aggressive response for the known individual.

What happens, however, if a bird hears his neighbor's call from an unusual place, for example, from the other side of his territory? This results in the most aggressive response of all—much more aggressive than the response to the sound of a strange bird calling nearby. This is presumably because the neighbor who is also willing to call from the other end of the bird's territory, is the greatest threat of all: He is violating any agreement about territorial boundaries. The bird will immediately want to know how he gets from one end to the other without passing through the bird's own territory and where else he may have been in the meantime without singing. This response to the familiar individual calling from an unfamiliar place suggests the kind of discrimination against cheaters that is necessary in order to gain the benefits of friendly relations with your neighbors without suffering the costs of negligence.

## RECIPROCITY INVOLVING HELPERS AT THE NEST

There are systems in birds, and also in social carnivores, characterized by so-called "helpers at the nest." Where these have been studied, it turns out that helpers are usually related to the individuals they are raising. So this system of altruism appears to be based on kinship. At first, people supposed that this was the only factor, but now we suspect that reciprocity is sometimes also a component of the system. We find that there are situations in which individuals will regularly help unrelated individuals raise their young, and reciprocity may come not from the parents but from the offspring. A year later they may help the helpers at their nest rather than their own parents. This may lead to some ambivalence on the part of parents toward the behavior of helpers, especially when those helpers are not related to them. That is, the parents would like to get help, but they do not want a friendly relationship growing between their chicks and the bird that is helping, since this may lead their chicks later to help the helpers.

In watching hunting dogs, James Malcolm and I believe we saw evidence of this kind of ambivalence. In one of the packs we were watching on the Serengeti Plains in Tanzania, there were three brothers who helped feed the young. The least dominant of the three regurgitated most of the food to the pups in the first few hours after a hunt, and, in general, regurgitated more than his share to the pups. The most dominant male, who was the father of the pups, was the last to regurgitate food, so if the others had regurgitated lots of food, he did not have to regurgitate much. He was quite content to see the third most dominant male regurgitate food to his pups. When this male, who genuinely seemed to like the pups, wanted to play with them, the dominant male was hostile, and he would snarl at the other male and chase him away from enjoying the companionship of the pups. The only evolutionary logic we could attach to this was that he was jealous of the possibility of a closer emotional relationship between the pups and their uncle than between the pups and himself, and the possible cost of this closer feeling is suggested by the studies of helpers in birds, namely that 2 or 3 years later, these pups, as adults, may form a coalition with their uncle—not their father—and hence lower their father's inclusive fitness.

## ARE DOLPHINS AND WHALES RECIPROCAL ALTRUISTS?

From the time of antiquity, dolphins and whales have been known for their altruism and for the ease in which these creatures extend this altruism beyond the boundaries of their own species. Ancient Greek coins depict dolphins rescuing humans. Similar unsubstantiated stories come from the present time. An entire book of the Bible tells the story of a man, Jonah, who spends 3 days in the belly of a whale in order to learn the lesson that you cannot run from God. Whether these stories are authentic or not, it is clear from a review by Richard Conner and Kenneth Norris (1982) that dolphins and whales often direct similar forms of altruism to members of other species. Likewise, their behavior shows a subtlety and sophistication that suggests they could easily appreciate the dilemma of human beings drowning and come to the rescue.

Carrying individuals to safety is easily derived from a common dolphin–whale habit, which is to give physical support to the sick, injured, or very young. This help comes in three forms: standing by, assistance, and support. Standing by occurs when an animal stays with another animal in distress but does not offer obvious aid. Often an individual will remain in a dangerous situation far longer than it would if there were no one in distress. Assistance includes approaching an injured comrade and showing excited behavior, such as swimming between the captor and its prey, biting or attacking capture vessels, and pushing an injured individual away from a would-be captor. Most of these examples come from descriptions of capture attempts. Support occurs when one or more animals maintain a distressed animal at the surface of the water. A supporting animal usually does not feed, stations itself below the sick animal—either right-side up or upside-down—and presses upward, leaving this position only long enough to breathe, but keeping the stricken animal at the surface. The behavior stops when the sick animal dies or recovers enough to swim by itself.

A striking feature of this help is that it is often extended to dolphins and whales of other species. Standing by has been observed at sea between members of widely different genera. For example, Kenneth Norris reports that during the capture of a young adult, female, Pacific pilot whale, a group of Pacific-striped dolphins stood by the struggling whale during capture and stayed even while the whale was being brought aboard the vessel. There is no doubt that whales and dolphins understand when another cetacean is being captured. They will often bite restraining lines of harpooned animals during capture, propel injured animals away from captors, and even attack the captors. An interesting example was again observed by Norris, in which an adult pilot whale was shot and killed instantly. It drifted toward the capture vessel. When it was a few meters from the vessel's rail, two other pilot whales rose on either side of the animal, and pressing their snouts on top of its head, took it down and away from the vessel so that it was never seen again. Notice that the dead whale was not supported in the usual fashion, but was spirited away from the would-be captors in exactly the opposite manner usually seen during support.

Support of injured comrades was probably derived from support of babies at birth. Dolphins and whales, unlike seals, give birth in the ocean, and often a second female assists in holding the newborn infant at the surface of the water so it can breathe. Females have also been seen removing a stillborn from its mother. A captive dolphin was observed to pull a hypodermic syringe from a tankmate during medical treatment; the helper then attacked the veterinarian. In nature, such behavior may be used to remove clinging remoras and similar ectoparasites.

Two other features of cetacean altruism are worth mentioning. First, there are several accounts of dolphins and whales sharing food. Sharing food is such a rare form of altruism in nature that these accounts are themselves of interest. For example, a whale may capture a fish, and instead of swallowing it, swim around among its schoolmates who feed off the fish. Likewise, dolphins often hunt cooperatively and encircle a school of fish. Through some unknown effect, the fish may become nearly immobilized so that a human observer can reach into such a school and pick up fish by hand at the surface. After such cooperative encirclement, the dolphins share the rewards.

Finally, dolphins and whales are subject to strong predation from sharks. They appear to travel in schools partly in order to gain mutual defense. They warn each other of the approach of predators, they may attack predators together, and, as we have seen, they will come to the assistance of an injured individual in a variety of ways. Indeed, scientists regard predation as the primary force favoring social living in dolphins and whales, and if so, this is probably similar to the recent evolutionary history of humans (see the following).

In addition to many examples of altruistic behavior, dolphins and whales are of interest to human beings because they appear to have evolved in a similar way, despite a very different background. Dolphins and whales are highly social creatures, spending their lives in social groups, whose constitution is sometimes very fluid. Dolphins and whales have evolved large brains relative to their bodies, so that they are relatively brainier than most other mammals except monkeys and apes. As one would expect, these large brains are associated with sophisticated learning abilities. This includes the ability to achieve what is called *second-order learning*. For example, rough-toothed dolphins were taught by standard conditioning methods to perform novel behavior in order to gain a reward. They soon made the intuitive leap that new behavior was required and began to pour out large numbers of invented patterns never before seen in captivity or sea, such as corkscrew swimming and gliding upside down with the tail out of the water. It is clear that individuals in a social group recognize each other as individuals, since they are able to form stable dominance hierarchies in captivity, sometimes including members of two different genera. Dolphins are able to recognize their trainers and sometimes have strong favorites among them. In turn, dolphin whistles are known to differ individually, and trained dolphins are known to discriminate unerringly between the whistles of several individuals. Finally, it is noteworthy that dolphins and whales are very long-lived animals, so that they have ample opportunity to form many individual associations lasting for many years. For example, the oceanic dolphin matures at between 9 and 12 years of age and reaches a maximum age of about 45 years. Sperm whales have been known to live for 75 years.

## Kinship or Reciprocity?

How are we to explain the unusual examples of altruistic behavior in dolphins and whales? The common approach is that of Wilson (1975) who imagines that altruistic behavior in the cetaceans may represent an innate behavior selected for on the basis of effects to close relatives, but this explanation immediately runs into two problems. First, altruism in the cetacea is directed very widely, to members of one's own species and to members of other species. Second, in some species, group structure is very fluid, yet altruism is common.

The frequent examples of interspecific altruism observed in captivity might be supposed to result from an unnatural association, but, in fact, interspecific associations in nature are very frequent. In some cases species travel together regularly, for example, Pacific bottlenose dolphins and North Pacific pilot whales. Groups are sometimes intimately mixed, and one species may imitate the behavior patterns of the other. Helping behavior has been reported between species that associate regularly as well as those that do not. Some of the partners in these exchanges look very different. For example, pilot whales and striped dolphins often travel together, and each species exhibits helping behavior toward the other. Striped dolphins are chunky, black, white, and gray animals reaching about 2 m in length and up to 90 kg in weight. Pilot whales are elongate, almost entirely black animals with bulbous heads, very large fins, and very long tails. They exceed 6 m in length and may weigh over 800 kg. As Connor and Norris (1982) point out, the best explanation for dolphin and whale altruism is that these animals possess "a generalized perception of distress. . . . In normal schools the altruism must extend to most members, and in situations where other species are present, often to them as well [p. 369]."

This interpretation is supported by two features of dolphin altruism. It is often expensive; indeed, animals may lose their lives trying to help a captured animal. When altruistic behavior is costly, we would expect animals to be especially careful about those they choose to help. Second, dolphins and whales appear to be very intelligent creatures, easily capable of making the appropriate discriminations. Nor does much of their altruistic behavior appear to be highly stereotyped. For example, dolphins and whales will offer aid even when this requires a new behavior pattern to do so.

The second factor that argues against kinship is dispersion. In some species, animals travel in separate groups (called pods), and these may remain distinct for many years. For example, groups of individually recognized Atlantic bottlenose dolphins showed little intermixing over a 10-year period, but in many species of dolphins there is good evidence that herds are composed of subgroups that may vary continually in composition. For example, a herd of 100 bottlenose dolphins living along a 40-km stretch of Florida coast did not intermix with adjacent herds, but, within the herd, traveling groups varied on a daily basis, although some association patterns were frequently seen. A herd of more than 50 South Atlantic bottlenose dolphins contained some subgroups that remained stable for months and then changed, whereas other subgroups were continually breaking up and being formed.

This degree of fluidity in group structure, combined with high altruism toward group members, is not what you would expect based on kinship. By contrast, the ability to recognize a large number of other animals and strong benefits to reciprocal interactions would both permit and encourage this kind of fluidity. Conner and Norris (1982) believe that it is predation that selects for this pattern. Dolphins and whales are vulnerable to sharks and travel in groups in order to minimize shark predation. Individuals warn each other of the approach of a predator; they aid each other in escaping the predator and come to the aid of an individual injured during predation. If predation pressure molded dolphin group formation and early altruism, then it must often have favored distantly related individuals traveling together for mutual defense. Dolphins and whales are long-lived, slowly reproducing animals, so that increase in group size via reproduction would be a very slow process. For this reason members of different species probably often travel together at least occasionally as opportunity arises for mutual protection. In these circumstances fluidity of social structure maximizes the possible number of altruistic relationships.

Predation also seems to favor mixed-species aggregations in fish. Individuals who feed near small clumps of coral and dart to safety in the coral are vulnerable when traveling from one piece of coral to another. I have frequently observed in Jamaica that such individuals wait until a school of fish passes by going in the right direction. The coral fish then joins the school, like getting on a bus, and leaves it when it reaches an attractive piece of coral.

## The Parallel Evolution of Humans and Dolphins

Dolphins and whales seem similar to humans in a number of respects, especially in their high intelligence, large brain–body ratio, high degree of sociality, and strong tendency to direct altruism beyond the bounds of immediate kinship. Connor and Norris (1982) suggest that the similarities between these widely divergent creatures is not accidental but results from a similar evolutionary step. Human ancestors descended from the trees some 5–20 million years ago and invaded a new zone, the savannah. In the case of dolphins and whales, these animals descended from four-legged, land-living mammals. They invaded a new zone, the ocean, and were very vulnerable to predation (and still are). Connor and Norris (1982) further believe that high interdependence led to strong reciprocal altruism that, in turn, led to high intelligence, and they state the argument as follows:

> We believe this marked increase in mutual dependence, contributed significantly to the evolution of the higher-order intelligences seen in humans and dolphins by producing strong selection pressures for individuals to practice reciprocal altruism with greater sophistication. This can be explained in terms of an increase in the costs and benefits of reciprocal interactions. In environments where mutual dependence is low (e.g., low predation pressures) individuals are by definition more self-reliant, and thus the costs an individual suffers are low because it can effectively provide for itself. The same reasoning applies to the benefits of receiving altruism in an equivalent exchange of successfully cheating. As mutual dependence increases, however, individuals are no longer able to provide for themselves as effectively, so the costs and benefits of their interactions with others increase; i.e., interactions have a greater effect on their fitness. This produces strong selection pressures for more sophisticated mechanisms for gaining the advantage in reciprocal interactions which are manifested as more complicated emotional systems, better memory and foresight, greater learning capacity, and the ability to make second-order abstractions, etc. (i.e., many of the components we associate with intelligence). The situation is further compounded when social communication is brought into the picture. Now, how one individual acts toward another may affect how the *society* acts toward it. The costs and benefits of a given interaction in this case will be enormously greater, as will the selection pressures for increased intelligence in animals that have been shunted into this evolutionary pathway [p. 371].

## THE PRISONER'S DILEMMA AND TIT FOR TAT

Game theorists have likened reciprocal altruism to the problem of the prisoner's dilemma. The prisoner's dilemma refers to the imaginary situation in which two individuals are imprisoned and accused of having cooperated to perform some crime. The prisoners are held separately, and attempts are made to induce each one to implicate the other. If neither one does, both are set free. This is the cooperative strategy. In order to tempt one or both to defect, each is told that a confession that implicates the other will result in his or her release and, in addition, a small reward. If both confess, each one is imprisoned, but, if one individual implicates the other, and not vice versa, then the implicated partner receives a harsher sentence than if both had implicated the other. We can symbolize the payoffs as follows. $T$ is the temptation to implicate the other; $R$ is the reward each one gets if neither one defects; $P$ is the punishment each one gets if both defect; and $S$ is the sucker's payoff, the penalty that one suffers if implicated by the partner. Thus, $T > R > P > S$.

The dilemma comes as follows. If each one thinks rationally, then each one will decide that the best course is to implicate the other. Thus both will be worse off than if each had decided to trust the other. Consider the problem from the standpoint of the first individual, who reasons as follows: If the partner fails to implicate her or him, then the individual ought to implicate the partner in order to gain $T$ instead of $R$, and, the individual reasons, if the partner implicates her or him, then it will also be better to implicate the partner and thus suffer $P$ instead of $S$.

The prisoner's dilemma mimics reciprocal altruism in the following way. Each stands to gain $R$ from reciprocal altruism, but each is tempted to enjoy the altruism without reciprocating, thereby gaining $T$. If neither reciprocates, however, then each only gains $P$, whereas the altruist who is not reciprocated does worst of all and ends up with only $S$. In single encounters there is no solution to the prisoner's dilemma except to cheat, and both individuals end up relatively badly off, but if prisoner's dilemmas are repeated a number of times, then it may be advantageous to cooperate on the early moves and cheat only toward the end of the game. It is possible to play repeated games of prisoner's dilemma in which each individual must decide which option to take without knowing what the other is simultaneously choosing, and each learns the results only after both have chosen. A new game then presents itself. When people know the total number of games to be played, they do, indeed, cheat more often in the final games.

The relationship between reciprocal altruism and the prisoner's dilemma is significant because the mathematics of the prisoner's dilemma is fairly well worked out. By conceptualizing reciprocal altruism as a series of prisoner's dilemmas, it is possible to derive some very interesting results. Axelrod and Hamilton (1981) discovered that one tactic is superior to all others in playing repeated games of prisoner's dilemma. This tactic is called *tit for tat*.

Axelrod discovered the superiority of the tit-for-tat strategy in an unusual way. He conducted a computer tournament. People were asked to submit strategies for playing 200 games of prisoner's dilemma. Fourteen game theorists in various disciplines such as economics and mathematics submitted entries. These 14 and a totally random strategy were paired with each other in a round robin. Some of these strategies were very intricate. For example, one modeled the opponent's behavior as a Markoff process and then used certain rules of mathematical inference to select what seemed to be the appropriate counterstrategy, but the result of the tournament was that the highest average score was attained by the simplest of all strategies submitted, tit for tat. Tit for tat had only two rules: On the first move, cooperate; on each succeeding move, do what your opponent did on the previous move. Thus, tit for tat may be characterized as a strategy of cooperation based on reciprocity.

Axelrod saw the computer tournament as an analogy to the evolutionary process. Imagine that a species finds itself in a situation in which individuals have about 200 opportunities to exchange altruistic acts with each other. We may imagine that mutation and recombination provide a series of possible strategies, including an entirely random one. These strategies then interact, and we see which one ends up gaining the greatest average benefit. Many people have pointed out that there is a similarity between genetic mutation and human mental innovation, but, so far as I know, Axelrod is the first person to use this similarity in order to gain deeper insight into the evolutionary process.

To intensify the competition between tit for tat and other strategies, Axelrod circulated the results of the first round robin and solicited entries for a second round. (In the second round, the *average* length of each game was 200 moves, with the probability that a given move would not be the last being slightly less than one.) This time there were 62 entries from six countries. Most of the contestants were computer hobbyists but included professors of evolutionary biology, physics, and computer science, as well as the disciplines represented earlier. Tit for tat was again submitted, and once again it won.

Each tournament may be considered a single generation of natural selection. So as to mimic the evolutionary process more exactly, Axelrod constituted the next generation by submitting entries according to their success in the previous interaction. The strategies were then played against each other in their new frequencies, and successive generations of selection were generated in the same way. The results showed that, as the less successful rules were displaced, tit for tat continued to do well. In the long run, it displaced all other rules and went to fixation. This provides further evidence that the simple strategy of what we might call *contingent reciprocity* is highly successful in competition with a variety of counterstrategies at various frequencies.

An analysis of the 3 million choices that were made in the second round identified three features of the tit-for-tat strategy as important in its success:

1. *It was never the first to defect*—that is, a tit-for-tat player begins by cooperating and defects only after the partner has defected.
2. *It was provoked into retaliation by a defection of the other.* The tit-for-tat player is a very cautious individual who immediately responds to non-reciprocation by cutting off additional altruism.
3. *It was forgiving after just one act of retaliation.* The tit-for-tat player is ever optimistic, taking any altruistic act by the partner as an invitation to reciprocity.

In summary, the tit-for-tat strategy consists of two rules. In the beginning, do unto others as you would have them do unto you. After that, do unto others as they have just done unto you.

Perhaps the most striking feature of the tit-for-tat strategy is the fact that one's memory extends only to the previous move in the relationship. One might imagine that it would be useful to know what one's partner had done 5 or 10 or 20 moves earlier, but in terms of immediate behavior, the only relevant question is this: What have you done for me lately?

## CONCLUSION

In summary reciprocal interactions were probably important in human evolution. They not only generated a series of emotions to regulate reciprocal tendencies, but they also generated a sense of fairness against which to measure the behavior of others and to detect subtle cheaters. Reciprocity is, in turn, not just found in humans. There is good evidence from other primates, especially baboons, that reciprocal interactions are important, and there is evidence from dolphins and whales that reciprocity may have been an important part of their social evolution. Regarding strategies of reciprocity recent work has shown that as long as interactions between potentially reciprocating pairs is sufficiently frequent, natural selection favors a tit-for-tat strategy. Individuals are favored to begin altruistically but to respond to any defection by the other with an immediate withdrawal of altruistic benefits. At present we have only tentative suggestions that monkeys, birds, and dolphins may discriminate against cheaters in their midst, but that they are favored to do so seems all but certain. If so, selection for a sense of fairness and for a simple tit-for-tat mentality governing reciprocal exchanges may be operating in many social species at present and may have evolved in our own lineage long before the advent of language.

## REFERENCES

Axelrod, R., & Hamilton, W. D. The evolution of cooperation. *Science*, 1981, *211*, 1390–1396.
Conner, R. C., & Norris, K. S. Are dolphins reciprocal altruists? *American Naturalist*, 1982, *119*, 358–374.
Hamilton, W. D. The genetical evolution of social behavior. *Journal of Theoretical Biology*, 1964, *7*, 1–52.
Packer, C. Reciprocal altruism in *Papio anubis. Nature*, 1977, *265*, 441–443.
Trivers, R. L. The evolution of reciprocal altruism. Quarterly Review of Biology, 1971, *46*(4), 35–57.
Wilson, E. O. *Sociobiology*. Cambridge, Mass.: Harvard University Press, 1975.

# Commentary and Critique: Sociobiological Approaches to Prosocial Development

## DENNIS KREBS

A graduate student once rushed up to me and exclaimed that Donald Campbell had included my name in a list of psychologists who had written about the genetics of altruism but who did not really know what they were talking about. Campbell was able to say this with dignity because he used some of his own past work to demonstrate the naiveté of psychologists who had ventured into the complexities of evolutionary theory. Having undergone a biological baptism, he felt comfortable chastising the rest of us for our limitations in this domain. By and large, his characterization of psychological biologizers was fair; Campbell deserves a great deal of credit for drawing psychologists' attention to the significance of evolutionary biology and for elevating their level of sophistication about its constructs.

The focus of Campbell's contribution to this volume is on the evolution of altruism in the social insects and the human species. In order to understand his arguments, it helps to review the development of his thought on this matter. In 1965 Campbell published an article in which he argued that although natural selection on an individual level would inevitably eliminate any altruistic tendencies that appeared in a population, the adaptive advantage of groups of altruists over groups of nonaltruists could cause self-sacrificial altruism to be selected at the group level. (Altruism here is defined as any behavior that enhances another's net genetic fitness at a net cost to one's own genetic fitness.) Over the years, however, Campbell changed his mind about the possibility that altruism could prevail through group selection. Although group versus group selection of many social behaviors may occur, there is a lethal problem with this type of selection when it applies to altruism. Although it is true that groups with a high proportion of individuals

61

willing to sacrifice their lives for the sake of the others may fare better in the "struggle for survival" than groups containing only selfish individuals, as long as there is variation in dispositions toward self-sacrificial altruism *within* the group (competition among the cooperators), the relatively nonaltruistic individuals will reap the rewards of the altruism of their fellows without suffering the costs (i.e., self-sacrifice). The altruists will diminish within the group, leaving the more selfish to prevail. Thus, concluded Campbell, genetic dispositions toward self-sacrificial altruism are doomed in all species in which there is competition within groups.

Convinced that the process of group selection was not, as he previously assumed, adequate to mediate the evolution of altruism in humans, Campbell (1975) recanted his earlier position. In a brilliant American Psychological Association presidential address, he argued that although true altruism could evolve in social insects who do not compete against one another genetically within groups (because they are sterile), true altruism could not have evolved in humans (where within-group selection would favor selfishness). Campbell went on to argue that humans have created prosocial cultural prescriptions to counteract natural, biologically based antisocial dispositions. This line of thought planted Campbell flat in the middle of an "original sin" conception of human nature—endowing humans with an innate core of individualistic selfishness held in check by social and cultural mores. Not satisfied with antagonizing the humanists in his audience, Campbell went on to goad the liberals by emphasizing that his analysis implied that people ought to have more respect for moral tradition. Needless to say, Campbell's 1975 address created quite a stir in the social sciences, evoking a spate of critical responses (see Wispé & Thompson, 1976). Campbell's contribution to the present volume can be viewed as a defense, refinement, and elaboration of some of the ideas he presented in 1975.

The central issue addressed by Campbell here is whether there is any route to altruism in the human species other than through group selection. To evoke an old cliché, did Campbell throw out the baby (innate dispositions toward altruism) with the bathwater (group selection)? At this point, no one has really supplied a definitive answer to this question. What I would like to do here is to review the five main routes to biologically based altruism that have been proposed by contemporary sociobiologists, and indicate why they fall short. I will then sketch out (or, more exactly, extend) a route that I believe may get us closer and discuss the relationship between biological and cultural evolution.

## RECIPROCITY

One of the main routes to altruism that Campbell considers is reciprocity. Campbell's ideas on reciprocity have been influenced by the work of Robert Trivers. It is appropriate, therefore, to digress from this discussion of Campbell's ideas and consider Trivers' contribution to this volume. Reading about Trivers' experiences in Kenya reminded me of the evenings I spent at his house when we were both graduate students at Harvard, totally enraptured by descriptions of his research on lizards. Trivers was working on his first paper on reciprocal altruism then, and, although many of us found his ideas extraordinarily creative, no one had any idea how influential they ultimately would become.

The central issue explored by Trivers in Chapter 2 concerns the conditions that mediate and control the development of systems of reciprocal helping in various species, especially humans. The first task he faces is to establish that individuals in the species he examines actually help one another. The second is to establish that the helping is supported by reciprocity. Trivers convincingly demonstrates that baboons and whales help one another. Baboons help subordinate males in their troops gain access to females by fending off other, often more dominant, males. Whales help others in distress; they share food; they help one another hunt; and they engage in mutual defense. In order to make his case that these helping behaviors are maintained through reciprocity, he must establish that (a) they are, in fact, reciprocated; and (b) they are not maintained by other processes such as kin selection. Trivers meets the first condition for baboons by citing the systematic observations of Packer. The data for dolphins is more anecdotal. Although it is logically impossible to meet the second condition fully (it would entail proving the null hypothesis), Trivers makes a good case that the helping behaviors he cites could not have developed through kin selection.

What most of us ultimately are concerned about is ourselves. Of the two comparison species—baboons and whales—baboons might seem to supply the better basis for extrapolations to humans. However, Trivers persuasively shows how what happened to whales may supply a better analogue to what happened to us. Both humans and whales underwent a radical ecological change millions of years ago that increased their individual vulnerability to predators and increased the adaptiveness of group hunting. These and other pressures forced, in a sense, these species to develop cooperative relations—individuals could not get along without one another. Cooperation entails checks and balances, controls, discriminations, and, when extended over time, the ability to remember. It is closely associated with the ability to communicate. It seems plausible that the adaptive advantages associated with balanced cooperation (perhaps especially tit-for-tat reciprocity) were instrumental in giving rise to brain enlargement and high order intelligence in both humans and whales (see Krebs & Miller, in press, for an elaboration of these ideas).

In addition to outlining the logic of reciprocal helping, Trivers outlines the necessity for checks and balances and speculates about the selection of innate dispositions in humans to experience emotions such as sympathy, gratitude, moralistic aggression, etc. The issue here is an old one; it involves the conflict between individual and society. Given certain conditions, it is in the best interest of individuals in a group to abide by the rules of reciprocity because if a significant number of them cheat, the system will disintegrate, leaving everyone with less. However, all social systems can tolerate a little deviance. Therefore, it is in each individual's selfish interest to preserve systems of reciprocity by preventing cheating by others but to cheat himself or herself when he or she can get away with it. With Trivers and Campbell, I believe that individuals inherit the "temptation" to cheat when they can get away with it, especially when the gains are large.

If individuals are disposed to cheat when they can get away with it, it is in the interest of others to monitor their behavior in order to prevent cheating. Furthermore, it is in the interest of individuals to monitor their own behavior in order to avoid transgressions that will be punished. Campbell raises the possibility that people acquire different "criterion images"—standards for detecting transgression—for the behavior of others than they do for their own behavior. The notion of a biologically based discrepancy between the criterion images individuals employ to evaluate the behavior of self and the behavior of others has implications for a wide array of issues in social and developmental psychology. In addition to the self–other differences in attribution theory and the use of various defense mechanisms such as rationalization, this notion may cast light on the phenomena of egocentricity and role-taking and, through them, moral development. One of the central shortcomings of existing tests of moral development such as Kohlberg's is that they tap only reasoning about hypothetical others. As found by Damon (1977) in some preliminary studies, children tend to use different criteria when making moral judgments that involve themselves. Cognitive–developmental theory would suggest that young children start with rather flexible cognitive criterion images that change with maturity. The notion that the development of role-taking ability (and morality) involves increasing the consistency between the standards (criterion images) applied to self and other seems worthy of more attention.

To return to the central issue, the question raised by the evidence on reciprocal helping is whether it supplies a route to "hard-core" altruism. Quite clearly, the answer is no. Although Trivers calls reciprocal helping reciprocal *altruism* (a label I tried unsuccessfully to talk him out of in 1970), this type of behavior does not involve suffering a net loss in the helper's fitness in order to elevate the fitness of another. Although reciprocal helping may meet the conditions for altruism when examined in a single instance, it will propagate only if it pays off for the helper in the future.

That reciprocal helping is not truly altruistic may detract from its purity, but it does not detract from its significance. Reciprocal helping clearly plays a far more important role in human social behavior than altruism. How often do we help others who cannot reciprocate (either to us, our kin, or to others who may then help us)? Even the prototypical case of sacrificing one's life in war is not immune from control by reciprocity because it could lead to benefits for one's kin. Considering the pervasiveness of reciprocity, we might wonder why there is so much ado about altruism. (One answer to this question is that, although pure altruism is relatively insignificant on a practical level, it entails a significant challenge to the reinforcement-based assumptions of several major theories of social behavior and, therefore, possesses considerable theoretical significance; see Krebs & Holder, 1982).

One last point about reciprocity and altruism: If we imagine with Axelrod and Hamilton (1981) that our "primeval" state was individualistic selfishness, how could a system of reciprocity ever have gotten started? Adopting a prisoner's dilemma format, why would anyone ever make an initial "cooperative" (i.e., altruistic at this point) response; and what would stop the recipient from taking advantage of it? Pure selfishness is an evolutionarily stable strategy. The answer suggested by Axelrod and Hamilton is based on kin selection—it is in an individual's best genetic interest to make an initial cooperative response toward a relative because the cooperator shares (genetically) in the gain. Once such a system gets started with kin, it can successfully invade a system of pure selfishness with nonkin. I have carried the notion that altruistic behaviors toward kin may generalize to others even further (see later), but for now it is sufficient to point out that kin selection may have been necessary for the evolution of reciprocity.

## GROUP SELECTION REVISITED ("STRUCTURED DEME THEORY")

If we abandon reciprocity as a viable route to hard-core altruism, we are left with two other possibilities. As it turns out, some biologists have been working on the group selection route that Campbell closed down in 1975. Recent revisions in the assumptions underlying models of group selection (especially corrections to the assumption that traits such as altruism are randomly distributed in breeding populations) remove some of the barriers that impeded the evolution of altruism in the old models. If these revisions extended to the evolution of all types of altruism, they would set Campbell back 20 years, to a more sophisticated version of his 1965 paper. However, the authors of the revisions—D. S. Wilson in particular—conclude that they do not supply a route to strong or "hard-core" self-sacrificial altruism. Although they supply a route to helping behaviors that instill greater gains in the fitness of the recipient than the fitness of the helper (i.e., they may give rise to weak or "soft-core" altruism), they also produce an absolute gain in the fitness of the helper. Thus, group selection may mediate the evolution of helping behaviors that come even closer to the criteria of pure altruism than the helping behaviors mediated by reciprocity; but group selection cannot take us all the way.

## FORCED "ALTRUISM"

An obvious way to get people to help you is to force them to. Campbell reviews the evidence that the tendency to force others to behave "altruistically" could have evolved biologically, as could the tendency for individuals to conform to such constraints as a second-choice strategy. However, forcing individuals to help in effect entails making it worth their while (even if only to avoid punishment or death). Thus, it does not meet the conditions for self-sacrificial altruism. Another dead end.

## THE ROUTE OF SOCIAL INSECTS

The social insects are the exemplars of altruism in the animal kingdom. We know a fair amount about how they got there; therefore, it makes sense to try this route for humans. Campbell traces the evolution of altruism in the social insects and asks whether it could have evolved in humans in the same manner. He attributes the evolution of self-sacrificial altruism (and other dimensions of "ultrasociality") in insects to a combination of kin selection and group selection. However, he concludes that altruism could not have evolved in humans through the same mechanisms because a central prerequisite of this process is the control over within-group competition made possible by the sterility of the altruists. Stopped short on this detour, let us turn to the route that has seemed most promising to contemporary sociobiologists—kin selection.

## KIN SELECTION

A major thrust of modern sociobiology is to show that individuals may propagate their genes in two ways: by fostering their own survival and reproductive success and by fostering the survival and reproductive success of those who carry replicas of their genes (i.e., their "blood relatives"). Although we take the self-sacrifice of parents for granted, a great deal of this behavior qualifies as hard-core altruism. (It enhances their offspring's fitness at a net loss to their own fitness.) Sociobiologists point out that the logic of evolution also permits individuals to sacrifice themselves to assist more distant relatives in some circumstances (i.e., to sacrifice individual fitness in order to foster inclusive fitness).

Campbell does not deny that kin selection may lead to self-sacrificial altruism toward relatives; however he argues that it is not sufficient to mediate the evolution of altruism to nonrelatives. I would like to pause at this intersection and outline what I believe may be a viable (even if tortuous) route around the central barrier to the evolution of altruism through kin selection. With Campbell, I assume that one of the major hurdles to primate sociality was "achieving cooperating groups of more than one family." Campbell suggests that this process was "hindered rather than helped by kin selection," but, on this point, I tend to disagree. I imagine that our early ancestors faced ecological changes that made altruism toward members of extended families adaptive. These changes probably related to hunting, food gathering, and defense against predators and other bands of early hominids. The question is, how could this altruism become extended to other families when it would be, in this form, genetically maladaptive? The answer that I have proposed centers around the proximal mechanisms that mediate altruistic responses. As Campbell points out, most animals, including humans, do not have the innate capacity to recognize kin. Therefore, they must infer kinship from reliable cues. Four such interrelated cues are physical similarity, proximity, familiarity, and in-group status. I believe it plausible that individuals may behave purely altruistically toward nonrelatives who possess the qualities of relatives as a sort of overgeneralization that has not been maladaptive enough to have been weeded out by natural selection during the past few thousands of years. In this view, pure altruism is an evolutionary anomaly (see Krebs & Holder, 1982; Krebs & Miller, in press). (Of course, if you want to get picky or pure, you could argue that even self-sacrificial helping toward relatives is not altruistic because it pays off at the genetic level; that is, it serves to propagate replicas of individuals' altruistic genes in relatives.)

## CULTURAL EVOLUTION

I do not know how much overgeneralization of kin selection Campbell would allow, but he insists that, whatever the genetically based dispositions to engage in altruism toward in-group members and other individuals who resemble relatives, these dispositions are limited mainly to primary groups and, therefore, do not explain the sacrifices made by individuals in large "ultrasocial" groupings (such as, for example, the alleged altruism of soldiers on behalf of their countries). According to Campbell, there is no way in which the disposition to sacrifice oneself in war or to abstain from procreation could have been selected biologically in species where there is "competition among the cooperators". The only route to these types of pure altruism, argues Campbell, is through social or cultural evolution.

In his 1975 address, Campbell emphasized the conflict between biological and cultural factors—the conflict between biologically based selfishness and culturally based altruism. He was roundly attacked for this polarity. Critics pointed out that biological and cultural evolution are inextrically bound. In his present contribution Campbell relents a little, implying that cultural evolution may be controlled by its ability to foster average inclusive fitness; however, he remains firm in his insistence that biological evolution alone could not have produced the behavioral tendency toward absolute altruism in the human species.

I am not certain that I understand why Campbell believes that cultural evolution can accomplish that which biological evolution cannot, but he seems to imply that the reason relates to the possibility that groups tend to develop homogeneous beliefs and that these sets of beliefs make group selection (and, thus, the selection of self-sacrificial altruism) possible. If this view is plausible, there must have been *groups* that varied drastically in their endorsement of beliefs that instilled the disposition to sacrifice one's own interest for the sake of the group, with little within group variation.

The notion of a conflict between biologically based urges and culturally based controls and incentives appeals to Campbell because it corresponds with the ubiquitous "original sin" models of human nature, whether based in religions such as Judeo-Christianity, in literary works such as those of Augustine and Tolstoy, or in psychological theories such as psychoanalysis. I would agree that this conflict constitutes an important part of human nature; however, I would argue in addition that in order to acquire a representative view of human nature, we must attend to (a) conflicts between biologically based dispositions; (b) conflicts between culturally based dispositions; (c) the ways in which biologically and culturally based dispositions complement and support one another; and (d) the form of the interaction between these types of influence. Focusing on (c), I have suggested that cultural norms such as the norm of reciprocity may evolve as extrapolations of natural laws. Individuals recognize, consciously or unconsciously, that their behavior conforms to a norm of reciprocity and that this behavioral strategy appears to work. Therefore, they preach it as a cultural prescription (see Krebs, 1978).

Of course, even if all of the biological routes to hard-core altruism fall short, it does not necessarily follow that culture can pave the way. To establish that helping behaviors that are caused by cultural inputs are altruistic, an investigator would have to establish that they do not pay off for the helper. This task is even more difficult at a cultural level than at a biological level of analysis and, indeed, has entertained philosophers of ethics for many centuries. The basic issue here involves the internalization of cultural prescriptions to behave altruistically. If you force someone to help others, the behavior is not altruistic. The question, then, is whether individuals ever really internalize altruistic prescriptions and, if so, whether behaving in a manner that is consistent with them is in any way reinforcing.

In closing, it is, perhaps, appropriate to put the biological approaches in this section in context. The central goal of both chapters is to explain how the disposition to engage in various prosocial behaviors evolved in human and nonhuman animals. The authors had little difficulty explaining the evolution of the vast majority of helping behavior. However, Campbell tried hard to explain how altruistic behaviors could evolve biologically in humans, but he failed to find a route. It should be clear that the role that altruism plays in human interaction undoubtedly is an extremely minute one. However, behaviors that seem altruistic present a monumental challenge to the theory of evolution—namely, to explain how individuals can acquire the disposition to engage in behaviors that by definition do not pay off for them (i.e., do not enhance their genetic fitness). It is common for readers of biological discussions of altruism to object that altruism is a uniquely human behavior that stems from high-order cognition and, thus, that it is silly to attribute altruism to nonhuman animals like whales and ants. This may be true when altruism is defined in terms of high-order cognitions such as intentions; however, this is not the way in which it is defined in biological analyses. If you want to play the biological game, you have to play by the biological rules. If you object strongly that the behaviors that sociobiologists call altruistic do not meet your criteria of altruism, then call them something else. Whatever you call them, these behaviors present an interesting challenge to the principle of natural selection and, thus, are worthy of attention.

# REFERENCES

Axelrod, R., & Hamilton, W. D. The evolution of cooperation. *Science,* 1981, *211,* 1390–1396.

Campbell, D. T. Ethnocentric and other altruistic motives. In D. Levine (Ed.), *Nebraska symposium on motivation.* Lincoln: University of Nebraska Press, 1965.

Campbell, D. T. On the conflict between biological and social evolution and between psychology and moral tradition. *American Psychologist,* 1975, *30,* 1103–1126.

Damon, W. *The social world of the child.* San Francisco: Jossey–Bass, 1977.

Krebs, D. L. A cognitive-developmental approach to altruism. In L. Wispé (Ed.), *Altruism, sympathy, and helping.* New York: Academic Press, 1978.

Krebs, D. L., & Holder, M. Evolution, altruism, and reinforcement. In D. Krebs (Ed.), *Readings in social psychology: Contemporary perspectives* (2nd ed.). New York: Harper & Row, 1982.

Krebs, D. L., & Miller, D. Altruism and aggression. In G. Lindzey & E. Aronson (Eds.), *The handbook of social psychology* (3rd ed.). Reading, Mass.: Addison–Wesley, in press.

Wispé, L. G., & Thompson, J. N., Jr. The war between the words: Biological versus social evolution and some related issues. *American Psychologist,* 1976, *31,* 341–384.

# PSYCHOLOGICAL AND PHILOSOPHICAL APPROACHES TO PROSOCIAL DEVELOPMENT

# The Early Appearance of Some Valued Social Behaviors

## DALE F. HAY and HARRIET L. RHEINGOLD

In this chapter we draw attention to some common social behaviors of very young children that until recently have gone largely unremarked but that carry a message of considerable import for views of human nature. As these behaviors arise in the course of ordinary social interactions, without direct tutelage, they provide a reservoir of capacities that, if properly nurtured, could lead to the betterment of humankind. The behaviors include sharing, giving care, cooperating, comforting, and helping; together they compose a class today labeled as *positive social behaviors* (Staub, 1978) or *prosocial behaviors* (Mussen & Eisenberg-Berg, 1977; Wispé, 1972). When performed by adults, they are valued; biblical injunctions and civil codes do indeed exhort us to share with, help, and comfort our fellows. Remarkable, then, is the occurrence of forms of these behaviors in children under 3 years of age—remarkable but not surprising, given the ample evidence that the human infant is a social, socializable, and socializing organism, capable from birth not only of interacting with others but also of modifying those interactions.

An appreciation of these early social behaviors can affect the view we hold of human nature. In turn, a revised view of human nature would in many ways affect our own behavior as persons, parents, and teachers, and even the behavior of legislators. We do not of course subscribe to simple views of human nature as good or bad. Nor are we assuming that the human infant is innately good or inevitably altruistic. Nonetheless, the very early appearance of valued social behaviors supports an optimistic view of human potentiality, informs efforts to realize it, and provides the conviction that it can be realized. Only as long as we cling to notions of

THE NATURE OF PROSOCIAL DEVELOPMENT

young children as dependent, egoistic, or antisocial, shall we be surprised to observe their active prosocial efforts.

At the outset let us admit that we have received criticism from some quarters for not balancing the evidence of prosocial behavior against that of aggressive behavior. Yet we are convinced that, had we presented data on aggression among children under 3 years of age, no one would have called for a counterportrayal of the behaviors we here call prosocial. Do adults—parents, teachers, and scholars alike—implicitly hold the view that the human child requires discipline to bring an unruly nature into conformity with society's demands? Or are we simply more likely to notice and respond to acts of aggression? Aggression, a behavior of high salience, serves as an important construct in ethological and psychoanalytic theories. Yet in a recent study of 1-year-old children's interactions with a peer of the same age (Hay & Ross, 1982), the children spent only about 5% of their time in conflict, and the use of force was rarer still; very instructive from our point of view was the mothers' noticing and commenting on those difficult interactions, while the children's cooperative play went nearly always unremarked. As the evidence we present here will show, it is because the prosocial behaviors are so common, low-key, and undemanding that they excite so little comment. Interestingly enough, parents usually cannot report when they first observed their children share with or help another person. At first they seem perplexed by our interest and then later are surprised (and pleased) when their children display these behaviors in our studies.

In this chapter, then, we provide evidence for a modified view of the social abilities of the child under 3 years of age, evidence gleaned from several sources. Some stems from reports from astute observers of the development of their own children (e.g., Darwin, 1877; Preyer, 1889; Stern, 1924). These anecdotes are extended by more recent controlled studies and systematic observations in the field. However, even the evidence from controlled studies bears the stamp of "real-life" behavior, unlike the artificial procedures used in much of the experimental work with older children. The behaviors are cataloged by their everyday labels—sharing, helping, comforting, and the like—that are found both in ordinary speech and in the literature on the prosocial behavior of adults and school-aged children. To be sure, the categories are interrelated and overlapping, just as they are when applied to the behavior of older persons. For example, one may share possessions with a companion in an effort to help, comfort, or cooperate with that person; the meaning assigned to a social action depends on the social and physical situation in which it is shown, as well as its topographical character. Nonetheless, the use of these familiar labels stresses important commonalities between the activities of very young children and the analogous transactions of older persons.

If all these behaviors can be shown to occur in the absence of direct tuition, how can their occurrences be explained? In an attempt to answer this question, we shall sketch a speculative account of their development. Then we shall consider what adjustment must be made in theoretical views of social development to incorporate the early flowering of prosocial activities.

## A CATALOG OF THE BEHAVIORS

### Friendliness and Affection

As early in the life of the human child as the various valued behaviors appear, they are nevertheless based on still earlier abilities and dispositions that were fostered by social experiences. Preeminent among these is the young infant's friendliness to other persons. Although friendliness and affection are seldom included in categories of prosocial behavior, they are here regarded as providing their firm basis.

Together with the interest infants characteristically accord other persons and their activities goes generally friendly behavior. When people approach or speak to them, even very young infants smile and vocalize (Bühler, 1931). By 3 months of age, they respond sociably to all persons, known and unknown. As they grow older and their power to distinguish among the persons increases, they behave in special ways to familiar persons. Signs of affection such as laughs, cries of joy, hugs, and cuddling are accorded their mothers, fathers, siblings, and other preferred persons (Banham, 1950). Then, as infants enter the second half of the first year of life, they respond somewhat differently to unfamiliar persons. They tend to watch these persons more intently (which may indeed reflect their interest in new people), take a longer time to smile, and approach them less often than they do familiar persons.

Nevertheless, friendliness is still apparent. An increasing number of studies show that, if the unfamiliar adult approaches an infant as people normally do—with a smile, a word or two, or a nod of the head (Shaffran, 1974)—the infant does not fret, cry, or flee. Furthermore, if friendly persons show them attractive toys and encourage the infants to approach, the infants draw near and engage in reciprocal play (Ross & Goldman, 1977). Even if adults remain quiet, only looking at the infant, they usually do not evoke a negative response (e.g., Eckerman & Rheingold, 1974). Infants' normally friendly responses to persons should not be lost sight of just because quite different behaviors appear in response to experimental attempts to measure adaptation to stressful events (e.g., Ainsworth & Wittig, 1969; Scarr & Salapatek, 1970).

As friendly as infants are to adults, they are even more so to other small children. This may commonly be observed wherever little children gather and has also been documented in the laboratory (Eckerman, Whatley, & Kutz, 1975; Ross & Goldman, 1977). Even 6-month-olds smile, vocalize, and reach out to each other (Bühler, 1931; Hay, Nash, & Pedersen, 1983).

In summary, the infants' friendliness can be viewed as the scaffold on which all later prosocial behaviors are built. Without a generally positive, outgoing disposition towards others, children would not likely share, help, or cooperate. Moreover, in its own right, friendliness needs no defense as a contributor to harmonious relations within a social group.

## Sharing Objects and Experiences

A common behavior of children under 3 years of age is the spontaneous sharing with other persons of objects and events that the children find of interest in the environment. We first observed this behavior while studying 12- and 18-month-old children's exploration of a suite of three playrooms in the laboratory (Rheingold, 1973). The children were tested individually, with their mothers seated in one of the rooms. The children did not hesitate to venture away from their mothers to investigate the other rooms and the toys they contained, but neither did they ignore their mothers. Rather, the children would frequently draw their mothers' attention to toys and other parts of the rooms by showing or giving them objects—that is, by pointing to or holding up objects for them to see, while looking at them as though checking to see if the message was received, and also by releasing objects into their hands or laps.

Because the behaviors of showing and giving have been reported in anecdotes at least since Tiedemann's observations in 1787 (Murchison & Langer, 1927) and because they seemed to correspond to the denotative definition of the term *sharing,* which ''implies that one as the original holder grants to another the partial use, enjoyment or possession of a thing,'' we deemed them worthy of further study. In a series of studies (Rheingold, Hay, & West, 1976), seven different samples of children were observed in the laboratory playroom. Each child was observed with the mother or the father; on occasion an unfamiliar adult was also present. Measures were taken of showing objects by pointing to them or holding them up for a person to see and of giving objects to a recipient. Not only did every one of the 111 15- or 18-month-old children in the seven samples spontaneously show or give objects to their companions, but most exhibited both behaviors several times. The children shared with mothers and fathers alike; many also shared with unfamiliar men and women. Although some classes of objects were shared more frequently than others, all but 1 of the 21 objects used in the studies were shared. Sharing was robust against several experimental manipulations: The children shared new toys as readily as familiar ones; they shared as much when their mothers were less as well as more responsive to their actions; and they gave toys whether the recipients requested them or not.

Field observations collected in airports, zoos, stores, and on campuses confirmed the laboratory findings. The most common behavior observed in the field was pointing, but children were also observed to give food and other objects to parents, siblings, other children and adults, and even to the observers. Incidental observations in the course of other studies in the laboratory revealed the occurrence of the behaviors before the first birthday. Two colleagues recorded instances of sharing by their infants at home; showing by holding an object was first observed at 9.3 months, giving at 9.5 months.

Subsequent studies extended the findings to older and younger ages. Children at 24 and 36 months of age, observed in the laboratory with age-appropriate toys, showed and gave objects to their mothers; however, they also drew the mother's attention to objects with words as well as gestures (Cook, 1977). In other studies, all but 3 of a total of 72 children at 12, 18, and 24 months of age, drawn from two different populations and tested in different settings, also shared objects with their parents (Cotton, 1976; Hay, 1979). Furthermore, in studies of peer relations in the second year of life, the children also showed and offered objects to peers, both familiar and unfamiliar (Eckerman *et al.*, 1975; Holmberg, 1980; Ross & Goldman, 1977).

These behaviors are worthy of note not only because they are means whereby both tangible objects and experiences are exchanged, but also because of what they reveal about the young child's social skills and understanding. For example, pointing to an interesting spectacle may be viewed as a means of sharing one's own observations with another person. Usually pointing is accompanied by words and then followed by glancing at the other person to ensure that he or she is attending and has perceived the object of interest. Just as often, the other person not only looks in the direction of the point but also verbally acknowledges that the spectacle has been seen. As this sequence of actions occurs between persons, pointing qualifies as a communicative gesture. Not as immediately obvious, however, is the evidence the gesture provides for the ability of each partner in the exchange to take the visual perspective of the other, an ability just naturally assumed by the one who points. Furthermore, as the ability to take the visual perspective of another person lies at the heart of speculations about role-taking and egocentrism, the age at which children first evidence the ability to draw another's attention to a distant object becomes important. Thus, the behavior of pointing was selected for special study.

In a laboratory setting containing several interesting objects, some moving or chiming on schedule, infants between the ages of 10 and 16 months showed a steady progression in pointing out these objects to their mothers (Leung & Rheingold, 1981). It was not until 12.5 months of age that a majority of them did so; by 16.5 months all of them did so. Their vocalizations, which were of a "look–see" nature, together with their visual regard of the mother, indicated that the gesture was truly one of social communication, a conclusion further supported by the mothers' verbally acknowledging the gesture and looking at the objects to which the infants pointed. In all respects the interaction between infant and mother resembled an "indicate and look" interaction between persons of any age.

## Giving Care

Gestures that permit a child to share objects and visual events constitute quite general skills that can be (and are) applied in a variety of circumstances. During the second year of life children also show they have acquired a more specific set of skills that would be called for in one particular type of prosocial encounter: situations in which another individual (usually another young child) requires care. Let us consider that the commonest prosocial activities are the behaviors of parents caring for their young children: feeding, bathing, grooming them, and so on. Then it may not be surprising that at an early age children demonstrate that they too know how to give care. Although children most commonly direct such behaviors to dolls and toy animals, they also on occasion direct them appropriately to people.

Field observations supply many instances of little children caring for others. The earliest example in our files describes how an 8-month-old girl fed zweiback to a dog. A later entry tells of a 2-year-old girl spreading a blanket over her mother when the mother said, "I'm cold." Children reared together in a residential nursery (Freud & Burlingham, 1944) similarly cared for each other's needs: A girl of 21 months fed a 15-month-old boy; a boy of 23 months put a sock on a 21-month-old girl's foot.

To assess young children's knowledge of various ways of giving care, the caregiving skills of 36 children, 12 each at 18, 24, and 30 months of age, were charted in an environment designed to promote them (Rheingold & Emery, in press). Equal numbers of girls and boys were observed individually with their mothers in a laboratory playroom furnished with child-sized domestic items—a high chair, cradle, dishes, baby bottle, a comb and brush, soap, and the like—together with dolls and toy animals as potential recipients of care. Not only did all the children at each age carry out many caregiving acts, but at least two-thirds of the children, even among the youngest group, displayed behaviors in at least five of the six predefined categories (i.e., put to bed, disciplined, fed, gave affection, groomed, and positioned or transported). Across all ages the commonest caregiving acts fell in the categories of positioning or transporting (i.e., carefully seating, carrying, or wheeling in a carriage), grooming (i.e., bathing, diapering, brushing hair), and feeding the dolls and animals. At least two-thirds of the children exhibited affectionate behavior in the course of bestowing care; in contrast, only 6 of the children hit or spanked the dolls or animals, and 5 of them did so only once. The caregiving activities were carried out by boys as well as by girls, with only minor differences in the types of behaviors represented: For example, more boys than girls at all ages transported the dolls and animals in the carriage, and more girls than boys tried to diaper them.

Approximately 25% of the caregiving acts, even those performed by the youngest children, were accompanied by appropriate speech. For example, a boy at 18 months of age said, "Night-night, bear" as he put the animal in the cradle, covered it with a blanket, and kissed it; a 30-month-old girl said, as she wrapped a blanket around a doll, "Oh, poor baby. Too cold. Too cold. I'll wrap you around." Such verbalizations revealed the children's intentions or perceptions of their own behavior and closely resembled parental speech to infants.

Further evidence of the nonrandom, planful nature of the behaviors was seen in the frequency of related acts within a sequence of caregiving; an average of 9–10 such sequences were exhibited by children at each age. As might be expected, the number of acts comprising the sequences increased with age. Thus, for example, a boy in the youngest group took a mattress from the cradle, placed it in the carriage with a pillow, put an animal in the carriage, and then pushed the carriage. An even longer sequence was displayed by a 30-month-old girl who placed a doll in the bathtub, rubbed soap on it, removed it from the tub, combed and brushed its hair, placed it in the carriage, and then completed the sequence by pushing the doll in the carriage.

Caregiving activities directed to dolls, of course, are usually interpreted as instances of mere play, despite their often being carried out with apparent seriousness. Nonetheless, giving care even to inanimate recipients indicates a considerable amount of prosocial knowledge; by giving care, the children demonstrate their awareness that the young have certain needs that can be met in particular ways. Confirmation of the anecdotal evidence (e.g., Freud & Burlingham, 1944) that very young children can translate this knowledge into action with *people* awaits further research.

## Cooperating and Complying with Requests

The planful caregiving sequences just described illustrate a major point about prosocial development: For effective prosocial action, children must not simply possess certain specific competencies, such as the ability to offer objects to other persons or to execute caregiving acts; they must also be able to coordinate these actions with other abilities *and* with the actions and words of other persons. The caregiving sequences exemplify the former type of coordination. The latter ability to organize one's actions with those of others is also manifested in the second year of life when children begin to take active roles in cooperative games and when they comply with the requests of others.

Even before the first birthday, infants are frequently invited by their parents to participate in structured games. At first, the infants' participation is relatively passive, but, after 6 months of age, they begin to take a more active role (e.g., Gustafson, Green, & West, 1979). For example, in the game of "peek-a-boo," infants begin to hide themselves as well as observing the mothers' disappearance and reappearance and permitting themselves to be hidden (Bruner & Sherwood, 1976). Similarly, a detailed analysis of the conventional game of "give-and-take" in one child from 3 to 12 months (Bruner, 1977) showed that the infant at first was a relatively passive recipient, then a more active one, and finally began eagerly to offer as well as accept objects.

When infants take active roles in social games, the ensuing interactions may qualify as early manifestations of cooperation, defined in common speech as two or more individuals working together toward a mutual goal. In games the mutual goal appears to be a sustained, coordinated interaction including the three hallmarks of game structure (Garvey, 1974; Ross & Goldman, 1977): (*a*) mutual involvement of the two persons who play the games, as by visual regard, supplementary actions, and speech; (*b*) repetition of particular actions, such that each partner has a distinctive role to play; and (*c*) alternation of turns, such that each person acts and then pauses while the partner takes a turn. To the extent that interactions meeting these criteria center on a task involving a common object or array of objects (e.g., a set of blocks to be stacked), the partners' mutual objective is even more apparent. Interactions meeting these criteria have been recorded for 1-year-old children with their parents (Hay, 1979), peers, and unfamiliar adults (Ross & Goldman, 1977). These interchanges were characterized by diverse themes (e.g., extended sequences of give-and-take, ball games, and representational episodes). Furthermore, the analysis of games played with peers revealed that three different types of role relations could be discerned, even in games in which 12-month-olds participated: There were imitative games, where both partners performed identical actions; complementary games, in which one partner's role was the complement of the other's (e.g., one person stacks blocks and the partner topples them); and reciprocal games, which were defined by two distinct actions that both partners performed in turn (most often exemplified by ball games in which each partner both threw and caught the ball).

As was the case with the sharing behaviors, cooperative games can be examined both as prosocial encounters in their own right and as arenas in which infants' emerging interactive skills are manifested, skills that may then be used in other types of prosocial encounters. For example, interactions between parents and infants in the first half of the first year of life are indeed coordinated and thus resemble dialogues, but they are initiated and maintained largely through the parents' efforts (for reviews see Cappella, 1981; Schaffer, 1978); the parents behave as if the infants are active, intentional contributors to the interchanges. As infants grow older, however, they take more responsibility for the enactment of their roles (i.e., repeating a distinctive action) and for the alternation of turns that mark an interaction as a game. Their understanding of the cooperative pattern of games and the roles therein is seen most clearly when a game for one reason or another has been interrupted. For example, a number of games were established between 12-month-old infants and a friendly adult experimenter (Ross, 1980). After each partner had taken about four turns in a given game, and it was judged to be proceeding smoothly, the adult interrupted the game for 10 sec by failing to take the next turn and instead merely gazing passively at the infant. Infants responded to the interruption with activities different from the ones they had displayed during the game itself. During the interruption period, they were more likely to gesture toward the toys, partially retake their own turns, or attempt to facilitate the adult's taking a turn, for example, by guiding the adult's hand to an appropriate object. The infants also watched the adult's hands and toys during the games, but, when the games were interrupted, the infants shifted their gazes to the adult's face. These reactions imply some understanding on the part of the infants of the rules of a cooperative game.

An analysis of cooperative interchanges between young children and their parents (Hay, 1979) showed that when parents were asked to remain seated throughout the observation period, the children themselves initiated most such interactions, thus determining their themes. Hence it was in their maintaining the structure of the games (by repeatedly enacting their roles and pausing while the partner responded), not in their initial overtures, that the cooperative nature of their activity became apparent. In many everyday situations, however, children may be asked to enter into an interaction initiated by someone else and thus cooperate with a plan developed by the other person; the literature on very young children's responses to parents' requests confirms their ability to do so. For example, "cooperation in dressing," an activity presumably initiated by the caregiver, is a normative item at 12 months on scales of infant development (Gesell & Amatruda, 1941). The pleasure little children display in carrying messages and following other simple requests comes through vividly in the anecdotal record (e.g., Stern, 1924). Between 9 and 12 months of age, predating the onset of speech, infants in their homes were observed to comply with such simple requests as "Come" and "Give it to me" (Stayton, Hogan, & Ainsworth, 1971). Then, in a laboratory play setting, 15-month-olds complied with an average of 66% and 24-month-olds with 53% of their mothers' requests to perform particular tasks (Schaffer & Crook, 1979). Such adaptations of one's actions to another's wishes are often requisite when one is helping another person. It also can be considered a socially valued achievement in its own right, even granted that a child's not complying may mark a nascent sense of independence that is also valued and that the value placed on unswerving obedience to authority in later life may certainly be questioned.

## Comforting Persons in Distress

The evidence just reviewed indicates that children in the first 3 years of life possess certain skills that in their own right indicate a basic prosocial orientation; at the same time these skills can also be used in response to other sets of circumstances calling for prosocial efforts. Another person's display of distress obviously constitutes one such circumstance. A variety of evidence indicates that very young children are likely to notice another's distress and, at least on occasion, may try to do something about it, using whatever skills and resources are at their command.

At the simplest level infants and toddlers pay attention to persons who cry or otherwise indicate they are experiencing pain or sorrow. For example, Murphy (1937) observed 2-year-olds approach and watch a crying peer. Young children's imitation of characteristic features of the distressed behavior of another child attests to their ability to attend to, recall, and recreate such events; Piaget's (1952) classic example of his 16-month-old daughter's reproduction of another child's temper tantrum is such an instance. With the onset of language, young children begin to talk about the distress of others; at times they may ask an adult why another child cries (e.g., Murphy, 1937). Indeed, they may comment on distress that is either not apparent to or is ignored by adults, such as the presumed discomfort of a plucked turkey (Church, 1966; Stern, 1924).

In addition to merely paying attention to another person's distress, infants and young children sometimes become distressed themselves. In such cases the distressed individual who triggers the child's own crying may be another child (Church, 1966; Hoffman, 1975), a caregiver (Darwin, 1877; Sully, 1896), an animal (Sully, 1896), or even an inanimate object: Preyer (1889) reported that his 27-month-old son "wept if human forms cut out of paper were in any danger of mutilation.'' Even newborns have been reported to be more likely to cry when presented with the tape-recorded sounds of another newborn's cries than when exposed to silence or a computer-generated synthetic cry (Sagi & Hoffman, 1976; Simner, 1971).

In an attempt to document such social facilitation of distress, pairs of 6-month-old infants were observed with their mothers, and the distribution of their distressed vocalizations was examined for signs of social influence (Hay, Nash, & Pedersen, 1981). The precise frequency, duration, and temporal distribution of one infant's distress could not be reliably predicted from comparable information about the peer; however, some indications of cumulative social influence could be discerned. The conditional probability of an infant's showing distress, given that the peer had been fussing or crying during a certain number of preceding 5-sec intervals, increased systematically as a function of the number of previous intervals in which the peer was distressed, that is, from $p = .04$ when the peer had been crying only in the last 5 sec to $p = 1.00$ when the peer had been crying for the 29 previous time intervals (about $2\frac{1}{2}$ min). In contrast, the conditional probability of an infant's showing distress, given that the peer had *not* been distressed for an equivalent number of preceding time intervals, never exceeded the value expected by chance. Thus, a cumulative model was needed to predict the effects of an infant's crying on an agemate's likelihood of also becoming distressed.

In addition to noticing and perhaps becoming upset by the distress of others, very young children also attempt to comfort the distressed persons, either by appealing to adults or by themselves offering consolation or distractions (e.g., A. Freud & Burlingham, 1944; Hoffman, 1975; Murphy, 1937). For example, a 15-month-old boy was observed to bring his own teddy bear to a crying peer; when that did not help, he brought the peer's security blanket from the next room (Hoffman, 1975). In a longitudinal study of children between the ages of 15 and 30 months (Zahn-Waxler, Radke-Yarrow, & King, 1979), mothers were trained to record their children's responses to persons who showed some form of distress in the children's presence. Two sets of distress-producing events were recorded: those in which the child, as a bystander, witnessed distress and those in which the child had actively caused another person to experience distress (e.g., by bumping into another child). The mothers reported that the children responded prosocially on about one-third of each type of distress episode. Their responses took the form of physically or verbally trying to comfort the distressed person, providing objects such as food or bandages, offering physical assistance, or locating other persons who could help. Approximately 10% of the time, the children's attempts to comfort other persons were accompanied by signs that the children themselves were distressed.

The preceding data represent responses made in the presence of overt distress cues such as crying. Can children less than 3 years of age also infer that another individual is likely to become distressed on the basis of situational information? Anecdotal accounts of children's attempts to prevent harm or anticipate the needs of other individuals suggest that they are indeed capable of inferring likely future distress (Murphy, 1937; Stern, 1924). In addition, the study of caregiving skills provided tangential information bearing on this question: The children's attempts to feed or put blankets around the dolls and toy animals, when accompanied by appropriate speech, suggested that they had acquired some awareness that being hungry or cold is unpleasant and might provoke distress, states that could be averted by a caregiver's attention.

## Helping Adults Complete Their Work

Children under the age of 3 may only infrequently witness another person's distress. Thus the frequency of this type of prosocial responding is likely to be limited not only by the children's abilities but also by the number of opportunities for its performance. Indeed, if such events are infrequent, many children may attend or possibly become upset themselves but not be able to mobilize their own reactions quickly. This is, of course, sometimes true for older persons who witness distress as well. In view of these considerations, it is important to examine a more common set of circumstances that also provides the opportunity for the young child to display prosocial behavior: the occasions when adults perform household tasks in the presence of their young children, who may then try to help.

As very young children follow their parents through a round of everyday activities, the children sometimes try to participate, executing behaviors that, if performed by older persons, would be described as helping (Church, 1966; Valentine, 1942). To substantiate the anecdotal accounts, 18-, 24-, and 30-month-old children were observed with either their mothers or fathers in a suite of rooms furnished to simulate a home environment (Rheingold, 1982). The rooms contained a number of ordinary, undone household tasks, including a table to set, a bed to make, books and cards to pick up from the floor, scraps to sweep up, and laundry to fold. The parents were instructed to perform as many tasks as they chose, in any order, pausing whenever they wished. They were requested to work slowly so that the children would have ample chance to participate. The parents were asked to talk about what they were doing but not to ask the children explicitly to help and not to tell them what to do. (While instructing the parents, the experimenter was careful to avoid the actual use of the term *help*.) After 25 minutes of observation, a research assistant (either male or female) entered the room with a bag of groceries, announcing the intention to put them away; the children's participation in the unfamiliar adult's task was also recorded.

All the children, even those at 18 months of age, joined in some of the tasks set by their parents. On the average, the parents were assisted by their 18-month-olds on 63%, by their 24-month-olds on 78%, and by their 30-month-olds on 89% of the tasks they performed. The children responded to their parents' tasks with alacrity: The median latencies over all tasks from the parents' first announcing their intentions or otherwise beginning the chore to the children's participation varied from only 16 to 20 sec across the different age groups. Almost all the children of each group helped the unfamiliar adult shelve groceries, with median latencies varying from only 18 to 28 sec across age groups.

Helping acts themselves could be as minimal as just holding the dustpan for the parent to sweep scraps into but were rarely so limited. Most often, for example, the children brought many items from a shelf to set the table, tried to sweep with the broom, and inserted into a box as many of the playing cards scattered on the floor as the adult left for them to do. Some not only placed dishes on the table but distributed them as though setting places. Others, after picking magazines up from the floor, stacked them and then straightened the pile. The older children of course were more competent than the younger ones at various tasks: For example, only 1 child at 18 months folded, rather than wadded, an item of laundry, whereas more than a third of the 30-month-olds folded items precisely. More than half of the children used the broom but no child at 18 months succeeded in sweeping scraps into the dustpan, a feat accomplished by 14 of the 20 30-month-old children.

These findings reveal that even by 18 months of age children have acquired a good deal of knowledge about the domestic tasks of everyday life as well as skills that enable them to participate in such tasks. The data also indicate that they are simultaneously acquiring more abstract knowledge about their own behavior, that is, that they have intentions and goals. The children's participation was often preceded or accompanied by statements germane to the task at hand. Even some of the youngest children could describe their actions; on 12% of the tasks they engaged in, they made such statements as "Sandy sweep" and "Fold clothes." By 30 months of age, children could express their intentions, for example, by saying, "I'm going to pick up these books" or "I'll put some of my cards in here." Furthermore, 19 of the 60 24- and 30-month-old children spontaneously incorporated the word *help* in their statements.

In addition to expressing their intentions, the children also indicated their opinions as to when the objectives of a task had been met. Overall the tasks that the children helped on, the percentage on which they signaled completion (verbally, for example, by saying "all picked up" or nonverbally, for example, by putting away the broom and dustpan) increased from 20% at 18 months to 39% at 24 months to 45% at 30 months. Verbal statements of completion accompanied 2% of the tasks of the 18-month-olds, 13% of those of the 24-month-olds, and 22% of those of the 30-month-olds. In meeting their own objectives, furthermore, the children spontaneously performed a number of behaviors that went beyond the completion of the task as verbalized or modeled by the parent. They stored various objects (e.g., placing the filled card box on a shelf or table; placing the folded laundry in the basket and then storing the basket under the table); they emptied the contents of one wastebasket into the other, thus collecting all the bits and papers in a single wastebasket; and they brought chairs from another room to complete the setting of the table, an omission no parent ever seemed aware of. These findings indicated that the children's actions within tasks represented diverse means to an overall goal, not just simple copying of the parents' specific behaviors. Furthermore, these data suggest that for very young children, as for adults, helping may qualify as creative action, in that helpers often reformulate their recipients' goals into their own terms and define suitable roles for themselves with respect to their own competencies and the demands of the task at hand.

Observations in the home corroborated the laboratory findings. In the course of collecting samples of 12 mothers' speech to their 2-year-old children, examples of the children's helping with household tasks were incidentally recorded.[1] All 12 children (5 boys and 7 girls) helped their mothers at least once during the observations, and 58 occurrences in all were recorded. The children often expressed their intentions, saying, for example, ''I gonna clean up mess'' or ''I help you, I hold that little light bulb.'' These counts may well be conservative because helping was not the original focus of study.

### Generality of the Evidence

The evidence on the early appearing valued behaviors is characterized by substantial consistency across different samples of children of both sexes observed at different times and in different settings. In the anecdotes and controlled studies, the reports revealed only a few minor differences by sex. Boys and girls alike, for example, helped their parents perform household tasks; boys and girls alike demonstrated their knowledge of caregiving skills. The evidence, furthermore, uniformly shows that these behaviors are extended not only to members of the family— mother, father, siblings, and relatives—but to unfamiliar persons of both sexes, children as well as adults.

Consistency also marked the findings across different samples of children. For example, studies of sharing yielded similar results whether the average level of parental education, a measure that roughly indexed socioeconomic status, was as high as 17 or as low as 12 years, with a range from 6 to 20 years. In addition, the evidence holds across different historical periods and different settings. The periods span almost 200 years from Tiedemann's observations of his son in 1787 (Murchison & Langer, 1927) to the present. The settings include homes, institutions, and laboratories in Germany, Austria, France, England, and the United States. Although the behaviors probably appear earlier and undoubtedly in greater variety in the home, they are easily reproduced in seminatural conditions in the laboratory when the parent is present and the children's movements are not constrained. Nor do variations from laboratory to laboratory produce reliably different measures of central tendency. Finally, field observations in all cases corroborated the laboratory findings.

### THE DEVELOPMENT OF THE BEHAVIORS

The anecdotal literature as well as the results of controlled studies suggest a regular progression of events in the course of early prosocial development (Table 3.1). During the first half of the first year of life, infants show a general responsive-

---

[1]Emery, G. N., personal communication (1977).

**TABLE 3.1**
*Milestones of Early Prosocial Development*

*Year 1: Birth to 6 months*

Responds positively to others
Participates in social games
Reacts emotionally to distress

*Year 1: 6–12 months*

Takes on active role in social games
Exhibits sharing behaviors
Displays affection to familiar persons

*Year 2*

Refines ability to point with index finger
Complies with simple requests
Indicates knowledge of rules of cooperative games
Shows knowledge of caregiving skills
Comforts persons in distress
Participates in the work of adults

*Year 3*

Draws person's attention to objects with words as well as gestures
Exhibits increasingly planful caregiving and helping sequences
Expresses own intentions to help and knowledge of task objectives

ness to the social world that constitutes the firm foundation for all their future prosocial efforts: They exhibit friendly behaviors, and they participate, at least to some extent, in social games. Of particular consequence for prosocial development are their attention and responsiveness to displays of emotion; they smile when others smile and sometimes cry when others cry. During the second half of the first year their interactive abilities change in several important respects. They take on increased responsibility for initiating and maintaining interactions, including cooperative games; they develop a repertoire of intentional, goal-directed actions that convey social meaning, including the behaviors of showing and giving objects to other persons; and they respond to familiar companions with special affection. Around the time of the first birthday, infants also evince their ability to comprehend the actions and words of other persons: They respond to verbal requests and demonstrate their awareness of the structure of cooperative games.

During the second year of life, young children refine these various skills—for example, the ability to point out objects to one's companions undergoes development during this time—and at the same time they acquire a host of other knowledge that enables them to comfort and offer care to other persons and to assist in others' tasks. During this year and the next, their prosocial activities become increasingly coordinated, and they become more and more capable of executing planful sequences. Furthermore, as their linguistic skills improve, they begin to supplement their actions with words and demonstrate their awareness of their own intentions and goals.

These achievements do not result from direct tutelage. Rather, early prosocial development proceeds in the theater of ordinary social interaction. New social abilities emerge throughout the period of infancy as a function of the infants' motoric and cognitive attainments. For example, with increased manual dexterity, infants are able to release an object into another person's hand or to sweep scraps of paper into a dustpan. With the onset of locomotion, they can initiate a greater variety of interactions (Green, Gustafson, & West, 1980), including prosocial ones. With the emergence of the ability to use diverse means to accomplish certain ends (Piaget, 1952), they become better able to comfort, cooperate with, and assist other persons. With increased understanding of language, they are more likely to be able to interpret the needs and desires of others. As such abilities emerge, they are facilitated and strengthened by the plentiful opportunities for learning afforded infants in the course of ordinary experience. When infants observe and experience the prosocial behaviors of other persons and when they note the consequences of their own actions, their own emerging prosocial skills are refined.

## OPPORTUNITIES FOR LEARNING

Opportunities for prosocial learning abound as infants observe their own care-givers. The relative motor helplessness of human infants requires care that is pre-eminently prosocial. Caregivers not only tend to the infants' basic needs, but also comfort them when they are distressed, show and give them interesting objects, and help them solve problems. These caregiving behaviors, being explicitly directed to the infants and producing pleasing consequences for them, would seem to acquire special distinctiveness as templates for duplication. Infants seem especially likely to imitate gestures performed by familiar persons (Valentine, 1942) that, when per-formed in turn by the infants, are clearly visible and thus can be monitored (Guil-laume, 1971); the prosocial actions of caregivers would so qualify. Furthermore, infants' imitation is especially likely if the modeled actions are presented in a repetitive sequence with ample time for the infant to respond (Kaye & Marcus, 1978). Parents often model showing, giving, and cooperative actions in exactly that way by enacting them in the course of social games. Evidence for infants' observa-tional learning from their own experiences of receiving care was provided by the studies of caregiving reported earlier and by parents' reports of their children's attempts to comfort others in the same distinctive ways in which the children themselves receive comfort (Church, 1966; Zahn-Waxler et al., 1979).

By observing their caregivers, infants not only perceive a variety of prosocial actions; they also observe complementary behaviors that encourage them to display their own prosocial responses. For example, parents may show and give objects to their infants, thus modeling those actions; at other times parents may request objects in the infants' possession and so provide an interactive slot into which the infants may slip a prosocial action. Such experiences inform infants about situations in which certain actions are socially appropriate and offer them opportunities for practicing and refining the actions. Thus, parents' performance of complementary behaviors, as well as their explicit modeling of the valued behaviors, may induce infants to perform those actions. This proposition was confirmed by observations of four groups of 12-month-old infants, who either observed an adult offer them objects (i.e., model the target action), request objects from them (i.e., perform the complementary action), both offer and request objects (i.e., try to induce a game of give-and-take), or merely chat with their mothers while displaying neither action (Hay & Murray, 1982). Infants who observed the model request objects and those who played give-and-take were reliably more likely than those in the control condition to offer objects to the model in turn. Furthermore, the give-and-take experience facilitated infants' later sharing with their own mothers.

These findings differ somewhat from the previous observation that, when mothers and unfamiliar persons requested toys from 15- and 18-month-old children, the frequency of giving was not increased above its spontaneous level (Rheingold et al., 1976). Perhaps observing the complement of a target act such as giving is especially facilitatory when an infant's ability to execute that act is first emerging; later, when the target act is firmly established in the child's repertoire, its spontaneous occurrence is more frequent and only information such as a verbal request may be needed to evoke it.

In addition to their experiences as recipients of care, infants also have many opportunities to observe the interactions of others. By observing other people, children presumably become better able to discriminate and assess the significance of facial expressions, vocalizations, and gestures (e.g., Borke, 1978) and to deduce the needs and emotions of others (Murphy, 1937). Children also soon observe the order their society has imposed on the physical environment. They learn how and when things are done in the world of adults, knowledge often requisite for effective prosocial action. For example, in the studies of helping, some children brought chairs from another room to complete the setting of the table, and others sought to wash the dishes from which they had pretended to eat; neither activity had been demonstrated in this setting or even suggested by the parents.

Infants of course are social agents as well as recipients, actors as well as observers. With maturation they develop numerous motor skills that permit them to act on the environment in many ways. Being social organisms, their actions soon become imbued with social meaning. As agents in a world of people, infants meet with responses from others that shape their succeeding acts. Even when they are too young to function as effective social agents, adults nevertheless tend to treat them as such (e.g., Rheingold & Adams, 1980; Schaffer, 1978). Thus, even very preliminary forms of prosocial behaviors (such as a child's resting an object on the parent's lap or picking up a scrap while the parent sweeps) are likely to be commented on and responded to in a way that places a prosocial construction on the child's behavior.

A telling example of parents' contingent responses to the early prosocial efforts of their offspring was documented in a laboratory study of mothers' verbal responses to the sharing behaviors of 12-month-old infants (West & Rheingold, 1978). Without being instructed to do so, the mothers responded 70% of the times their infants showed them objects and 93% of the times their infants gave them objects. Furthermore, when the infants accompanied their showing and giving with vocalizations, the likelihood that their mothers would respond was increased. The mothers' responses extended beyond undifferentiated attention or arbitrary reinforcement; rather, they typically provided socially appropriate reactions, for example, naming an object that was shown or expressing thanks for a gift. Such contingent responding by parents appears not to be restricted to just the relatively discrete actions of showing and giving; in the studies of helping, for example, parents very frequently praised their children's attempts to help.

Infants as agents of course display actions that are other than prosocial, and direct them to recipients other than their parents. Nonetheless, the parents' reactions to such behaviors may also contribute to prosocial development. For example, the way in which mothers reported they typically responded when their own children caused another child to become distressed (e.g., by bumping into a peer or starting to play with a peer's toy) predicted their children's subsequent responses to the distress of others (Zahn-Waxler et al., 1979). When mothers explained the consequences of their children's actions, emphasizing the peer's discomfort, the children were subsequently more likely to make reparations in similar incidents and to respond sympathetically to distress even when they were merely bystanders.

Despite the importance of the models infants observe and the consequences that accrue to their own actions, early prosocial behavior should not be viewed as slavish imitation or mechanical responding. Infants in the first year do imitate, but even then their imitation is selective, not automatic, and often represents considerable effort. Furthermore, the reproduction of another's act does not necessarily imply that it is performed without awareness or meaning. As in their use of language, young children generate variations and compose new sequences of acts. For example, when 1-year-old children were trained to play cooperative games with adults and were then observed with peers who had been similarly trained, they were more likely to invent new games than to repeat the ones learned during training (Ross, 1982). The innovative nature of the children's acts while participating in the parents' household tasks provides another example. Indeed, prosocial behaviors are flexible, generalizing across recipients, objects, and settings. Consider, for example, the case of helping, an activity that takes diverse forms, depending on the nature of the task, and includes various component actions even within a single task. Simple imitation would not suffice. Rather, the observation of helpful models probably promotes the abstraction of a principle that can be applied in other appropriate situations. Similarly, although the importance of response consequences should not be overlooked, the task-oriented yet cheerful manner in which infants and young children offer their prosocial acts (e.g., the alacrity with which they entered into the tasks set by their parents in the study of helping) bespeaks the rewarding properties of the acts themselves. Indeed, failures to train prosocial behavior in somewhat older children may partially stem from a use of less meaningful rewards or punishments that interfere with intrinsic ones.

## SOME IMPLICATIONS FOR EXISTING THEORIES

No current theory of socialization predicts prosocial behavior on the part of infants. The major perspectives that have been applied to the topic of moral development—social learning theory, Piaget's theory of cognitive development, and psychoanalytic theory—appear to assume that one need not search for manifestations of moral behavior much below the age of 6 years. Perhaps this is because prosocial acts are thought to be the products of conscience, and conscience is usually attributed only to mature, reflective, and socialized individuals.

Investigators working within a social learning perspective on prosocial development (see review by Bryan, 1975) have typically ignored infants and only recently remarked the existence of preschool-aged children. Rather, with older children as subjects, they manipulated variables in experimental settings that were assumed to approximate socializing events in the course of development. Thus, when social learning accounts of prosocial development are proposed, older children are studied; when social learning analyses are applied to infancy, only the topic of attachment to parents comes into focus. The evidence presented here is not incompatible with a social learning perspective; however, the evidence challenges investigators within this tradition to determine whether the processes thought to underlie socialization may not in fact be at work in the first years of life.

The failure of social learning theorists to examine very early development thus seems a case of neglect; the failure of S. Freud (e.g., 1938) and Piaget (1932) to do so seems more a matter of theoretical persuasion. In both perspectives, infancy is regarded as a period during which the capacity to comprehend the social world is limited; in both theories, infants are viewed as having some difficulties in distinguishing the boundaries between themselves and the rest of the world. Such confusion between self and other could conceivably foster empathic reactions and thus actually facilitate prosocial responding, as some theorists (Guillaume, 1971; Hoffman, 1975; Murphy, 1937) have speculated; however, many contemporary investigators of prosocial behavior appear to have interpreted the term *egocentrism* in its pejorative sense and thus have eschewed the study of infants.

Although neither Freud nor Piaget presented an account of the development of overt prosocial activity, both did describe moral development as the outcome of conflicts occurring in later childhood. In psychoanalytic theory, the capacity for prosocial action presumably awaits the resolution of the oedipal conflict and the consequent development of the superego. In Piaget's theory, the transition from heteronomous to autonomous moral reasoning arises from children's experience with and accommodation to the demands of their peers. If conflicts such as these are required to impel moral growth, then early childhood would not seem a reasonable domain in which to discover the first manifestations of socially valued behavior.

These traditions have probably ignored the early signs of prosocial behavior not only because of the emphases on the egocentricity of infants and on the need for growth through conflict, but also because the followers of Freud and Piaget have focused on different sorts of empirical questions. Freud's stress on cathexis and aggression may have prevented attention to prosocial behavior; psychoanalytic discussions of morality may place more emphasis on guilt than on altruism. Hence, when Freudian concepts were first translated into the terminology of social learning theory, young children's overtures to parents and peers were interpreted not as prosocial actions, but as manifestations of dependency (Sears, 1963). Similarly, investigators of early cognitive development have focused more on the knowledge about the world indexed by infants' acts than on their social interactive implications; thus, an observer in this tradition may indeed remark a game of give-and-take but classify it as a circular reaction.

Hence, there exists a need to extend current theories of socialization in light of the prosocial behaviors of very young children. The occurrence of the behaviors bears witness against a narrow use of the construct of egocentrism and suggests also that social behavior in infancy extends beyond attachment responses to caregivers. Furthermore, if any of these theories are to account for the development of a socially competent, moral human being, the mechanisms proposed and the variables investigated must be tested in the laboratory of early childhood.

## CONCLUDING REMARKS

The primary purpose of this chapter has been to draw attention to these noteworthy behaviors of very young children. However labeled, the behaviors and their early appearance merit consideration. The behaviors provide evidence of an impressive amount of learning about activities especially suited for harmonious social interaction, and they mark social achievements that have not yet found their place in developmental scales. When formal instruction does begin, it already has at hand a considerable number of social skills to build upon. To paraphrase Sully's words of 1896, the young child is well fitted to learn to become a member of a "good and virtuous community." It remains only for the persons in the child's environment to continue to provide benevolent models, to respond with encouragement and not impatience to children's earliest prosocial efforts, and, perhaps above all, to provide opportunities, even within the course of their ordinary routines, for children to display their emerging skills.

## REFERENCES

Ainsworth, M. D. S., & Wittig, B. A. Attachment and exploratory behavior of one-year-olds in a strange situation. In B. M. Foss (Ed.), *Determinants of infant behavior IV*. London: Methuen, 1969.

Banham, K. M. The development of affectionate behavior in infancy. *Journal of Genetic Psychology,* 1950, *76,* 283–289.

Borke, H. Piaget's view of social interaction and the theoretical construct of empathy. In L. S. Siegel & C. J. Brainerd (Eds.), *Alternatives to Piaget: Critical essays on the theory.* New York: Academic Press, 1978.

Bruner, J. S. Early social interaction and language acquisition. In H. R. Schaffer (Ed.), *Studies in mother–infant interaction.* London: Academic Press, 1977.

Bruner, J. S., & Sherwood, V. In J. S. Bruner, A. Jolly, & K. Sylva (Eds.), *Play: Its role in development and evolution.* Harmondsworth, England: Penguin Books, 1976.

Bryan, J. H. Children's cooperation and helping behaviors. In E. M. Hetherington (Ed.), *Review of child development research* (Vol. 5). Chicago: University of Chicago Press, 1975.

Bühler, C. The social behavior of the child. In C. Murchison (Ed.), *A handbook of child psychology.* Worcester, Mass.: Clark University Press, 1931.

Cappella, J. N. Mutual influence in expressive behavior: Adult–adult and infant–adult dyadic interaction. *Psychological Bulletin,* 1981, *89,* 101–132.

Church, J. (Ed.),*Three babies: Biographies of cognitive development.* New York: Random House, 1966.

Cook, K. V. *The verbal and nonverbal sharing of 2- and 3-year-old children.* Unpublished master's thesis, University of North Carolina, 1977.

Cotton, N. S. *The developmental course and interpretation of sharing during the second year of life.* Unpublished doctoral dissertation, Tufts University, 1976.

Darwin, C. A biographical sketch of an infant. *Mind,* 1877, *2,* 285–294.

Eckerman, C. O., & Rheingold, H. L. Infants' exploratory responses to toys and people. *Developmental Psychology,* 1974, *10,* 255–259.

Eckerman, C. O., Whatley, J. L., & Kutz, S. L. Growth of social play with peers during the second year of life. *Developmental Psychology,* 1975, *11,* 42–49.

Freud, A., & Burlingham, D. *Infants without families: The case for and against residential nurseries.* New York: International University Press, 1944.

Freud, S. *An outline of psychoanalysis.* London: Hogarth, 1938.

Garvey, C. Some properties of social play. *Merrill–Palmer Quarterly of Behavior and Development,* 1974, *20,* 163–180.

Gesell, A., & Amatruda, C. S. *Developmental diagnosis: Normal and abnormal child development.* New York: Hoeber, 1941.

Green, J. A., Gustafson, G. E., & West, M. J. Effects of infant development on mother–infant interactions. *Child Development,* 1980, *51,* 199–207.

Guillaume, P. [*Imitation in children*]. (E. P. Halperin, Trans.) Chicago: University of Chicago Press, 1971.

Gustafson, G. E., Green, J. A., & West, M. J. The infant's changing role in mother–infant games: The growth of social skills. *Infant Behavior and Development,* 1979, *2,* 301–308.

Hay, D. F. Cooperative interactions and sharing between very young children and their parents. *Developmental Psychology,* 1979, *15,* 647–653.

Hay, D. F., & Murray, P. Giving and requesting: Social facilitation of infants' offers to adults. *Infant Behavior and Development,* 1982, *5,* 301–310.

Hay, D. F., Nash, A., & Pedersen, J. Responses of six-month-olds to the distress of their peers. *Child Development,* 1981, *52,* 1071–1075.

Hay, D. F., Nash, A., & Pedersen, J. Interaction between six-month-old peers. *Child Development,* 1983, *54,* 557–562.

Hay, D. F., & Ross, H. S. The social nature of early conflict. *Child Development,* 1982, *53,* 105–113.

Hoffman, M. L. Developmental synthesis of affect and cognition and its implications for altruistic motivation. *Developmental Psychology,* 1975, *11,* 607–622.

Holmberg, M. C. The development of social interchange pattern from 12 to 42 months. *Child Development,* 1980, *51,* 448–456.

Kaye, K., & Marcus, J. Imitation over a series of trials without feedback: Age six months. *Infant Behavior and Development*, 1978, *1*, 141–155.

Leung, E. H. L., & Rheingold, H. L. Development of pointing as a social gesture. *Developmental Psychology*, 1981, *17*, 215–220.

Murchison, C., & Langer, S. Tiedemann's observations on the development of the mental faculties of children. *Pedagogical Seminary and Journal of Genetic Psychology*, 1927, *34*, 205–230.

Murphy, L. B. *Social behavior and child personality: An exploratory study of some roots of sympathy*. New York: Columbia University Press, 1937.

Mussen, P. H., & Eisenberg-Berg, N. *Roots of caring, sharing, and helping*. San Francisco: Freeman, 1977.

Piaget, J. *The moral judgment of the child*. New York: Harcourt Brace, 1932.

Piaget, J. [*The origins of intelligence in children*]. (M. Cook, Trans.) New York: INternational Universities Press, 1952.

Preyer, W. [*The mind of the child*]. (H. W. Brown, Trans.) New York: Appleton, 1889.

Rheingold, H. L. Independent behavior of the human infant. In A. D. Pick (Ed.), *Minnesota Symposia on Child Psychology* (Vol. 7). Minneapolis: University of Minnesota Press, 1973.

Rheingold, H. L. *Little children's participation in the work of adults, a nascent prosocial behavior*. *Child Development*, 1982, *53*, 114–125.

Rheingold, H. L., & Adams, J. L. The significance of speech to newborns. *Developmental Psychology*, 1980, *16*, 397–403.

Rheingold, H. L., & Emery, G. N. *The early reenactment of nurturant behaviors*. Manuscript in preparation, in press.

Rheingold, H. L., Hay, D. F., & West, M. J. Sharing in the second year of life. *Child Development*, 1976, *47*, 1148–1158.

Ross, H. S. *Infant's use of turn-alternation signals in games*. Paper presented at the International Conference on Infant Studies, New Haven, Conn., April 1980.

Ross, H. S. Establishment of social games among toddlers. *Developmental Psychology*, 1982, *18*, 509–518.

Ross, H. S., & Goldman, B. D. Establishing new social relations in infancy. In T. Alloway, P. Pliner, & L. Krames (Eds.), *Advances in the study of communication and affect* (Vol. 3). *Attachment behavior*. New York: Plenum, 1977.

Sagi, A., & Hoffman, M. L. Empathic distress in the newborn. *Developmental Psychology*, 1976, *12*, 175–176.

Scarr, S., & Salapatek, P. Patterns of fear development during infancy. *Merrill–Palmer Quarterly*, 1970, *16*, 53–90.

Schaffer, H. R. Acquiring the concept of the dialogue. In M. H. Bornstein & W. Kessen (Eds.), *Psychological development from infancy: Image to intention*. Hillsdale, N. J.: Erlbaum, 1978.

Schaffer, H. R., & Crook, C. K. Maternal control techniques in a directed play situation. *Child Development*, 1979, *50*, 989–996.

Sears, R. R. Dependency motivation. In M. R. Jones (Ed.), *Nebraska Symposium on Motivation* (Vol. 11). Lincoln: University of Nebraska Press, 1963.

Shaffran, R. Modes of approach and the infant's reaction to the stranger. In T. G. Decarie (Ed.), [*The infant's reaction to strangers*]. (J. Diamanti, Trans.) New York: International Universities Press, 1974.

Simner, M. L. Newborn's response to the cry of another infant. *Developmental Psychology*, 1971, *5*, 136–150.

Staub, E. *Positive social behavior and morality* (Vol. 1). *Social and personal influences*. New York: Academic Press, 1978.

Stayton, D. J., Hogan, R., & Ainsworth, M. D. S. Infant obedience and maternal behavior: The origins of socialization reconsidered. *Child Development*, 1971, *42*, 1057–1069.

Stern, W. [*Psychology of early childhood up to the sixth year of age*] (3rd ed.). (A. Barwell, Trans.) New York: Holt, 1924.

Sully, J. *Studies of childhood*. New York: Appleton, 1896.

Valentine, C. W. *The psychology of early childhood*. London: Methuen, 1942.

West, M. J., & Rheingold, H. L. Infant stimulation of maternal instruction. *Infant Behavior and Development*, 1978, *1*, 205–215.

Wispé, L. Positive forms of social behavior: An overview. *Journal of Social Issues*, 1972, *28*, 1–20.

Zahn-Waxler, C., Radke-Yarrow, M., & King, R. A. Child rearing and children's prosocial initiations toward victims of distress. *Child Development*, 1979, *50*, 319–330.

# Benevolent Babies:
# Emergence of the Social Self[1]

### DIANE L. BRIDGEMAN

## INTRODUCTION

The historical roots of prosocial inquiries can be traced to the moral philosophy tradition of the 1920s with its focus on altruism and morality. Arguments within the field at that time are not unlike the debates of today. For example, current theorists of morality (e.g., Hogan, 1973; Kohlberg, 1969), employing a stage model of moral development, assume that early stages embody less moral understanding or a type of conventional reasoning. Similarly, the utilitarians, such as La Rochefoucauld, employed reductionism with the construct of altruism, viewing it as a degenerate form of egotism. Durkheim (1925), however, criticized this reductionism and clearly stated that altruism and egotism are not derived from each other but are "both rooted in our nature—a nature of which they only express two aspects implying and mutually complementing one another [p. 222]."

Contemporarily, Turiel's (1978) work on social cognition, for example, supports antireductionism tendencies. He reports that reasoning around issues of societal concerns constitutes social conventional thinking rather than a lower form of moral reasoning, which is defined by principles of justice prescriptive of behavior. He has proposed that social convention is part of a conceptual domain that is distinct from the moral domain and that social convention, as part of the societal domain, refers to concepts of social systems and social organizations.

[1]I thank the University of California, Santa Cruz, for a faculty research grant that provided partial support for this research.

THE NATURE OF PROSOCIAL DEVELOPMENT

The research discussed in this chapter reaffirms a nonreductionistic, yet parallel view of social development, in its finding that certain types of prosocial behaviors in preschool children seem to develop congruently with specific self-centered behaviors. Further validation is given to recent claims (Rheingold, Hay, & West, 1976; Zahn-Waxler, Radke-Yarrow, & King, 1979) of the presence of prosocial behavior at earlier levels of development than theoretically assumed. This finding is discussed with respect to its contradiction of the traditional socialization view, which holds that the very young child is not initially social and that only through later modifications and instrumental behavior the child becomes social. In addition to an exploration of the theoretical and social significance of the existence of early prosocial behavior, there is the thornier conceptual issue of self-centered and prosocial development as parallel processes.

The following observational method was used to qualitatively and quantitatively assess two primary areas of inquiry: prosocial behaviors and self-centered behaviors between parent and young child. The design, procedure, and subjects were the same for both investigations. Two separate coding and scoring systems were developed and are presented prior to the summary of results for each inquiry. Correlations between the prosocial and the self-centered behaviors are also summarized.

## THE STUDY

### Sample

Twenty-four families participated in this study. They were contacted through day-care centers and birth announcements in a local newspaper. The families included children at $1\frac{1}{2}$, $2\frac{1}{2}$, and $3\frac{1}{2}$ years of age ($\pm 8$ weeks), with even distribution over the three age groups. The equal number of both sexes at each age therefore included 12 males and 12 females. Three selection criteria were: (a) that families had only one child or had a child whose younger sibling was no more than 6 months old; (b) that families were Caucasian and of middle socioeconomic class; and (c) that they were monolingual.

The subjects were screened by means of two preliminary interviews. The first, conducted by telephone, served to establish rapport with the subjects, and to explain the details of the taping procedure. The second interview consisted of a 15-min visit to the homes of the families. This session was to meet the child and parents and to administer a brief questionnaire that assessed demographic variables. It was explained to the parents that the child should be well fed and rested prior to taping, and the schedule of the filming session was planned.

### Data Collection

The interactions of parents and children were videotaped. Subjects were situated in a room at home in which the parents and children typically played. The camera was set up in full view of the subjects; no special zoom techniques or other special focusing effects were used and the camera remained in a relatively fixed position. A high-quality monophonic audio track was obtained on the videotape. Subjects were asked to play as they usually would. For purposes of standardization across families, they were asked to use a basket of assorted toys that were provided by the experimenters. These toys included a house containing the characters of The Three Bears, a doctor's kit, a panda bear with an adhesive bandage strip on his head, and assorted plastic people and vehicles. There were three 8-min taping sessions counterbalanced by age and sex of the child and by the three conditions—mother–child, father–child, and combined parents and child—for a total of 24 min of recorded time per family. If the family desired, the tape was played back after the filming was completed. The videotape equipment permitted manual control of the direction and speed of tape movement so that segments of the tape could be reviewed and verbal content transcribed. Each transcription was made by two observers.

Experimenters completed a postobservation assessment to evaluate their perceptions of the subjects' degree of naturalness and cooperativeness and of the taping session in general. Their perceptions of the sessions were found to be consistent with the subjects' reported self-perceptions of the sessions. Modifications in the design of this study over most studies in this area were: the use of the natural home environment; the inclusion of separate episodes with mother–child, father–child; and both parents and child; very young children as subjects; and the consideration of possibly antithetical behaviors within the same population. Limitations are the modest sample size (24 families) and restricted taping time of only 24 min per family because of the young ages of the subjects.

### Prosocial Behavior Coding System

All subjects, parents and children, were scored for six prosocial behaviors. The working definitions for the targeted behaviors were as follows:

*Sharing*—Giving away or allowing temporary use of an object previously in one's possession

*Helping*—Attempting to meet another's needs. This often included giving useful information or assisting with a task

*Nurturing*—Concerned and supportive behavior toward another

*Cooperating*—Working together with another for a common purpose

*Sympathizing*—Expressing regret at the distress of another

*Praising*—Giving approval to another person, often including encouragement

Both qualitative and quantitative assessments were obtained. Quantitatively, the frequency for the occurrence of each prosocial behavior by each subject was scored. The qualitative levels of prosocial behavior were scored using the following scale: (*a*) minimally present behavior; (*b*) clearly present with more elaborate development, which often included examples; (*c*) well-developed prosocial behavior, which often included the use of reasoning about the behavior. This level sometimes entailed a call for prosocial action. Both a verbal and a nonverbal notation were made. Nonverbal behaviors were given a 4, 5, or 6, with 4 signifying that the behavior was minimally present, 5 signifying clearly present, and 6 signifying very well developed. If a behavior had a verbal and a physical component, it was rated for the behavior that was the more prosocial, with an indication that both had occurred.

Next to each behavior was a column that indicated who had initiated and who had been the recipient. Duration was measured and rounded off to the nearest 5 sec. Two similar prosocial activities were considered separate behaviors if 4 or more sec elapsed between them.

The context in which the prosocial behaviors occurred and the experiences that elicited the behaviors were scored, since the subjects were too young to be interviewed. This scoring also helped to minimize the problems of inference (inherent in data based solely on observations) and to gain a clearer understanding of possible cognitive and motivational factors.

## ELICITING OF BEHAVIORS

Perceived eliciting behavior was rated for all subjects using the following categories:

1. A result of the present ongoing activity
2. Spontaneous
3. A response to a request
4. Modeling or imitation (behavior appeared to result from copying or observing another, usually a child copying the parents' actions
5. From preaching (lecturing about doing a prosocial act, but with no explanation)
6. Reasoning (explanation given about importance of a prosocial behavior)
7. Directive (directing to another person: "Could you help daddy?") or
8. Ambiguous (did not fit into any of the other categories).

## CONTEXT

The perceived *context* from which a behavior occurred was also coded but only for the children in the study. The categories were as follows:

1. Acceptance, obedience or compliance
2. Attention (acted prosocially to gain parent or parents' attention
3. Antisocial, such as throwing a toy, followed by a prosocial behavior
4. Fear of punishment
5. Rewards or privileges
6. Sympathy or kindness
7. Supportive, helpful

8. Imitation (clearly followed from watching another person—delayed imitations were not included)
9. Other (not appropriate to any of the previous categories)

There was also a column for additional comments, intended to give more information about the specific nature of each transaction. Scoring of all the tapes was completed by three undergraduate assistants; interrater reliability was 86%.

## METHODS OF DATA ANALYSIS

Repeated-measures analyses of variance were employed where sex and age were the two nonrepeated factors. The first repeated factor consisted of condition (either mother–child, father–child, or mother–father–child). The second consisted of either the type (sharing, helping, etc.) or level (as just described) of the exhibited behavior. The independent variable was the frequency of levels or the frequency of types of prosocial behaviors observed within each condition.[2]

## Prosocial Results

### VERBAL BEHAVIOR

Total frequency of child's verbal prosocial behaviors was found to significantly increase with age ($F = 5.48$; $df = 2,18$; $p < .02$). This corresponds to a Pearson correlation coefficient of .44. No significant differences were found for sex of child or for condition. A significant level by age interaction was also found in the analysis of child's levels of verbal prosocial behavior ($F = 4.16$; $df = 8,72$; $p < .001$). No significant statements can be made concerning behaviors at Levels 2–5.

A comparison of the mother's and father's levels of verbal prosocial behaviors exhibited a drop-off effect after Level 1, indicating that the ability to detect even more of a continuum of prosocial behaviors would require further refinement. A conventional explanation for an increase in verbal behavior across age is the development of verbal skills and cognitive abilities during this period.

A significant level by condition interaction was found for mothers' level of verbal prosocial behavior ($F = 5.75$; $df = 4,72$; $p < .001$). Once again, Levels 2–5 are

---

[2]Parametric methods of analysis of variance with repeated measures were used, with assigned variables such as levels of sophistication of prosociality. Types of prosociality were used as classifying second-repeated factors under the first-repeated factor of condition. Although these data can be thought of as dependent scores, they are taken here as independent factors, because they were assigned prior to the scoring procedure, facilitating analysis by repeated-measures ANOVAs. Nonparametrics statistics were considered, but since ANOVAs are very robust toward deviations from a normal distribution of events, and, given that the dependent variable is interval type (frequency of behavior), the more powerful parametric procedure was used. This decision was made for both the prosocial and the self-centered aspects.

minimally present. Overall, mothers tended to show more verbal prosocial behavior when with their spouse (and child, of course) than when alone with their child. The analysis of fathers' levels of verbal prosocial behavior found no significant differences with age or sex of child or with condition. Once again, fathers' behaviors are predominantly Level 1.

NONVERBAL BEHAVIOR

Mothers and fathers both showed a high incidence of the lowest level of nonverbal prosocial behavior. No significant difference in mothers' nonverbal prosocial behavior was elicited by child's sex or age, nor by condition. The fathers showed varying levels of nonverbal prosocial behavior dependent upon condition (level by condition interaction: $F = 6.38$; $df = 2,36$; $p < .004$). Overall, the lowest level of behaviors was again most prevalent.

*Types.* In general, the children showed the greatest incidence of prosocial behavior in the mother–father–child condition, less in the mother–child condition, and least in the father–child condition. The most striking example of this, and a significant finding in itself, is found in the children's *nurturance* behavior, where children tended to exhibit higher levels of nurturance in both conditions where the mother was present ($F = 3.65$; $df = 2,36$; $p < .04$). The differences between conditions are not significant for the other types. Nurturance and helping seem to be the most prevalent prosocial behaviors appearing in these children. Praising, cooperating and sharing were all at minimal levels. Sex and age were nonsignificant.

Mothers, fathers, and children all showed a greater frequency of prosocial behaviors in the mother–father–child condition ($F = 4.83$; $df = 1,18$; $p < .05$). This suggests an overall prosocial catalytic effect. The fathers' and mothers' prosocial patterns were almost identical (no significant differences were found). Parents seem to exhibit a greater frequency of praising and helping, unlike sharing, sympathy or cooperation and, to an even lesser extent, nurturance.

Concerning the interactive effects of parents' and children's prosocial behavior, the children's overall prosocial behaviors were not significantly correlated with either the mothers' or the fathers' prosocial tendencies. With respect to specific types of prosocial behaviors, mothers' sharing behavior was significantly correlated with the children's sharing (Pearson $r = .57$; $p < .01$), yet not with fathers' sharing behaviors. Caution must be exercised, however, with this correlation, as sharing generally was very sparse. It is interesting, however, to note that children tended to share when mothers shared.

*Elicitation and Context.* There appeared to be no sex differences in the way prosocial behaviors were *elicited*. For both boys and girls, most behaviors were equally distributed between the context of the present ongoing activity (42%) and requests (42%); 6% were from spontaneous behavior and 8% from modeling.

There were also few sex differences in the *context* from which the behaviors arose, with 29% from apparent compliance and 39% from sympathy and kindness; 16% occurred out of a desire to be supportive and helpful. There was a small percentage of behaviors that appeared to stem from immediate imitation (4%), a surprisingly low incidence considering that imitation is thought to be a primary means for learning in certain theoretical orientations (Bandura, 1977; Mischel, 1977). These findings imply that, although the children often responded from the present activity rather than spontaneously (not unusual for such young children), they still showed a sense of thoughtfulness about their behavior. The lack of difference with respect to sex of child and the degree of prosocial behavior, eliciting of that behavior, or context in which it occurred is consistent with most studies in the field (Krebs, 1970).

No distinct differences were found between parents' elicitations of prosocial behavior. For both males and females, prosocial behaviors were elicited by present activity 82% of the time and in response to requests 10% of the time.

PARENTS' PROSOCIAL REASONING

At the conclusion of the taping session mothers and fathers separately were asked to consider three hypothetical dilemmas regarding their attitudes about social interactions. In these brief inquiries the parent was asked how certain instances were typically rendered within their family. For example, "Their child had a package of crackers. Several neighbor children joined the child in play. A grappling over the crackers then ensued." A composite prosocial reasoning score was determined for each parent based on the responses to the inquiries. The results seem to reflect, for the mothers at least, a similarity between attitude and behavior regarding prosocial experiences. The mothers' prosocial attitudes were positively correlated with their total prosocial behavior as determined by the taping session observations ($\rho = .44$; $p < .04; N = 24$). A similar analysis of the fathers' responses and behaviors did not reach significance.

## Self-Centered Behavior Coding System

The same videotaped sessions were the source of ratings for both prosocial behavior and the quantity and quality of self-centered behaviors. Each scoring was completed independently. The term *self-centered*, as it was employed in this study, is defined as "absorbed in oneself." This term is intended to be descriptive and nonpejorative.

LEVELS

A $2 \times 3 \times 3 \times 2$ repeated-measures ANOVA was employed. The first three factors were the same as those used in the prosocial analyses (sex, age, condition), whereas the second repeated measure was the rater-perceived level of sophistication of the self-centered behavior observed, scored using the following scale: (*a*) minimally present self-centered behaviors; and (*b*) clearly present self-centered behaviors with the inclusion of an example or developed reasoning.

## CONTEXT

A 2 × 3 × 3 × 2 repeated-measures ANOVA was used. For qualitative purposes a second repeated measure was the perceived context in which the behavior occurred. The following scale was employed:

1. The child's self-centered behavior deprives the parent. (No instances of this behavior were found.)
2. The child's self-centered behavior is exhibited with little benefit to the child.
3. The child's self-centered behavior is oriented to benefit the child.

## TYPES

A 2 × 3 × 3 × 4 repeated-measures ANOVA was employed where the second repeated factor was scored using the following scale:

1. Self-referencing behavior. Child labels something as "mine," when it is not his or hers (i.e., "That's mine;" "Oh my bottle," etc.).
2. Demand for action from parent (i.e., "Put this on me;" "Open it.")
3. Child specifying desires (i.e., "No, I don't want it.")
4. Child reasoning from his or her own experience base (i.e., "Any teri-drops left?")

## ELICITATION

A 2 × 3 × 3 × 4 repeated-measures ANOVA was used, where the second repeated factor was scored using the following scale (these categories describe the situations that evoked the perceived self-centered behaviors):

1. Self-centered behavior in response to present activity (child's behavior is congruent with the ongoing context of the situation)
2. Self-centered behavior in response to request by parent
3. Answer to question by parent
4. Spontaneous self-centered behavior

Inter-rater reliability for scoring of the self-centered behavior by two undergraduate assistants was 88%. Differential attrition occurred when scoring the self-centered aspect of the study. Two 1½-year-old children—one of each sex—were dropped from the self-centered scoring as their speech was unintelligible to the raters.

## Self-Centered Results

### LEVELS

The only significant finding was a main effect for level of behavior ($F = 16.87$; $df = 1,15$; $p < .001$). There were more minimal self-centered behaviors than there were highly developed levels of behavior. This is to be expected as the subjects are very young and just developing their cognitive and verbal abilities. Level 1 included both verbal and nonverbal expressions of self-centeredness. Age was not found to be significant.

### CONTEXT

There were no significant main effects for sex, age, or condition on context. A significant three-way interaction accounts for this, involving the factors of context by condition by age ($F = 2.70$; $df = 4,30$; $p < .05$). All of the post hoc analyses executed in an attempt to determine the source of the interaction yielded nonsignificant results. These analyses included examination of trends within Context 1 and Context 2, as well as examination of trends within the father-alone condition.

### TYPES

A significant main effect for type of behavior was found, suggesting differences in the occurrences of the four types of self-centered behaviors ($F = 3.07$; $df = 3,45$; $p < .04$). Again, there were no significant effects for age or sex. A high degree of behavior consisting of demands for parent action was found. There were no significant differences between self-referencing behavior, specification of desires, and reasoning from the child's experience base. Collapsing of individual types of self-centered behaviors yielded no finding of significant differences between sex, age, and condition.

### ELICITATION

A main effect was found for the way the self-centered behavior was elicited ($F = 21.82$; $df = 3,45$; $p < .001$). The majority of behaviors were elicited in response to present activity, next from parent questioning; however, this was not significantly different from spontaneous behavior (Type 4), whereas it was significantly different from response to request from parent (Type 2) ($F = 5.57$; $df = 1,20$; $p < .05$).

## Relationship between Prosocial and Self-Centered Findings

In order to correlate the prosocial and the self-centered aspects, one single index of representative behavior for each aspect was chosen. This index was defined as the total frequency of prosocial, or of self-centered, behavior exhibited across the conditions of the corresponding aspect.

A central finding was a positive correlation between total prosocial and total self-centered behaviors exhibited by the children ($r = .50$; $p < .03$, $N = 21$), which suggests that self-centered and prosocial behaviors develop simultaneously in a child and that they are not antithetical constructs. As the indexes of both aspects of behavior were total frequency of behaviors elicited, one plausible explanation for this significant correlation is that activity or verbal level of the child may account for the increases of both simultaneously.—that is, children who are more active and more verbal overall might exhibit more and better developed self-centered and prosocial behaviors than children who are less so.

Consequently, an index of verbal activity level was developed to determine the relative role of verbalness. The three assessments of verbal activity that were used were based on two of the three conditions (mother with child and father with child):

1. Mean length of child's utterances (MLU)
2. Total number of words spoken by child (NW)
3. Total number of child's utterances (NU)

Both the prosocial and the self-centered indexes were adjusted for the child's activity level using computer statements with correlations calculated between the adjusted indexes.

It was found that a significant relationship between verbal activity level and prosocial behavior exists (using MLU scores across conditions, $r = .59$; $p = .003$), whereas no corresponding trend for self-centered behavior was apparent.

From the literature it might be assumed that prosocial and self-centered behaviors would be negatively correlated; that is, a child who is prosocial is unlikely to be self-centered and vice versa. A significant relationship between prosocial behavior and self-centered behavior, however, was found in this study. After adjusting for verbal activity level, however, the two constructs were found to coexist but not to be correlated.

Consequently, knowing a child's level of prosocial behavior would not predict his or her level of self-centered behavior. A reason for this finding is the higher correlation between prosocial behavior and verbal level. Therefore, previous assumptions from the literature of a negative correlation are not supported by these data. If both of these behaviors are more evident in children who exhibit more developed verbal behaviors, then the self-centered and the prosocial behaviors will be correlated.

## DISCUSSION

In reviewing the significant prosocial results from this study, one of the areas that yields an intriguing pattern is that of the mother's influence. Her presence seems to enhance the quantity and quality of positive social behavior. First, there was significantly more nurturant behavior by the child when the mother was present than when she was absent. There was a significant correlation between mother's sharing and the child's sharing. There was also generally more verbal prosocial behavior when the mother was present. It appears that the positive impact of the mother's role affects the father and interacts with the father's presence, since several of the conditions show the greatest degrees of prosocial behavior when both parents were present, less when the child was alone with the mother, and the least when the child was alone with the father.

Furthermore, both parents exhibited the most prosocial behavior in the combined condition, and the mothers showed more prosocial behavior when with the spouse. This effect was not found for the fathers. Whether these results are due to the mere presence of the mother on the father, her modeling or teaching, the opportunities she presents, or the combined effect of both parents together, is unclear; yet these results indicate that the mother holds a pivotal position with respect to positive social interaction. Further consistency in the mothers' interactions is noted in the significant correlation reported in the mothers' prosocial attitudes, from the interview questions, with her prosocial behavior as noted in the videotape observations.

The very existence of prosocial behavior in $1\frac{1}{2}$–$3\frac{1}{2}$-year-olds is one of the most noteworthy findings of this study, although the majority of these behaviors were at the lowest levels of the assessment scale. Perhaps the fact that these behaviors are relatively undifferentiated and infrequent in occurrence accounts for the paucity of research attesting to its existence until recently.

With slightly differing methods, goals, and age span of subjects, 3 separate groups of researchers' results (Rheingold, Hay, & West, 1976; Zahn-Waxler, Radke-Yarrow, & King, 1979; and this author's current research) confirm the existence of prosocial behaviors in very young children. We now need to proceed beyond affirming the presence of these behaviors in preschoolers and move from descriptive accounts to an understanding of their cognitive and social significance. More global assessments are in order where structured interviews, observations, and interventions are combined within one study in home and school settings with family and peers.

In comparing studies across the prosocial literature, it is necessary to examine subjects' experience level, the social context, methods, definitions, and types of prosocial behaviors examined. Along with these specifications is the frequent conceptual call for a more direct measure of the reasoning behind social behavior (Krebs, 1978). A cognitive analysis of prosocial development is therefore necessary. One fruitful approach that meets and goes beyond these requirements, especially in light of the consistent finding of the importance of social interaction in the development of social knowledge, is the social cognitive research by Turiel (e.g., 1978, 1979). His work explores the specific domains of children's social knowledge as applied in judgments about social behavior. He views social development as the formation of systems of knowledge about social interactions and suggests that future research focus on the conceptual similarities and differences in children's reasoning about constraint-oriented and positive events (Turiel, 1978).

Along with cognitive studies that consider the nature of the system of social knowledge, especially in searching for origins of prosocial behavior, it would be useful to examine infants' and young children's accommodations to prosocial interactions and when and where they anticipate, are surprised, or angered by specific transgressions or prosocial experiences. How would the results of such inquiries influence our existing theories of social development and what implications have they for education, child rearing and development in general?

Earlier work by Murphy (1937) has been appropriately revived and cited as an example of a study that reports the existence of infrequent prosocial behavior in preschoolers. A more fully developed set of insightful observational studies, including an integrative psychoanalytical and Piagetian perspective by the British researcher Susan Isaacs (1924), however, has been sorely overlooked. The current finding that prosocial and self-centered behavior coexist in very young children is expressed in Isaacs's early work, although her conceptual conclusions differ somewhat.

In her observations with 2–6-year-olds, Isaacs (1924) prefaced a section on "friendliness and cooperation" with the statement that "there were countless minor incidents of mutual helpfulness and common activity throughout the observations [p. 93]." Not unlike the results described in this chapter, the overall incidence seems infrequent, yet the consistency of the presence of prosocial behavior for such young children is striking. One of Isaacs's conclusions, agreeing with Piaget, states that "he is basically right about egocentrism dominating the behavior of children under five years of age depending partly on his social experience [p. 214]." Yet she continues, "A great deal of the children's behavior was naturally of a marginal kind, showing strands of true egocentrism *interwoven* with a limited but genuine appreciation of the point of view of playmates, and with the recognition of independent but complementary roles in co-operative play [Isaacs, 1924, p. 214]." Examples of clear prosocial behaviors are found in all volumes of her work.[3]

Regardless of theoretical persuasion, social scientists have not developed frameworks that include or predict prosociality in preschoolers. It has not been expected, nor looked for, and, if noted, its low incidence has rendered it less noteworthy.

---

[3]Accompanying Isaacs's study, results, and theory are extensive and rich narrative accounts of the children's exact interactions. For example, in the volume *Social Development in Young Children: A Study of Beginnings*, Isaacs (1924) cites the following observations:

> 7.11.24. Frank (age 4) had hurt Harold's (age 4) leg in a quarrel, and Harold lay on the floor with his head buried in his hands. Presently Dan (age 3), who was modelling, went to Harold and asked "Is it better now? Will you come and do plasticine?" . . . Soon Dan went to him again, and asked the same questions; and after a time, he said again, "Won't you come now and do some plasticine?" Harold then joined the others and became cheerful again. The children were all modelling, very quietly, and Dan made a boat and gave it to Benjie (age 4). Benjie told the others, "He has made a boat for me." Dan remarked, "Yes, I like you very much, and I'm going to kiss you." He kissed Benjie's hand. Benjie told the others, "He likes me." Dan then said to Harold, "I like you, and I'm going to kiss you," and kissed Harold's hand. Harold said, "He's a dear little thing," and all the others agreed [p. 93].

Both psychoanalytic and cognitive–developmental orientations posit the years of 5–7 as likely to be the onset of positive social behaviors. Piagetians argue for the development of cognitive functions such as operational thought in general before prosocial behaviors occur, whereas Freudians' preoccupation with guilt and self-degradation to enforce standards limits the consideration of prosociality. In psycho-analytic thought even the development of the sociality and morality of the child were thought to have to await oedipal resolution, the core conflict, along with the fascinating ramifications of neurosis. In his 1920 preface to the fourth edition of the "Three Essays on Infantile Sexuality," Freud (1953–1966) stated, however, that the essays would not have had to be written had we been able to learn from direct child observation.

## IMPLICATIONS FOR THEORY

Current investigators, led by cognitive-developmentalists and ethologists, are beginning to rethink the degree to which young children have social experiences. Even infants are now thought to be more socially competent and more willing and ready to interact. Possibly infants' early accidental discovery of their impact on the physical world, coupled with opportunities and joys of social interactions and later language development, leads to further reciprocal interactions and a parallel sense of self and other. This would, in turn, yield more developed reciprocal interactions and actual perspective-taking.

As Lewis and Brooks-Gunn (1979) have suggested, the knowledge of others in the social world is acquired through interactions at the same time and in the same manner as the knowledge of self. A review presented later of a few representative studies of young children's construction of their social world seems to reflect a "bandwagon" effect regarding researchers' views of preschoolers' sociality. These tentative, descriptive findings however, are beginning to yield a consistent picture that is difficult to deny. It is, in fact, of social beings who immediately interact with their social world. For example, Sander (1977) found that as early as the sixth day of life, babies respond with dismay if the mother's face is masked during feeding. Mimicking of mother's facial expression is reported at 2 weeks (Lichtenberg, 1981), and smiling in social interaction is found at 8–12 weeks (Spitz, 1965).

More important for understanding the origins of prosocial or affective develop-ment is Trevarthen's (1978) study, which demonstrates that babies listen to and watch their mothers in face-to-face orientation and enter into social *engagement* at 2 months of age. Engaging in communication about using objects and playing games by perceiving objects in an interpersonal framework occurs around 6 months to a year (Hubley & Trevarthen, 1979). In another study, Trevarthen and Hubley (1978) observed that cooperative understanding becomes effective at approximately 9 months of age.

Trevarthen proposes that the developmental process consists of a tension between perception and cognition on one hand, and an intense psychological process biased for social cooperation on the other. The conventional instrumental conceptions of interaction (e.g., Bandura, 1977; Mischel, 1977) pose a different view. It is seen as a closed system where reciprocity is possible within a causal-functional chain of activity. The Trevarthen perspective requires an interpretive, consensual element that implies joint action of two subjects in an open system where intersubjectivity, not instrumentality, is central. The distinctions are clear and important, with the intersubjectivity analysis assuming that cognitive development in early childhood is integrated with social development.

The role of language is also important in our understanding of early social cognition. The preverbal cooperative interactions just referred to are most likely enhanced by the onset of language. Bates, Bretherton, Shore, and Carpen (1979) found naming of objects emerging as a communicative act as early as 10–13 months. Recall that, in this author's previously described study, there was a significant correlation between the prosocial interactions and the child's level of verbal activity. Bretherton and Bates (1979) caution, however, that it is premature to state whether "early harmonious quality of interaction in play as well as other cooperative sequences is related (or not related) to later discourse skill [p. 96]."

A beginning degree of intentionality seems to be a key quality in early social development. When it is associated with an initial sense of self differentiated from other, as developed in Lewis and Brooks-Gunn's (1974) work with 1-year-olds and as hypothesized in the theory of James Mark Baldwin (1895), this intentionality contributes to early role-taking and empathy (as reported, for example, by Zahn-Waxler, Radke-Yarrow, & King, 1979). In turn, these processes allow early sharing, helping, and other prosocial behaviors to develop as described in the primary research in this chapter with $1\frac{1}{2}$–$3\frac{1}{2}$-year-olds. A similar integration of the relationship of these social experiences is reported in Lempers, Flavell, and Flavell's (1977) work, where effective accommodation to another's viewpoint is achieved through pointing, showing, and hiding behaviors in 1–2-year-olds. See Table 4.1 for an integrative scheme of levels of early social affect based on the representative studies just cited.

The relationship of prosocial behavior to role-taking was examined by this author in a study with older children. It was found that cooperative interactions (specifically cooperative, interdependent learning groups) enhanced fifth-grade students' level of role-taking, and earlier studies with the same paradigm showed the use of the cooperative groups to enhance self-esteem (Bridgeman, 1981). The results provide intervention-based support for Piaget's (1965) assertion that cooperative peer exchange promotes perspective-taking and that, through the active process of resolving social and cognitive conflicts, the child learns to construct his or her way of viewing the world. Piaget (1965) has stated that "it is *cooperation* that leads to the primacy of intentionality, by forcing the individual to be constantly occupied with the point of view of other people so as to compare it with his [pp. 189–190]." Both Piaget (1928) and, later, Mead (1934) hypothesized the direction of these social relationships. Their assumption was that the ability to role-take is necessary to the

**TABLE 4.1**

*Early Social Affect and Prosocial Development: A Modest Integrative Scheme Based on Representative Studies*

| Level | Concept | Approximate age |
|---|---|---|
| Level 1 | *Initial joint regard* | |
| | A. Interacting with mother in negative way when mother's face is masked during feeding (Sander, 1977) | 6 days |
| | B. Mimicking of mother's facial expression (Lichtenberg, 1981) | 2 weeks |
| | C. 1. Smiling in social interactions (Spitz, 1965) | 8–12 weeks |
| |     2. Listening, watching, and entering into social engagement (Trevarthen, 1978) | 8–12 weeks |
| Level 2 | *Development of effective, positive interaction* | |
| | A. Engaging in communication about the use of objects and playing of games in interpersonal framework (Hubley & Trevarthen, 1979) | 6–12 months |
| | B. Cooperative understanding becomes effective (Trevarthen & Hubley, 1978) | 9 months |
| Level 3 | *Initial communication and self-recognition* | |
| | A. Emergence of concept that objects have names, can be recognized, and can serve as communicative acts (Bretherton & Bates, 1979) | 10–13 months |
| | B. Emergence of knowledge of self and others and of one's relationship to others (Lewis & Brooks-Gunn, 1979) | 12 months |
| Level 4 | *A more developed understanding of self, other, and of prosocial concepts* | |
| | A. 1. Evidence of accomodation to another's viewpoint through pointing, showing, and hiding behaviors (Lempers, Flavell, & Flavell, 1977) | 1–3 years |
| |     2. Evidence of role-taking and empathy (Zahn-Waxler, Radke-Yarrow, & King, 1979) | 1–3 years |
| |     3. Evidence of self-centered and prosocial behaviors (Rheingold, Hay, & West, 1976; Bridgeman, current chapter) | 1–3 years |

development of self, for a totally egocentric mind cannot be conscious of its own processes. Mead, perhaps more than Piaget, stressed the central constructive role of social experience in the development of social cognitive abilities. Mead's contention is that self-awareness can only be attained by an individual indirectly, through mediation of social activity and that the development of self is *concurrent* with the ability to take roles.

The evidence for early social reciprocity in infants and young children suggests that the parent–child social unit provides the basis for later essential peer interactions. The peer relationship as described earlier has a special mutuality in status, and a give and take quality which often is of a conflicting nature, whereas with the very young, a more tolerant yet challenging exchange is available through interactions with parents. The latter also benefits from intuitively developed synchrony, rhythmicity, and reciprocity, so that a foundation for the roots of trust, intimacy, friendship, and other prosocial interactions can flourish.

This emphasis on the importance of experiencing oneself as an affective, emotional, and interpersonal social agent, coupled with the current work reported in this chapter where prosocial and self-centered behaviors coexist in early development, suggests a parallel process in which the social self begins to differentiate itself from others through interactions with others. This constructive process then incorporates perspective-taking and allows a beginning level of prosocial behavior to develop.

The findings that prosocial behaviors are (a) exhibited in the very young, and (b) seem to coexist with self-centered behaviors seem, at first blush, to contradict the conventional theories of the psychoanalytical and cognitive–developmental traditions. Freud, however, centered solely on the reconstruction of early childhood experiences whereas Piaget's efforts primarily embraced the nonsocial development of the child. Therefore, it is not surprising that the theories do not reflect the socially competent young child. More important, however, Piaget's egocentric child and Freud's child with an undifferentiated self are perhaps more similar to each other than generally assumed. Freud posited that each phase of undifferentiation is superseded by differentiation that leads to a new level of integration. The undifferentiated child and the egocentric child are both limited in their ability to distinguish self from other. The pattern of parallel development of prosocial and self-centered behaviors may be compatible with both these perspectives, since the very young child's prosocial behavior is, in fact, undifferentiated and broad based. At one moment early social behavior appears to be prosocial with nurturing and loving behaviors abounding. At the next it is self-centered, with relentless demands and need for attention, dependent on context, motivation, and the types of social systems with which the child interacts. Perhaps these early, distinct but related, social behaviors are gradients of actual "selfless" behavior, during which prototypical levels of prosocial or even presocial behaviors are seen that are infrequent, undeveloped, and reflect little reasoning. As the child has opportunities to construct social knowledge through reciprocal social interactions, the self begins to differentiate from others through an active social-grappling process. A beginning level of perspective-taking then evolves, and better-developed prosocial behavior (clearly differentiated from self-centered behavior), the prosocial behavior we are more familiar with, starts to flourish, complete with beginning levels of reasoning.

These conclusions are consistent with Durkheim's (1956) early thought:

> At bottom, egotism and altruism are two concurrent and intimately intertwining aspects of all conscious life. As soon as there is consciousness, there is a subject who thinks of himself as distinct from everything that is not he—a subject who says "I." When he thinks of himself in that manner and concentrates his activity on himself, thus represented, he acts like an egotist. To the degree that he represents to himself external beings as external and takes them as the objects of his activity, there is altruism. One form of activity cannot exist without the other. . . . Consequently, egoism and altruism are two abstractions that do not exist in a pure state; one always implies the other, at least to some degree; although in a

given, concrete situation they are never developed in the same degree. We can therefore rest assured that the child is not the purely selfish person often described to us. By the very fact that he is a conscious being, no matter how rudimentary his consciousness may be, he is capable of some altruism; and he is capable of it at the very threshold of his life [p. 217].

## ACKNOWLEDGMENTS

Appreciation is extended to Elliot Turiel for a critical reading of this chapter; to Janet Burton for her excellent editorial advice; to the parents and children who served as subjects; and to the dedicated undergraduate assistants, especially to Neil Guterman and Juliet Musso.

## REFERENCES

Baldwin, J. M. *Mental development in the child and the race.* New York: Macmillan, 1895.
Bandura, A. *Social learning theory.* Englewood Cliffs, N. J.: Prentice–Hall, 1977.
Bates, E., Bretherton, I., Shore, C., & Carpen, K. *The emergence of symbols in language and action: The role of contextual support.* Paper presented at the biennial meeting of the Society for Research in Child Development, San Francisco, Calif. March 1979.
Bretherton, I., & Bates, E. The emergence of intentional communication. In I. C. Uzgiris (Ed.), *New directions for child development: Social interaction and communication during infancy* (Number 4). San Francisco: Jossey–Bass, 1979.
Bridgeman, D. L. Enhanced role taking through cooperative interdependence: A field study. *Child Development,* 1981, *52,* 1231–1238.
Durkheim, E. [*Moral education: A study in the theory and application of the sociology of education*] (translated by Everett K. Wilson and Herman Schnurer from the 1925 edition). Glencoe, Ill.: Free Press, 1956.
Freud, S. *The standard edition of the complete psychological works of Sigmund Freud* (24 vols.). (James Strackey, Ed.) London: Hogarth, 1953–1966.
Hogan, R. Moral conduct and moral character: A psychological perspective. *Psychology Bulletin,* 1973, *79,* 217–232.
Hubley, P., & Trevarthen, C. Sharing a task in infancy. In I. C. Uzgiris (Ed.), *New directions for child development: Social interaction and communication during infancy* (Number 4). San Francisco: Jossey–Bass, 1979.
Isaacs, S. *Social development in young children: A study of beginnings.* London: Routledge & Kegan Paul, 1924.
Kohlberg, L. Stage and sequence: The cognitive-developmental approach to socialization. In D. Goslin (Ed.), *Handbook of socialization theory and research.* New York: Rand McNally, 1969.
Krebs, D. L. Altruism—an examination of the concept and a review of the literature. *Psychological Bulletin,* 1970, *73,* 258–302.
Krebs, D. L. A cognitive-developmental approach to altruism. In L. Wispé (Ed.), *Altruism, sympathy, and helping.* New York: Academic Press, 1978.
Lempers, J. D., Flavell, E. R., & Flavell, J. H. The development in very young children of tacit knowledge concerning visual perception. *Genetic Psychology Monographs,* 1977, *95,* 3–53.
Lewis, M., & Brooks-Bunn, J. Toward a theory of social cognition: The development of self. In I. C. Uzgiris (Ed.), *New directions for child development: Social interaction and communication during infancy* (Number 4). San Francisco: Jossey–Bass, 1979.
Lichtenberg, J. D. Implications for the psychoanalytic theory and research on the neonate. *International Review of Psychoanalysis,* Vol. 1, Part 1, 1981, 35–52.
Mead, G. H. *Mind, self and society.* Chicago: University of Chicago Press, 1934.

Mischel, W. The interaction of person and situation. In D. Magnusson & N. S. Endler (Eds.), *Personality at the crossroads: Current issues in interactional psychology.* Hillsdale, N. J.: Erlbaum, 1977.

Murphy, L. B. *Social behavior and child personality.* New York: Columbia University Press, 1937.

Piaget, J. *Judgment and reasoning in the child.* New York: Harcourt Brace, 1928.

Piaget, J. *The moral judgment of the child.* New York: Free Press, 1965.

Rheingold, H., Hay, D. & West, M. Sharing in the second year of life. *Child Development,* 1976, *47,* 1148–1158.

Sander, L. W. The regulation of exchange in the infant caregiver system and some aspects of the context–content relationship. In M. Lewis & L. A. Rosenblum (Eds.), *Interaction, conversation and the development of language.* New York: Wiley, 1977.

Spitz, R. *The first year of life.* New York: International Universities Press, 1965.

Turiel, E. Social regulations and domains of social concepts. In W. Damon (Ed.), *New directions for child development* (Vol. 1). San Francisco: Jossey–Bass, 1978.

Turiel, E. Distinct conceptual and developmental domains: Social convention and morality. In C. B. Keasey (Ed.), *Nebraska symposium on motivation, 1977.* Lincoln: University of Nebraska Press, 1979.

Trevarthen, C. Communication and cooperation in early infancy: A description of primary intersubjectivity. In M. Bullowa (Ed.), *Before speech: The beginnings of human communication.* London: Cambridge University Press, 1978.

Trevarthen, C., & Hubley, P. Secondary intersubjectivity: Confidence, confiding and acts of meaning in the first year. In A. Lock (Ed.), *Action, gesture and symbol: The emergence of language.* New York: Academic Press, 1978.

Zahn-Waxler, C., Radke-Yarrow, M., & King, R. A. Child rearing and children's prosocial initiations toward victims of distress. *Child Development,* 1979, *50,* 319–330.

# Affective Perspective-Taking, Exhortations, and Children's Prosocial Behavior[1]

CATHLEEN L. SMITH, MARY DRIVER LEINBACH,
BARBARA J. STEWART, and JANE M. BLACKWELL

## INTRODUCTION

Contemporary theories of prosocial behavior generally acknowledge the contributions of both the person and the situation to the performance of behavior that benefits other people. The person in this case is the young child. In the first section of this chapter, we emphasize the child's ability to take the emotional perspective of others (i.e., affective role- or perspective-taking). The cognitive processes involved in recognition and understanding of other people's affect are presumed to be important in prosocial development, but what do young children know about other people's emotions? On what basis do they determine what another is feeling? To what extent does this knowledge predispose intervention on another's behalf? In this chapter we review what is known about children's capacity for taking the emotional perspective of another, examine some methodological issues involved in "knowing what children know," so to speak, and report an investigation that looked at affective perspective-taking and comforting behavior in the preschool child.

In the second section of this chapter, we examine external or situational factors contributing to children's prosocial behavior. Although a variety of situational factors have been implicated in prosocial development, we focus on the effects of verbal communications from adults exhorting prosocial behavior in children. Do such exhortations foster either immediate or enduring prosocial inclinations? What

[1]Our work described in this chapter was supported in part by a grant to the first author from the Portland State University Research and Publications Committee.

113

types of verbalizations are most effective? We review the evidence concerning verbalizations exhorting charity in children, examine methodological issues in the experimental study of verbal influence, and report an experiment that looked at the role of exhortations in encouraging helping, sharing, teaching, and comforting in preschool children.

## CHILDREN'S UNDERSTANDING OF THE EMOTIONS OF OTHERS

The emotions of other people are surely among the most salient features of the young child's world, and it is intuitively plausible that children's ability to perceive and understand the affective states of others could influence responses in situations inviting such acts as helping, sharing, or comforting. Empathy, or responsiveness to others' emotions, has in fact been proposed as a motivational factor underlying various forms of altruistic behavior (e.g., Feshbach, 1975; Hoffman, 1975, 1981; Iannotti, 1975b; Mussen & Eisenberg-Berg, 1977; Shantz, 1975a). Some investigators see empathy as a cognitive response and are concerned with the child's recognition and understanding of another's emotion (Borke, 1971; Chandler & Greenspan, 1972). Others, however, require in addition that the subject's own feelings match those of the other person (Feshbach & Roe, 1968; Iannotti, 1978). Yet even where empathy is considered primarily an emotional response to others' affect, the importance of cognitive processes in recognizing and understanding emotions is acknowledged, and these are the processes with which we are concerned.

Investigations of children's ability to understand the emotions of others have been carried out against the background of Piaget's characterization of preoperational children as egocentric, trapped within their own subjective experience and unable to assume the perspectives of other people (e.g., Piaget, 1959; Piaget & Inhelder, 1956). Viewed in this way, the child's cognitive development involves progressive structural change from early egocentrism to the mature ability to put one's self in another's place, to *infer* the subjective experience of the other person. Consequently, much of the research concerning egocentrism in children has investigated their ability to take another's point of view (i.e., role- or perspective-taking, which has been considered the converse of egocentrism; Ford, 1979), and has questioned when or whether children can make nonegocentric judgments or charted developmental changes in their ability to do so. Selman (1980), for example, has proposed a stage model of interpersonal understanding based on children's ability to distinguish the alternative perspectives held by characters in filmed vignettes involving sociomoral dilemmas. Turiel (1978), noting the wide range of ages at which children can succeed at various perspective-taking tasks, considers this ability a "method" or way of obtaining information rather than a "structural–developmental dimension [p. 102]" of the child's thought. In his view, children construct conceptual frameworks or ways of organizing their understanding of the world, which change qualitatively as development proceeds and interaction with the environment occurs. As the level of conceptual development advances, the child will be able to apply information-gathering methods such as perspective-taking to material of greater variety and complexity.

The preceding views of perspective-taking suggest a unitary dimension or skill, but other researchers have distinguished among perceptual, cognitive, and affective aspects of this ability—that is, one may ask, respectively, what another sees, knows, or feels, and perspective-taking tasks have been categorized according to these distinctions. Although such separations run counter to Piaget's concept of the child as a structural whole (Chandler, 1977), a number of studies have attempted to understand children's interpersonal behavior in terms of the ability to assume the emotional perspectives of others.

Taking the affective perspective of another person involves mentally placing one's self in another's emotional situation and must necessarily include recognition of that person's emotional state. Even 3-year-olds may display this basic ability (Borke, 1971), and children as young as 4 or 5 show consensus in their expectancies with regard to the affective outcomes of various experiences (Barden, Zelko, Duncan, & Masters, 1980). Such abilities alone, however, are not sufficient as evidence against egocentrism (Chandler & Greenspan, 1972). Since even young children tend to agree about emotional expressions and their situational referents, there is really no way to determine in the ordinary course of events whether another person's affective state has been perceived accurately. In particular, one's own probable emotion in a comparable situation or the most likely response of people in general may have been attributed to the other person. These latter responses have been designated projective and normative judgments, respectively. Only empathic judgment, the accurate identification of the feelings of specific others, entails assuming another's emotional perspective. Projecting one's own probable reaction onto another is considered an egocentric response, and, although not necessarily egocentric, a normative judgment based upon knowledge of how most people would feel in a given situation is generally not considered empathic (Shantz, 1975b). Following this line of reasoning, it appears impossible to distinguish empathic judgments from those that are projective or normative except in situations where the emotion displayed is not what would ordinarily be expected in that context.

## Unexpected Emotion: The Incongruent Items Paradigm as a Measure of Affective Perspective-taking

In one approach to this problem, children are shown drawings, photographs, or videotaped episodes depicting a character whose facial expression is at odds with the rest of the information given (Burns & Cavey, 1957; Iannotti, 1975a; Kurdek & Rodgon, 1975; Urberg & Docherty, 1976). For example, in one of Burns and Cavey's (1957) picture stories, a child is portrayed as smiling despite the approach of a doctor wielding an oversized hypodermic syringe. The target character's affective perspective is thought to have been assumed if his or her emotion is specified on the basis of the facial expression rather than situational cues.

Unfortunately, use of this incongruent items paradigm has yielded no clear developmental insight into children's ability to judge the affect of others. Whereas Burns and Cavey (1957) found that 5- and 6-year-olds were more likely than children under 5 to use the facial expression in judging the target character's affect, Kurdek and Rodgon's (1975) results with a kindergarten through sixth-grade sample suggested a developmental trend *toward* egocentrism, in that projective (i.e., situationally based) responses were more prevalent at higher grade levels. Moreover, in a study of 6- and 9-year-old boys, Iannotti (1975a) found no relationship between age and naming a character's emotion on the basis of either facial or situational information.

## Relating Perspective-Taking Measures to Prosocial Behavior

Given the preceding pattern of results, it is hardly surprising that performance on affective perspective-taking tasks has not consistently been found to be related to prosocial behavior. Strayer (1980) found children's naturally occurring helping, comforting, and giving positive reinforcement to be "modestly [p. 821]," albeit nonsignificantly, related to their performance on two measures of perspective-taking (one of which used the incongruent items paradigm). Performance on these measures was also unrelated to a measure of donations to a poor child. Iannotti (1975a) found no relationship between the use of either facial or situational cues in judging a story character's emotion and the number of candies children shared with an absent needy child. On the other hand, Buckley, Siegel, and Ness (1979) found a positive relationship between scores on a measure similar to that used by Borke (1971) and children's helping and sharing. Thus, although it is reasonable to expect that accurate perception of others' feelings will enhance the probability of treating people well, evidence for this notion has been equivocal where children are concerned.

The inconsistent findings with respect to the incongruent items paradigm indicate several possible methodological and conceptual problems. First, the few studies that have assessed the construct validity and internal consistency of affective perspective-taking measures have not been encouraging (Ford, 1979; Kurdek, 1978; Rubin, 1978). In addition, a forced choice between facial expression and situational information in specifying another's emotion may indicate too narrow a conceptualization of the ability to understand others' emotions. It is at least necessary to determine what such a choice means for the child, and to do this the reasoning process behind the response must be considered. Furthermore, the ability to integrate both expressive and situational cues is unlikely to be related only to a decline in egocentrism but may instead reflect improvement in the capacity for attending and processing information in general. Children may fail at perspective-taking tasks for reasons that have little to do with the ability to escape one's own outlook and take another's point of view (Borke, 1971; Ford, 1979). A task may be too complex or the content too unfamiliar for the child to understand; such failures are not solely attributable to egocentrism as a limitation in cognitive structure, although they may be accommodated within Turiel's (1978) definition of perspective-taking as a way of obtaining information.

Moreover, attempts to relate measures of perspective-taking to prosocial behavior encounter problems in selecting an appropriate criterion response. Differences in the frequency and presentation of events that invite prosocial responses, as well as in expected base rates for various behaviors, undoubtedly contribute to inconsistent findings. Available normative data indicate that young children's prosocial acts such as helping, sharing, and especially comforting are relatively infrequent occurrences (Eisenberg-Berg & Lennon, 1980; Murphy, 1937; Yarrow & Waxler, 1976). Consequently, if one wishes to study such behaviors solely as they occur in natural settings, the dross rate (i.e., the ratio of irrelevant material to useful information; Webb, Campbell, Schwartz, & Sechrest, 1966) may be somewhat high. More importantly, since prosocial acts are most likely to occur in response to events rendering another person in need, field observations may not fully take into account differences in opportunity to engage in the target behaviors. Hence comparisons of rates of occurrence per unit of observation across subjects or behavioral categories defy meaningful interpretation. Strayer (1980), in reporting prosocial and "empathic" behaviors as proportions of observed affect displays to which subjects responded, has begun to deal with this problem; her work represents an important corrective to methodology in this area. Differential opportunity to display particular behaviors can also be controlled by presenting natural-appearing eliciting events uniformly to all subjects (e.g., Buckley, Siegel, & Ness, 1979; Yarrow & Waxler, 1976). Such structured observations provide a useful and reasonable adjunct to observations of naturally occurring behavior, provided the simulation represents an adequate approximation of events in a natural context.

## A Study of Affective Perspective-Taking, Knowledge of Intervention Strategies, and Comforting in Preschool Children

We have recently completed a study that examined relationships among measures of affective perspective-taking, children's knowledge of strategies for intervening when another person is in distress, and comforting in response to an ostensibly injured peer (Leinbach, Smith, & Stewart, 1980). Thirty-six boys and girls, ages 33–75 months, were tested at their day-care center. Comforting behavior was assessed in a setting in which two adult female experimenters, a child confederate (a 6-year-old girl), and each individual subject played a game. Following the temporary departure of the two experimenters, the child confederate opened a small trunk, pretended to slam the lid on her hand, and exclaimed, "Oh! I slammed my hand in the trunk! It really hurts!" Children's responses to the injured child were rated on a 5-point scale for evidence of attempts to comfort the victim, and their efforts to inform the returning experimenters of the incident (cf. Staub, 1971) were also recorded.

Affective perspective-taking and knowledge of intervention strategies were assessed in a single session prior to the session measuring comforting. Borke's (1971) materials, modified as in Kurdek and Rodgon (1975), were used to investigate affective perspective-taking (Task 1). Eight stories about children in familiar situations were illustrated by line drawings. The facial expression and story situation were congruent in four of the items, but mismatched in the remaining four. Subjects were asked to specify and explain the character's emotion. The congruent items were scored for *social comprehension* (correct specification of the emotion illustrated) and rated for *explanation of affect* (ability to justify the emotion specified). For the incongruent items, an *empathic judgment* was scored if the emotion named matched the pictured expression, and a *projective judgment* if the response was based on the situational cues. In addition, these items were rated for *awareness of discrepancy* (ability to detect and reconcile the conflicting cues).

A picture–story technique was also used to investigate children's knowledge of intervention strategies (Task 2). Subjects were presented with four scenarios in which one character observed while another experienced some mild form of distress, such as falling out of a wagon. As in Task 1, subjects were asked to identify the characters' emotions, and these responses were scored for social comprehension. Children's statements of what they would do upon observing the portrayed mishaps were rated for knowledge of *intervention strategies,* using a 5-point scale closely paralleling that used for rating responses to the child confederate's injury.

In light of the inconsistent findings and meager evidence for reliability in affective perspective-taking tasks, the psychometric properties of our measures were a major concern. Consequently, extensive item analyses were conducted before items were combined to form scales. Item intercorrelations were positive and generally significant for all measures except those based upon the incongruent items; here, one item was consistently unrelated to the other three and was therefore excluded from the empathic judgment, projective judgment, and awareness of discrepancy scales. Estimates of internal consistency reliability (coefficient $\alpha$, Nunnally, 1978) for all measures except Task 1 social comprehension and empathic judgment were considered satisfactory or better for research purposes (.67–.96). The latter relationships were more marginal (.47 and .53, respectively), and caution is required in interpreting results obtained with these measures.

Relationships among the Task 1 and Task 2 measures and age were also assessed. Although the number of correlation coefficients computed suggests a cautious interpretation of the results, some clear patterns emerged. Five of the seven measures (all but empathic and projective judgments) were quire strongly intercorrelated ($.44 \leq r \leq .69; .01 \geq p \geq .001$). Since these variables were also highly related to age, partial correlations, controlling for age, were obtained; the relationships generally remained quite strong. These measures appear to have a great deal in common and may be tapping a fairly broad category of social cognition. They are also related, no doubt, to overall cognitive development and verbal skill. Attempting to distinguish between empathic and projective judgments on the basis of children's attention to facial expressions rather than situational cues, however, does not fit into this picture. Children who made empathic judgments were somewhat more aware of the discrepancy between facial expression and story ($r = .33; p < .05$), but there were no other significant relationships between either empathic or projective judgments and any of the other measures. Furthermore, empathic judgments were not correlated with age for either sex, whereas projective judgments were more prevalent in older boys($r = .49; p < .05$).

In this study 28% of the children comforted another child who appeared to be hurt, and 42% reported the injury to the experimenters. Neither age nor sex influenced the probability of a comforting response. No part of the affective perspective-taking measure predicted comforting, nor were children who suggested a sympathetic course of action in response to the plight of a story character more likely to comfort the injured child in the live distress situation than those who did not, although knowledge of intervention strategies, along with the ability to recognize and explain situationally consistent emotions, was related to reporting the incident to the adult experimenters. Since only one measure of comforting was used, however, a possible relationship between comforting and children's perception and understanding of others' emotions was less likely to have been detected than if multiple measures of the behavior had been employed (see Green, 1978, on the need for multiple measures). The relationship between comforting and affective perspective-taking, therefore, has not been disconfirmed. Work that we currently have in progress makes use of a greater number of behavioral events in continuing to explore this possibility.

Whether perspective-taking is seen as an aspect of cognitive structure or as a way of gathering information as Turiel (1978) suggests, one would expect older children to be more successful than younger ones on any particular perspective-taking task. Thus, if the faculty of assessing another person's emotional state nonegocentrically is really indicated by predicting affect on the basis of expressive cues when these are at odds with the context in which they occur, empathic judgment scores should have increased with age and should, logically, have been quite strongly related to the other cognitive skills. Similarly, if situationally based judgments indicate a lack of perspective-taking ability, evidence that projective judgments increase among older children defies ready explanation. Furthermore, on the basis of empathic judgment scores alone, one cannot argue that perspective-taking has occurred. Our awareness of discrepancy measure indicated that some children who correctly named the emotion pictured did so without indicating any understanding of the situation. Their responses suggested that attention was focused only or primarily on the expressive cues, and thus provided evidence only for recognition of emotion, not perspective-taking. However, other children took both expressive and situational cues into account. For example, some who recognized the sad expression on the face of a child holding an ice cream cone described as his or her favorite food asked, ''Why is he sad?'' or ''Then how come he's crying?'' These responses indicate that the feelings of the child in the picture were unexpected, since the congruent items provoked no such questions. This level of awareness of the conflicting cues suggests some ability to recognize a perspective differing from the child's own. Still other children not only detected the discrepancy but offered explanations by which it could be reconciled. In response to a picture of a smiling child dreaming of being chased by a ferocious tiger, one girl said that the child in the picture was happy, '' 'cause she can run faster than the tiger!'' Similar responses were obtained from children as young as $4\frac{1}{2}$ years, and show that, in some situations at least, preschool children not only can recognize but also can explain an emotional perspective that differs from their own probable feelings.

## Considerations for the Further Study of Affective Perspective-Taking

The issue of establishing an acceptable criterion for determining whether or when children are able to discern the emotional perspectives of others has not been successfully resolved. Certainly more attention must be given to methodological issues. Individual items in affective perspective-taking tasks vary in complexity, some of the situations described may be more familiar or believable than others, and the different emotions may vary in their ability to be expressed and understood. Hence the practice of combining items to form scales without establishing internal consistency reliability cannot be defended. Differences in stimulus materials need to be explored systematically if the homogeneous items needed for reliable scales are to be developed. More specifically, we believe that use of the incongruent items paradigm as a measure of affective perspective-taking is of little value unless the task is structured so that the choices themselves have clear implications (e.g., Gove & Keating, 1979) or children's explanations of their judgments are probed, as in the awareness of discrepancy measure in this study.

Even if all methodological issues are resolved, the use of facial expressions rather than situational information as the standard for nonegocentric judgment of affect poses conceptual problems. Piaget has asserted that nonegocentric assessment of another's point of view requires construction of alternative perspectives by inference rather than direct perception (Piaget & Inhelder, 1956, 1962). Thus, the incongruent items paradigm seems to entail a contradiction, since making an inference about another's feelings on any basis other than situational information requires direct perception of the other's expressive cues. Furthermore, as noted previously, a situationally based judgment is not necessarily egocentric, even though the perspective of a particular person has not been assumed. A judgment based upon knowledge of how most people would feel in a given situation (i.e., normative judgment, Shantz, 1975b) would not constitute entrapment within one's own point of view, but cannot be distinguished in the incongruent items paradigm from the projection of one's own feelings onto another. Despite the shortcomings of current measures employing incongruent items, however, these stimulus materials might be used productively to explore the relative contributions of expressive and situational information to children's perception and understanding of the emotions of others.

We suggest that children may recognize others' emotions at a very early age, although they may not differentiate them from their contextual determinants (Gove & Keating, 1979). As knowledge of the world is acquired, however, situational information may assume greater significance or utility. The child may learn to rely on normative judgments, which would reduce the amount of effort required to process each person–situation interaction. In addition, children must eventually come to realize that people do not always express their emotions veridically. In these cases, situationally based judgments may predominate. In fact, Jones (1979) has reviewed evidence that under some circumstances adults not only will infer the affective state of another person solely on the basis of situational cues (e.g., judge a target person awaiting electric shock to be anxious, even though he or she displays no signs of anxiety) but will attribute a generalized emotional disposition to that individual (in the example just cited the target individual is an anxious person). Furthermore, observers and actors alike may have been taught to suppress the expression of their own feelings and to refrain from commenting on the affect displays of others. And, of course, one may ultimately learn to make inferences about the emotions of others who are absent, on the basis of descriptions of their plight alone. Although as they get older, children become increasingly able to infer the inner states of others (Flapan, 1968), especially, perhaps, where situational information cannot account for an emotion displayed, we suspect that people do not learn to ignore the context of emotion but to integrate situational and expressive cues.

Much remains to be learned regarding what children perceive and think about others' emotions and how these cognitive processes influence their behavior toward other people. We do not believe that assuming another's perspective is a discrete ability that one either has or does not have, nor that egocentric responding can ever be overcome once and for all. Viewing the world through another's eyes—or feelings, as it were—may indeed predispose intervention on the other's behalf, but this ability may also be used to one's own advantage at another's expense. Intrapersonal differences in temperament and mood may alter the likelihood that concern for others will be shown, and such concern may be tendered differentially toward different persons. People, even very young ones, differ in the skills and knowledge they bring to social situations and in the motivation to use the abilities they have, and situations vary in the opportunities they present for prosocial actions as well as in the relative salience of social cues. The interrelationship of social cognition, motivation, and behavior is complex, and this richness must be reflected in our measures if we are to understand children's prosocial responses to the needs and feelings of others.

## ADULTS' EXHORTATIONS AND CHILDREN'S
## PROSOCIAL BEHAVIOR

Although affective perspective-taking and other cognitive influences on prosocial behavior have received increasing attention from researchers in the past several years, an emphasis on cognition is clearly not sufficient to provide a complete picture of prosocial development. Just as we have seen that situational cues figure prominently in the evaluation of emotional states, so it is the case that the situational context exerts a profound influence on other behaviors implicated in prosocial development. The extent to which adults will engage in helping behavior, for example, has been shown to be influenced by seemingly irrelevant variations in the situation, such as the weather, the mood of the potential helper, and the number of other people present. (See Rosenhan, Moore, & Underwood, 1976, for a review of situational determinants of adult helping behavior.) With regard to children's prosocial behavior, the contribution of some situational factors, such as the provision of prosocial models, has been thoroughly documented. (See reviews by Mussen & Eisenberg-Berg, 1977; Rushton, 1980; Staub, 1978.) The impact of other situational variables, such as external reinforcement and verbalizations from adults exhorting charity (i.e., preaching), has also been demonstrated, but the extent to which these represent examples of brief social influence or more generalized learning in children has been questioned. Mussen and Eisenberg-Berg (1977), for example, classified modeling as a "socialization determinant" of prosocial behavior because of the ecological validity of some of the laboratory studies of modeling and the degree of correspondence between results from laboratory and field (i.e., home or school environments). In contrast, both reinforcement and preaching were categorized by these authors as "situational determinants" of prosocial behavior because of the brevity of exposure to reinforcement or preaching in most studies and the relative lack of information about the impact of these variables in other than laboratory settings. However, with respect to reinforcement effects, Gelfand and Hartmann (1982) have reviewed research conducted in children's natural environments that indicates that contingent use of positive reinforcers does produce generalized and enduring increases in children's sharing and other prosocial behaviors.

The effectiveness of preaching, on the other hand, remains questionable. Although we shall review evidence that verbal communications from adults exhorting charity have immediate effects on children's donating behavior, there is a paucity of evidence for more generalized and longer-lasting change. Furthermore, it is not clear what types of exhortations seem to be most effective, nor what relationships exist between content of verbal directives and subject characteristics such as age. Finally, methodological issues pertaining to how one might assess the effects of verbal communications in experimental settings have not been successfully resolved.

In comparison with other situational factors, the relative lack of information concerning the effects of verbal communications is curious, particularly in light of current theoretical accounts of prosocial development which assign a prominent role to some kinds of verbal influence. For example, it has been suggested that a specific type of verbal communication labeled *induction,* in which the socializing agent reasons with the child in an attempt to change his or her behavior, is especially influential in the internalization of moral values and prosocial action (Hoffman, 1963, 1970; Hoffman & Saltzstein, 1967; Walters & Grusec, 1977). These verbal influence procedures are contrasted with more *power-assertive* child-rearing methods, which rely on aversive control and use or threats of force, and are not generally associated with advanced levels of moral development. The original conceptualization of induction by Hoffman and his associates referred to emphasizing to children the negative consequences of their misbehavior following an occurrence of a misdeed. Particular emphasis was placed on statements that stressed the effect of the child's transgression on other people (other-oriented induction). However, when response suppression is not an issue and the concern is with the encouragement of prosocial behavior, "positive induction" (Staub, 1975, p. 116) may be used, in which the potential positive consequences for other people of the child's future desirable behavior are highlighted by the socializing agent.

The use of induction is an excellent illustration of the interface between situation and cognition, in that the effects of a situational factor such as inductive verbalizations are presumed to be cognitively mediated. For example, it is thought that induction may foster an understanding of other people's need states (Hoffman, 1970), including their emotional states, thus engendering affective perspective-taking, which presumably mediates helpful actions. Additionally, induction may minimize the intrusiveness of external pressure, leaving children to attribute their prosocial behavior to their own morality and internal value systems (e.g., "I'm the kind of person who helps") rather than to external coercion (Walters & Grusec, 1977). In other words, inductive statements may be just sufficient to motivate prosocial action but not so forceful as to be seen by the child as mandating the behavior. (See Lepper, 1981, for a discussion of this minimal sufficiency principle as applied to the socialization process.)

A second reason for focusing on verbal influence procedures in relation to prosocial behavior has been suggested by Staub (1975, 1979). Verbal communications that succeed in inducing individuals to participate in some form of positive behavior, even if only on a single occasion, may foster a kind of "natural socialization" process (Staub, 1979, p. 7), in which participation in prosocial behavior itself leads to the likelihood of further prosocial acts. According to this analysis, responsibility to behave prosocially will lead to internalization and subsequent displays of positive behavior in future situations, as long as "undue force" (Staub, 1979, p. 204) is not used to compel such participation in the first place.

However, what constitutes undue force? Obviously, verbalizations to children exhorting charitable behavior can take a number of different forms and will compel behavior to greater or lesser extents. What types of instructions or exhortations seem to be most effective in fostering generosity in children? Can a verbal message to a child to behave prosocially increase the likelihood of subsequent similar behaviors in situations where the socializing agent is not present to effect compliance with the charitable request?

## Effects of Charitable Exhortations
## on Children's Immediate Donating Behavior

Before we turn to an exploration of these questions, a few general comments are in order. A number of carlicr studies examined, in an experimental setting, the effects of exposure to an adult who both preached and practiced generosity (e.g., Bryan & Walbek, 1970a, 1970b; Midlarsky & Bryan, 1972; Rushton, 1975). However, our concern here is limited to those investigations in which the adult only preached, without actually donating (Dlugokinski & Firestone, 1974; Eisenberg-Berg & Geisheker, 1979; Grusec, 1972; Grusec, Saas-Kortsaak, & Simutis, 1978; Rice & Grusec, 1975). These experiments have found that verbal communications exhorting children to behave charitably are effective social influence techniques. In tests of donating behavior immediately following such exhortations, children exposed to such statements generally give more than children who receive either neutral or no communications.

### CONTENT OF THE VERBAL COMMUNICATION

Despite the robustness of this general effect, we still do not understand whether and to what extent the content of the verbal communication promotes children's charitable behavior. Earlier research paid scant attention to what was actually said to the child. More recent studies compared other-oriented inductive communications with normative statements about the appropriateness of donating ("It's good to give.") and/or communications clearly specifying that the child should donate ("You are expected to share."). For example, in two experiments Eisenberg-Berg and Geisheker (1979) informed their subjects (each of whom had been given 50¢ for his or her participation) that they did not have to but could choose to donate some of their earnings to poor children. In both experiments, children who were given further "empathic" preaching statements that detailed the plight of needy children and the positive consequences for the recipient of the child's charitable behavior were subsequently more generous than children who were given no additional information about the poor children. However, children given these "empathic" verbalizations were not more generous than children who heard "normative" exhortations (e.g., "It's really good to donate. . . . Sharing is the right thing to do [p. 170]" delivered by their school principal (Experiment 1 only) or a person who they thought might teach at their school the next year (Experiment 2). Dlugokinski and Firestone (1974) found that inductive appeals stressing the pronounced need of the recipients of the charity were more effective only with children who identified their mothers' child-rearing style as inductive. Children whose professed socialization history was power-assertive, in contrast, tended to give more in response to power-assertive appeals emphasizing that the school authorities thought they should give. Other investigators have also noted the effectiveness of more constraining verbal communications. Weissbrod (1980) found that responsible instructions clearly specifying the expectation that the child would donate were more effective than permissive verbalizations that stressed to children the optional nature of their donating behavior.

EFFECTS OF REHEARSAL OF GENEROUS BEHAVIOR

In all of the studies on verbal influence just cited, children were left alone to make their contributions "anonymously" shortly after being exposed to the preaching of adult experimenters. The number of donations made by children in the absence of surveillance by the original socializing agent (i.e., the experimenter) has been a customary operational definition of internalization of moral standards (e.g., Grusec, Kuczynski, Rushton, & Simutis, 1978), or "true" generosity (Rushton, 1976). However, suppose the experimenter remains with the children for a period of time to encourage them to practice, or rehearse, the generous behavior. Under these circumstances the results are remarkably consistent. Providing children with opportunities to practice a charitable behavior in the experimenter's presence, and insuring that they do so with explicit reminders or instructions to donate, leads to subsequent displays of generosity in the experimenter's absence or when the instructions are eliminated (Dressel & Midlarsky, 1978; Gelfand, Hartmann, Cromer, Smith, & Page, 1975; Grusec, Kuczynski, Rushton, & Simutis, 1978; White, 1972).

## Durability and Generalizability of Verbal Communication Effects

In virtually all of the studies just reviewed, the experimental paradigm was similar; children were exhorted to make donations (of marbles, money, or gift certificates they had earned or had been given) to an unknown and unseen needy child, and the extent to which the verbal communications were effective in eliciting donating behavior was assessed shortly thereafter. An important question is whether these statements have effects that endure beyond the immediate training situation or generalize to other kinds of prosocial behavior. Unfortunately, only a handful of studies have addressed these issues.

The research reviewed earlier provided little evidence for the durability or generalizability of the effects of verbal communications. Although Rice and Grusec (1975) found that children who heard an adult exhort charity were more generous 4 months later than controls, White (1972) found that children who had previously rehearsed a donation response in the experimenter's presence were no more generous 5 days later than controls. Grusec, Saas-Kortsaak, and Simutis (1978) found that children who had heard either ''specific'' exhortations (telling them they should donate to those less fortunate in order to make them happy) or ''general'' exhortations (telling them they should donate because it is a good thing to make people happy by helping in any way one can) were somewhat more likely to donate 3 weeks later than controls who had heard no preaching statements, although this tendency was of only marginal statistical significance. The latter study was also one of the few investigations to assess both immediate and delayed effects of exhortations on behaviors other than donating. In generalizability tests immediately following the experimental manipulation, there was some indication that children who had been given either specific or general exhortations were actually *less* likely than controls to spontaneously pick up objects the experimenter dropped. However, boys who received specific exhortations shared more pencils with children who could not participate than boys who received general exhortations and somewhat ($p < .10$) more than controls. Exhortations did not affect girls' sharing of pencils. On generalization tests 5 weeks after the initial donation opportunity, only children who had been given general exhortations and had not also been previously exposed to a generous model collected more craft items for sick children than controls.

## Age and the Effects of Exhortations

There is little information about the effects on the very young child of verbal communications exhorting generous behavior. Subjects in the studies reviewed here ranged from kindergarten children (Gelfand *et al.*, 1975) to ninth graders (Dressel & Midlarsky, 1978). Only one investigation found an interaction between age and preaching effects: Dlugokinski and Firestone (1974) found that fifth graders gave more under power-assertive appeals, whereas eighth-graders were more responsive to inductive appeals. One might surmise that inductive communications pointing out the positive consequences of the child's prosocial behavior for others might be ineffective with preschool children, who have been characterized as having little appreciation for the needs of others. However, there is reason to believe that preschool children may be able to understand and respond to inductively worded statements. Eisenberg-Berg and Neal (1979) have shown that 4- and 5-year-olds are able to verbalize a rudimentary understanding of others' physical and psychological needs when questioned about their own spontaneous sharing, helping, and comforting, and that sharing, at least, is related to such needs-oriented reasoning (Eisenberg-Berg & Hand, 1979). We suspected that if young children justify their own spontaneous prosocial behavior by reference to the needs of other people, these rationales should be equally understandable when delivered by an adult in a socializing context.

Most importantly, however, with very young children for whom prosocial repertoires are not yet firmly established, direct participation in prosocial behavior (Staub, 1979) may be the most important source of learning and a crucial determinant of whether or not delayed or generalized prosocial responses occur. This line of analysis would lead us to predict that to the extent that either power-assertive commands or inductive verbal communications result in the practice, or rehearsal, of prosocial behavior in the young child, such influences will tend to promote the internalization of that behavior as well.

## Methodological Considerations in the Experimental Study of Verbal Influence

In our discussion of the effects of verbal communications from adults urging generous behavior in children, we reviewed evidence of the effectiveness of exhortations that clearly specify the expectation of the experimenter that the child will donate. We also discussed evidence that children who are induced to behave generously in the presence of an experimenter will tend to display the same behavior in his or her absence. This pattern of results, although generally interpreted by researchers as evidence of internalized behavior change in children, can perhaps be explained in another way. When children are placed in a relatively unusual situation with an unfamiliar adult who specifies what behavior is expected, the safest course of action is to do what one is told. The notion of experimental demand (Orne, 1962) is, of course, not new, nor is the criticism of the artificial, momentary, and nongeneralizable nature of some of our experimental interventions in the laboratory (e.g., Bronfenbrenner, 1977). These criticisms seem especially potent, however, when applied to the experimental study of the effects of instructions or other verbal communications on the prosocial behavior of children. Although it is not immediately clear how laboratory researchers could proceed to separate the demand variable from the theoretically meaningful variable of instructional set, the continued reliance on the standard paradigm of donating to an absent needy peer has not been overly helpful in this regard. The children's behavior in this situation is entirely constrained: Their options are to donate or not to donate. When behavioral options are few, and intermediate, diversionary, or alternative responses are not available, we can perhaps be less confident that we are measuring something other than the effects of experimental demand. Even when the effects of verbal communications are measured over time, as they have been in a few of these studies, rarely have responses that are not identical to those acquired during training (i.e., donating) been included as dependent measures, and the extent to which this donating behavior can be generalized to other kinds of prosocial responses, or even to sharing in general, is questionable. In fact, one of the few studies that reported the correlation between a measure of donation and a measure of sharing (Grusec, Kuczynski, Rushton, & Simutis, 1978) found no relationship between the two.

## A Study of the Effects of Verbal Communications on the Prosocial Behavior of Preschool Children

These methodological considerations led us to design a study of the effects of verbalizations exhorting prosocial behavior (Blackwell, Smith, Stewart, & Jennings, 1980) in which the situation was kept as natural as possible, the responses of the children were not constrained but allowed to vary widely, and several types of prosocial responses were assessed. Sharing (in the form of donating to an absent needy other) has, of course, been the most frequent, and in most cases, the only prosocial behavior examined in previous studies. Our study looked not only at sharing, but at helping, teaching, and comforting behaviors as well, and, as in most naturally occurring opportunities for prosocial action, the recipient of the prosocial response in all cases was present and an active participant in the interaction.

Our general methodology was heavily influenced by the work of Yarrow, Scott, and Waxler (1973) and of Yarrow and Waxler (1976), who described a technique for observing and rating prosocial behavior in an experimental setting designed to be maximally similar to situations children actually encounter in their daily lives. In our study with 4- and 5-year-old children, standardized opportunities to behave prosocially were embedded as unobtrusively as possible into a stream of events involving nurturant interaction and play on some activity, such as planting seeds. Only the child and two experimenters were present. Opportunities to behave prosocially were introduced by means of statements, which we termed *verbalizations of need,* designed to provide relatively unambiguous indications that the experimenter needed help. In all cases, however, the expressions of need stopped short of directly asking the child to intervene. For example, helping opportunities were provided when one of the experimenters appeared to have dropped objects accidentally (e.g., "Oh! I spilled the sticks."), when objects ostensibly became lost, or when materials needed to be moved or cleaned up. Sharing opportunities occurred when the experimenter indicated her desire for an object in the child's possession previously labeled as belonging to the child (e.g., "I'd like to plant seeds, but I don't have a cup."). Teaching opportunities occurred when one of the experimenters acknowledged that she did not know how to do a simple task that the child had just been taught by the other experimenter (e.g., "I don't know how to make a glitter picture."). Finally, opportunities to comfort were provided when one of the experimenters appeared to injure herself accidentally and demonstrated mild distress and appropriate nonverbal cues (e.g., "Oh! I bumped my knee. It really hurts.").

Each child participated in three sessions several days apart. Table 5.1 lists the various opportunities for the child to behave prosocially and their temporal order within each session. Session 1 measured baseline levels of prosocial behavior; the child was presented with three opportunities (each) to help, share, and teach and one opportunity to comfort an allegedly injured experimenter. To avoid the modeling of nonintervention and to focus responsibility for prosocial action on the child, all verbalizations of need were presented by one of the experimenters while the other had temporarily left the room. Each experimenter delivered an equal number of need verbalizations but did not praise or acknowledge any prosocial behavior. Neither did she comment when the child failed to respond prosocially. Two observers behind a one-way glass independently rated the child's response to each expression of need on a 6-point scale ranging from 0 (child actively refuses to intervene) to 5 (child displays a prosocial response with special involvement—e.g.,

**TABLE 5.1**
*Temporal Order of Prosocial Opportunities*

| Session 1 (planting seeds) | Session 2 (painting) | Session 3 (play dough) |
|---|---|---|
| Help move planting materials to table | Help move chairs to table | Help move bags to suitcase |
| Share cup | Share paint | Share play dough |
| Teach how to plant seeds | Teach how to make blow picture | Teach how to make colored play dough |
| Comfort adult with hurt knee | Help pick up spilled papers | Comfort adult with bumped elbow |
| Teach how to water seeds | Teach how to make glitter picture | Teach how to make striped pancake |
| Help pick up spilled sticks | Share stars | Help pick up spilled cookie cutters |
| Share flower sticker | Help look for lost pen | Teach how to make smile cookie |
| Teach how to make stick flower | Teach how to make crayon picture | Share sparkle |
| Help look for lost box | Share candy kisses | Help find lost red food coloring |
| Share animal crackers | | Share chocolate mints |

child shares *all* of his or her remaining cookies or immediately picks up *all* dropped objects).

During Session 2, children in a control condition ($N = 16$) were again given standardized opportunities to help, share, and teach (comforting was not assessed for any subject during Session 2), using the same general procedure as in Session 1. The remaining children were divided into two treatment conditions, those given *power-assertive* statements ($N = 16$) and those given *inductive* statements ($N = 16$). In these conditions both experimenters remained in the room; following each need verbalization by one of the adults, the other adult delivered a statement exhorting prosocial behavior. Children given power-assertive statements were commanded to behave prosocially (e.g., "When I play with you, I want you to help. Help move the chairs to the table."). Those given inductive statements, on the other hand, were supplied with a description of the other person's need and a rationale that pointed out the consequences of the child's behavior for the other person (e.g., "Jenny doesn't have any candy kisses. If you share your candy kisses, then she'll have some too."). In order to maximize the probability that the child would actually rehearse the prosocial behavior, children who failed to respond prosocially (scale points 4 or 5) to the initial verbalization were given a further command or inductive statement. If the child did not intervene following this prompt, a second and final prompt was given. If the child still failed to respond prosocially, the adults made no comment and resumed the play activity as before.

Incidentally, the mean number of prompts required by children was not significantly different across the two treatment conditions. There were some children in both groups, however, who failed on one or more occasions to respond prosocially (i.e., rehearse) even after they were prompted. We do not know much about who these children are, since we did not include an independent assessment of person variables (e.g., intelligence, locus of control, need for approval, sociability) which might have mediated children's responsiveness to our verbal communications. However, we do know that the number of prompts given to children in the treatment groups tended to be negatively correlated with their Session 2 scores as well as their scores on each behavior at Session 1. Perhaps children who are initially disinclined to behave prosocially may require more reminders to participate in prosocial action, although our data suggest that providing repeated reminders does not guarantee that the behavior will be displayed.

To ascertain the extent to which the child had learned to behave prosocially in the absence of exhortations and the original experimenters, a third session approximately 1 week later involved the child and two unfamiliar adult women. As in previous sessions, a context of friendly interaction and playful activity provided an occasion to present the child with natural-appearing opportunities to help, share, and teach. An opportunity to comfort was also included at Session 3 to assess whether the effects of the exhortations would generalize to a behavior that had not been instructed. The need verbalizations were again administered with only one adult present, and no exhortations or prompts were given. The new experimenters at Session 3 were unaware of the experimental condition of the subject. So that the observers would likewise remain unaware, Session 2 was videotaped and scored after the child was observed at Session 3.

Interobserver reliabilities, calculated using percentage agreement, revealed that exact agreement ranged from 76% (comforting) to 86% (helping and sharing) and reached 98% for all measures when disagreements within one point on the 6-point scale were included. Since helping, sharing, and teaching behaviors at each session were highly intercorrelated within each response class, a mean score for each child on each behavior at each session was calculated.

The four prosocial behaviors were moderately intercorrelated at Session 1 (.30 $\leq$ $r \leq .52; .02 \geq p \geq .001$), with the correlations involving helping lower than correlations involving the other variables. Perhaps helping represents a different class of prosocial behavior than sharing, teaching, or comforting, one involving less personal involvement or self-sacrifice (Eisenberg-Berg & Hand, 1979; Yarrow & Waxler, 1976).

The results of our experimental interventions can be summarized quite briefly. Analysis of covariance procedures (with Session 1 scores as the covariate) indicated that children who were exhorted to behave prosocially displayed significantly more prosocial behavior at Session 2 than control children ($p \leq .001$ for all measures). Furthermore, children who received inductive statements emphasizing the positive consequences of their behavior for others showed just as much helping, sharing, and teaching as children who heard power-assertive instructions commanding them to behave prosocially.

Although an assessment of the effectiveness of these verbal communications in eliciting rehearsal is valuable in its own right, a more important question is the extent to which prosocial behavior was displayed at a later time in the absence of exhortations and the original socializing adults. Here again our results were quite clear, at least for the behaviors of sharing and teaching: Children in the exhortation groups demonstrated significantly more sharing ($p \leq .004$) and teaching ($p \leq .001$) during the delayed session with different experimenters than did children who had heard no verbal communications. Again, the two exhortation groups did not differ. These results for Session 3, as well as the group differences for Session 1 and Session 2, are illustrated for the prosocial behavior of sharing in Figure 5.1. The results for the prosocial behavior of helping showed that only girls continued to be affected by the verbal communications at Session 3 ($p \leq .002$). Helping scores of exhorted boys did not differ from controls.

Finally, children in the inductive and power-assertive groups showed more comforting at Session 3 to an ostensibly injured adult ($p \leq .02$) than did children who received no exhortations (again, the two treatment groups did not differ). This finding is especially important, since it suggests that the effects of exhortations regarding specific prosocial behaviors may generalize to other acts of intervention on another's behalf which have not been elicited in this way.

What determined Session 3 scores? We employed a hierarchical multiple regression procedure to ascertain to what extent Session 3 helping, sharing, teaching, and overall prosocial scores (computed by averaging standardized Session 3 helping,

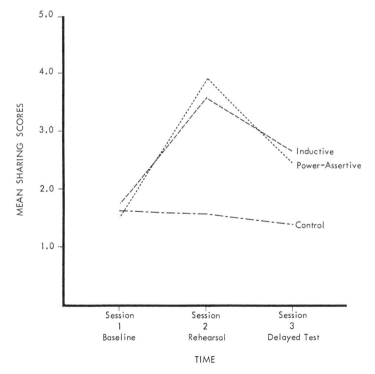

**FIGURE 5.1.**   Mean sharing profiles for the three conditions across sessions.

sharing, and teaching scores) could be predicted from the child's baseline prosocial behavior (i.e., Session 1 scores), whether the child at Session 2 had received verbal communications of either type or not, and the child's rehearsal of the corresponding prosocial behavior (i.e., Session 2 scores). Baseline prosocial behavior accounted for from 9.7% (helping) to 16.7% (teaching) of the variance in Session 3 prosocial behavior. After the contribution of the Session 1 scores was partialed out, receipt of exhortations (or not) was found to account for an additional 18.6% (sharing) to 33.4% (overall prosocial) of the Session 3 variance. Finally, after both the baseline and exhortation effects were partialed out, rehearsal of prosocial behavior at Session 2 was found to contribute from 4.7% (sharing) to 14.8% (teaching) of the variance in Session 3 scores. Together, the three predictor variables (i.e., baseline scores, receipt of exhortations or not, rehearsal scores) accounted for from 38.5% (sharing) to 56.1% (overall prosocial) of the variance in Session 3 scores. With the exception of the rehearsal effects for sharing, all other stepwise contributions to Session 3 variances were significant at $p \leq .05$ or better.

We also checked whether any of the interactions among our three predictor variables predicted Session 3 scores. Of the four possible interactions, only the exhortation $\times$ rehearsal interaction was significant ($p \leq .05$). Separate regression analyses for the experimental and control subjects revealed that after controlling for Session 1 scores, rehearsal was a significant predictor ($p \leq .01$) of Session 3 sharing, teaching, and overall prosocial behavior for the control group only. (Rehearsal on helping was not a significant predictor of Session 3 helping even for controls.)

We do not believe that rehearsal of prosocial behavior is inconsequential for young children. Instead, we suspect that our inability to demonstrate a contribution of rehearsal to Session 3 scores in our experimental groups was likely due to a restriction of range in the Session 2 scores for these groups. In other words, both our power-assertive and inductive exhortations were so generally effective in eliciting rehearsal of prosocial behavior that there was little variability in Session 2 scores for either group, thus perhaps obscuring the contribution of the children's actual participation in prosocial behavior.

In general, we are convinced that adults can enhance the helping, sharing, teaching, and comforting behaviors of preschool children by furnishing them with exhortations to behave prosocially and opportunities to rehearse, or practice, the behaviors. How such prosocial behavior is cognitively mediated, however, remained unexamined in this study. Had it been possible to do so without affecting the behavioral data, it would have been interesting to question the children in all conditions about their reasons for behaving prosocially at Session 3. There is evidence that young children may fail to recognize the compelling effects of instructions and other forms of verbal influence (Smith, Gelfand, Hartmann, & Partlow, 1979). As a matter of fact, even adults may dismiss as inconsequential, or actually fail to notice, what are in reality highly constraining instructions (Jones, 1979). Thus it is not clear that the subjective meaning of the experimental manipulations (Damon, 1977; Kuhn, 1978) differed for our two treatment groups, or that the children themselves would see their own prosocial behavior differently as a result of having experienced one condition rather than the other. Statements that pointed out the potential positive consequences of the child's behavior for others and those that directly told the child how to behave appear to have been equally effective. Both kinds of exhortations induced immediate rehearsal of prosocial behavior, and both fostered delayed and generalized change. Furthermore, and perhaps importantly, both kinds of exhortations were delivered in a nurturant context, with no punishment for noncompliance. As a result, even the verbalizations we called *power-assertive* may not have been perceived by the children as overly coercive demands but as statements of rules or norms for appropriate behavior in the experimental situation. In natural childrearing contexts when children misbehave, mothers report that they do use such rule statements, but often in conjunction with pronounced affective loading (Zahn-Waxler, Radke-Yarrow, & King, 1979) or more punitive techniques such as spanking, threats, withdrawal of privileges, or forced compliance (Grusec & Kuczynski, 1980). However, once verbal control of the rule or norm over the child's behavior is firmly established, the more aversive techniques can often, if not always, be eliminated. When one is attempting to inculcate intervention on others' behalf in situations where the child has not transgressed, the verbal techniques may be entirely sufficient, as our rehearsal and Session 3 data would suggest.

Situational factors such as verbal communications that induce participation in prosocial action do appear to have a potent influence on young children's prosocial learning. In everyday situations of home and school, opportunities to offer exhortations such as those delivered in this study must abound. We do not yet know whether parents regularly avail themselves of these opportunities or whether they generally intervene only when their child has transgressed. Ultimately, we must include an examination of these influences in natural childrearing contexts as we continue to explore the role of verbal communications in the socialization of prosocial responses.

## CONCLUSION

The effectiveness of exhorting children to behave prosocially demonstrates the potential strength of situational events. Situational variables, however, can only exert influence as their input is mediated by characteristics of the individual person, and even young children may vary greatly in the skills, knowledge, and expectancies with which they meet the world. Whether one chooses to regard the meaning children extract from situational influences as, for example, the child's own active construction brought about by interaction with others, especially peers (Piaget, 1932), the acquisition of "scripts" ("conceptual representations of stereotyped event sequences, [Abelson, 1981, p. 715]"), or the ability to make "successively more abstract generalizations from initially concrete schemas [Lepper, 1981, p. 196]," a viable model of prosocial development must take these cognitive factors into account. As Mischel and Mischel (1976) have emphasized, actions stem from the constructive interplay of environmental events and the cognitive activity by which each person construes information and generates potential behaviors; a model of prosocial development should ultimately be able to specify the nature of this interaction.

Our work has several implications for the development of such a model. First, our investigation of one paradigm used frequently to assess children's ability to assume the emotional perspectives of other people highlights the need for greater rigor and sophistication in measuring such cognitive constructs. Second, we would do well to investigate the child's cognitive competencies in conjunction with situational variability. For example, it is not enough to claim that a child—or an adult, for that matter—is or is not egocentric. We should also inquire into the conditions under which children are likely to display whatever ability they may have to take another's point of view. Finally, if we were to generalize from our own research, we might be inclined to conclude, as have others (e.g., Rosenhan, Moore, & Underwood, 1976), that situational factors are preeminent in the determination of prosocial behavior. Although we must not overlook the fact that environmental events are cognitively mediated, compelling situational factors may at times override intrapersonal influences. A model of prosocial development that fails to recognize the contribution of situational variables ignores a potent force for positive change.

## ACKNOWLEDGMENTS

We wish to express our sincere appreciation to Beverly I. Fagot, Donna M. Gelfand, Donald P. Hartmann, and Peter Jusczyk for their critical comments on an earlier version of this chapter.

## REFERENCES

Abelson, R. P. Psychological status of the script concept. *American Psychologist,* 1981, *36,* 715–729.

Barden, R. C., Zelko, F. A., Duncan, S. W., & Masters, J. C. Children's consensual knowledge about the experiential determinants of emotion. *Journal of Personality and Social Psychology,* 1980, *39,* 968–976.

Blackwell, J. M., Smith, C. L., Stewart, B. J., & Jennings, J. D. The effects of instructions on prosocial behavior of preschool children. Paper presented at the meeting of the Western Psychological Association, Honolulu, May 1980.

Borke, H. Interpersonal perception in young children: Egocentrism or empathy? *Developmental Psychology,* 1971, *5,* 263–269.

Bronfenbrenner, U. Toward an experimental ecology of human development. *American Psychologist,* 1977, *32,* 513–531.

Bryan, J. H., & Walbek, N. H. Impact of words and deeds concerning altruism upon children. *Child Development,* 1970, *41,* 747–757. (a)

Bryan, J. H., & Walbek, N. H. Preaching and practicing generosity: Children's actions and reactions. *Child Development,* 1970, *41,* 329–353. (b)

Buckley, N., Siegel, L. S., & Ness, S. Egocentrism, empathy, and altruistic behavior in young children. *Developmental Psychology,* 1979, *15,* 329–330.

Burns, N., & Cavey, L. Age differences in empathic ability among children. *Canadian Journal of Psychology,* 1957, *11,* 227–230.

Chandler, M. J. Social cognition: A selective review of current research. In W. F. Overton & J. M. Gallagher (Eds.), *Knowledge and development* (Vol. 1). New York: Plenum, 1977.

Chandler, M. J., & Greenspan, S. Ersatz egocentrism: A reply to H. Borke. *Developmental Psychology,* 1972, *7,* 104–106.

Damon, W. *The social world of the child.* San Francisco: Jossey–Bass, 1977.

Dlugokinski, E. L., & Firestone, I. J. Other centeredness and susceptibility to charitable appeals: Effects of perceived discipline. *Developmental Psychology,* 1974, *10,* 21–28.

Dressel, S., & Midlarsky, E. The effects of model's exhortations, demands, and practices on children's donation behavior. *Journal of Genetic Psychology,* 1978, *132,* 211–223.

Eisenberg-Berg, N., & Geisheker, E. Content of preachings ard power of the model/preacher: The effect on children's generosity. *Developmental Psychology,* 1979, *15,* 168–175.

Eisenberg-Berg, N., & Hand, M. The relationship of preschoolers' reasoning about prosocial moral conflicts to prosocial behavior. *Child Development,* 1979, *50,* 356–363.

Eisenberg-Berg, N., & Lennon, R. Altruism and the assessment of empathy in the preschool years. *Child Development,* 1980, *51,* 552–557.

Eisenberg-Berg, N., & Neal, C. Children's moral reasoning about their own spontaneous prosocial behavior. *Developmental Psychology,* 1979, *15,* 228–229.

Feshbach, N. D. Empathy in children: Some theoretical and empirical considerations. *The Counseling Psychologist,* 1975, *5*(2), 25–30.

Feshbach, N. D., & Roe, K. Empathy in six- and seven-year-olds. *Child Development,* 1968, *39,* 133–145.

Flapan, D. *Children's understanding of social interaction.* New York: Teachers College Press, 1968.

Ford, M. E. The construct validity of egocentrism. *Psychological Bulletin,* 1979, *86,* 1169–1188.

Gelfand, D. M., & Hartmann, D. P. Social learning and cognition: Two contributors to prosocial behavior. In N. Eisenberg (Ed.), *The development of prosocial behavior.* New York: Academic Press, 1982.

Gelfand, D. M., Hartmann, D. P., Cromer, C. C., Smith, C. L., & Page, B. C. The effects of instructional prompts and praise on children's donation rates. *Child Development,* 1975, *46,* 980–983.

Gove, F. L., & Keating, D. P. Empathic role-taking precursors. *Developmental Psychology,* 1979, *15,* 594–600.

Green, B. F. In defense of measurement. *American Psychologist,* 1978, *33,* 664–670.

Grusec, J. E. Demand characteristics of the modeling experiment: Altruism as a function of age and aggression. *Journal of Personality and Social Psychology,* 1972, *22,* 139–148.

Grusec, J. E., & Kuczynski, L. Direction of effect in socialization: A comparison of the parent's versus the child's behavior as determinants of disciplinary techniques. *Developmental Psychology,* 1980, *16,* 1–9.

Grusec, J. E., Kuczynski, L., Rushton, J. P., & Simutis, Z. M. Modeling, direct instruction, and attributions: Effects on altruism. *Developmental Psychology,* 1978, *14,* 51–57.

Grusec, J. E., Saas-Kortsaak, P., & Simutis, Z. M. The role of example and moral exhortation in the training of altruism. *Child Development,* 1978, *49,* 920–923.

Hoffman, M. L. Parent discipline and the child's consideration for others. *Child Development,* 1963, *34,* 573–588.

Hoffman, M. L. Moral development. In P. H. Mussen (Ed.), *Carmichael's manual of child psychology* (Vol. 2) (3rd ed.). New York: Wiley, 1970.

Hoffman, M. L. Developmental synthesis of affect and cognition and its implication for altruistic motivation. *Developmental Psychology,* 1975, *11,* 607–622.

Hoffman, M. L. Is altruism part of human nature? *Journal of Personality and Social Psychology,* 1981, *40,* 121–137.

Hoffman, M. L., & Saltzstein, H. D. Parent discipline and the child's moral development. *Journal of Personality and Social Psychology,* 1967, *5,* 45–57.

Iannotti, R. J. The many faces of empathy: An analysis of the definition and evaluation of empathy in children. Paper presented at the meeting of the Society for Research in Child Development, Denver, April 1975. (a)

Iannotti, R. J. The nature and measurement of empathy in children. *The Counseling Psychologist*, 1975, *5*, 21–25. (b)

Iannotti, R. J. Effect of role-taking experiences on role-taking, empathy, altruism, and aggression. *Developmental Psychology*, 1978, *14*, 119–124.

Jones, E. E. The rocky road from acts to dispositions. *American Psychologist*, 1979, *34*, 107–117.

Kuhn, D. Mechanisms of cognitive and social development: One psychology or two? *Human Development*, 1978, *21*, 92–118.

Kurdek, L. A. Perspective-taking as the cognitive basis of children's moral development: A review of the literature. *Merrill–Palmer Quarterly*, 1978, *24*, 3–28.

Kurdek, L. A., & Rodgon, M. M. Perceptual, cognitive, and affective perspective-taking in kindergarten through sixth-grade children. *Developmental Psychology*, 1975, *11*, 643–650.

Leinbach, M. D., Smith, C. L., & Stewart, B. J. Affective perspective-taking and sympathy in young children. Paper presented at the meeting of the Western Psychological Association, Honolulu, May 1980.

Lepper, M. R. Intrinsic and extrinsic motivation in children: Detrimental effects of superfluous social controls. In W. A. Collins (Ed.), *Minnesota symposia on child psychology* (Vol. 14). Hillsdale, N. J.: Erlbaum, 1981.

Midlarsky, E., & Bryan, J. H. Affect expressions and children's imitative altruism. *Journal of Experimental Research in Personality*, 1972, *6*, 195–203.

Mischel, W., & Mischel, H. N. A cognitive social-learning approach to morality and self-regulation. In T. Lickona (Ed.), *Moral development and behavior*. New York: Holt Rinehart & Winston, 1976.

Murphy, L. B. *Social behavior and child personality: An exploratory study of some roots of sympathy*. New York: Columbia University Press, 1937.

Mussen, P. H., & Eisenberg-Berg, N. *Roots of caring, sharing, and helping*. San Francisco: Freeman, 1977.

Nunnally, J. C. *Psychometric theory* (2nd ed.). New York: McGraw–Hill, 1978.

Orne, M. T. On the social psychology of the psychological experiment: With particular reference to demand characteristics and their implication. *American Psychologist*, 1962, *17*, 776–783.

Piaget, J. *The moral judgment of the child*. London: Kegan Paul, 1932.

Piaget, J. *The language and thought of the child* (3rd ed.). London: Routledge & Kegan Paul, 1959.

Piaget, J., & Inhelder, B. *The child's conception of space*. London: Routledge & Kegan Paul, 1956.

Piaget, J., & Inhelder, B. *Le développement des quantités physiques chez l'enfant* (2nd ed.). Neuchâtel: Delachaux & Niestlé, 1962.

Rice, M. E., & Grusec, J. E. Saying and doing: Effects on observer performance. *Journal of Personality and Social Psychology*, 1975, *32*, 584–593.

Rosenhan, D. L., Moore, B. S., & Underwood, B. The social psychology of moral behavior. In T. Lickona (Ed.), *Moral development and behavior*. New York: Holt Rinehart & Winston, 1976.

Rubin, K. H. Role taking in childhood: Some methodological considerations. *Child Development*, 1978, *49*, 428–433.

Rushton, J. P. Generosity in children: Immediate and long-term effects of modeling, preaching, and moral judgment. *Journal of Personality and Social Psychology*, 1975, *31*, 459–466.

Rushton, J. P. Socialization and the altruistic behavior of children. *Psychological Bulletin*, 1976, *83*, 898–913.

Rushton, J. P. *Altruism, socialization, and society*. Englewood Cliffs, N. J.: Prentice–Hall, 1980.

Selman, R. L. *The growth of interpersonal understanding*. New York: Academic Press, 1980.

Shantz, C. U. The development of social cognition. In E. M. Hetherington (Ed.), *Review of child development research* (Vol. 5). Chicago: University of Chicago Press, 1975. (a)

Shantz, C. U. Empathy in relation to social cognitive development. *The Counseling Psychologist*, 1975, *5*, 18–21. (b)

Smith, C. L., Gelfand, D. M., Hartmann, D. P., & Partlow, M. E. Y. Children's causal attributions regarding help giving. *Child Development*, 1979, *50*, 203–210.

Staub, E. A child in distress: The influence of nurturance and modeling on children's attempts to help. *Developmental Psychology*, 1971, *5*, 124–132.

Staub, E. To rear a prosocial child: Reasoning, learning by doing, and learning by teaching others. In D. J. DePalma & J. M. Folley (Eds.), *Moral development: Current theory and research*. Hillsdale, N. J.: Erlbaum, 1975.

Staub, E. *Positive social behavior and morality* (Vol. 1). New York: Academic Press, 1978.

Staub, E. *Positive social behavior and morality* (Vol. 2). New York: Academic Press, 1979.

Strayer, J. A naturalistic study of empathic behaviors and their relation to affective states and perspective-taking skills in preschool children. *Child Development*, 1980, *51*, 815–822.

Turiel, E. Social convention and morality: Two distinct conceptual and developmental systems. In C. B. Keasey (Ed.), *Nebraska symposium on motivation* (Vol. 25). Lincoln: University of Nebraska Press, 1978.

Urberg, K. A., & Docherty, E. M. Development of role-taking skills in young children. *Developmental Psychology*, 1976, *12*, 198–203.

Walters, G. C., & Grusec, J. E. *Punishment*. San Francisco: Freeman, 1977.

Webb, E. J., Campbell, D. T., Schwartz, R. D., & Sechrest, L. *Unobtrusive measures: Nonreactive research in the social sciences*. Chicago: Rand McNally, 1966.

Weissbrod, C. S. The impact of warmth and instructions on donation. *Child Development*, 1980, *51*, 279–281.

White, G. M. Immediate and deferred effects of model observation and guided and unguided rehearsal on donating and stealing. *Journal of Personality and Social Psychology*, 1972, *21*, 139–148.

Yarrow, M. R., Scott, P. M., & Waxler, C. Z. Learning concern for others. *Developmental Psychology*, 1973, *8*, 240–260.

Yarrow, M. R., & Waxler, C. Z. Dimensions and correlates of prosocial behavior in young children. *Child Development*, 1976, *47*, 118–125.

Zahn-Waxler, C., Radke-Yarrow, M., & King, R. A. Child rearing and children's prosocial initiations toward victims of distress. *Child Development*, 1979, *50*, 319–330.

# What's It to Them? The Value of Considerateness to Children

AMY E. SIBULKIN

> Altruism is essential for the existence of society. The question
> of how it is that a human being, brought into the world with
> apparently no other thought than its own gratification,
> eventually becomes capable of living its life with concern for
> others, is of central importance.
>
> Rushton, 1980 [p.viii]

This quote, taken from the preface of a literature review, explicitly states adults'
value of prosocial behavior and endorsement of its acquisition, but what about kids?
Do children share our concern? A review of research on children's "prosocial" or
"altruistic" behavior reveals a major gap in knowledge about this popular topic.
Despite a proliferation in the number of variables used to refine our understanding
of the nature of children's prosocial behavior, little attention has been given to its
value to children themselves, although correlates such as popularity indirectly suggest prosocial behavior is highly regarded among peers.

Much research effort continues to be expended on describing prosocial behavior
and studying how it develops, how it is socialized, and how it can be actively
trained. Along with this concern on the part of adult researchers, the question of
whether children value prosocial behavior as much as adults do has not been
considered. The purpose of this chapter is to present the results of a research
project[1] that was designed to address this question of children's value of consid-

[1]This research was supported by a grant from the New York State College of Human Ecology at
Cornell University, Ithaca, New York. It was undertaken for a dissertation submitted to the Graduate
School of Cornell University.

THE NATURE OF PROSOCIAL DEVELOPMENT

erateness by using new measures as well as incorporating methodological improvements into measures typically used.

Critical to inferring a value of considerateness are the concepts of salience and preference. A first step in acting considerately, for either adults or children who are not under adult supervision, is to notice the opportunity to act considerately. Additionally, the child must prefer considerate behavior to the often conflicting alternatives present. In other words, a valid test of children's value of considerateness would include, but not be limited to, providing a choice of behavioral alternatives. Also, these alternatives should be as representative of everyday life as possible and should compete for attention with other stimuli, a situation that in itself is more representative of everyday life. These aspects of preference and salience are regarded as essential parts of a value of considerateness, along with acting considerately.

*Considerate behavior* will be used to refer to kind, nurturant, helpful, and polite words or actions that enhance or do not diminish the physical or emotional well-being of others. It does not require any self-sacrifice by the actor and is compatible with the expectation either of reward or no reward as a result of the behavior. Hence, it is almost equivalent to "prosocial" behavior, perhaps best thought of as a large subset.

The term *considerateness,* as used here, indicates the extent to which an individual values considerate social behavior. The idea that values are constructs inferred from a wide variety of types of data is taken from Kluckhohn (1951), who defines values as conceptions or criteria of the desirable, thus providing the basis for selecting among alternative thoughts, feelings, and actions. Values are an aspect of the broader concept of "motivation" and can be multiply motivated. We would expect children's value of considerateness to be influenced by other than "purely altruistic" motives, which imply sacrifice to the actor, and will present some evidence on what these might be. (For a discussion of the criteria for classifying behavior as "prosocial" versus "altruistic," see Krebs, 1970; Rushton, 1980; Schwartz, 1977; Staub, 1978.)

Our last detour before presenting this research is to illustrate the conceptual and methodological problems it addresses via some representative examples from the literature. The purpose is not to criticize studies for inadequately measuring children's value of considerateness; the point is to review previous research and its lack of concern with this issue. Even the few studies that do address values use measures that do not permit a strong inference of a value of considerateness, as defined here, given their lack of representativeness of common forms of considerate behavior and lack of stimulus choice.

## SOME PREVIOUS RESEARCH ON CHILDREN'S PROSOCIAL BEHAVIOR

Rubin and Schneider (1973) had 7-year-olds participate in several perspective-taking, moral judgment, and altruistic tasks. Their generosity task, one of the most frequently used measures of altruism, consisted of giving each child the opportunity to donate previously earned candies to poor children. The amount of candy privately donated was the measure of altruism. Although this procedure is fairly representative of the way donations are solicited in everyday life, children are ordinarily involved in a much wider array of more frequently occurring and subtle forms of considerate behavior. This is not to deny the importance of understanding the valued social behavior of donating, but children are not called upon to donate their earnings or rewards as often as they routinely encounter helping, defending, teasing, and pushing, to name a few of the common considerate and inconsiderate behaviors among peers. In the same study Rubin and Schneider also used a helping task in which the child was paired with a younger child in a room with new toys. They were told they could play with the toys after completing a task consisting of counting out piles of tickets. The older child, who was given fewer tickets, finished first and could choose between helping the younger child finish or playing. The measure of altruism was the number of ticket piles one child finished for the other younger child. Children are more likely to find themselves with such an opportunity to help another child than to be solicited for a donation. Also, they were not explicitly given the option of helping, as in the donating task, hence their attention was not directed to it by the experimenter. However, we have no clues as to whether the children who did not help were unaware of the opportunity or did not help for other reasons, such as thinking it was not allowed. We also do not know whether the children who did help would have if other activities had been available. These problems are common to the vast majority of studies on prosocial behavior. Hence, we do not know if children notice and respond to events that usually vary in salience and compete for their attention.

A few studies have been designed to directly measure what authors have called "other-directedness" and an "altruistic value." Children rank-order statements according to how important the described behavior is to them, or they indicate their liking for pictures depicting considerate or inconsiderate behaviors (e.g., Dlugokinski & Firestone, 1973, 1974; Guilford, 1974; Hoffman, 1975; Hoffman & Saltzstein, 1967). Although these types of measures attempt to directly assess children's values, two problems occur that the research to be presented attempted to solve. First, the statements to be rank ordered do not usually refer to commonly occurring, everyday behavior but rather to future aspirations (e.g., "getting a job that helps other people," "being a good caretaker of my family"). The second problem is that statements describing alternative values are not systematically provided. It seems that a stronger test for a value of considerateness would result from forcing considerate behavior to be weighed against other attractive and socially acceptable behaviors. The remainder of this chapter describes a study that used four sets of indicators to assess children's value of considerateness among peers.

## A STUDY OF CHILDREN'S VALUE OF CONSIDERATENESS

In order to study children's interest in, concern with, and awareness of this issue, four measures focusing on specific and commonly occurring considerate behaviors among peers were employed. Additionally, competing stimuli were introduced, thereby incorporating the critical elements of preference and salience into the design. The first set of indicators was intended to be the most direct assessment of the value and was a self-ranking of preference for statements describing considerate behavior, as well as other socially approved behaviors. The second was a measure of sensitivity to others' distress, designed to totally avoid directing the children's attention to stimuli related to considerateness in order to determine what was salient to them. The third and fourth measures of peer nominations and teacher ratings were designed to provide information on behavior that corresponded to the self-reported rankings. The advantages of these measures over previously used ones will be further explicated in the following sections.

The participants were 30 third-graders, 30 fourth-graders, and 30 fifth-graders (mean age = 10.0 years). An equal number of boys and girls were in each grade. All of the children were white, and 86% attended a rural school serving families with a below-average income. The other 14% attended a suburban school with children from families with an average to above-average income. Each child participated individually on all of the tasks.

## Self-Choice Measure of Preference for Considerate Behavior

This procedure was intended to be a direct measure of children's preference for considerate behavior, relative to other socially valued or acceptable behavior, based on the rationale that a value influences what one prefers. The results are used in two ways. First, the preference for considerate behavior as compared with conscientious, clean, and carefree behavior is of interest. Second, individual differences in the rank ordering of considerate behavior are compared with individual differences on the other three sets of indicators. In other words, the nature of the value will be studied through the intercorrelations of these different measures.

The four categories of behavior to be compared were (a) considerate; (b) conscientious; (c) clean; and (d) carefree. Four statements describing a person in action were used to represent these four groups. Each statement was on a card, thus totaling 16 cards. The set used for girls appears in Table 6.1. An equivalent set with boys' names was used with male participants. The children were asked to rank order their preference to be like the four people described by the four cards for that trial. It is important to note that the four "considerate" statements are worded in two different ways: "helps out other kids who can't do something" and "sticks up for another girl/boy that kids make fun of" are stated positively, meaning that doing what is referred to is considerate. The items "does not say mean things to hurt other kids' feelings" and "does not cut in front of kids already in line" are stated negatively, meaning that not doing what is referred to is considerate behavior. This distinction becomes critical in interpreting later results.

The experimenter placed the cards in front of the child, one at a time, having the child read each one aloud. After the first four were in place, the experimenter asked

**TABLE 6.1**
*Self-Choice Statements*

| Value | Trial # |
|-------|---------|
| | 1 |
| Clean | _____ Debbie keeps her room neat |
| Considerate | _____ Mary helps out other kids who can't do something |
| Carefree | _____ Ann always wants to have a good time |
| Conscientious | _____ Sue works very hard on schoolwork |
| | 2 |
| Considerate | _____ Barbara does not say mean things to hurt other kids' feelings |
| Carefree | _____ Ellen always tries new things |
| Conscientious | _____ Karen remembers to do things |
| Clean | _____ Carol brushes her teeth twice a day |
| | 3 |
| Conscientious | _____ Michelle is ready to go places on time |
| Clean | _____ Laura keeps her clothes clean |
| Considerate | _____ Judy will stick up for another girl that kids make fun of |
| Carefree | _____ Jenny never worries about things |
| | 4 |
| Carefree | _____ Beth always stays up late watching TV |
| Conscientious | _____ Sally does not lose things |
| Clean | _____ Jean always wipes her feet at the door |
| Considerate | _____ Joan does not cut in front of kids already in line |

who the child would most want to be like, and the selected card was removed and set aside. The experimenter then asked, "Who would you next most want to be like?" and the child made the second selection and then the third one, thus fixing the fourth choice.

These "considerate" items were adapted from the descriptive statements used in the previously mentioned studies but refer to concrete and specific behaviors rather than to abstractions or generalities. Also, this measure provides a more systematic assessment of the preference for considerate behaviors in that these are pitted against three other categories an equal number of times. Additional rigor was introduced by having children in a pilot study rank order their preferences within each of the four value groups as well as across groups as just described. These results were used to put the most preferred descriptions from Value Groups 1, 2, 3, and 4 together to form the material for one trial. The second most preferred statements were put together to form another trial, etc. We cannot say the groups contained four equally attractive statements, but disparity in the attractiveness of the statements within each group was minimized. Hence, the children were given a choice, and this choice presumably was not systematically influenced by social desirability, given the contents of the statements.

The score for each of these four "self-choice" items was its rank order on the trial in which it was presented. A 4 was scored if it was chosen first, a 3 if it was chosen second, etc. Hence, the scores for each ranged from 1 to 4.

Table 6.2 shows the means and standard deviations of the sums of the four ranks within each value category. We see that the sum of ranks for the "considerate" statements is highest, followed by the "conscientious," "carefree," and "clean" statements, in descending order. Since these mean sum of ranks are not independent of each other, given the forced ranking procedure, each was compared to the mean expected by chance, rather than to each other. If the children were ranking the statements randomly, then each statement would be ranked once in first, second, third, and fourth places over the four trials, giving a sum of ranks of 10. $T$ tests comparing the means in Table 6.2 to the chance value of 10 showed that "considerate" was quite reliably ranked higher than expected by chance, with a near zero probability level. "Clean" was as reliably ranked lower than expected by chance, and "conscientious" and "carefree" statements did not differ from chance.

To obtain more detailed information as to the relative preference for the "considerate" statements, similar $t$ tests were done to compare how frequently they were preferred over each of the other types of statements. We would expect that the "considerate" statements would be chosen over, or ranked higher than, the "conscientious" statements two out of the four times by chance, and the same for the "clean" and "carefree" statements. Table 6.3 shows the average number of times the "considerate" statements were preferred over the other ones. Similar to the mean sum of ranks of "considerate" statements, the mean number of times these "considerate" statements were chosen over the other statements does not differ greatly from chance expectancy. However, these differences are quite reliable and show that the "considerate" statements were preferred over each of the other three categories. Boys and girls did not differ on their mean rankings of the "considerate" statements, however gender differences were observed on several other variables used in this study and will be discussed later.

Of course, these four categories do not exhaust all the conventional values that children subscribe to, and this task was not intended as a full-scale investigation of children's values. In fact, pretesting with other categories showed that "obedience to authority" items such as "always follows the rules at school" and "does not do something wrong that other kids say to do" were ranked far higher than other items,

**TABLE 6.2**

Mean Sum of Ranks for Each Self-Choice Value Category

|  | Value | | | |
|---|---|---|---|---|
|  | Considerate | Conscientious | Carefree | Clean |
| Mean | 11.30 | 10.07 | 9.64 | 9.01 |
| SD | 2.75 | 2.10 | 3.39 | 2.31 |
| $t$ | 4.49 | .30 | −1.00 | −4.07 |
| $p$ | .000 | .764 | .322 | .000 |

**TABLE 6.3**
*Mean Number of Times Considerate Statements Ranked Higher Than
Other Value Statements over Four Trials*

| Comparison | Mean | SD | t | p |
|---|---|---|---|---|
| Considerate > conscientious | 2.36 | 1.11 | 3.03 | .003 |
| Considerate > clean | 2.60 | 1.00 | 5.67 | .000 |
| Considerate > carefree | 2.33 | 1.27 | 2.49 | .015 |

including "considerate" ones. However, we can imagine that preferences for all the items could partly be motivated by obedience to authority and, in fact, we will later see evidence that considerateness is likely to be so motivated. Given that a preference for obedience to authority may uniformly underlie choices across all the categories used here, the top ranking of the "considerate" items seems to indicate a preference for considerate behavior in its own right.

## Measure of Sensitivity to Distress

In addition to preferring considerate behavior even over other approved behavior, we would expect children with a value of considerateness to selectively attend to the presence and absence of considerate-related themes in the environment. We would expect distress to be a particularly salient event to a child who valued considerateness; much of childhood distress is caused by other people's inconsiderateness. Also, "empathy," often studied as a reaction to others' distress, has long been considered a motivator of positive social behavior, and the instrument we will describe shares some similarities with others that assess reactions to distress. However, such previously used tasks do not allow for a choice of stimuli. In Feshbach and Roe's (1968) widely used test, children are asked how they feel and how story characters involved in happy and sad events feel. The accuracy of the match between these is used to index empathy. Research on the associations between empathy and prosocial behavior does not show clear findings, resulting partly from using different operationalizations of empathy and prosocial behavior and from the desire for approval, which may influence children to indicate they feel like the character in the story does (Eisenberg-Berg & Lennon, 1980; J. Strayer, 1980).

The instrument used here consisted of seven pictures, selected from children's books, and two of them are shown in Figures 6.1 and 6.2.[2] All the pictures depicted at least one character experiencing distress common in children's everyday lives, with the exception that one scene was set in an Indian camp. Pictures were selected in which the characters experiencing distress were not the picture's focal point, but were surrounded by other characters and activities, thereby not commanding the

---

[2]Descriptions and sources of the other five pictures can be obtained from the author.

**FIGURE 6.1.** Picture 3. *Baseball*. Illustration by George Wilde from *Wanted . . . A Brother* by Gina Bell. Copyright © 1959 by Abingdon Press. Used by permission.

viewer's attention to the exclusion of other content. In other words, the distress-related material had to appear at an appropriate level of prominence in order to elicit individual differences in how much attention the subjects paid to it. One picture was included because it was known from pretesting to elicit very few distress and considerate responses. It was always shown first to familiarize the child with the

**FIGURE 6.2.** Picture 6. *Party*. Copyright © 1959 by Reiner Zimnik. Reprinted from *The Snow Party* by Beatrice Schenk DeRegniers, illustrated by Reiner Zimnik, by permission of Pantheon Books, a Division of Random House, Inc.

procedure and is referred to as the "trial" picture. The other six pictures were presented in various randomly selected orders.

The selection of pictures was based on the rationale that children who valued considerateness among peers would notice its presence and absence (i.e., stimuli of children in distress and helping or being kind to each other should be salient to them). The rationale is also based on the assumption that one effect of heightened motivation is to lower the threshold of response to a stimulus configuration.

After being shown each picture, the children were asked what the most important things about the picture were and what was important about those things. Additionally, they were asked what they would like to happen next and why. Finally, they were asked what they liked and disliked most about the picture and for what reasons. The children were encouraged to give as many answers as they wished to the questions of what was important and what they would like to happen.

Although this procedure is similar to standard projective techniques, particularly thematic apperception tests, it has three advantages over them. First, the stimuli are better representative of real life, since an array of social events is presented rather than just the main character in a standard picture. Second, the instructions and scoring are congruent. In this procedure, the children are asked, "What are the most important things about the picture to you?" and their responses are scored to index just that: attention to, importance of, and concern with others' needs or distress. Third, the inference that noticing distress and opportunities for helping and comforting are generalizable to how frequently these are noticed in real life is more plausible than the inference that stories about a main character reflect a wish or need. Finally, this measure stands in contrast to commonly used ones in that the child's attention is not focused on considerate behavior by the experimenter. By presenting the relevant stimuli along with other events, thus allowing for stimulus choice, the inference that children's reports indicate a value is sounder.

Two types of responses to the pictures were scored.[3] A point was scored each time the child identified someone experiencing or potentially experiencing either distress, discomfort, inconvenience, or considerate behavior such as helping, sharing, or kindness. The second type of responses scored were answers to what they would like to happen and what they liked and disliked. A point was scored if they suggested things that enhanced the emotional or physical state of the characters, if they liked things referring to a positive state of the characters, or they disliked things referring to a negative state. Asking for a reason after each response was done in order to verify that the response was related to distress or considerateness. For instance, a common response to "what's important?" for Picture 3 (Figure 6.1) was "the boy climbing the tree." This was counted, if in response to "what was important about that?" the child said, "He'll get hurt if he falls," but it was not counted if the child said, "It's fun." All the points for each picture were added up to produce a total picture score. Thus, each child had seven picture scores.

Interrater reliability based on the picture scores of 30 randomly selected children

---

[3]The complete coding manual for scoring the pictures is available from the author.

# TABLE 6.4
### Correlation Coefficients for All Variables ($N = 90$)[a,b]

| | Self | | | | Peer | | | | Teacher | | | | Picture trial | Picture | | | | | | Age | Gender | SAT |
|---|---|---|---|---|---|---|---|---|---|---|---|---|---|---|---|---|---|---|---|---|---|---|
| | Help | Not cut in line | Not say mean things | Stick up for | Help | Not cut in line | Not say mean things | Stick up for | Help | Not cut in line | Not say mean things | Stick up for | Picture trial | Picture 1 | Picture 2 | Picture 3 | Picture 4 | Picture 5 | Picture 6 | Age | Gender | SAT |
| Self–Help | 1.00 | | | | | | | | | | | | | | | | | | | | | |
| Self–Not cut in line | .13 | 1.00 | | | | | | | | | | | | | | | | | | | | |
| Self–Not say mean things | .34 | .16 | 1.00 | | | | | | | | | | | | | | | | | | | |
| Self–Stick up for | .16 | .02 | .08 | 1.00 | | | | | | | | | | | | | | | | | | |
| Peer–Help | .22 | .05 | .19 | -.12 | 1.00 | | | | | | | | | | | | | | | | | |
| Peer–Not cut in line | .20 | .07 | .35 | -.01 | .47 | 1.00 | | | | | | | | | | | | | | | | |
| Peer–Not say mean things | .10 | .09 | .32 | .05 | .37 | .65 | 1.00 | | | | | | | | | | | | | | | |
| Peer–Stick up for | .15 | .07 | -.05 | .20 | .24 | .02 | -.01 | 1.00 | | | | | | | | | | | | | | |
| Teacher–Help | .24 | .00 | .09 | .15 | .23 | .03 | .17 | .23 | 1.00 | | | | | | | | | | | | | |
| Teacher–Not cut in line | .09 | -.07 | .11 | -.07 | .09 | .36 | .26 | -.25 | .04 | 1.00 | | | | | | | | | | | | |
| Teacher–Not say mean things | .13 | .23 | .18 | -.04 | .29 | .54 | .38 | -.16 | .15 | .55 | 1.00 | | | | | | | | | | | |
| Teacher–Stick up for | .08 | -.00 | -.05 | .08 | .16 | .13 | .13 | .07 | .40 | .05 | .13 | 1.00 | | | | | | | | | | |
| Picture trial | .15 | .01 | .07 | .10 | .01 | .02 | .03 | .24 | .28 | -.10 | -.14 | .17 | 1.00 | | | | | | | | | |
| Picture 1 | .13 | .08 | .20 | .16 | .10 | .20 | .28 | .08 | .21 | -.05 | .06 | .08 | .39 | 1.00 | | | | | | | | |
| Picture 2 | .22 | -.02 | .18 | .18 | .06 | .15 | .20 | .04 | .21 | -.12 | .01 | .08 | .27 | .49 | 1.00 | | | | | | | |
| Picture 3 | .22 | -.05 | .29 | .12 | -.02 | .04 | .05 | .11 | .22 | -.01 | -.07 | -.01 | .33 | .58 | .56 | 1.00 | | | | | | |
| Picture 4 | .10 | -.18 | .22 | .22 | -.05 | .11 | .11 | .12 | .27 | .11 | .04 | .13 | .34 | .33 | .39 | .56 | 1.00 | | | | | |
| Picture 5 | .24 | .01 | .35 | .22 | .25 | .31 | .28 | .10 | .13 | .01 | .04 | .10 | .31 | .64 | .52 | .62 | .43 | 1.00 | | | | |
| Picture 6 | .20 | .03 | .23 | .07 | .00 | .21 | .16 | -.03 | .15 | .12 | .03 | .04 | .31 | .58 | .41 | .46 | .29 | .53 | 1.00 | | | |
| Age | .03 | -.10 | -.01 | -.01 | -.01 | -.13 | -.15 | .03 | -.13 | -.14 | -.21 | -.01 | -.05 | .02 | -.01 | -.05 | -.14 | -.02 | -.07 | 1.00 | | |
| Gender | .11 | -.12 | .36 | -.06 | .39 | .53 | .54 | -.21 | .13 | .36 | .35 | .11 | .11 | .26 | .23 | .25 | .19 | .43 | .25 | -.04 | 1.00 | |
| SAT | .20 | .03 | -.04 | -.14 | .41 | .26 | .29 | -.10 | .20 | .32 | .34 | .15 | -.00 | -.00 | .02 | -.18 | -.15 | -.09 | .03 | .03 | .19 | 1.00 |

[a]Correlations of .207 and .270 are significantly different from 0 at the .05 and .01 levels.
[b]Girls = 1; Boys = 0.

proved quite high. The correlations ranged from .88 to .98 with an average of .91. Across the 90 children, scores on the pictures were not related to Stanford Achievement Test (SAT) reading scores.

## Relationship between Preference for Considerate Behavior and Sensitivity to Distress

The intercorrelations among the four "self-choice" items and among the seven picture scores are shown in Table 6.4, and they are all positive as expected. The average correlation between "self-choice" and picture scores is only .13. However, the correlation between the sum of the scores within each group of items, shown in Table 6.5, is a much higher .31, the usual result of combining items.

We have evidence that children in late elementary school value considerate behavior in terms of preferring it relative to other adult-approved behavior. This preference is somewhat related to the salience of others' distress. However, we can draw more inferences about the nature of this underlying value by considering evidence from two other indicators, which were used in the same study of third, fourth, and fifth graders. It was hypothesized that the value of considerateness would not only influence a preference for considerate behavior, as measured by the "self-choice" items and a tendency to selectively attend to its presence and absence in the environment, as measured by the pictures, but that it would also influence everyday considerate behavior, as measured by the children's reputation among their peers and teachers. These four measures were used to obtain evidence concerning the generality of children's value of considerateness. The results also provided indirect evidence for the nature of considerateness, in terms of its multiple motivations.

## Reputation for Considerate Behavior as Judged by Peers

Each child was shown a sheet of paper with his or her classmates listed alphabetically by first name and asked to indicate which three boys or girls were the most like 12 descriptive phrases. Each phrase was written on a card and appears in Table 6.6 in the order in which it was presented. Statements 3 (peer–help), 6 (peer–not

**TABLE 6.5**
*Correlations among Composite Variables*

|          | Self | Peer | Teacher | Pictures |
|----------|------|------|---------|----------|
| Self     | 1.00 |      |         |          |
| Peer     | .28  | 1.00 |         |          |
| Teacher  | .19  | .39  | 1.00    |          |
| Pictures | .31  | .22  | .16     | 1.00     |

**TABLE 6.6**
*Peer Nomination Statements*

Which three boys or girls . . . ?
1. are the tallest
2. are the shortest
3. help out other kids who can't do something
4. do not help out other kids who can't do something
5. cut in front of kids already in line
6. do not cut in front of kids already in line
7. draw the best
8. draw the worst
9. say mean things to hurt other kids' feelings
10. do not say mean things to hurt other kids' feelings
11. stick up for another boy or girl that kids make fun of
12. do not stick up for another boy or girl that kids make fun of

cut in line), 10 (peer–not say mean things), and 11 (peer–stick up for), which made up the peer nomination group of items, were constructed to correspond to the four "self-choice" items. In this way a lack of consistency between the children's preference and reputation could not be attributed to objective differences in the kind of considerate behavior being described. The scores for each item were the sum of the nominations received for that item. Hence, each child's score could range from zero to the number of children in his class.

## Reputation for Considerate Behavior as Judged by Peers

The children's classroom teachers were asked to rank order their respective classes on the same six dimensions used for the peer nominations. They grouped the children into five categories, which ranged from most likely to least likely to behave as the statement indicated over a typical 2-week period. Again, the "considerate" items of "teacher–help," "teacher–not cut in line," "teacher–not say mean things," and "teacher–stick up for" were intended to be parallel to the "self-choice" and "peer" items.

## FURTHER RESULTS

### Generality of the Value of Considerateness

Table 6.4, previously referred to, shows the intercorrelations among the 19 indicators. The order of the variables listed in this and subsequent tables has been changed from the order in which they were discussed. This was done to facilitate comparisons of the parallel items across the first three groups.

The .39 correlation (Table 6.5) between the summed peer and teacher scores indicates that the teachers and peers agreed moderately well on how considerate the children were, consistent with previous findings (e.g., Bar-Tal & Raviv, 1979; Hartshorne, May, & Maller, 1929). However, these two measures of reputation were not as strongly related to the previous two measures of preference and salience. This is also consistent with previous studies, which show lower correlations with decreasing task similarity or type of prosocial behavior being rated or observed (e.g., Eisenberg-Berg & Hand, 1979; Eisenberg-Berg & Lennon, 1980; Green & Schneider, 1974; O'Bryant & Brophy, 1976; Payne, 1980; Rubin & Schneider, 1973; Rutherford & Mussen, 1968; Severy & Davis, 1971; Yarrow & Waxler, 1976).

Despite the clustering into groups along the lines of behavioral versus cognitive–affective aspects of considerateness and low correlations at the level of individual items, a series of confirmatory and exploratory factor analyses strongly supported the validity of a general factor, interpreted as a value of considerateness. However, these factor analyses also provided evidence that the value of considerateness is itself related to other important variables in the child's social world; these latter results will be focused on here. Evidence for the distinctiveness of the positively and negatively worded items appears repeatedly, thus leading to the supposition that they were indicating the influence of other variables. Since these speculations were derived from the original factor analyses, an explanation and summary of those results will be given first.

Recall that there are 19 indicators of a value of considerateness—seven pictures and four items each for the self-choice, peer, and teacher measures. These last three sets were designed to measure the same behavior by different methods. It was hypothesized that a pattern of five factors would reproduce the matrix of correlations among these 19 indicators. A general factor would correspond to the value of considerateness, which influences all the indicators, and four group factors would correspond to the four different methods of measuring considerateness. As discussed by Campbell and Fiske (1970), it is typically found in personality research that correlations among different methods of measuring the same traits are lower than correlations among different traits measured by the same method. Although we do not have a multitrait–multimethod matrix, evidence for the validity of a value of considerateness would be provided by intercorrelations among all the indicators that do not vanish when method variance is controlled.

Holzinger's (in Harman, 1976) "bifactor" model was hypothesized to fit the observed correlations. The objective was to test how well this model, in which each indicator is affected by a general and group factor, fits the empirical correlations in Table 6.4. In other words, the question is how much discrepancy exists between the empirical correlations and those estimated or predicted from the model via the factor loadings. The next step is to obtain estimates of these factor loadings. The method of maximum likelihood was chosen because of certain statistical properties. Also, a statistical test of significance can be done to determine the adequacy of the fit between the estimated and empirical correlations via the significance of a chi square $(\chi^2)$ value.[4]

Joreskog and Sorbom's (1978) LISREL IV program was used to obtain the estimates shown in Table 6.7. The lower part of Table 6.7 shows the hypothetical correlations among the group factors that were required to adequately reproduce the observed correlations. (The original bifactor model with uncorrelated group factors proved inadequate and was rejected.) The overall model is accepted, given the high $p$ value, which is interpreted differently from more common significance tests.[5]

## Considerateness, Activity, and Assertiveness

Contrary to the expectation that all the variables would correlate positively with the general factor, seven variables have negative loadings. With the exception of "peer–help" which is negligible, they involve all the negatively worded behaviors—"not cut in line" and "not say mean things." One explanation for this pattern is that the general factor of considerateness is correlated with an even more general factor of activity level, responsiveness, or assertiveness. Besides involving considerateness, the "help" and "stick up for" behaviors require some kind of activity in the form of assertiveness or initiative, as well as other personality characteristics such as confidence and self-esteem. "Stick up for" seems to involve very assertive behaviors; not only does it require action, but one is usually advocating an unpopular cause—the person being victimized. It follows then that "not say mean things" and "not cut in line" may in part reflect inactivity or low responsiveness rather than considerateness. The child who refrains from cutting in line or saying mean things may also not talk a lot or run down the halls, whereas those who help other kids or stick up for other kids might do these other things as well. This hypothesis of a general activity factor could have been tested by including indicators that did not involve considerateness, such as talking and running, and these would load only on the activity factor. The indicators used in this study would be hypothesized to load on both the activity and considerateness factors.

An association between activity level or frequency of social interaction and prosocial behavior is often found in observations of preschoolers' free play. Going back to Murphy (1937), who observed naturally occurring "sympathetic" behavior, frequency of sympathetic behavior was positively correlated with aggressive behavior. Both increased with age, presumably concomitant with the increasing frequency of all social interaction with age. Friedrich and Stein (1973) found summed scores of cooperation and nurturance to be significantly correlated with

---

[4]For further description of the maximum likelihood approach to confirmatory factor analysis, see Joreskog (1969), Kenny (1979), Long (1976), and Mulaik (1972).

[5]The chi square is a measure of the badness of fit of the model, and the null hypothesis is that the model does fit. A low $p$ value means the probability of getting a fit that poor or poorer due to chance is low, and the hypothesis that the model fits is rejected. Alternatively, a low chi square and a $p$ value above an agreed upon level leads to accepting the hypothesis that the model fits.

**TABLE 6.7**
*Maximum Likelihood Factor Loadings and Factor Correlations Estimated by LISREL[a,b,c]*

| | Factors | | | | | | |
| Variables | General | Self method | Peer method | Teacher method | Picture method | $h^2$ | $U^2$ |
|---|---|---|---|---|---|---|---|
| Self–Help | .09 | .54 | | | | .30 | .70 |
| Self–Not cut in line | −.12 | .18 | | | | .05 | .95 |
| Self–Not say mean things | −.11 | .67 | | | | .46 | .54 |
| Self–Stick up for | .17 | .21 | | | | .07 | .93 |
| Peer–Help | −.05 | | .56 | | | .31 | .69 |
| Peer–Not cut in line | −.46 | | .80 | | | .86 | .14 |
| Peer–Not say mean things | −.22 | | .68 | | | .51 | .49 |
| Peer–Stick up for | .35 | | .21 | | | .17 | .83 |
| Teacher–Help | .61 | | | .75 | | .93 | .07 |
| Teacher–Not cut in line | −.46 | | | .43 | | .40 | .60 |
| Teacher–Not say mean things | −.55 | | | .66 | | .74 | .26 |
| Teacher–Stick up for | .19 | | | .37 | | .17 | .83 |
| Picture trial | .34 | | | | .39 | .27 | .73 |
| Picture 1 | .13 | | | | .76 | .59 | .41 |
| Picture 2 | .18 | | | | .63 | .44 | .56 |
| Picture 3 | .24 | | | | .74 | .61 | .39 |
| Picture 4 | .19 | | | | .53 | .32 | .68 |
| Picture 5 | .05 | | | | .82 | .68 | .32 |
| Picture 6 | .05 | | | | .65 | .43 | .57 |

| | General | Self method | Peer method | Teacher method | Picture method |
|---|---|---|---|---|---|
| General | 1.00 | | | | |
| Self method | 0 | 1.00 | | | |
| Peer method | 0 | .54 | 1.00 | | |
| Teacher method | 0 | .36 | .54 | 1.00 | |
| Picture method | 0 | .54 | .41 | .20 | 1.00 |

[a]$\chi^2$ (127) = 127.66.
[b]$p$ = .47.
[c]Blank entries indicate the parameter was fixed at 0.

summed physical and verbal aggression, perhaps for the same reason. Yarrow and Waxler (1976) actually controlled for level of casual social interaction, which caused the correlation between girls' frequency of sharing/comforting and aggression to drop to nonsignificance. F. Strayer, Wareing, and Rushton (1979) observed that "empathic" behaviors of looking at, approaching, and/or comforting were consistently negatively related to helping and cooperating, although nonsignificantly. The evidence for the association among prosocial and aggressive behavior and activity level may account for these negative correlations. The empathic activities of approaching and looking (comforting never occurred) are much less active than the prosocial activities. Hence, the empathic children may interact little with the other children, giving them low scores on prosocial behavior. Measures of aggression and activity level are rarely included in studies of older children's prosocial behavior. An exception is Barrett and Yarrow (1977) who found that prosocial behavior was related to assertiveness among 5–10-year-olds who scored high on giving accurate explanations for a change in characters' behavior.

Although the relationship between considerateness as measured in the study presented here and activity level, assertiveness, or aggressiveness may not be simple, we see that inclusion of relevant measures would have aided in the interpretation of the findings. Results from some additional analyses, presented later, further support the notion that a value of considerateness is best understood in the context of other variables.

## Considerateness and Obedience to Authority

Returning to the results of the first factor analysis shown in Table 6.7, the nature of the general factor is difficult to interpret in the traditional sense, given its negative loadings and that it is not calculated prior to the group factors. However, the inclusion of this general factor definitely provided a better fit to the data. A model with just four correlated group factors, without the general factor, was estimated and the fit was significantly worse. Therefore, a principal components analysis was done on the 19 indicators with the hope of obtaining more evidence for the nature of the relationship among the items. Characteristic of the method, the first principal component is actually extracted first (rather than simultaneously as in the LISREL model) and is expected to have all positive loadings. The solution is shown in Table 6.8, where it is seen that the first principal component does have all positive loadings, with the picture items having the highest. As in the LISREL model, the distinctive quality of the negatively worded items—"not cut in line" and "not say mean things"—shows up. The highest loadings on the second principal component are for "not cut in line" and "not say mean things" in the peer and teacher groups (.69, .57, and .59, .75). The corresponding self items are the highest in their group (.21, .25). This second component was called "considerate by default," based on the hypothesis that certain forms of considerate behavior may be motivated partly by a desire not to annoy other children or to avoid unpleasant peer interactions, behaviors that would be consistent with the general idea of a lower activity level.

Considerateness by default could also be motivated by obedience to authority. Not cutting in line and not saying mean things refer to common school behavior. It is likely that teachers admonish children not to cut in line or say mean things more often than directing them to help out other children who cannot do something or to stick up for another child being made fun of. Evidence for the effect of obedience to

**TABLE 6.8**
*Principal Components of the 19 Indicators*

| Variables | Components | | | | | $h^2$ | $U^2$ |
|---|---|---|---|---|---|---|---|
| | 1 | 2 | 3 | 4 | 5 | | |
| Self–Help | .42 | .12 | .22 | .28 | .45 | .52 | .48 |
| Self–Not cut in line | .06 | .21 | .12 | .56 | .29 | .46 | .54 |
| Self–Not say mean things | .48 | .25 | −.17 | .35 | .27 | .52 | .48 |
| Self–Stick up for | .26 | −.21 | .20 | .01 | .51 | .41 | .59 |
| Peer–Help | .31 | .50 | .41 | .18 | −.40 | .70 | .30 |
| Peer–Not cut in line | .47 | .69 | −.03 | .06 | −.19 | .75 | .25 |
| Peer–Not say mean things | .47 | .57 | .00 | .04 | −.22 | .60 | .40 |
| Peer–Stick up for | .18 | −.21 | .66 | .24 | −.10 | .58 | .42 |
| Teacher–Help | .42 | −.00 | .56 | −.33 | .16 | .63 | .37 |
| Teacher–Not cut in line | .14 | .59 | −.29 | −.45 | .25 | .71 | .29 |
| Teacher–Not say mean things | .23 | .75 | −.06 | −.17 | .20 | .69 | .31 |
| Teacher–Stick up for | .23 | .11 | .51 | −.46 | −.02 | .53 | .46 |
| Picture trial | .47 | −.36 | .23 | −.10 | −.09 | .42 | .58 |
| Picture 1 | .74 | −.21 | −.15 | .07 | −.20 | .66 | .34 |
| Picture 2 | .66 | −.26 | −.11 | .02 | −.07 | .52 | .48 |
| Picture 3 | .71 | −.39 | −.22 | −.02 | .04 | .71 | .29 |
| Picture 4 | .59 | −.26 | −.07 | −.38 | .15 | .59 | .41 |
| Picture 5 | .80 | −.13 | −.16 | .12 | −.15 | .72 | .28 |
| Picture 6 | .64 | −.15 | −.31 | .01 | −.06 | .54 | .46 |

authority is provided by Staub (1971). Seventh-grade girls working on a task were (*a*) told they could go into another room; (*b*) given no information; or (*c*) told not to enter. Those given permission to enter did so, in response to cries from a same-aged girl, significantly more often than the other two groups, which did not differ. Additional evidence comes from the self-choice ratings. Although considerate behavior was the most preferred of the available four groups, pretesting showed that obedience to authority behaviors were even more preferred.

### Considerateness and Friendship

The reverse pattern occurred on the third principal component. The highest loadings were for the ''peer'' and ''teacher'' items of ''help out other kids who can't do something'' and ''stick up for another boy or girl kids make fun of'' (.41, .66 and .56, .51). The self-choice ''help out'' and ''stick up for'' were the highest ones in the self group (.22, .20). This third component may tap group or clique membership. The experimenters' impression was that groups of friends would stick up for each other, and they may also help each other more than nonfriends, making reciprocity a key element. This clique membership would be apparent to teachers as well as peers, and self-choice of these active behaviors could indicate a desire to be part of a group.

Although the notion that considerateness is partly motivated by friendship is speculative, it seems a reasonable source of hypotheses, given recent literature on the nature of children's friendships. Much research on children's friendships grows out of cognitive-developmental theory, and investigators attend to changes in children's conceptions of friendship with age. Damon (1977) reviews his own work and that of Youniss (1975) and Selman (1976), all of whom identified progressive levels in children's conceptions through interviewing them. Although they emphasize different aspects, reciprocity is a core concept. Youniss describes 6-year-olds as defining friendship in terms of sharing thoughts and feelings. These ideas were also present in their conceptions of kindness. For 6-year-olds, sharing material goods was kind, and for 10-year-olds helping out someone in need was kind. Selman views emerging conceptions of friendship as driven by advances in social perspective-taking skills, thus the 8–12-year-olds' view that friends help out each other stems from their understanding that each party is evaluating the others' actions. Damon describes three levels of 5–13-year-olds' conceptions of friendship. The youngest children emphasize sharing and playing together as the basis of friendship, without a sense that people are liked for their stable personality characteristics. Children in middle childhood stress helping and being considerate as important criteria for friends. Each party is expected to act in the other's interest, and this "niceness" is seen as a stable characteristic across activities. The oldest children stress psychological aspects of helping, such as comforting, and that friends understand each other. Other researchers who apply cognitive–developmental theory to children's conceptions of friendship expect to find an increase in the number and complexity of the concepts used to describe friends with age, and Mannarino (1980) describes some of this work.

Little research exists on elementary schoolers' spontaneous prosocial behavior towards friends versus nonfriends. Rather, correlates of children's popularity, a conceptually distinct notion (Mannarino, 1980), have received much more attention. The effects of friendship on standardized sharing tasks has been studied, and Berndt (1981) reports that these results are equivocal. In his own work, Berndt found that only boys distinguished between friends and acquaintances but shared more with acquaintances. He attributed this to greater competition among friends, given that the task was designed to be competitive (i.e., sharing the crayon meant less time coloring and getting less reward). Although Berndt's methodology distinguished between friends and acquaintances better than most previous work, the competitive sharing task is problematic for our purpose of studying considerateness in the context of preference and salience.

Most research in the area of prosocial behavior and friendship has involved observations of nursery school children, and considerable evidence exists for reciprocity, meaning that children usually receive the amount and kind of responses from peers that they initiate. However, the questions of whether the reciprocating children form stable groups and whether the group members are friends have not been as fully investigated. F. Strayer (1980) did find that preschoolers were altruistic to the children they sought proximity to (affiliative behavior). Although the affiliative bonds of preschoolers may be equivalent to their friendship bonds, the same may not be true for grade-school children, for whom maintaining visual contact does not appear to be a necessary criterion for friendship, based on the cognitive-development literature. Also, Foot, Chapman, and Smith (1980) note that some studies have found children's selections of "best friends" do not correspond to whom they interact with the most.

Methodological and conceptual problems regarding the measurement of friends and everyday prosocial behavior make the limited evidence difficult to interpret. It seems warranted, though, to hypothesize that the consistent patterning of the positively and negatively worded "considerate" items in the research reported here is in part reflecting a distinction between considerateness resulting from active involvement with friends versus considerateness as a result of other motivations, such as obedience or shyness.

## Gender Differences

Despite common stereotypes of differences between boys' and girls' prosocial behavior and correlates, observational studies of preschoolers rarely show gender differences in the frequency of prosocial behavior. In standardized tasks, few differences are reported on donation tasks; girls occasionally score higher on generosity ones but often not significantly (Bryan, 1975; Krebs, 1970; Rushton, 1980; Staub, 1978, 1979). On standardized helping tasks, girls sometimes help more, but these differences change with varying experimental conditions. Girls consistently but unreliably make more precise matches on affect-matching measures of empathy but are not usually more skilled in recognizing or understanding the reasons for others' emotions (Hoffman, 1977).

Given this background, the gender differences found in the research reported here were not expected; girls scored significantly higher on 11 of the 19 indicators. Beginning with the pictures, they talked about more distress-related themes on Pictures 1, 2, 3, 5, and 6. Unlike previous empathy measures, the pictures were designed to measure the salience and concern with others' distress given a variety of competing stimuli. Although cognitive and affective aspects are involved, accuracy is not relevant.

Girls' greater sensitivity may be explained in terms of modeling and identification from a social learning perspective. Controversy in the area of the social learning of, for example, aggressive behavior, concerns how early children selectively observe same-sex models and use this information to monitor their own sex-appropriate behavior (Maccoby & Jacklin, 1980; Tieger, 1980). However, by the time girls are 8 years old, the youngest age of the participants in this study, they have observed mothers and fathers for a long time in a natural setting. On the assumption that mothers model nurturance and awareness of others' needs more than fathers do and that girls identify more with their mothers than with their fathers, it follows that girls would learn to be more sensitive to others' distress than boys. They are probably not only observing more of this behavior in a same-sex model but are actively socialized to be aware of others' needs by being given more child-care responsibilities than boys. This is particularly relevant since the pictures all involved a child in distress.

Concerning the "help," "not cut in line," "not say mean things," and "stick up for" items, again the second and third were distinguished from the first and last. Girls scored higher on five of the six negatively worded ones—"self–not say mean things," "peer–not cut in line," "peer–not say mean things," and "teacher–not say mean things." Hence, girls are higher on the "considerate by default" component, perhaps motivated by obedience to authority. No gender differences were found on the active "help" and "stick up for" items, supporting the idea that a general activity factor can be further refined by the considerate by default and friendship components. Perhaps girls avoid cutting in line and saying mean things to avoid trouble with teachers and peers but are as likely as boys to support their friends.

## DISCUSSION

The intention of the research presented in this chapter was to step back and begin to explore children's interest and concern with considerateness, rather than continuing to investigate prosocial behavior without cognizance of its importance to children. This importance was explored in two ways. First, considerate behavior was found to be preferred to other socially approved behavior, within the limited range of value categories used in this first attempt. Second, characters undergoing distress were noticed as important events amid competing activities in their respective pictures. Although we can not quantitatively compare the salience of these distress-related events to the salience of alternative ones, as done in the preference measure, the two measures lend validity to the concepts of preference and salience in terms of their moderate correlation. Further evidence for the preference of considerate behavior would be obtained by using pictures that included both distress-related themes and themes from other value categories. This would be extremely difficult, however, since the stimulus configurations would have to differ only in the salience of the themes being compared and not in nontheme stimuli (e.g., colors, style of pictures). A more viable approach to further validating the notions of preference and salience would be to replicate the association between the preference measure and picture measure of sensitivity to distress for another value category, such as obedience to authority. Although not designed to, the pictures also elicited obedience themes, which could be correlated with preference measures. Preference for obedience proved so strong, however, that other more attractive competing statements would have to be included. Of course, new pictures could be selected that depicted other themes.

The preference and salience measures were correlated more highly with each other than either was with reputation for considerate behavior, as judged by teachers or peers. However, all of these performances are legitimately thought of as being aspects of a value of considerateness, the construct proposed to underlie performance on this wide variety of tasks.

The coherent results from the factor analyses and gender differences led to the hypothesis that this value is better thought of as multiply motivated, itself the result of other goals. This idea comes from the pattern of factor loadings across three sets of parallel items with equivalent contents but measured by different methods. The two items describing the active behaviors of helping other kids and sticking up for another boy or girl fell together on a separate principal component from the items of not cutting in line and not saying mean things, behaviors that are considerate by the absence of or refraining from doing something. Further evidence for the distinctiveness of these two types of considerate behavior came from the confirmatory factor analysis in which the active behaviors had positive loadings on the general factor and the less active behaviors had negative loadings on it. Taken together, a picture emerged of considerateness being motivated in part by general activeness and/or assertiveness. This influence was further refined by the idea that the active items may be indicating behavior among friends and the passive items may be indicating obedience to authority.

It is emphasized that these results concerning the nature of the value of considerateness were unexpected. However, they are consistent with previous research showing the distinctions among different forms of considerateness. Hampson (1979), Payne (1980), and Suda and Fouts (1980) found that desire for approval and extroversion seem to differentiate types of prosocial behavior, consistent with the hypotheses concerning assertiveness and obedience to authority previously discussed. In fact, prosocial behavior in most standardized situations often unexpectedly changes as a result of seemingly minor modifications in the experimental procedure (e.g., Green & Schneider, 1974; O'Bryant & Brophy, 1976; Rubin & Schneider, 1973; Staub, 1979). These unplanned effects can be retrospectively interpreted partly in terms of other motivations.

The influence of other motivations on considerate behavior and the role of salience could be experimentally tested, as Staub (1978, 1979) would advocate. The value of considerateness and, for example, assertiveness, could be regarded as person variables in a paradigm that tested for person–situation interactions. Children with different patterns of high and low scores on considerateness and assertiveness could be placed in situations in which an opportunity to be considerate or assertive first had to be noticed, thus applying the salience notion to a behavioral situation and further testing its status as a cognitive and affective, rather than behavioral, aspect of considerateness. Children high on considerateness but low on assertiveness, for example, would be predicted to notice opportunities but not respond. Research along these lines may aid in understanding the role of what is noticed in acting considerately and help account for the lack of association among behavioral and nonbehavioral variables.

This attention to salience as a previously unexplored aspect of considerateness is not intended to negate the value of previous work but rather to promote its inclusion into studies using more typical measures. Learning more about salience is unlikely to directly facilitate enhancement of prosocial behavior, but it seems to be an important element of a value of considerateness and worthy of further exploration. Perhaps salience could be incorporated into studies that use modeling techniques to induce observational learning of prosocial behavior. It is possible that modeling, or otherwise training children to notice opportunities to be considerate, may have longer term payoff with respect to generalizability to situations in which a mentor is not present. The importance of including salience and preference in studies of prosocial behavior will be confirmed only by doing such research. The evidence presented in this chapter suggests that studying more about children's interest and concern with this issue, in conjunction with other motivators, may lend coherence to the literature and provide insights on how to intervene in promoting prosocial behavior.

## ACKNOWLEDGMENTS

This chapter is based on dissertation research, and I gratefully acknowledge the advice and assistance of my thesis adviser, John S. Harding. I also thank Sharon Nelson-LeGall and Margaret S. Clark for their careful reading of the chapter manuscript and cogent criticisms.

## REFERENCES

Bar-Tal, D., & Raviv, A. Consistency of helping-behavior measures. *Child Development,* 1979, *50,* 1235–1238.

Barrett, D., & Yarrow, M. Prosocial behavior, social inferential ability, and assertiveness in children. *Child Development,* 1977, *48,* 475–481.

Bell, G. *Wanted . . . A Brother.* Nashville, Tenn.: Abingdon, 1959.

Berndt, T. J. Effects of friendship on prosocial intentions and behavior. *Child Development,* 1981, *52,* 636–643.

Bryan, J. H. Children's cooperation and helping behaviors. In E. M. Hetherington (Ed.), *Review of child development research* (Vol. 5). Chicago: University of Chicago Press, 1975.

Campbell, D. T., & Fiske, D. W. Convergent and discriminant validation by the multitrait–multimethod matrix. In G. Summers (Ed.), *Attitude measurement.* Chicago: Rand McNally, 1970.

Damon, W. *The social world of the child.* San Francisco: Jossey–Bass, 1977.

DeRegniers, B. S. *The snow party.* New York: Pantheon Books, 1959.

Dlugokinski, E. L., & Firestone, I. J. Congruence among four methods of measuring other-centeredness. *Child Development,* 1973, *44,* 304–308.

Dlugokinski, E. L., & Firestone, I. J. Other-centeredness and susceptibility to charitable appeals: Effects of perceived discipline. *Developmental Psychology,* 1974, *10,* 21–28.

Eisenberg-Berg, N., & Hand, M. The relationship of preschoolers' reasoning about prosocial moral conflicts to prosocial behavior. *Child Development,* 1979, *50,* 356–363.

Eisenberg-Berg, N., & Lennon, R. Altruism and the assessment of empathy in the preschool years. *Child Development*, 1980, *51*, 552–557.

Feshbach, N., & Roe, K. Empathy in six- and seven-year-olds. *Child Development*, 1968, *39*, 133–145.

Foot, H., Chapman, A., & Smith, J. *Friendship and social relations in children*. New York: Wiley, 1980.

Friedrich, L. K., & Stein, A. H. Aggressive and prosocial television programs and the natural behavior of preschool children. *Monographs of the Society for Research in Child Development*, 1973, *38* (4, Serial No. 151).

Green, F. P., & Schneider, F. W. Age differences in the behavior of boys on three measures of altruism. *Child Development*, 1974, *45*, 248–251.

Guilford, J. S. Maturation of values in young children. *Journal of Genetic Psychology*, 1974, *124*, 241–248.

Hampson, R. Peers, pathology, and helping: Some kids are more helpful than others. Paper presented at the biennial meeting of the Society for Research in Child Development, San Francisco, 1979.

Harman, H. H. *Modern factor analysis (3rd ed.)*. Chicago: University of Chicago Press, 1976.

Hartshorne, H., May, M. A., & Maller, J. B. *Studies in the nature of character* (Vol. II). *Studies in self-control*. New York: Macmillan, 1929.

Hoffman, M. L. Sex differences in moral internalization and values. *Journal of Personality and Social Psychology*, 1975, *32*, 720–729.

Hoffman, M. L. Sex differences in empathy and related behaviors. *Psychological Bulletin*, 1977, *84*, 712–722.

Hoffman, M. L., & Saltzstein, H. D. Parent discipline and the child's moral development. *Journal of Personality and Social Psychology*, 1967, *5*, 45–57.

Joreskog, K. A general approach to confirmatory maximum likelihood factor analysis. *Psychometrika*, 1969, *34*, 183–202.

Joreskog, K., & Sorbom, D. *LISREL IV—Estimation of linear structural equation systems by maximum likelihood methods*. Chicago: National Educational Resources, 1978.

Kenny, D. A. *Correlation and causality*. New York: Wiley, 1979.

Kluckhohn, C. Values and value-orientations in the theory of action: An exploration in definition and classification. In T. Parsons & E. Shils (Eds.), *Toward a general theory of action*. Cambridge: Harvard University Press, 1951.

Krebs, D. L. Altruism—an examination of the concept and a review of the literature. *Psychological Bulletin*, 1970, *73*, 258–302.

Long, J. S. Estimation and hypothesis testing in linear models containing measurement error. *Sociological Methods and Research*, 1976, *5*, 157–206.

Maccoby, E. E., & Jacklin, C. N. Sex differences in aggression: A rejoinder and reprise. *Child Development*, 1980, *51*, 964–980.

Mannarino, A. P. The development of children's friendships. In H. Foot, A. Chapman, & J. Smith (Eds.), *Friendship and social relations in children*. New York: Wiley, 1980.

Mulaik, S. A. *The foundations of factor analysis*. New York: McGraw–Hill, 1972.

Murphy, L. B. *Social behavior and child personality*. New York: Columbia University Press, 1937.

Mussen, P. H., & Eisenberg-Berg, N. *Roots of caring, sharing, and helping*. San Francisco: Freeman, 1977.

O'Bryant, S. L., & Brophy, J. E. Sex differences in altruistic behavior. *Developmental Psychology*, 1976, *12*, 554.

Payne, F. D. Children's prosocial conduct in structured situations and as viewed by others: Consistency, convergence, and relationships with person variables. *Child Development*, 1980, *51*, 1252–1259.

Rubin, K. H., & Schneider, F. W. The relationship between moral judgment, egocentrism, and altruistic behavior. *Child Development*, 1973, *44*, 661–665.

Rushton, J. P. *Altruism, socialization, and society*. Englewood Cliffs, N. J.: Prentice–Hall, 1980.

Rutherford, E., & Mussen, P. Generosity in nursery school boys. *Child Development*, 1968, *39*, 755–765.

Schwartz, S. H. Normative influences on altruism. In L. Berkowitz (Ed.), *Advances in experimental social psychology* (Vol. 10). New York: Academic Press, 1977.

Selman, R. The development of interpersonal reasoning. In A. Pick (Ed.), *Minnesota symposia on child psychology* (Vol. 10). Minneapolis: University of Minnesota Press, 1976.

Severy, L. J., & Davis, K. E. Helping behavior among normal and retarded children. *Child Development*, 1971, *42*, 1017–1031.

Staub, E. Helping a person in distress: The influence of implicit and explicit "rules" of conduct on children and adults. *Journal of Personality and Social Psychology*, 1971, *17*, 137–145.

Staub, E. *Positive social behavior and morality* (Vol. 1). *Social and personal influences*. New York: Academic Press, 1978.

Staub, E. *Positive social behavior and morality* (Vol. 2). *Socialization and development*. New York: Academic Press, 1979.

Strayer, F. F. Child ethology and the study of preschool social relations. In H. Foot, A. Chapman, & J. Smith (Eds.), *Friendship and social relations in children*. New York: Wiley, 1980.

Strayer, F. F., Wareing, S., & Rushton, J. P. Social constraints on naturally occurring preschool altruism. *Ethology and Sociobiology*, 1979, *1*, 3–11.

Strayer, J. A naturalistic study of empathic behaviors and their relation to affective states and perspective-taking skills in preschool children. *Child Development*, 1980, *51*, 815–822.

Suda, W., & Fouts, G. Effects of peer presence on helping in introverted and extroverted children. *Child Development*, 1980, *51*, 1272–1275.

Tieger, T. On the biological basis of sex differences in aggression. *Child Development*, 1980, *51*, 943–963.

Yarrow, M. R., & Waxler, C. Z. Dimensions and correlates of prosocial behavior in young children. *Child Development*, 1976, *47*, 118–125.

Youniss, J. Another perspective on social cognition. In A. Pick (Ed.), *Minnesota symposia on child psychology* (Vol. 9). Minneapolis: University of Minnesota Press, 1975.

# Differentiation of Domains and Prosocial Behavior

**JUDITH G. SMETANA, DIANE L. BRIDGEMAN, and ELLIOT TURIEL**

Over the past 20 years, developmental psychologists have become increasingly concerned with a realm termed *prosocial*. This interest has taken two forms: Some have been concerned with prosocial behavior and more recently, others, with prosocial reasoning. Developmentalists' interest in this area was preceded by a large body of social–psychological research on the personality and situational determinants of prosocial or altruistic behaviors. The terms *prosocial* and *altruistic,* often used interchangeably, have been applied to a wide range of behaviors that are presumed to have positive effects on others.

In many instances the social–psychological paradigms have been used in research with children. In keeping with a general trend toward developmental psychologists' greater concern with the cognitive aspects of social development, some have attempted to analyze judgments regarding prosocial behavior. This chapter is primarily concerned with social cognitive analyses as they are applied to concepts of prosocial behavior or altruism. Our aim is to raise a series of questions about the epistemological bases of such social cognitive analyses in an effort to delineate the parameters of the category. Research is reported in which attempts were made to determine the domains of social knowledge that children apply to judgments about what have been referred to as *prosocial behaviors*. Our analysis begins with a look at the types of issues and events typically used in research on prosocial behavior.

## STUDIES OF PROSOCIAL BEHAVIOR

A representative definition of altruism was provided by Macauly and Berkowitz (1970), who stated that it is "behavior that is carried out to benefit another without

163

anticipation of rewards from external sources [p. 73]." Consistent with this general definition, Latané and Darley (1970) began their volume *The Unresponsive Bystander: Why Doesn't He Help?* with descriptions of three actual events, occurring in the late 1960s, that received a good deal of publicity in the public media:

> Kitty Genovese is set upon by a maniac as she returns hom from work at 3 A.M. Thirty-eight of her neighbors in Kew Gardens come to their windows when she cries out in terror; none come to her assistance even though her stalker takes over half an hour to murder her. No one even so much as calls the police. She dies.

> Andrew Mormille is stabbed in the stomach as he rides the A train home in Manhattan. Eleven other riders watch the 17-year-old boy as he bleeds to death; none come to his assistance even though his attackers have left the car. He dies.

> An 18-year-old switchboard operator, alone in her office in the Bronx, is raped and beaten. Escaping momentarily, she runs naked and bleeding to the street, screaming for help. A crowd of 40 passersby gathers and watches as, in broad daylight, the rapist tries to drag her back upstairs; no one interferes. Finally, two policeman happen by and arrest her assailant [pp. 1–2].

Of course, the most striking aspect of each event is that people failed to help individuals who were being physically attacked and in danger of being killed. Because of the extremity of these incidents—two actually did result in death—they received widespread publicity and became models for research by Latané and Darley and others. Undoubtedly, the publicity and the research concerns stemmed from the view that the bystanders, the witnesses to the event, had an obligation to act in an attempt to prevent physical harm or death from befalling another person— especially when they would not be risking harm to themselves, as in the first two incidents.

The reason one might think that the bystanders had an obligation to help is that the event itself—one person harming another—is generally considered a moral transgression. Indeed, the second striking feature of the incidents is that they involved one person causing great harm to another. Even in the absence of unresponsive bystanders, such incidents do not go unnoticed by the media or the legal authorities. Accordingly, each of the incidents highlighted by Latané and Darley has two components: one person harming another and person or persons failing to help ("Why doesn't he help?"). All this is obvious. The purpose of explicitly drawing a distinction between the two components is to point out that in these cases "helping" is within the particular context of preventing harm to another. Helping, of course, can pertain to other contexts. The possibility exists, therefore, that in some other contexts helping may not entail a moral obligation.

As an example, suppose that an individual who inherits a substantial amount of money is aware of someone who would like some of that money to go on a vacation. Should the inheritance be shared in that circumstance? Is there a moral obligation to do so? Or suppose that one person gives an expensive present to a friend. Would that form of prosocial behavior be of the same type as helping another in distress? Conversely, suppose that the murderer of Kitty Genovese had requested a bystander to aid him in the deed. Helping in that case would not have the same meaning as what Latané and Darley had in mind. The moral obligation to help in the emergency situations just described does not necessarily apply to all situations in which a person desires or requests help from others. The same sorts of differentiations could be relevant to several classes of prosocial or altruistic behaviors that have been the object of research: generosity, sharing, cooperating, showing sympathy or concern. In turn, such differentiations are applicable to the general terms of prosocial or altruism themselves. A similar point has been made by Krebs (1978), who cogently argued for the importance of examining the meanings individuals attribute to prosocial situations, rather than focusing solely on behavior and its situational determinants.

The point can be illustrated through examples of the variety of events used in research on prosocial behavior with adults or children. Latané and Darley reported a series of studies that included both nonemergency and emergency situations. In the nonemergency situations assessments were made of people's responsiveness to requests for one's name, directions, and small amounts of money. In the emergency situations the assessments were of responsiveness to another person's accident, to one child beating another, to a person who has an epileptic seizure, as well as whether or not a witnessed theft is reported. Examples of events used in other studies (see Krebs, 1970, for a review) include: donating to charity; volunteering to give blood; willingness to collect for charity; stopping on the road to help fix a tire; donating for a gift; returning a lost wallet; expressing sympathy; and cooperating in a game. In research with children, events have included: helping a person in distress; helping an adult pick up paper clips; donating money earned in the experiment to charity; willingness to visit other children who had been hospitalized or writing letters to them; and sharing marbles.

All these behaviors have been placed under the same rubric for two reasons. The first stems from theoretical propositions regarding social (including moral) behaviors. Socialization models, including behavioristic, social-learning and psychoanalytic ones, have assumed that social development entails the transformation of an initially self-interested, instinctually bound or need-oriented child into one with increased self-control and greater concern for others. Accordingly, a dichotomy is established between self-interest and other-interest, with corresponding measures of the extent to which behaviors are self-interested or altruistic. A second reason all the fore-mentioned behaviors have been placed under the same rubric stems from efforts to operationalize the self-interest–altruism dichotomy. Empirically, the concept of altruism has been defined as behaviors that benefit others (i.e., any forms of helping or giving). For the most part, the provision that the behavior is carried out without anticipation of rewards from external sources has been much more difficult to operationalize and is left unaddressed in research.

We suggest that the operationalization of altruism through behaviors that benefit others glosses over possible differences in other aspects of the motivations and evaluations of the behaviors—that is, the examples we contrasted with events like the one involving Kitty Genovese point to the possibility that prosocial behaviors do not stem from a unitary source. Research findings also indicate that behaviors fitting operational definitions of prosocial or altruism may reflect more than one type of behavior. Studies have shown that situational variables and personality traits account for no more than 10% of the variance in prosocial responses (Sarason, Smith, & Diener, 1975). Furthermore, experimental and naturalistic studies with children also point to the multifaceted nature of prosocial behaviors. For instance, Payne (1980) examined fourth- and sixth-grade children's responses to experimental prosocial situations. These included donating goods to strangers, donating services to strangers, and cooperating with a classmate. Correlations between responses to the various behaviors were moderate to low. Behaviors clustered into two components: donating goods and services and helping; and sharing and cooperating. Similar findings were reported by Radke-Yarrow and Zahn-Waxler (1976). Employing both naturalistic observations and experimentally manipulated situations, they found that both sharing and comforting were moderately correlated (.32) but that neither was related to helping ($r = -.13, .10$, respectively).

One means of examining possible distinctions between different types of prosocial behaviors would be to consider their underlying conceptual justifications. It may be that different kinds of judgments are made about different types of prosocial behaviors. If so, social development would be viewed not as the acquisition of control over needs and self-interest but as entailing the formation of systems of knowledge about social interactions.

## THE DEVELOPMENT OF SOCIAL JUDGMENTS

As mentioned earlier, developmental psychologists have recently become increasingly concerned with the relations between social cognition and behaviors operationalized as prosocial or altruistic. Typically, the focus has been on the development of moral judgments. In a number of studies, the usual altruistic behaviors (helping another in distress, sharing, cooperation, etc.) have been correlated with measures of the development of moral judgments, such as those of Piaget (1932/1948) and Kohlberg (1969). Generally, the aim of these studies is to determine whether the child's developmental level or stage of moral judgment is predictive of behavior (see Blasi, 1980, for a comprehensive review). The underlying assumption of the studies, that altruistic behaviors would be associated with more advanced levels of moral judgment development, has been supported (Blasi, 1980). However, since these findings are based on correlational methods, the evidence for the hypothesized causal relation between moral judgment and prosocial acts is inconclusive. As the tendency to respond prosocially has been found to be highly related to age (Bryan, 1975; Krebs, 1970; Staub, 1975), correlations between the two measures may reflect age effects rather than the effect of development in moral judgments.

A different approach to the study of the conceptual basis of altruism is taken by Krebs (1978). He has argued for the importance of directly assessing the organization or patterns of thinking about altruism. Krebs proposed that: (*a*) altruism is one of several components of moral reasoning; (*b*) children's reasoning about altruism is consistent with their patterns of reasoning about moral issues in general; and (*c*) developmentally, the meaning and significance of altruism would change in conjunction with changes in the organization of moral judgments. Accordingly, Krebs proposed correspondences between the development of altruistic thinking and the sequence of moral judgment stages proposed by Kohlberg (1969, 1971). In this way, Krebs (1978) provides descriptions of qualitative differences in conceptions of altruism: "The quantity of helping would not necessarily increase at each stage. However, . . . the quality of helping should improve at each stage. It should become more exactly attuned to the needs, rights, and duties of individuals as they relate to the needs, rights, and duties of other individuals in the social order [p. 157]."

Two assumptions are made by Krebs and others. One is that altruistic behaviors are related to the organization of moral judgments. The second assumption, which follows from the first, is that developmental changes occur in concepts of altruism insofar as the organization of moral thinking undergoes developmental transformations. We are in agreement with the view that altruistic or prosocial behaviors can and often do entail moral judgments. The types of real emergency situations described by Latané and Darley (as well as in some experimental conditions) do involve moral obligations, since the witnesses were observing a moral transgression (to put it mildly). However, as indicated earlier, there are forms of helping or other ways of acting to benefit others that are not clearly situations that could be classified in the moral domain. If this is correct, prosocial behavior is not synonymous with moral behavior; all prosocial behaviors are not moral behaviors. The question as to whether all moral behaviors are prosocial is a more complex one whose answer depends on how far one stretches the meaning of the word *prosocial*. For instance, antisocial behavior can clearly bear on moral considerations (e.g., the killing of Kitty Genovese). However, the moral concern for the welfare of the victim of an antisocial act does have "prosocial" connotations. Moreover, as is discussed shortly, there are acts that may be regarded as antisocial, but which are regarded as such for nonmoral reasons (i.e., transgressions of social conventions).

It appears to us that further definition and classification of the conceptual underpinnings of prosocial actions is required. As with any effort to study the acquisition or development of knowledge, it is necessary to consider the nature of the system of knowledge (cf. Chomsky, 1979; Piaget, 1970). The shift from the exclusive reliance on behavioral analyses in this realm to the study of judgment brings with it a series of epistemological questions. In the first place, it is not necessarily the case that the specific set of actions used in behavioral analyses, such as helping, cooperating, or sharing, constitute the most appropriate units of analysis for social cognitive research. Although the term *prosocial* matches a set of operational behaviors, it may not match a category of social judgment. At least implicit in some of the social cognitive research is the idea that prosocial judgments are an important class of moral judgments. However, further discriminations would be helpful in this regard.

If prosocial behaviors are not to be entirely subsumed under the moral category and if there is not a straightforward distinction between prosocial and antisocial acts or judgments, then a multiplicative classification system is required. Both prosocial and antisocial actions can be subsumed under more general classes of moral and nonmoral judgments.

For instance, coming to the aid of another person to save a life or sharing to relieve suffering or even to achieve an equitable distribution of resources are acts to which most individuals may apply moral judgments. Other forms of helping and giving may be regarded as personal choices. To say that one has an obligation or duty to help or to share is a different kind of judgment from that entailed in statements that it is desirable or merely positive to help or share (Dworkin, 1978). In empirical research, a variety of different sharing behaviors have been used as indices of prosocial actions. Studies of sharing have varied as to whether the recipient was described as in need (e.g., Emler & Rushton, 1974; Rubin & Schneider, 1973) or not (Dreman, 1976; Dreman & Greenbaum, 1973; Wright, 1942a, 1942b). Whereas the former set of situations may more clearly entail justice and welfare concerns, the latter circumstances, usually referred to as examples of generosity, may not. Similarly, situations in which respondents are asked to donate or share their own possessions, as in the previous examples, may be judged differently from situations in which respondents are asked to share or distribute limited or public resources (e.g., Damon, 1977).

These findings can be understood within the context of recent research on distinctions between domains of social–cognitive development. Three domains, the moral, social–conventional, and personal, have been identified as part of children's structuring of the social world. Moral concepts, or concepts of harm, rights, or fairness, are constructed from interactions involving psychological harm or benefit to another, trust, responsibility, and the scarce distribution of resources. Moral judgments entail prescriptive judgments about how people ought to behave towards others (Turiel, 1983, in press). These develop through an awareness of the factors intrinsic to actions, such as the violation of rights, the harm inflicted upon others, or the effects of actions upon others' welfare. From this perspective, prosocial events within the moral domain would include those that pertain to fairness and the rights or welfare of others.

Moral events can be distinguished from social conventions. *Social conventions* refer to the behavioral uniformities that serve to coordinate social interactions and maintain social systems. They are generated through an understanding of regularities in the environment, such as regularities in modes of address, manners, dress, sexual mores, and sex roles. Unlike moral events, social conventional events are not in themselves intrinsically prescriptive. Rather, this domain pertains to the arbitrary and consensually determined uniformities that coordinate interactions with social systems.

Finally, the personal domain pertains to actions that are perceived to be outside of societal regulation and moral purview. It has been hypothesized (Nucci, 1977, 1981) that control over personal issues is central to the establishment of the "self" in society. Societies may or may not define their control over individuals more extensively than individuals might prefer. Through the consideration of an action, event, or issue as a personal matter, the individual places that event under his or her own authority. Personal issues are organized around concepts of the actor as an autonomous individual and issues related to the maintenance of the self. This includes actions that are perceived to pertain only to individuals and to be of minor consequence to others. Positive social acts may lack the prescriptive or obligatory nature of moral events or the social regulatory or organizational function of social–conventional events. These events, although perhaps considered "nice" or "good," would also be regarded as discretionary behaviors (for example, giving an expensive present to a friend). These events may be considered within the personal domain.

Although concepts in each domain have been found to be transformed with increasing age, the ability to distinguish between domains is not. Research indicates that from a young age children consider moral rules more important and moral transgressions more serious offenses than social conventional rules and trangressions (Nucci, 1981; Smetana, 1981a, 1981b; Turiel, 1978; Weston & Turiel, 1980). More importantly, the research also shows that children apply different criteria to each domain; they evaluate social conventional events as relative to the social context and contingent upon the presence of rules and authority dictates, whereas moral events are not (Nucci, 1981; Smetana, 1981a; Turiel, 1978; Weston & Turiel, 1980). Finally, it has been found that different actions are associated with events in the two domains (Nucci & Nucci, 1982a,b; Nucci & Turiel, 1978; Smetana, 1983).

These studies also point to ambiguities in the distinction between constraint-oriented or antisocial events and prosocial events. All constraint-oriented events are not treated alike in that children do distinguish between constraint-oriented moral and nonmoral events. If the same distinctions apply to positive social acts, then it would also be necessary to distinguish between moral and nonmoral events. Thus, a further research question concerns the conceptual similarities and differences in children's reasoning about constraint-oriented and positive events.

Consider the following examples: Both stealing a drug to save a woman's life and violating school dress codes can be considered constraint-oriented or antisocial events in that both are governed by specific rules and negative sanctions. Conversely, both sharing food with a hungry child and acknowledging a friend's birthday with a birthday card may be viewed as positive, or prosocial, events. Which events are conceptually more similar? Although stealing a drug and distributing scarce resources differ in that one is constrained by specific rules or prohibitions and the other is not, both events are structured by moral concepts. Similarly, whereas ignoring dress codes entails a transgression and sending greeting cards does not, both are regulated by social conventions or social expectations.

## DIFFERENTIATION OF DOMAINS
## IN SOCIAL JUDGMENTS

We have begun to explore the types of social knowledge that underlie positive or prosocial events—without assuming that all positive social events fall within the same category. One study, conducted by Smetana, examined the criteria used in judging transgressions and positive acts in different domains. Assessments were also made of justification in reasoning about those actions.

## Research Procedures

The subjects in this study were 62 adolescents at four grade levels. There were 15 subjects each at the fifth and eighth grades, 16 subjects in the eleventh grade, and 16 subjects who were sophomores in college. All subjects were administered two classification tasks and a measure of reasoning, which will be described.

Subjects were presented with a total of 30 pen-and-ink pictures of positive and negative events classified in the moral, social conventional, and personal domains. Five events in each of the three domains depicted positive actions, and five events in each domain depicted transgressions. The positive events classified in the moral domain were representative of actions that have been examined in previous studies of prosocial reasoning. The five items were: sharing a lunch with a child who has none; comforting a young child; helping an old person across the street; donating to charity; and returning a lost wallet. Positive social conventional actions are customary or polite acts that help to maintain the social order but are not in themselves prescriptive in that other actions could serve the same function. The five stimulus items classified as social conventional were: raising hands to answer questions in class; dressing up to go to worship; wearing a school uniform; holding a door open for someone; and celebrating holidays and birthdays by sending cards. These events were contrasted with a third set of items in the personal domain. These included: writing in the diary; getting a haircut; going to the movies; sleeping late on a weekend morning; and joining a club.

The 15 positive events were contrasted with 15 negative social events. The moral transgressions included hitting, cheating, taking someone's notebook, telling a lie, and writing in a borrowed book. Transgressions within the social conventional domain included calling a teacher by her first name in class; coming into class late; eating with fingers; not following school codes about hair length; and not lining up in the schoolyard after recess. Personal events included: watching television on a sunny day; playing with children whom others do not like; not wanting to play with other children in the schoolyard; playing the radio loud when alone; and having a long phone conversation.

First, subjects were presented with 10 sets of three pictures: 5 sets included positive events, one from each of the domains; 5 sets included transgressions, also one from each of the domains. For each of the 5 sets of positive events, subjects were asked to *rank* the pictures in order of their *rightness*. For each of the 5 sets of transgressions they were asked to rank them in order of their *wrongness*. After ranking each set of events, subjects were asked to provide justifications for their rankings.

Although the rankings provided relative ratings of the three types of events, a classification task, based upon a procedure employed successfully elsewhere (Nucci, 1981; Smetana, 1981b), was employed to assess the extent to which the positive and negative events were judged to be within the moral and personal domains. In previous research the criterion of rule contingency has been used as an indication of the subject's domain classification of social events. Events in the moral domain, in contrast with conventions, are judged wrong even in the absence of rules pertaining to the act. Although the previous research has dealt solely with transgressions, the rule contingency criterion was also applied here to positive social events. Thus subjects were given the entire set of 15 positive events and asked to *sort* the events that are always right whether or not they are governed by rules, laws, or social expectations. At the same time, subjects were asked to indicate the events that should be the person's own business and that are not issues of right or wrong. According to Nucci (1981), this provides an indication of events within the personal domain. An equivalent procedure was repeated for transgressions.

## Results

The results are consistent with our hypotheses. The classification tasks and justifications regarding the event rankings indicated that subjects between the ages of 10 and 20 discriminate domains of positive social events and that these correspond to distinctions made among transgressions.

First consider the rankings. Separate one-way analyses of variance for ranked data (Winer, 1971) performed on ranks collapsed across grade levels yielded a highly significant effect ($p < .001$) for domain. As Table 7.1 indicates, planned comparisons using correlated $t$ tests for rankings by domain revealed that subjects of all ages ranked positive moral items significantly more right than positive social

**TABLE 7.1**

*Mean Rankings of Positive and Negative Moral, Social–Conventional, and Personal Events by Grade*

| Moral | 5th | 8th | 11th | College | $t$ |
|---|---|---|---|---|---|
| Positive | 1.08 | 1.07 | 1.06 | 1.08 | $- .07$ |
| Negative | 1.13 | 1.05 | 1.06 | 1.04 | |
| | | | | | prosocial $= -25.67***$ |
| | | | | | transgressions $= -30.23***$ |
| *Social–conventional* | | | | | |
| Positive | 2.06 | 2.05 | 2.06 | 2.02 | $-1.13$ |
| Negative | 2.04 | 2.00 | 2.03 | 1.98 | |
| | | | | | prosocial $= -17.82***$ |
| | | | | | transgressions $= -26.51***$ |
| *Personal* | | | | | |
| Positive | 2.85 | 2.88 | 2.88 | 2.91 | 1.30 |
| Negative | 2.83 | 2.95 | 2.91 | 2.99 | |

$***p < .0001$.

conventional items ($p < .001$) and positive social conventional items significantly more right than positive personal items ($p < .001$). Across grade levels, 93% of the positive moral events were ranked most right; 82% of the social conventional events were ranked more right; and 93% of the personal events were ranked right. These results were comparable to the findings obtained for transgressions. Of all moral items, 94% were ranked as most wrong; 87% of the social conventional transgressions were ranked as less wrong; and 93% of the personal events were ranked least wrong. Thus, the rankings closely corresponded to the domain classification of the item. Moreover, analyses of variance performed on scores within each domain yielded no significant effects for age (see Table 7.1).

There were also no significant differences in the rankings assigned to positive versus negative moral, social conventional, and personal items at each grade level. All subjects consistently considered moral actions better (or worse) than social conventional actions, and social conventional actions better (or worse) than personal actions. Similar distinctions were made for both positive and negative events.

The results on rankings of events provide evidence that evaluations of right and wrong, in a quantitative sense, are based on domain and not on whether the act is positive and negative. Results from the two other assessments—justifications and the sorting task—bear on the types of judgments subjects made regarding the events presented. The results point to (a) differences in conceptualization of events in accordance with domains, and (b) similarities in conceptualization, within a domain, for positive and negative characteristics of events.

Subjects' justifications for their rankings were analyzed using a coding system developed in previous research by Nucci (1981). The coding categories formulated by Nucci correspond to the three domains examined in this study. The following justification categories are associated with the moral domain: (a) welfare (harm or benefit); (b) justice or fairness; (c) an action's categorical rightness or wrongness; (d) the moral character of the actor; and (e) the fair distribution of resources. The justification categories associated with conventions are as follows: (a) explicit rule violations or maintenance; (b) normative, (in)appropriate, or deviant acts; (c) social order; (d) politeness, courtesy, or consideration; and (e) minor or inadvertent offenses. Finally, the following justification categories pertain to the personal domain: (a) consequences that only affect the actor; (b) the person's own business; and (c) the neutral (neither right nor wrong) nature of the act.

In this study, this coding system was applied to justifications for both positive and negative events with high interjudge agreement (92% for 20% of the justifications). A summary of the frequency of types of justifications provided for positive events is in Table 7.2, whereas Table 7.3 summarizes justifications for the negative events. Analyses of variance were then performed separately on the justifications provided for moral, social conventional, and personal acts.[1]

---

[1]Separate repeated-measures analyses of variance were performed on (arcsine) transformed proportions of justifications provided within each of the three superordinate classes (moral, conventional, and personal) for both positive and negative events. For each of the analyses, grade level (fifth, eighth,

(footnote 1 continued on bottom of page 174)

**TABLE 7.2**

*Frequency (%) of Justifications Given for Rankings of Positive Events*

| Moral | Most right (moral) | | | | More right (social conventional) | | | | Right (personal) | | | |
|---|---|---|---|---|---|---|---|---|---|---|---|---|
| | 5th | 8th | 11th | College | 5th | 8th | 11th | College | 5th | 8th | 11th | College |
| 1. Welfare (benefit) | 40 | 40.4 | 39.4 | 58.3 | 4.3 | 3.8 | 3.8 | — | — | 2.0 | — | — |
| 2. Just act | 15.6 | 8.8 | 23.5 | 20.8 | 4.3 | 3.8 | — | 3.9 | — | 2.0 | — | — |
| 3. Moral character of actor | 4.4 | 8.8 | 5.9 | 2.1 | — | — | — | — | — | — | — | — |
| Subtotal | 60.0 | 58.0 | 68.8 | 81.2 | 8.3 | 7.6 | 3.8 | 3.9 | 0 | 4.0 | 0 | 0 |
| *Social–conventional* | | | | | | | | | | | | |
| 4. Rule maintenance | 4.4 | — | — | — | 13.0 | 19.3 | 23.1 | 13.7 | — | 6.1 | 8.2 | 6.0 |
| 5. Normative or appropriate act | 2.2 | 15.8 | 25.3 | 2.1 | 13.1 | 11.5 | 15.4 | 17.6 | — | — | 2.0 | 6.0 |
| 6. Politeness, courtesy, or consideration | 4.2 | — | — | 6.3 | 26.1 | 26.9 | 34.5 | 31.4 | 2.2 | 4.0 | 4.0 | 2.0 |
| 7. Act helps maintain order | — | 1.8 | — | — | 4.3 | 13.5 | 1.9 | 11.7 | 2.2 | 2.0 | — | — |
| Subtotal | 10.8 | 17.6 | 25.3 | 8.4 | 56.5 | 71.2 | 74.0 | 74.4 | 6.6 | 16.1 | 14.2 | 14.0 |
| *Personal* | | | | | | | | | | | | |
| 8. Consequences (only) to self | 8.9 | 12.3 | 3.9 | — | 10.9 | 9.6 | 11.5 | 3.9 | 22 | 24.5 | 35 | 24.0 |
| 9. Action is OK | — | — | — | — | — | 3.8 | 1.9 | 1.9 | 26.7 | 14.0 | 10.1 | 18.0 |
| 10. Personal matter | — | — | — | — | 6.5 | 3.8 | 5.8 | 1.9 | 24.4 | 35.0 | 28.6 | 30.0 |
| Subtotal | 8.9 | 12.3 | 3.9 | 0 | 17.4 | 13.4 | 19.2 | 7.7 | 83.3 | 73.5 | 73.7 | 72.0 |
| Unscorable response | 2.2 | 12.3 | 1.9 | 10.4 | 17.4 | 7.7 | 1.9 | 11.8 | 12.2 | 10.2 | 12.2 | 14 |

As expected, the analysis for positive events revealed that moral justifications were more likely to be provided for events ranked most right than for events ranked less and least right. Subjects at all grade levels were more likely to consider the *welfare (benefit) to another* (e.g., ''You're helping somebody who needs it''; ''She needs your help and someday you may need help too''), or the *good character of the actor* (e.g., ''It shows that you're a good person'') when ranking an act most right rather than less or least right.[2]

Moral justifications were also more likely to be provided for events ranked most wrong than for events ranked less and least wrong. Subjects at all grade levels were more likely to consider events ranked most wrong *unjust acts* (c.g., ''It's not fair to the other kids if he cheats''); *categorically wrong* (e.g., ''That's terrible thing to do. It's always wrong to hit.''); or an *unfair distribution of resources* (e.g., ''You're taking something that's not yours; it's his and you should respect that'').

Significantly more social conventional justifications were provided for events ranked less right than for events ranked most or least right ($p < .0001$). Subjects either considered events ranked less right *normative or appropriate acts* (e.g., ''It's customary to get dressed up; it's the socially accepted thing'') or used *politeness, courtesy, or consideration,* (e.g., ''That's the polite way of doing things.'' ''That's just plain common courtesy'').

Social conventional justifications were also more likely to be provided for events ranked less wrong than for events ranked most and least wrong ($p < .0001$). Subjects ranking events less wrong considered these events *impolite acts* (e.g., ''In our society it's not accepted because it's rude''). In addition, fifth-grade subjects provided significantly greater frequencies of social conventional justifications for events ranked less wrong than subjects at the other grade levels ($p < .05$).

Personal justifications were more likely to be provided for events ranked least right than for events ranked most or less right ($p < .0001$). Personal justifications were also more frequent for acts ranked least wrong than for acts ranked most or less wrong ($p < .0001$). Subjects at all grade levels considered actions ranked least wrong *OK* (e.g., ''It's no big deal, it's not bothering anyone'').

Whereas the ranking procedure assessed subjects' relative ranking of stimulus events in the three domains, the sorting task provides an independent assessment of subjects' classification of items into domains. Table 7.4 presents the results of individual items analyses by grade levels. Stimulus items were sorted either as right (or wrong) whether or not the act is governed by a rule, law, or social expectation, or as the person's own business.

---

(footnote 1 continued from page 172)

eleventh, or college sophomore) was the between-group factor; action severity (rank) and justification category were the within-group factors. To avoid spuriously inflated overall $F$s due to the extremely low frequencies of responses associated with at least one of the three ranks, analyses were conducted on the proportions of reasons provided for the predicted action-severity ranking and proportions of reasons provided for the other two ranks combined.

[2]These analyses entailed planned pairwise comparisons ($t$ tests for related measures) on the response frequencies for individual justification categories. All comparisons were significant at $p < .001$ or greater unless otherwise noted.

**TABLE 7.3**

Frequency (%) of Justifications Given for Rankings of Transgressions

| Moral | Most wrong moral | | | | Less wrong social–conventional | | | | Least wrong personal | | | |
|---|---|---|---|---|---|---|---|---|---|---|---|---|
| | 5th | 8th | 11th | College | 5th | 8th | 11th | College | 5th | 8th | 11th | College |
| 1. Unfair, unjust act | 8.3 | 11.6 | 20.8 | 26.6 | 10.2 | 8.9 | 5.8 | 6.0 | 0 | 0 | 0 | 0 |
| 2. Welfare (harm) | 15 | 27.5 | 16.7 | 28.1 | 0 | 0 | 4.3 | 0 | 0 | 0 | 0 | 0 |
| 3. Act is categorically wrong | 16.7 | 11.6 | 13.9 | 10.9 | 3.4 | 3.0 | 1.4 | 1.5 | 0 | 0 | 0 | 0 |
| 4. Moral character of actor | 20 | 10.1 | 18 | 7.8 | 1.7 | 1.5 | 2.9 | 0 | 0 | 0 | 0 | 0 |
| 5. Unfair distribution of resources | 11.6 | 10.1 | 12.5 | 10.9 | 3.4 | — | 1.4 | 1.5 | — | 1.6 | — | — |
| Subtotal | 71.6 | 70.9 | 81.9 | 84.3 | 18.7 | 13.4 | 15.8 | 9.0 | 0 | 1.6 | 0 | 0 |
| *Social–conventional* | | | | | | | | | | | | |
| 6. Rule violation | 14.9 | 11.6 | 8.3 | 1.6 | 15.3 | 13.4 | 17.4 | 17.9 | 0 | 4.8 | 2.3 | 0 |
| 7. Act creates disorder | 0 | 1.4 | 0 | 1.6 | 3.4 | 16.4 | 13 | 19.4 | 0 | 0 | 0 | 0 |
| 8. Normative, inappropriate, or deviant act | 0 | 0 | 0 | 0 | 5.1 | 6.0 | 11.6 | 10.4 | 0 | 0 | 1.6 | 0 |
| 9. Impolite | 0 | 4.3 | 1.4 | 0 | 13.6 | 13.4 | 19.8 | 14.9 | 0 | 1.6 | 0 | 0 |
| 10. Minor offense/inadvertent violation | 0 | 2.8 | 1.4 | 1.6 | 8.5 | 13.5 | 10.1 | 11.4 | 5.4 | 3.2 | 3.3 | 1.6 |
| Subtotal | 14.9 | 20.1 | 11.1 | 4.8 | 45.9 | 62.7 | 71.9 | 74.0 | 5.4 | 9.6 | 7.2 | 0 |
| *Personal* | | | | | | | | | | | | |
| 11. Consequences only to self | 6.6 | 1.4 | 1.4 | 0 | 10.2 | 3.0 | 4.3 | 6.0 | 5.4 | 14.5 | 14.7 | 18.3 |
| 12. Action is ok | — | — | — | — | 10.2 | 7.5 | 5.6 | 6.0 | 41.1 | 40.3 | 47.5 | 33.5 |
| 13. Personal matter | — | 1.4 | — | — | — | — | — | — | 41.1 | 38.7 | 39.3 | 61.7 |
| Subtotal | 6.6 | 1.4 | 1.4 | 0 | 22.1 | 13.5 | 10.1 | 12.0 | 84.0 | 83.8 | 91.7 | 98.5 |
| Unscorable | 6.6 | 7.2 | 5.6 | 10.9 | 13.6 | 10.4 | 2.9 | 6.0 | 10.7 | 4.8 | 0 | 0 |

**TABLE 7.4**

*Numbers of Subjects at Each Grade Level Sorting Event as "Wrong/Right–No Rule" and "Should Be Person's Own Business"*

| Moral | 5th[a] W | 5th[a] PB | 8th[a] W | 8th[a] PB | 11th[b] W | 11th[b] PB | College[b] W | College[b] PB |
|---|---|---|---|---|---|---|---|---|
| Hitting | 12 | 0 | 15 | 0 | 16 | 0 | 16 | 0 |
| Cheating at cards | 12 | 0 | 14 | 0 | 15 | 0 | 15 | 0 |
| Taking someone's notebook | 10 | 0 | 15 | 0 | 16 | 0 | 16 | 0 |
| Telling a lie | 14 | 0 | 15 | 0 | 16 | 0 | 15 | 0 |
| Writing in borrowed book | 12 | 0 | 15 | 0 | 14 | 0 | 16 | 0 |
| Sharing lunch | 11 | 3 | 13 | 1 | 14 | 1 | 15 | 1 |
| Helping older person | 10 | 3 | 12 | 1 | 13 | 1 | 13 | 3 |
| Returning lost wallet | 14 | 0 | 15 | 0 | 15 | 0 | 16 | 0 |
| Comforting child | 11 | 3 | 14 | 1 | 15 | 0 | 12 | 3 |
| Giving to charity | 12 | 3 | 9 | 4 | 12 | 3 | 13 | 3 |
| *Conventional* | | | | | | | | |
| Eating with fingers | 7 | 5 | 4 | 2 | 4 | 2 | 1 | 3 |
| Not following dress code | 1 | 1 | 1 | 2 | 0 | 1 | 1 | 5 |
| Not lining up | 7 | 1 | 6 | 2 | 6 | 1 | 5 | 0 |
| Calling teacher by first name | 3 | 6 | 4 | 0 | 2 | 0 | 2 | 0 |
| Coming to class late | 4 | 1 | 6 | 0 | 3 | 0 | 5 | 0 |
| Raising hand in class | 9 | 0 | 9 | 1 | 9 | 0 | 5 | 1 |
| Celebrating holidays | 6 | 6 | 6 | 6 | 7 | 4 | 5 | 6 |
| Dressing for worship | 6 | 6 | 6 | 5 | 1 | 6 | 3 | 3 |
| Wearing uniform | 1 | 1 | 2 | 2 | 0 | 0 | 2 | 4 |
| Holding door open for someone | 7 | 3 | 10 | 2 | 8 | 1 | 8 | 4 |
| *Personal* | | | | | | | | |
| Watching TV | 0 | 15 | 0 | 14 | 0 | 16 | 0 | 16 |
| Playing with disliked child | 0 | 15 | 0 | 14 | 0 | 15 | 0 | 13 |
| Playing alone | 0 | 15 | 1 | 12 | 1 | 15 | 0 | 16 |
| Talking on phone | 1 | 12 | 0 | 15 | 0 | 15 | 0 | 15 |
| Playing radio | 3 | 8 | 0 | 13 | 0 | 12 | 0 | 15 |
| Writing in diary | 0 | 14 | 2 | 13 | 0 | 16 | 0 | 16 |
| Sleeping late | 1 | 12 | 0 | 15 | 0 | 16 | 1 | 15 |
| Getting a haircut | 0 | 13 | 1 | 12 | 0 | 14 | 0 | 15 |
| Joining a club | 0 | 15 | 1 | 14 | 0 | 16 | 0 | 14 |
| Deciding to go to the movies | 0 | 15 | 0 | 15 | 0 | 16 | 0 | 16 |

[a]$(N = 15)$ 7.5 subjects would be expected to sort an event in either category on a chance basis; $p < .02$ or greater when 12 or more subjects sort an action in a given category; $p < .001$ when 14 or more subjects sort an item in a given category using $\chi^2$ goodness-of-fit test.

[b]$(N = 16)$ 8 subjects would be expected to sort an event in either direction on a chance basis, $p < .05$ when 12 or more subjects sort an action in a given category; $p < .01$ when 13 or more subjects sort an action in a given category, and $p < .001$ for 14 or more subjects using $\chi^2$ goodness-of-fit tests.

Eighth-grade, eleventh-grade, and college subjects sorted nearly all items classified as moral in the moral category at statistically significant frequencies, as indicated by chi-square goodness-of-fit tests. The one exception, "giving to charity," was sorted on a chance basis by eighth-grade subjects. Fifth-grade subjects sorted all five hypothesized prosocial moral items in the expected direction; two items, "returning a lost wallet" and "giving to charity" were statistically significant, while three items were sorted in the expected direction but did not reach conventional levels of significance ($p < .07$). All moral transgressions were placed in the moral category at significant frequencies (at the $p < .05$ level or greater) for all subjects, except for fifth graders. They sorted "taking someone's notebook" on a chance basis.

Table 7.4 indicates that all of the items classified as personal issues were sorted in the personal category at significant frequencies ($p < .05$). There were no age differences in subjects' sorting of personal issues. One item, "playing the radio," was sorted on a chance basis by fifth graders.

In addition to the individual item analyses, comparisons were made between children's sorting of all positive versus negative events across the three domains. Children at all four grade levels did not differ significantly in their classification of prosocial events and transgressions as moral, social conventional, or personal. Thus children were found to make the same distinctions among positive and constraint-oriented events.

## THE BOUNDARIES BETWEEN JUDGMENTS OF POSITIVE AND CONSTRAINT-ORIENTED ACTS

The study just reported represents an initial effort at comparing acts characterized in positive terms (e.g., helping another in need) with acts characterized in negative terms (e.g., avoidance of the infliction of physical harm to another). By combining the positive–negative dimension with domain classifications, it was shown that there is considerable consistency in the criteria used to classify positively and negatively characterized acts within a domain and that different criteria are applied to positive or negative acts in the different domains. Events in the moral domain were considered nonrule contingent in that they were judged to be right or wrong regardless of the presence or absence of explicit rules or normative expectations. Correspondingly, the justifications given for evaluations of positive and negative acts differed primarily by domain. As expected, positive and negative moral acts were evaluated on the basis of justice, welfare, and the fair distribution of resources whereas social conventional events were evaluated on the basis of politeness, courtesy, consideration, and adherence to culturally prescribed standards for behavior. In other words, negatively or positively stated prescriptions may, indeed, have a similar conceptual source. For example, the prescription that one should not hit another can be justified (and subjects often did) on the grounds that it is wrong to harm persons (the welfare category). The proposition that one should help another through an altruistic act (e.g., fishing out of the river someone who is drowning) can be justified on the grounds that it is right to benefit another and aid in the avoidance of harm (again, the welfare category).

Therefore, the results of the study conducted by Smetana indicate that the prosocial category is multifaceted in that there are important differences in the ways an individual thinks about various prosocial events. The results also suggest that the boundaries between prosocial and constraint-oriented situations may not be clearcut. Subjects regarded both positive and negative acts as right or wrong regardless of the existence of a rule. An implication of this finding may be that regulations, based on moral grounds, would be regarded as legitimate for both types of acts. A pilot study conducted by Bridgeman and Turiel yielded preliminary data regarding children's judgments of the boundaries between prosocial acts and constraints imposed by rules and authority.

The study included 48 subjects, with 12 from each of the following grades: kindergarten, second, fourth, and sixth. A series of questions regarding rules were posed about three briefly described hypothetical situations. Two of the situations (sharing and helping) were characterized in prosocial terms and one (stealing) in antisocial terms.

The sharing situation described the following scenario: The subject and another student are engaged in painting for a classroom art project; the other student has only two jars of paint, whereas the subject has six jars of paint. In a second situation the subject comes by another young person lying on the street. In the third situation the subject witnesses one classmate stealing a dollar from another classmate. For each of these situations subjects were asked the following questions pertaining to the existence and desirability of regulations:

1. Is there a rule that says what we should do in a situation like this? If so, why does the rule exist?
2. Should there be a rule and why?
3. If no rule exists, what would you do?

The findings are preliminary and should be taken only as suggestive, but they do point to the plausibility of the hypothesis that children do not regard constraint as independent of prosocial actions. Table 7.5 presents the percentage of subjects at each grade who stated that rules exist pertaining to sharing, helping, or stealing. Table 7.6 presents the percentage of subjects stating that a rule should exist with regard to each of the actions.

Table 7.5 shows a gradation from helping to sharing to stealing regarding the existence of social regulation. Most subjects assumed that rules exist for the act of stealing; about half of the subjects stated that sharing is regulated, and the majority of subjects maintained that helping behavior is unregulated. However, when given the opportunity, a large number of subjects (particularly those below the sixth grade) expressed the view that prosocial acts should be subject to constraint. As shown in Table 7.6, the majority of kindergarten, second-grade, and fourth-grade

**TABLE 7.5**
*Frequency (%) of Subjects Stating Rule Exists*

| Grade | Action | | |
|---|---|---|---|
| | Sharing | Helping | Stealing |
| Kindergarten | 58 | 42 | 55 |
| Second | 42 | 25 | 92 |
| Fourth | 50 | 25 | 58 |
| Sixth | 33 | 17 | 75 |

subjects stated that the prosocial acts ought to be constrained by social regulation. It was primarily the oldest subjects in the study (the sixth graders) who separated rule-constraint from the acts of sharing (50%) and helping (75%), which were regarded as acts that should not be governed by rules.

Accordingly, children do conceptually transform prosocial acts to include the necessity for constraint. Such transformations cannot simply be explained as a general tendency for young children to, when asked, say that rules should govern social acts. When these subjects were posed with the same question in regard to sex-role conventions, the majority of subjects responded that such rules ought not to exist. An alternative explanation stems from subjects' justifications for their responses that rules exist and/or should exist. It appears that there are commonalities in children's underlying judgments for positive evaluations of prosocial acts and negative evaluations of antisocial acts.

The analysis of justifications in this pilot study yielded categories that closely correspond to the justification coding categories used in the Smetana study. Generally, subjects justified the necessity for rules in the helping and stealing situations in similar ways. Some subjects said that rules did or should exist because the acts were categorically wrong or right. More commonly, the rules were justified by the necessity for protecting the welfare of persons (e.g., "because other people who fell down and got hurt would get more hurt if there wasn't a rule;" "because then people wouldn't have any money and they couldn't have any food").

**TABLE 7.6**
*Frequency (%) of Subjects Stating Rule Should Exist*

| Grade | Action | | |
|---|---|---|---|
| | Sharing | Helping | Stealing |
| Kindergarten | 92 | 75 | 80 |
| Second | 92 | 83 | 92 |
| Fourth | 92 | 58 | 83 |
| Sixth | 50 | 25 | 92 |

Justifications for rules pertaining to sharing were also based on the moral categories. In many cases the sharing rule justifications were coded with the same categories as the helping and stealing rules: welfare and the categorical rightness of the act. Among the older subjects (fourth and sixth graders), however, the rule was justified with reference to fairness and equality (e.g., "It is good to have an equal amount because it is fair.").

In addition to the increased use of the fairness category on the part of older subjects, it also appears (see Tables 7.5 and 7.6) that more of the oldest subjects rejected the necessity of rules with regard to sharing and helping (but not stealing). In the absence of data from subjects older than the sixth-grade group, we cannot ascertain whether the findings reflect a general age trend or are specific to an age period. It may be that with increasing age children make sharper separations between constraint and prosocial actions. Or it may be that the separation is specific to children of about 11 or 12 years of age. However, the types of reasons given by some of the sixth graders for the rejection of rules in the sharing and helping situations suggest an alternative explanation—namely, that they took more factors into account than the younger children. For example, several subjects regarded helping situations of the sort described as ambiguous in that they may not be what they appear and actually pose risks for the actor (e.g., the person lying on the street could be unhurt and intending to harm the passerby). The existence of a rule, according to these subjects, would limit the actor from making a judgment about the physical danger entailed in the situation. Nevertheless, these subjects recognized the obligation to act in the sharing and helping situations. Almost all the sixth-grade subjects stated that they would help or share even in the absence of a rule. Interestingly, more of the younger subjects (but still a minority of them) stated they would not help or share if there were no rule.

We must reiterate that the results of the Bridgeman and Turiel pilot study are presented solely to suggest hypotheses. However, they do provide, along with the Smetana findings, good indications of the multifaceted nature of judgments about prosocial acts. The prosocial realm cuts across domains and has features that are shared with evaluations of antisocial or constraint-oriented actions. The inconsistencies frequently found in prosocial research are likely to be due not solely to a lack of consistency in the subject's orientation to the category, but also to systematic distinctions made by the subject concerning the type of social knowledge involved.

Findings from two types of studies of children's prosocial behaviors provide evidence for the proposed relation of the domain of judgment and behaviors. One set of findings comes from research on friendship and sharing (reviewed in Berndt, 1983). We might expect that the propensity for children to act altruistically would be increased by the closeness of the relationship between the children. Contrary to such an expectation, it has been found that children are more likely to share with a stranger than with a friend, insofar as the stranger is perceived to be in greater need than the friend. In that case, it appears that even young children treat moral considerations as more important than the relationship between the children.

Another form of intersection between domain and behavior was evident in a series of studies (Staub, 1971) that examined the effect of implicit or explicit rules of conduct on helping behavior. Children in an experimental situation were either given permission to enter an adjoining room or they were given no instructions as to the permissibility of entering that room. They were left alone to complete a task when they heard cries of distress coming from the adjoining room. The experimental measure was the frequency with which they either actively sought to help or volunteered information about the situation to the experimenter. Children who were not given permission to enter almost uniformly did not help whereas those who were given permission helped in nearly half of the instances. Responses in a prohibition condition in which respondents were explicitly instructed not to enter the other room were similar in lack of helping responses to the no-instruction condition.

Experimental situations of this sort can be seen to entail a conflict between the social conventions of the experimental situation and the moral obligation to help a person in distress. The results suggest that changing the social conventions in such a way as to alleviate the conflict facilitated helping behavior. Although the children's reasoning about the situation was not directly assessed, one interpretation of the results is that children's behavior was consistent with the meaning they ascribed to the situation. When the situation was constructed as an unambiguously moral one, the likelihood of helping was greatly increased.

Further research can fruitfully attend to the multiple classifications of acts termed *prosocial*. This would entail the use of criteria for the classification of social acts that includes more than a characterization of their positive or negative features. Our research indicates that children use consistent criteria to distinguish among categories of social knowledge and that children apply these categories to both prosocial and antisocial acts. A consideration of the type of social knowledge that underlies social acts may not only clarify the development of children's reasoning about prosocial or altruistic acts. We suggest that this also may provide an understanding of the motivational source of children's positive social behavior.

## REFERENCES

Berndt, T. Social cognition, social behavior, and children's friendships. In E. T. Higgins, D. Ruble, & W. H. Hartup (Eds.), *Developmental social cognition: A sociocultural perspective*. New York: Academic Press, 1983.

Blasi, A. Bridging moral cognition and moral action: A critical review of the literature. *Psychological Bulletin*, 1980, *88*, 1–45.

Bryan, J. H. Children's cooperation and helping behaviors. In E. M. Hetherington (Ed.), *Review of child development research* (Vol. 5). Chicago: University of Chicago Press, 1975.

Chomsky, N. *Language and responsibility*. New York: Pantheon, 1979.

Damon, W. *The social world of the child*. San Francisco: Jossey–Bass, 1977.

Dreman, S. B. Sharing behavior in Israeli school children: Cognitive and social learning factors. *Child Development*, 1976, *47*, 186–194.

Dreman, S. B., & Greenbaum, C. W. Altruism or reciprocity: Sharing behavior in Israeli kindergarten children. *Child Development,* 1973, *44,* 61–68.

Dworkin, R. *Taking rights seriously.* Cambridge, Mass.: Harvard University Press, 1978.

Emler, N. P., & Rushton, J. P. Cognitive–developmental factors in children's generosity. *British Journal of Social and Clinical Psychology,* 1974, *13,* 277–281.

Kohlberg, L. Stage and sequence: The cognitive–developmental approach to socialization. In D. Goslin (Ed.), *Handbook of socialization theory and research.* New York: Rand McNally, 1969.

Kohlberg, L. From is to ought: How to commit the naturalistic fallacy and get away with it in the study of moral development. In T. Mischel (Ed.), *Cognitive development and epistemology.* New York: Academic Press, 1971.

Krebs, D. L. Altruism—an examination of the concept and a review of the literature. *Psychological Bulletin,* 1970, *73,* 258–302.

Krebs, D. A cognitive–developmental approach to altruism. In L. Wispé (Ed.), *Altruism, sympathy, and helping.* New York: Academic Press, 1978.

Latané, B., & Darley, J. M. *The unresponsive bystander: Why doesn't he help?* New York: Appleton–Crofts, 1970.

Macauley, J., & Berkowitz, L. (Eds.). *Altruism and helping behavior.* New York: Academic Press, 1970.

Nucci, L. Social development: Personal, conventional and moral concepts. Unpublished doctoral dissertation, University of California, Santa Cruz, 1977.

Nucci, L. The development of personal concepts: A domain distinct from moral or societal concepts. *Child Development,* 1981, *52,* 114–121.

Nucci, L. P., & Nucci, M. S. Children's social interactions in the context of moral and conventional transgressions. *Child Development,* 1982, *53,* 403–412. (a)

Nucci, L. P., & Nucci, M. S. Children's responses to moral and social–conventional transgressions in free-play settings. *Child Development,* 1982, *53,* 1337–1342. (b)

Nucci, L. P., & Turiel, E. Social interactions and the development of social concepts in pre-school children. *Child Development,* 1978, *49*(2), 400–407.

Payne, F. D. Children's prosocial conduct in structured situations and as viewed by others: Consistency, convergence, and relationships with person variables. *Child Development,* 1980, *51,* 1252–1259.

Piaget, J. *The moral judgment of the child.* Glenco, Ill.: Free Press, 1948. (originally published, 1932.)

Piaget, J. Piaget's theory. In P. Mussen (Ed.), *Carmichael's manual of child psychology* (3rd ed.). New York: Wiley, 1970.

Radke-Yarrow, M. R., & Zahn-Waxler, C. Z. Dimensions and correlates of prosocial behavior in young children. *Child Development,* 1976, *47,* 118–125.

Rubin, K. H., & Schneider, F. W. The relationship between moral judgment, ego-centrism, and altruistic behavior. *Child Development,* 1973, *44,* 661–665.

Sarason, I. G., Smith, R. E., & Diener, E. Personality research: Components of variance attributable to the person and the situation. *Journal of Personality and Social Psychology,* 1975, *32,* 199–204.

Smetana, J. Preschool children's conceptions of moral and social rules. *Child Development,* 1981, *52,* 1333–1336. (a)

Smetana, J. Reasoning in the personal and moral domains: Adolescent and young adult women's decision-making about abortion. *Journal of Applied Developmental Psychology,* 1981, *2,* 211–226. (b)

Smetana, J. Infants' and toddlers' social interactions regarding moral and social–conventional transgressions. Paper presented at the Biennial Meetings of the Society for Research in Child Development, Detroit, 1983.

Staub, E. Helping a person in distress: The influence of implicit and explicit rules of conduct on children and adults. *Journal of Personality and Social Psychology,* 1971, *17,* 137–145.

Staub, E. To rear a prosocial child: Reasoning, learning by doing, and learning by teaching others. In D. DePalma & J. Foley (Eds.), *Moral development: Current theory and research.* Hillsdale, N.J.: Erlbaum, 1975.

Turiel, E. Social regulations and domains of social concepts. In W. Damon (Ed.), *New directions for child development: Social cognition*. San Francisco: Jossey–Bass, 1978.

Turiel, E. *The development of social knowledge: Morality and convention*. Cambridge: Cambridge University Press, 1983.

Turiel, E. Domains and categories in social cognition. In W. Overton (Ed.), *The relationship between social and cognitive development*. Hillsdale, N.J.: Erlbaum, in press.

Weston, D., & Turiel, E. Act–rule relations: Children's concepts of social rules. *Developmental Psychology*, 1980, *16*, 417–424.

Winer, B. J. *Statistical principles in experimental designs* (2nd ed.). New York: McGraw–Hill, 1971.

Wright, B. A. Altruism in children and the perceived conduct of others. *Journal of Abnormal and Social Psychology*, 1942, *37*, 218–233. (a)

Wright, B. A. The development of ideology of altruism and fairness in children. *Psychological Bulletin*, 1942, *39*, 485. (b)

# Altruism and Moral Development

## BILL PUKA

What is so great about altruism? Much behavior, perhaps most behavior going under that name, seems designed to win friends and gain approval, or to boost sagging self-esteem, or even to play out maternal fantasies. The most dramatic cases of altruism seem to border on masochism. Is any of this especially noble?

Worse yet, altruism seems discriminatory from the moral point of view. Justice bids us to render each her or his due. Certainly we must count ourselves equal to anyone else, equally worthy of our due. Why then is it better to fulfill someone else's interest or enhance someone else's welfare rather than our own? In fact, why is it not worse to be altruistic than to be just or even to be self-interested? After all, altruism involves a significant loss to someone, a sacrificing of one's interest for another, whereas self-interest does not, justice need not. More interests would be served, it would seem, if we each catered to our own, for the most part.

Still, there seems to be something more praiseworthy about going out of your way for others than merely doing your part. Our moral exemplars are not drawn primarily from among the merely fair or just and certainly not from among the selfish or prudent. We admire those who have conscientiously dedicated themselves to their community or to humankind in general and at some personal cost. Are our feelings misplaced here, or do we admire merely the unselfishness of these rare people?

The extraordinary virtues of altruism derive from four main sources. One is altruism's tendency to increase overall welfare or the ratio of benefit over burden. The other three involve desirable traits expressed in altruistic acts or embodied in altruistic character, that is, preference for the good; insight and sensitivity; and self-

185

mastery. Altruism typically occurs where others are in dire need or are liable to experience great benefits that they cannot partake of unassisted. Increased good accrues from altruistic acts largely because there are many others and only one self.

The personal sacrifice involved is not desirable in itself but necessary as a means that is outweighed by the benefit to others. From the perspective of consequences, altruism should not be considered preferable to justice, or even to prudence, except where this ratio of benefits between self and other holds. The example just offered of a dyadic relationship in which one person merely sacrifices her or his interest to satisfy the like interest of another is not especially worthy (at best). It also is not especially frequent. Even in close love relationships where such altruism might occur most, the altruist presumably reaps great satisfaction from what is more an expression of love than an act of sacrifice, a means of communicating devotion, enhancing bonds of affection, and bettering the relationship generally.

Altruists are admirable both because they make the right choice of values and because they make that choice at some sacrifice to their self-interest. Either in a particular decision to act or in the many choices which contribute to developing altruistic motivations, the altruist puts good-enhancing values generally above self-enhancing ones. For this effort in behalf of the good, she or he merits our appreciation.

We typically associate the character trait of altruism with personal wisdom and maturity. Altruists are often valued because they seem to have an especially high level of understanding regarding their own nature and value and that of others. We are tempted to think that being altruistic requires a high degree of self-mastery and personality integration, bringing feelings and attitudes into line with moral principles and freeing oneself from fears, anxieties, and insecurities regarding the dangers that others and life in general present. Altruists must have a well-developed self-concept and high self-esteem, we think. How else could they afford to risk and give away so much? Must they not be inwardly expansive to be outwardly so?

Though it is difficult to demonstrate precisely which character traits are valuable, from the moral point of view, traits of deep understanding, personality integration, empathy, and high self-esteem will surely fall on the list. When we add in the additional qualities of sensitivity and compassion that normally accompany true altruism, its worth seems assured. In the truly altruistic act we see these traits and the character they compose in action. We value such acts largely because of the personal qualities they express.

Psychological research has verified some of our common-sense beliefs regarding the motivations and traits of altruists, especially as concerns locus of control and role-taking ability. (See, for example, Staub, 1978.) Due to the focus of this research, however—its emphasis on childhood and the relation of situational variables to behavior—little has been discovered about the comparative level of personality integration or cognitive "maturity" of altruists. Limited research by cognitive developmentalists suggests that level of cognitive–moral structure significantly affects choice and behavior, with greater conceptual sophistication leading to more principled and morally valid judgment. (See, for example, Haan, Smith, & Block,

1968; Krebs & Rosenwald, 1977.) If, in fact, our level of understanding is related to altruism as our commonsense beliefs suggest, we should expect more adults than children to be characteristically altruistic, where factors other than cognitive structure are equal. We should also expect to find more instances of true altruism, altruism motivated by altruistic motives, among adults. Moreover, we should expect to find an inordinate number of altruists at the highest levels of cognitive–moral development. The highest levels of moral–cognitive structure should embody the moral logic of altruism.

Surprisingly, the most widely discussed and empirically supported conception of moral-cognitive development, Kohlberg's moral stage theory, portrays *justice* as the highest level of moral cognition and moral logic. His research suggests that altruistic motivations do not demonstrate superior levels of moral understanding, but merely particular desires to go beyond the call of duty, perhaps even beyond the call of morality. (See the appendix for a brief account of Kohlberg's view.)

## ALTRUISM AND JUSTICE STRUCTURE

Among the many psychologists and philosophers who have objected to the justice emphasis in Kohlberg's theory, some have been motivated by a preference for altruism. They find it hard to believe that someone whose rationales for acting are merely fair and righteous can be more morally sophisticated than someone who is kind and compassionate. They see much of what they like (i.e., caring, concern, love, and community) at Kohlberg's Stage 3, and they wonder if his ordering of stages and interpretation of data is not skewed to his ideological tastes or even gender identity.

There is much that can be said in reply to these reactions. For one thing, they often fail to take seriously Kohlberg's crucial distinction between structure and content. Critics such as Gilligan (1977) simply will not let Kohlberg confine his scope to cognitive-moral structure, as he defines it. Instead we find Kohlbergian stages portrayed as levels of personality development, as ego stages, perhaps, in which *styles* of thought and behavior, attitudes toward personal liberation and love, are figured into "stage" transitions. There is no reason to think that a person reasoning at the highest stage of justice could not use some lessons in caring and warmth, in taking on and feeling the power of responsibilities. There are certainly more and less humane world views that are open to someone at a certain cognitive stage, not to mention different moral beliefs and skills. Some of these nonstructural aspects may be crucial to moral judgment (more crucial than structure), especially where reasoning relates to behavior. Still, this is not the stuff of Kohlberg's stages. It is the *structure* or logic of caring, compassion, and altruism that must be contrasted with his stage of justice.

Critics often make unfair comparisons between the least desirable motivations that can underlie justice (judgmentalism, self-serving prudentialism, begrudging egalitarianism) and the ideal motivations for altruism (e.g., love and compassion).

At the moral root of justice, however, is a respectfulness for the value, autonomy, and uniqueness of each individual. Kant described this motivation as a kind of nondiscriminating reverence and love. Critics should reformulate their argument by comparing the best motivations of both perspectives and showing how love and compassion surpass reverence and respect. The altruist must be portrayed as feeling that she or he should do what the just person considers nonobligatory but admittedly better. Here the superiority of altruism would be based on the assumptions of justice; altruism is justice and something more.

The rationale one finds for altruism at Stage 3, however, is clearly something less. It is a conventional altruism of "in-group conformity" for the most part. Those who support this stage against principled stages fall into the sort of trap Kohlberg has set even for himself in caricaturing altruism as a set of adolescent "feelings". To merit a hearing, critics must offer rationales of altruism that are as sophisticated philosophically and as integrated and differentiated conceptually as Kohlberg's highest stages. They must portray altruism as an overall theory of morality rather than a special emotion or particular set of obligations and virtues.

This is not an easy matter. Conceptions of altruism as a general moral "stance" on life are more spirit than refinement. The lack of clarity in even traditional philosophical theories of benevolence or love, (agape) make them less adequate than theories of justice in performing crucial moral functions such as resolving conflicts of interest. Moreover, utilitarian views, which embody an altruism of sorts, are flawed in ways that make altruism seem inappropriate for morality altogether. Let us consider this point briefly.

Put very simply, the rationale of utilitarian obligation is that we should act so as to foster the maximum welfare of all. This is an altruistic principle in that each individual often will be required to sacrifice her or his own interest, even surrender her or his rights, where this will increase the well-being of others. Such a view does not account for our recognition that some less than ideal activities are not wrong, but merely less than best. It makes every ideal thing we could do obligatory on pain of immorality.

It might be possible to reconstruct utilitarianism so that it offers an additional set of weak or imperfect obligations to do best or better. Such a view would then have to provide a way to order or balance these two sorts of obligations and in a way that somehow renders justice inviolate while giving altruism "punch." This would be difficult and would detract from the traditional virtue of utilitarian theory, which is simplicity. Moreover, even if the altruistic obligations of utility could be worked out, there would still be the problem of ordering goods or utilities by their moral importance and of protecting individuals from majority tyranny.

Consider the first point. If we defined altruism merely in terms of maximizing good or social welfare or of enhancing the happiness or satisfactions of others, then our moral exemplars would come from among the ranks of famous comedians and rock'n'roll stars rather than, for example, civil rights leaders or servants of the poor. This is so, at least, where the former celebrities were devoted to their audiences and where the latter devotees ruffled feathers or worked obscurely in small locales.

Sacrificing oneself for interests of any sort—to increase soap opera watching opportunities in America, for example—hardly qualifies for moral commendation. Sacrificing one's desires for social justice to help sadists or Nazis derive their most treasured pleasures in the suffering of others is despicable altruism.

Utilitarianism mistakenly has been viewed as a moral principle, when in fact it is a principle of social interest and prudent choice in a conventional or positivistic sense. It has a "pro social" orientation in much the way psychological research in this area has. Moral psychology, moral development research, by contrast, is concerned with what society or the individual *should* want, from the *moral* point of view. Altruism in the moral sense involves enhancing the well-being of others in certain ways and, ideally, for certain reasons. It serves the best interests of others and fosters morally permissible (merely permissible) ones, primarily as a way of respecting or caring for their possessors.

On utilitarian principles we may be obliged to infringe the free choice of others where they are unwilling to cooperate in social progress, to foster the greater good of the many. This is the majority tyranny problem. The legacy of human nature theory, especially before behaviorism got hold of it, is that our psychology is organized by its cognitive, active, willful side. At least this is how it should be seen where we are considering how to relate to others, to cooperate or contend. To respect and value persons, which is what morality is all about, we must view their aims through their perspectives, as they choose to set priorities and pursue them. Any moral view that sees people primarily as experiencers or welfare-holders misses the point. Coerced or coercive altruism, paternalistic or otherwise, is morally unacceptable, regardless of its good effects overall.

## JUSTICE AND MORALITY

Despite these problems in defining a structure of altruism, there seems good reason to be dissatisfied with justice alone as the defining concept of moral development. Even those who view justice as the centerpiece of moral thought and development speak of going beyond the call of duty, of acting in supererogatory fashion. As mentioned previously, we associate our moral exemplars with kindness and love rather than mere fairness. Kohlberg and the schools of moral theory with which he identifies concentrate on moral obligations, on rights and duties that, at the highest (Stage 6) level, will apply to all persons equally. Yet when we speak of going beyond the call of duty we do not mean going beyond morality. Those who exemplify love and kindness in their stance toward others are exemplary and admirable within the moral realm, whether they act out of obligation or not. A most adequate form of moral thought should accommodate this moral logic. A highest stage of moral reasoning should incorporate supererogatory rationales and correctly.

A careful look at Kohlberg's Stage 6 indicates that a great deal of behavior we would intuitively consider altruistic is required by justice. This follows primarily from his interpretation of the Kantian principle of nondiscrimination which bids us to weigh the value of our interests equally with those of others in rendering each her or his due. Kohlberg portrays this principle best through the logic of his ideal role-taking or "moral musical chairs." Two examples might suffice:

1. If someone needed a ride to get to an appointment and you are the only person willing (or able) to drive her or him, you are obligated to do so as long as the cost to you is not greater than the loss would be to the person missing the appointment.
2. If you are walking over a bridge and see someone drowning whom only you could feasibly help, you are obligated to rescue that person so long as this would not increase the likelihood of your drowning beyond that of his or her drowning or make it likely that both of you will drown.

According to Kohlberg, these are the only conclusions you could come to if you really had to occupy all the relevant positions in each dilemma. You would consider it legitimate to expect the person to drive or rescue you and you would be willing, in good faith, to inconvenience yourself or even seriously risk your life "in return."

As we normally understand duty, both of these cases would go beyond it. It might be a bit callous of you not to drive someone in need to an appointment. It might even be wrong or unfair of you not to do so when that person really needs it and it would be "no big thing" for you to help out. However, you need not take on his or her situation, take on his or her utility prospects, feeling obliged to bear almost as much inconvenience in helping as he or she would if not helped. This would ignore that person's responsibility for having made the appointment, for conducting her or his life in a way that leads to such foreseeable needs and dilemmas.

Likewise in the drowning person case, no one owes another a 45–50% risk to one's life on grounds of mere fairness. We are not being unfair to someone when we have insufficient courage to "play hero." It is true that it might be better to set up our interrelations so that people could depend on this much aid from each other, as much as we now expect from a close family member, but this would not represent the merely just society. It would be the humane society in a true sense. The potential savior is not obliged to right the tragedies of nature or accident, even if her or his conceptions of just desert should not rest upon them. (We should not fault or reward people morally for what they cannot help.) When asked, "Why won't you bear the risk I am bearing? Why do you choose to stay safe and dry while I am the one to drown?" The potential saviour can answer, "Because you are the one who fell in the water, not me." This may sound too heartless to bear if we do not add to his reaction, "But, my God, how I wish it had never happened to you, how I wish I could save you without putting my life in dire peril, without knowing that, if I jumped in, there's as much chance I'll never come out as not." The person who respects the high and equal value of human life should feel this way but need not jump in the water.

We may even feel that the potential saviour *should* attempt a rescue and that we are morally obliged to be heroic to some extent, if not to this great extent. I would agree. This obligation, however, if it exists, is an obligation to go beyond the call of justice or fairness. It is an obligation of benevolence or kindness in some moderated form. In these ways, Kohlbergian justice at the highest stage can be said to accommodate altruism but not in the right way. Stage 6 is structurally inadequate in assimilating the moral logic of moral altruism.

In ancient ethical texts, justice was seen as the moral virtue that organized all other virtues and balanced them in proper, relative proportions. No doubt this approach influenced Kohlberg, as an avowed Platonist, in choosing justice to define moral thought. However, these ancient conceptions lacked content. They directed us to be properly courageous or generous or honest without indicating how and where to draw the line of propriety. Moreover, many virtues they placed under justice's wing would fall outside the realm of universal rights and duties that justice commands in Kohlberg's stages. It is mistaken to think that only justice, rather than one of these other virtues, can provide the general structure for organizing the moral domain. Benevolence and prudence have also been tried in that position; utilitarianism is the evidence.

Modern justice is a particular moral concept that performs certain limited roles in morality. It falls in the moral category of right, as does rights, rather than in that of good or ideals. In his early writings such as "From Is to Ought," Kohlberg (1981) defines the role of morality as ordering competing claims and resolving conflicts of interest among persons. Kohlberg's moral judgment interview presents moral dilemmas to get at moral reasoning in this way. According to Kohlberg, morality does its job best when it resolves such dilemmas by showing impartial respect for the equal value and autonomy (rights) of those involved, regarding their occurrent, nonwrongful interests.

Actually, resolving such conflicts, and in this impartial way, is the special function of justice. When considering what we should do morally, we might also wonder how to assess the relative quality of interests, values, or intentions and how to advance them. We might consider how to set ideals for character development, life-style, and career choice, or for social progress. When considering how to treat people, we may accord respect to their potential for development, their best and ideal interests (seen as possible future interests) rather than to their actual interests alone. Moral reasoning must be concerned with all these moral issues.

Importantly, however, justice is commitedly neutral regarding the relative quality of interests, values, and ideals. The impartial respect it renders people as equals requires that their different conceptions of the good life and worthy character be ignored. In this way, justice can never be expected to tell the whole story; it must rely on other moral concepts to complement its role. In the particular school of justice with which Kohlberg aligns, that is, deontological justice, this concept functions as a filter device on values and a side constraint on their pursuit. It does not guide our behavior, development, or forms of interaction toward ideals. It does not exhort or oblige us to be better. Rather it sets minimal standards of acceptable behavior and takes a neutral stance toward all values, interests, or pursuits that are permissible or nonwrong. The very definition of deontology implies this for justice. It defines any concept in the moral category of right as logically independent from the concept of good and as not forwarding or maximizing good.

Seen from the category of right, deontological justice is normally concerned with according respect to individual autonomy. It ranks equal individual liberty absolutely (or near absolutely) above all considerations of value and above all interests. In this way, it takes freedom out of the realm of values, making equal respect for persons as autonomous beings a prior-to-value consideration. This is a far cry from any teleological conception that defines right (and justice) solely as promoting values. Moreover, because respect for persons normally accords persons equal *maximum* freedom (as much freedom as each can exercise without infringing on each other's freedom), deontological justice normally includes no teleological component at all. It cannot obligate people to advance the good once it has said that anything an individual may want to do is morally acceptable, so long as it does not coerce others. Being unwilling to develop kindly motivations or to make a social institution more humanistic does not involve coercing someone. It does not violate anyone's rights.

A moral concept that excludes so many moral concerns on principle cannot represent the logic or structure of morality as a whole. However, it could be argued that once we see what justice implies, once we recognize the deontological truth that equal respect for the autonomy of persons is primary, the primacy of justice in morality must be accepted also. It is not that justice excludes all other moral considerations, it is that other moral considerations become dubious or unruly beside it or that they must be subsumed within it. On the first view it is recognized that teleological (good-enhancing) obligations to advance overall good oblige us to infringe personal liberty if necessary. This places supposedly moral principles in the uncomfortable position of requiring immorality. Thus there is no place for them within the realm of obligation. Such principles might represent "hypothetical imperatives" for supererogation, however—"if you want to be saintly, loving or admirable, do such and such."

On the second view, teleological principles could be used to support justice and respect for liberty. Thus we should develop certain virtues of courage, honesty, sympathy, and generosity regarding the needs and burdens of others; we should promote a willingness to compromise our interests and cooperate in joint projects insofar as this fosters commitment to the principles of justice and compliance with them.

Neither view is likely to satisfy the altruist. It is not merely a question of *if* you happen to want to be loving. You *should* want to be! Altruism should not merely foster justice and stop short of going beyond it. It should strive to go beyond justice and strive mightily, and it should inspire others to do the same. Altruists and nonaltruists alike may sense that the trouble with justice, its tendency to dominate morality, comes from its obsession with coercion. Put another way, the modern conception of justice, and of deontological justice in particular, is tailored to providing a moral foundation for the coercive nature of political and legal systems. The conception of justice provided by John Rawls (1971) and which Kohlberg often cites to explicate Stage 6, is explicitly designed for that purpose. Like other deontological conceptions, it arises from the social contract tradition that asks how a government can have the authority to order its citizens around, to set rules for them, to threaten them with fines and imprisonment, and to make good on these threats through direct coercion. The answer this tradition offers is that citizens reasonably can be expected to accord government these powers voluntarily, to legislate these powers on themselves by unanimous, if tacit, consent. Citizens would do this to provide assurance that interpersonal conflicts of interest or over fairness will be resolved peaceably and in a regular, nonarbitrary fashion, and that shared expectations for fair cooperation will be set publicly and followed. (Such publicized expectations will avert unresolvable conflict and resentment down the road.)

How does government assure that people will abide by its rules? By force! The government is a coercive power monopoly (among other things) that backs its procedures with threats. The rights we surrender it to create this power, legitimately, are rights to *enforce* our rights. We do not surrender the rights themselves. Consider—we not only have the right to life, but, most likely, the right to enforce that right. This is the right to infringe the liberty of someone threatening our life, perhaps even to violate her or his right to life, in defense of our (right to) life. The logic of enforcing rights, of rights to enforcement, is different from that of morality generally or even of rights, that is, *moral* rights, in particular. Enforcement, after all, is coercion. Coercion is a prima facie moral wrong. The moral question of coercion is one of when it is legitimate to do what would otherwise be wrong. This would be a question of justifiability or excusability rather than a question of right, per se. Normally enforcement deals with how to deal with people who have committed injustices, not merely with people as autonomous beings worthy of equal respect. Moreover, when enforcing rights we must worry about the evils of making a mistake or of abusing power much more than in normal cases of respecting life or liberty.

Given these special and atypical considerations of enforcing morality and the special social contractarian need to rally unanimous consent among divergent individuals, it is no wonder that the principles of justice derived emphasize individual freedom above all, maximum toleration of diverse interests. No one would be willing to risk having the values of some enforced by government on others, even if these values seemed best, and, indeed, why should anyone be so willing? Whether or not deontological principles or rights should be enforced (over the noncoercive opposition of pacifists and anarchists), teleological principles or duties should not, in general. This does not make them supererogatory or hypothetical. It merely leaves them matters of morality per se.

Consider the issue of enforcement in the context of utilitarianism. What is the problem of majority tyranny? It is that some are allowed or obliged to coerce others, to make them suffer burdens they would not choose to bear, to advance the good of others. The few, here, have done nothing wrong. They do not deserve to be discriminated against at the expense of their liberty and welfare. Suppose, however, that we confined morality to its proper realm, the realm of noncoerce advice-giving, or guidance; inspiration and the setting of legitimate expectations, and so forth. Here utilitarian principles would direct us to initiate good actions, develop good traits in ourselves and foster them in others, and seek cooperation in socially progressive ventures. These principles would form the basis for *exhorting* others to do likewise, for *praising* them when they did, or *criticizing* them when they did not. Such principles would not advise that we coerce others but offer strong advice or apply strong pressure. Coercion or the threat of coercion is precisely what morality is designed to avoid.

Of course such a pragmatic basis for morality may seem insufficient. It may be most practical for some individual in some particular instances to bend others to her or his will if she or he can get away with it. No good-enhancing principle, including utilitarianism, has come up with a totally acceptable way to guarantee each individual, or moral practice generally, against coercion. At the same time, so-called *ideal utilitarian principles* have been advanced which argue for the high quality of freedom and equality as values and direct us to maximize them. These may be combined with rule–utilitarian principles, which direct us to adhere strictly and foremost to a rule of equal individual liberty as the best means of advancing overall good. Here we approach the deontological good quite closely. We could go even farther in transcending the crude categories of deontology and teleology altogether by adopting a narrower conception of morally acceptable liberty to make room for direction on how to use some liberties better. These two types of principles would then combine in what is termed a *mixed conception,* protecting right and fostering good in a more balanced way.

The point is that deontological justice, as embodied in Kohlberg's Stage 6, does not represent, should not dominate, and cannot subsume morality adequately. Somehow it must be complemented, conceptually, with significant rationales for promoting values. Put another way, if people naturally develop to Stage 6 and if Stage 6 truly represents the structure of their moral reasoning on the whole, then Stage 6 structure is not morally adequate. It is not the highest level of moral reasoning. Of course, it may be the highest level of *natural* development in moral reasoning, since the moral competence people develop spontaneously through social interaction may not be very high.

A more reasonable assessment of Stage 6, and one with which Kohlberg recently has come to agree, is that it represents reasoning about matters of justice in particular, not morality in general. After all, it was generated empirically (insofar as it has been supported empirically) by a research technique that pulled for fair resolutions to conflicts of interest. This instrument also focused on questions of law—should someone be punished for doing wrong, what is the relation of law to society—which is the special province of deontological justice. Since stage descriptions account for responses to such questions, we can expect a justice bias, a political or legal bias as well, in Kohlberg's theory. We can expect, also, that teleological rationales of utility and perfection will be represented as nonstructural or orientational components of moral judgment, where they arise empirically. This has occurred in Kohlberg's work on substages.

To fill out the empirical basis for defining stages of moral development, we must pose different sorts of moral questions that concern ideals of character and community development or ordering of values. We may then discover that moral reasoning on the whole does not develop naturally and in Piagetian stages or that the structure of moral development does not correlate neatly with justice development; Stage 6 justice may not occur in Stage 6 morality. More likely we will discover that the structure of reasoning about nonjustice issues is compatible with the structure of justice but alters importantly the precise nature and extent of obligations.

## IF NOT JUSTICE, THEN WHAT?

### Objections to Love as an Alternative to Justice

As noted, various conceptions of altruism, benevolence, or love (agape) have been advanced as alternatives to justice theory. Although they are inspiring and imaginative, they are too vague to be of much practical use to the moralist. Love has been defined, for example, as an intuitive union with the essence of another person or all persons. (Consider the modern conceptions of love offered by humanistic psychologists such as Fromm, Maslow, and May.) If such conceptions are not practical, we must doubt that they could ever define a natural structure of cognitive–moral thought. Such structures arise, after all, as solutions to conceptual problems that occur as people interact with others. Utilitarianism as a form of benevolence theory is much more detailed and practicable than love theories, but it is seriously flawed, as we have seen.

In Kohlberg's offhand rejection of love conceptions, love has appeared either as a particular (moral) emotion or virtue that cannot organize the structure of moral reasoning or as a rationale of supererogation that cannot place obligations on all people. Recently, in his book *The Philosophy Of Moral Development*, Kohlberg (1981) placed certain conceptions of universal love in a metaphorical "Stage 7." Here they function as a kind of religious or spiritual metaphysic that lends meaning and worth to being moral in general. In answering the question "why be moral," they have great value for moral thought, yet they are not really part of that thought.

Perhaps the most pointed criticism Kohlberg has offered of a sophisticated principle of love concerns its inadequacies in resolving moral dilemmas. Love cannot resolve some dilemmas at all because it is totally on the side of each conflicting party. Kohlberg often raises the hypothetical case of two altruists slowly dying of thirst on a desert despite a canteen containing enough water to save one of them. On one interpretation of altruism, they may each feel obliged to empty the canteen into each other and thus they may end up passing the canteen back and forth, without either drinking, until they both die. (Of course, if one dies first. . . .)

On a second interpretation of love or altruism, or regarding other sorts of dilemmas, total concern for each person may lead to equal sharing. Here altruism or love will reduce to justice. Yet since justice is a more clarified concept with a more explicit rationale, we should prefer it to love where their effects are the same. Last, if loving concern does not lead to equal justice when it resolves a conflict of interests, it is objectionable because it is discriminatory or unjust. On all these grounds justice is to be preferred.

## Responses to Objections to Love

A plausible response can be offered to each of the previous objections against love or altruism. The vagueness and impracticability problem can be handled by merely specifying a clear conception of these concepts, a conception of love or altruism that is as explicit as that of Stage 6 justice. How this can be done will be considered in a moment. Insofar as such an account can portray love or altruism as a general moral principle, criticisms of love as a particular (moral) emotion or virtue or pantheistic metaphysic will be beside the point.

Transforming supererogatory conceptions of love or altruism to morally obligatory ones is primarily a matter of building in moderation. To require that all people be altruistic is inappropriate only because it asks more than we can reasonably expect of people. In effect, it discriminates against the vast majority who do not have the extraordinary degree of compassion, self-esteem, etc., to fulfill duties of love in stride. Note that being just, especially in Kohlberg's sense, often requires sacrificing strong self-interests. Duties of justice will be easier to fulfill for those who are especially empathetic or moralistic. However, we feel that justice does not ask so much of anyone that she or he could not reasonably expect the same of others in return. The problem with good-enhancing or teleological priniciples is that they direct us to *maximize* the good across all persons. This is not an accident. Given the nature of value and the virtue of rational prudence, which all moral principles should embody, it would make no sense to prefer less good to more or most. By contrast, the teleological tradition needs a principle of right that will be rational for each person and will give equal consideration to the moral burdens each bears. Such a principle would direct each of us to promote the welfare of all to a sizable (but not overly burdensome) extent.

Two substantial problems would have to be faced in formulating such a principle. The first is one of precision—where to draw the line of moderation. Do we require people to advance 75% of the welfare that utilitarian altruists would predictably generate, or to exert 65% of the effort they would exert in maximizing good? The second is how to guarantee equality. It is possible that the approximate equality needed in bearing altruistic obligations could be established by a rule–utilitarian principle, as suggested previously, but this is unclear.

An alternative approach might be to construct an altruistic logic through a complex of different principles that limit, balance, or moderate each other. In a sense, deontological justice is designed to do this, to place side-constraints of right on the pursuit of good. Unfortunately justice does not pose sufficient obligations to foster good that might then be limited by an arena of permissible slacking off. I will take the balancing approach in posing an altruistic stage of moral cognition, a stage of moderate altruism. Its great advantage is that it can build in rival principles, a circumscribed principle of justice, for example, thereby borrowing the virtues of these alternatives. Where justice is guaranteed as a component of altruism, we can meet the criticism that loving resolutions of conflicts of interest will not only be nonjust, but *un*just. We can also fend off the criticism that such conflicts cannot be resolved. If justice can resolve them, our justice-and-more can resolve them also. This is true at least where the revisions of and additions made to a justice rationale do not decrease its validity or hamper its effectiveness. The component principles of a complex love rationale have to be combined or ordered in a clear-cut and regularized manner. Only in this way can we avoid uncertainty in deciding what weight each will have relative to each other in deciding a case.

It is important that we assess the merits and demerits of a love or altruism rationale against those of justice structure. Just as altruism may have difficulty resolving conflicts of interest, justice may have difficulty (if it has anything to say at all) prescribing ideals of character and community. (A mixed or complex conception of love or altruism could deal with both issues.) Where love may sometimes be nondiscriminating regarding who gets what or whether anyone gets the goods, justice may be unacceptably indifferent as to what goods people should pursue.

The justice advocate can hardly fault love or altruism for reducing to justice in some instances. Yet it is a mistake to think that because love may resolve conflicts of interest fairly, it is limited to fairness in handling all moral problems. The structure of altruism that I will suggest, however, usually would add additional considerations to fairness even in resolving conflicts of interest. However, many of the standard Kohlberg dilemmas happen to be structured so that the additional obligations of altruism cannot take hold. I see this as a methodological problem in Kohlberg's research that we will consider shortly.

## ALTRUISM AS JUSTICE AND MORE

Defining the precise structure of a Stage 6 level altruism would be equivalent to defining the logical foundations of an ultimately valid moral philosophical theory. This is too long (and too technical) a story to tell here. Moreover such a story may have limited relevance to moral development, since *natural* development may not extend this far. The structure of a cognitive–moral stage in the Kohlbergian sense, must be derived meticulously from data.

It may be useful to consider, however, how such data might be generated and what structure it would show. We might also speculate on how moral rationales that have shown up in the data, which define various Kohlbergian stages, might be integrated and differentiated to form a principled altruism. Since stage progression shows moral logical progress through integration and differentiation of this sort, our speculative account might represent a plausible hypothesis of how more than just development would proceed.

As I read Kohlberg, the main rationales that arise and recur in moral stages are an individual rights rationale, prominent at Stages 2, 4, and 5A; a liberal egalitarian justice rationale, prominent at Stages 3B and 6 (if there is a Stage 6); a utilitarian rationale, most prominent in Stages 4B and 5B; and a value hierarchy that ranks life over liberty over property, with greater clarity as development progresses. Subsidiary or less frequent rationales also arise along the course of development: a just deserts rationale, at Stages 2A and 4A in particular; a catering-to-needs rationale, most prominent in Stage 3; and a perfectionist rationale, which occurs at various B substages and especially at Stages 3B and 5B. (Perfectionist rationales direct us to develop our natural gifts and virtues on the individual level and to foster excellence or exemplary individuals in our society.) All the foregoing rationales of natural development are prominent within moral philosophical theory in more refined form. They provide the building blocks for a principled stage of altruism.

The main conceptual problem to be solved at the highest level of moral cognition is how to accommodate the conflicting demands of deontological right and teleological good. Within Stage 5, for example, Kohlberg describes an opposition between an individual rights rationale, respects the equal autonomy of each individual, and a rule–utilitarian rationale, which tries to tailor this respect to practices that advance the overall good of society. According to Kohlberg, until these rationales are universalized and ordered so that all persons as persons are respected equally (not merely as members of particular societies) and equal respect is made prior to advancing the good (advancing the good becomes a form of rendering equal respect), the greatest level of structural adequacy cannot be achieved. Ideally we might wish to show how this problem can be solved by combining the primary rationales of Stage 5 in a way that embodies the logic of altruism and meets the Kohlbergian criteria of integration, differentiation, reflective equilibrium, reversibility, correlativity, universality, prescriptivity, abstractness, etc. This would build the case for a structure of altruism on the structural and philosophical foundations Kohlberg accepts—a formalist, deontological altruism. Of course, these criteria are challengeable, and we may wish to challenge Kohlberg's philosophical assumptions, especially, in making our case. We do not have to tailor altruism to the peculiar structural difficulties of Stage 5 insofar as this stage is defined with a bias toward justice.

For now let me suggest that a promising way around the deontological–teleological problem, the problem of infringing individual liberty for the greater welfare, is through a principle of perfectionism. People will be altruistic voluntarily, finding the self-sacrifice quite bearable, where they have developed and strengthened other-oriented motivations such as empathy and caring. Through such development, also, we can foster true altruism or love, altruism rendered out of altruism, loving acts expressing loving. This development can be stimulated and reinforced during childhood years, primarily, thereby mitigating problems of indoctrination and authoritarianism. Before a child has a developed sense of autonomy and an elaborated self to determine, the fostering of certain character traits will not be an imposition, nor need it feel like one. Early training of this sort can also help motivate compliance in later life with obligations to make oneself, and others, more spontaneously giving.

By itself, a principle or rationale of perfectionism is not strong enough to support altruism. People who develop kindly feelings slowly, who are at present underdeveloped, or who hearken most to nonaltruistic motivations (and obligations) will exhibit precious little altruism in their daily behavior. Therefore, we might add a rule–utilitarian principle that ranks the value of altruistic motivations and their predictable aims highly. This would be termed an *ideal* utilitarian principle because it would place certain values (ideals) above others and would rank morally worthy or desirable ones highest.

Let us assume, for the sake of prudence and clarity, that both of the above principles define right or obligation in terms of *maximizing* altruism. Now we will need some way to moderate these obligations without sapping away their strength. For this purpose I would suggest circumscribed individual rights, accompanied by a limited principle of egalitarian justice. In designing these rationales we want to limit the permissible use of liberty so that our perfectionist and ideal utilitarian obligations can hold sway; it is not OK, morally, to act in ways that neglect or impede the development and expression of altruism. At the same time we want to respect the equal autonomy of persons. Positing equal rights, as opposed to a general liberty principle, allows us to pick the sorts of liberties we will sanction morally. Duties will not be placed on others to refrain from interference in any nonwrong thing a person wants to do. Rather, people will be given specific rights to do specific things, or types of things, and we will be duty-bound to give them right of way. (Consider the Bill of Rights as an example of this rationale, although such rights are political.) By defining these rights so that less than a maximum amount of general liberty is sanctioned—even within particular rights, perhaps—altruistic obligations are given room to operate. At the same time, the essential moral personality, that core of each person we respect as an equal, is guaranteed room to function autonomously. In an ideal account of moral rights, we might wish to sanction only those liberties that express the traits of the morally essential personality.

An egalitarian justice rationale would be added to the structure of altruism to distribute moral obligations and unearned welfare equally among persons. Obligations to help others at personal sacrifice would be distributed equally thereby, avoiding the majority tyranny and unequal burden problems of utilitarianism. (Ideally, subrationales of just desert and need should form parts of this principle, weighted or ranked relative to each other.)

It is an important defect of Kohlbergian (and Rawlsian) justice that the particular needs and meritorious efforts of individuals are all but ignored in deference to respect for the equality of essential personhood. Kohlberg talks at Stage 6 of the equal value of life and, only indirectly, of respect for equal liberty. Yet respondents to Kohlberg interviews talk of just deserts, rewards and punishments for accomplishments and faults, and of the value of property. Why is Stage 6 justice silent on these aspects of human personality and activity? Is it not more cognitively sophisticated to differentiate both the moral core and the moral fringe of human personality, as well as the interests and deserving "claims" of each, and then to integrate these in one's rationale of respect?

It is important to ask how the sorts of moral rationales I have just identified have been differentiated and integrated in Stage 6 structure. It seems to me that the liberal justice bias in Kohlberg's view has suppressed strong natural rights and just deserts aspects of justice as well as teleological rationales. By contrast, the structure of altruism I propose distinguishes many aspects and roles of justice and respect. It relegates that portion of Stage 6 justice that invokes altruism (e.g., risking one's life to save a drowning person) to appropriately good-enhancing rationales.

Yet how are these rationales to be integrated? There are several possibilities. To accomplish our goals of moderating altruism and equalizing its moral demands, we might rank-order rationales as follows: rights over equal liberty over perfectionism over ideal rule–utilitarianism. This retains the primacy of right over good as the deontologist demands. It relieves the few of extraordinary sacrifices to enhance the many. Yet above all it protects basic liberties even from the tyranny of betterment, while giving betterment a fighting chance.

Working out the details of this structure would be extremely difficult. The particular rights to be granted and their scope would have to be specified and justified, as would the relative weight of just deserts to claims of need. The precise implications of ranking perfectionism absolutely over ideal utilitarianism would have to be explicated. Would people be able to hide behind their own self-development—leave me alone, I am working on my empathy—to avoid being generous or boosting ideals of community? Are the combined rationales of altruism reversible and universalizable? Do they match the criteria of adequacy as well as justice alone does at the Stage 6 level?

Perhaps the most complex problems arise in ranking the ideals to be advanced by the rationale of ideal utility and in justifying the overall superiority of altruistic ideals and motivations. With regard to the perfectionist principle as well, we might ask, "Why should we develop our propensities for love; why not courage, honesty or integrity? Why not appreciation of beauty?" My reliance on the perfectionist principle as the key to generating structural altruism is highly problematic. Of all rationales appearing in Kohlberg's data, this is one of the most infrequent. If my speculation regarding moral structure is to have any empirical relevance, how can it rest so heavily on such an undistinguished feature of observed natural development?

In my view, the sorts of stimuli that would elicit statements about duties to (altruistic) development have not been presented in Kohlberg's research. On the contrary, the sorts of questions Kohlberg's moral interview asks make perfectionist responses inappropriate. Consider the Heinz dilemma, for example, in which a man is so desperate to save his wife's life that he is contemplating robbery to acquire needed medicine. In such a last minute and desperate situation, with life hanging in the balance, can we contemplate Heinz's possible obligation to feel empathy for the greedy druggist who will not sell the lifesaving drug at less than an outrageously high price? Should Heinz use this occasion to practice stoic acceptance or instruct the druggist on virtue? Might he return to his wife empty handed and consider with her what she might learn from this disappointment in her waning moments of suffering and consciousness? (I am caricaturing the perfectionist stance, but hopefully one gets the drift.) Lifeboat dilemmas that ask whom to throw overboard to save a sinking ship are similarly inhospitable to developmental suggestions.

Consider next the story of a father who heartlessly reneges on a promise to his son. The question asked on Kohlberg's interview is whether the son should respect the father's unjust request. A respondent is very unlikely to say that the son should go to his father and try a little developmental stimulation. Nor would we expect the son to take it upon himself to act so as to develop his own character. This would be nice, but hardly to be expected of children under the (psychological) gun or of those considering what children in that situation should do. The situation wreaks of injustice and pulls for a just resolution.

Developing one's moral virtues or those of others takes time and perhaps some informal planning. It usually occurs within stable but expanding social contexts, not bizarre and terminal ones. The moral aims approached by perfectionist duties involve what sorts of persons to become, what sorts of relationships to establish and how to steer their growth, what kinds of community to aim for. To get at reasoning about these issues, we might pose situations in which people are asked to give moral advice or instruction on developmental issues. "Should I stay with my boyfriend (or husband) and try to work out our problems even now that the feeling has faded and a romantic alternative stands temptingly in the wings?" "Should I bring my child up in a religion? If not, how should I deal with my religious mother-in-law as the time for each religious rite of passage arises and is missed?"

We also might pose alternative career choices. The first places one in joint enterprise with high energy materialists pursuing economic gains. The second weds one to burned-out social activists struggling haltingly toward lofty but unlikely ideals. "Subjects" might be asked which option one should choose and why. Such choices might be posed in terms of competing duties: Should one devote oneself to one's own moral development when there are people in need of aid or where there are gross injustices to be opposed? Should one forego the developmental environment of a social change organization to pursue a high salary that could be used to bankroll this organization? The same sorts of questions could be generated regarding our choice of friends or mates.

Questions of these sorts will not only produce evidence, pro or con, for a naturally developing perfectionist rationale, but will also show how people rank values and ideals, and whether or not they can justify these rankings. There is a values clarification exercise that presents succinct paragraphs posing various approaches to life; the approach of hedonism, striving for individual accomplishment and success, devotion to spiritual enlightenment or cultural pursuits. "Subjects" could be asked to assess the relative merits of these styles as conceptions of the morally worthy or good life: "Do you feel that it is wrong to pursue life-style $X$ in preference to life-style *Y*? Do you feel we are obliged to pursue one life-style more than the other, or would it merely be better to do so, or is morality indifferent to such choices? Are these choices irrelevant to morality?''

Based on the evaluations of ideals people offer and their reasons for them, we may be able to define an expanded, naturally developing value hierarchy that is a logical extension of stage structure. The relativity we normally associate with value judgments may then be explained away, at least in part, as a function of inadequate stage development. Some rankings will reflect the structural inadequacies of lower stages. Hopefully the motivations and ideals of altruism and love would tend to be ranked highest by people at principled stages. This would provide some basis for arguing that there are ideals that all people tend to recognize as superior and toward which all people might be expected to strive.

## APPENDIX

Kohlberg has outlined the assumptions of cognitive developmental theory as follows:[1]

> 1. Basic development involves basic transformations of cognitive structure which cannot be defined or explained by the parameters of associationistic learning and which must be explained by parameters of organizational wholes or systems of internal relations.
> 2. Development of cognitive structure is the result of processes of interaction between the structure of the organism and the structure of the environment, rather than being the direct result of maturation or the direct result of learning (in the sense of a direct shaping of the organism's responses to accord with environmental structures).
> 3. Cognitive structures are always structures (schemata) of action. While cognitive activities move from the sensorimotor to the symbolic to verbal-propositional modes, the organization of these modes is always an organization of actions upon objects.
> 4. The direction of development of cognitive structure is toward greater equilibrium in this organism-environment interaction i.e., of greater balance or reciprocity between the action of the organism upon the (perceived) object (or situation) and the action of the (perceived) object upon the organism.
>
> Social development is, in essence, the restructuring of the (1) concept of self; (2) in its relationship to concepts of other people; (3) conceived as being in a common social world with social standards: Social cognition always involves role-taking, i.e., awareness that the other is in some way like the self, and that the other knows or is responsive to the self in a system of complementary expectations. Accordingly developmental changes in the social self reflect parallel changes in conceptions of the social world.
>
> The core of the cognitive–developmental position, then, is the doctrine of cognitive stages. Cognitive stages have the following general characteristics:
> 1. Stages imply distinct or qualitative differences in children's modes of thinking or of solving the same problem at different ages.
> 2. These different modes of thought form an invariant sequence, order, or succession in individual development While cultural factors may speed up, slow down, or stop development, they do not change its sequence.

[1]Source: From L. Kohlberg, ''Stage and sequence: The cognitive–developmental approach to socialization. In D. A. Goslin (Ed.), *Handbook of socialization theory and research*. Chicago: Rand McNally, 1969. Pp. 348–353.

3. Each of these different and sequential modes of thought forms a "structured whole." A given stage-response on a task does not just represent a specific response determined by knowledge and familiarity with the task or tasks similar to it.

4. Cognitive stages are hierarchical integrations. Stages form an order of increasingly differentiated and integrated structures to fulfill a common function.

### Kohlberg's Levels and Stages of Moral Judgment[2]

*Level I—Preconventional*

*Stage 1.* It is right to avoid breaking rules backed by punishment, to obey for its own sake, to avoid physical damage to persons and property, to avoid the superior power of authorities.

Egocentric point of view: Doesn't consider the interests of others or recognize that they differ from one's own; doesn't relate two points of view. Actions are considered physically rather than in terms of psychological interests of others. Authority's perspective is confused with one's own.

*Stage 2.* One should follow rules only when it is to someone's immediate interest; acting to meet one's own interests and needs and letting others do the same. Right is also what's fair, what's an equal exchange, a deal, an agreement. You should serve your own needs or interests in a world where you have to recognize that other people have their interests, too.

Concrete individualistic perspective: Aware that everybody has his own interest to pursue and these conflict, so that right is relative (in the concrete individualistic sense).

*Level II—Conventional*

*Stage 3.* One should live up to what is expected by people close to you or what people generally expect of people in your role as son, brother, friend, etc. "Being good" is important and means having good motives, showing concern about others. It also means keeping mutual relationships, such as trust, loyalty, respect and gratitude. You must be a good person in your own eyes and those of others. You must care for others and believe in the Golden Rule. You desire to maintain rules and authority which support (stereotypically) good behavior.

Perspective of the individual in relationships with other individuals: Aware of shared feelings, agreements, and expectations which take primacy over individual interests. Relates points of view through the concrete Golden Rule, putting yourself in the other guy's shoes. Does not yet consider generalized system perspective.

*Stage 4.* You must fulfill the actual duties to which you have agreed. Laws are to be upheld except in extreme cases where they conflict with other fixed social duties. Right is also contributing to society, the group, or institution. You must keep the institution going as a whole, to avoid the breakdown in the system "if everyone did it," or the imperative of conscience to meet one's defined obligations.

Differentiates societal point of view from interpersonal agreement or motives: Takes the point of view of the system that defines roles and rules. Considers individual relations in terms of place in the system.

*Level III—Postconventional*

*Stage 5.* You should be aware that people hold a variety of values and opinions, that most values and rules are relative to your group. These relative rules should usually be upheld, however, in the interest of

*(continued)*

[2]Source: Adapted from L. Kohlberg, "Moral stages and moralization: The cognitive developmental approach." In T. Lickona (Ed.), *Moral development and behavior.* New York: Holt, Rinehart, and Winston, 1976. Pp. 34–35.

---

*Level III—(Continued)*

---

impartiality and because they are the social contract. Some nonrelative values and rights like life and liberty, however, must be upheld in any society and regardless of majority opinion. You must have a sense of obligation to law because of your social contract to make and abide by laws for the welfare of all people's rights. A feeling of contractual commitment, freely entered upon, to family, friendship, trust, and work obligations. Concern that laws and duties be based on rational calculation of overall utility—"The greatest good for the greatest number."

Prior-to-society perspective: Perspective of a rational individual aware of values and rights prior to social attachments and contracts. Integrates perspectives by formal mechanisms of agreement, contract, objective impartiality, and due process. Considers moral and legal points of view; recognizes that they sometimes conflict and finds it difficult to integrate them.

*Stage 6.*   One must follow self-chosen ethical principles. Particular laws or social agreements are usually valid because they rest on such principles. When laws violate these principles, one acts in accordance with the principle. Principles are universal principles of justice, the equality of human rights and respect for the dignity of human beings as individuals. As a rational person one must believe in the validity of universal moral principles and a sense of personal commitment to them.

Perspective of a moral point of view from which social arrangements derive: Perspective is that of any rational individual recognizing the nature of morality or the fact that persons are ends in themselves and must be treated as such.

---

# REFERENCES

Gilligan, C. In a different voice: Women's concepts of self and morality. *Harvard Educational Review.* 1977, *47,*(4), 481–517.

Haan, N., Smith, M. B., & Block, J. The moral reasoning of young adults: Political–social behavior, family background and personality correlates. *Journal of Personality and Social Psychology,* 1968, *10,* 183–201.

Kohlberg, L. *The philosophy of moral development* (Vol. 1). New York: Harper & Row, 1981.

Krebs, D., & Rosenwald, A. Moral reasoning and moral behavior in conventional adults. *Merrill–Palmer Quarterly,* 1977, *23,* 79–84.

Rawls, J. *A theory of justice.* Cambridge, Mass.: Harvard University Press, 1971.

Staub, E. *Positive social behavior* (Vol. 1). New York: Academic Press, 1978.

# Commentary and Critique: Psychological and Philosophical Approaches to Prosocial Development

**DENNIS KREBS**

"Original sin" conceptions of human nature and human development permeate the social sciences. Infants are viewed as essentially selfish, aggressive, and amoral, and the task of parents and other "socializing agents" is seen as civilizing them—training them to behave in the ways deemed appropriate in their society. Consider for example the following statement by Professor Alberta Siegal of Stanford (cited by Brown & Solomon in Chapter 11, this volume):

> A horde of untutored savages arrives in our midst annually; these are our infants, who come among us knowing nothing of our language, our culture, our values. . . . The child starts life totally ignorant of . . . decency, gentleness, compassion, sympathy, kindness. . . . Twenty years are all we have to civilize these barbarians. . . .

It is not surprising that during the past few decades the goal of most research on socialization has been to investigate techniques for inhibiting in children their "natural" disposition to behave antisocially and instilling in them the "unnatural" disposition to behave prosocially or altruistically. The chapters by Dale Hay and Harriet Rheingold (Chapter 3) and Diane Bridgeman (Chapter 4) supply compelling antidotes to this trend.

Hay and Rheingold review research that establishes quite clearly that infants display prosocial behaviors on their own if given half a chance. Shortly after birth they react negatively to the distress of other infants; in the early months of their life they respond positively to other people; before the end of their first year they share their possessions quite spontaneously with both adults and peers, and, by 2 years of age, they engage in playful caregiving activities with toys and dolls, initiate at-

THE NATURE OF PROSOCIAL DEVELOPMENT

tempts to comfort others who appear to be distressed, and help their parents. Indeed the amount of assistance they give their parents increases steadily from age $1\frac{1}{2}$–2 to $2\frac{1}{2}$ (and, although not reported by Hay and Rheingold, but established unequivocally by my own experience, diminishes to nothing during the early teens!).

Diane Bridgeman reports the results of a set of naturalistic observations on $1\frac{1}{2}$–$3\frac{1}{2}$-year-old children interacting with their parents in their homes. She found that children of these ages display a significant amount of sharing, helping, nurturance, cooperation, sympathy, and supportiveness, although in a rudimentary forms. Behaviors of this sort are most likely to occur in the context of an ongoing activity or in response to a request by a parent; however, some appear to occur spontaneously. Although about a third of the observed behaviors were rated as "compliant," more than half appeared to stem from sympathetic, kind, supportive, and helpful motives.

The evidence reviewed in Chapters 3 and 4 indicates that many prosocial behaviors are not instilled in children through exhortation or reinforcement. Of course parents exhort their children to behave prosocially, and they reward them in various ways when they do; but as Diane Bridgeman shows, prosocial behaviors evoked in these ways are in a minority. Similarly, although children clearly learn through modeling, Bridgeman observed a "surprisingly low incidence" of modeled prosocial behavior (4%) in her subject sample.

Considered in the context of other research, the findings presented in Chapters 3 and 4 should be interpreted less as a disconfirmation of original sin models of socialization than as an exemplification of their limitations. As documented by Bridgeman, young children often behave in selfish ways. However, the total number of self-centered behaviors emitted by the children observed by Bridgeman correlated .50 with the total number of prosocial behaviors they displayed. The findings from the studies described in Chapters 3 and 4 indicate that the primary function of socialization techniques is often much more to indicate how, in a general sort of way, a natural motive may be expressed than to stifle an antisocial desire. Also, as pointed out by Hay and Rheingold, children are not mechanical imitators; like the languages they develop, the behaviors they emit are creative—their own expression of the meanings they seek to convey.

If the original sin model of human nature is limited, with what should it be supplemented or replaced? The authors of Chapters 3 and 4 appear to want to supplement it with a fair amount of original benevolence. I share this inclination, but I feel somewhat tentative about the data on which it is based. The observations reported in Chapters 3 and 4 are observations of *behavior*. It makes sense to call most of the behavior "prosocial" in a general, descriptive sense because its *effect* on other people is desirable. However, models of human nature are based on motives. In evaluating them we must go beyond behavior; we must attempt to determine why children do the things they do and, more specifically, whether the motives underlying their prosocial behavior are intrinsically prosocial.

This difficult question remains unanswered in the research reviewed in Chapters 3 and 4, although a call for studies that address it is noted. Bridgeman reports on the context in which the prosocial behaviors occurred, which supplies some clue to their motives (i.e., in response to a direct command versus in response to the need of another); however, the attribution of motives from contextual cues is necessarily inferential. If I were to put my money on a motive underlying the prosocial behaviors that were observed, I would put it on something like the desire to acquire and express competence. The sketch of the young child that emerges in this research is of one who is actively reaching out to understand, cope with, and fit into the social world. Sometime between 6 months and a year of age, the young child begins to give things to other people. Because he or she wants to do something nice for them? Perhaps, but I would guess it is for the same reason why children of this age push a mobile back and forth—to make an effect on the world, to evoke a reaction, to see what will happen, to practice a new behavioral skill. The fact that Hay and Rheingold include pointing in their list of sharing behaviors supports this view. The same goes for helping around the house. (Tell a young child that you do not want any help—that is, construe the behavior as not prosocial—and see whether he or she retains the motive to become involved in the activity.) Finally, Diane Bridgeman's finding that children's level of verbal behavior correlates highly with their prosocial behavior suggests that children who display the most prosocial behavior may not be the most prosocially-motivated children; rather, they may be the most active.

The authors of these chapters discuss the implications of their findings for existing theories of development. Hay and Rheingold state quite flatly that ''no current theory of socialization predicts prosocial behavior on the part of infants,'' and Bridgeman states that ''both psychoanalytic and cognitive developmental orientations posit the years of 5–7 as likely to be the onset of positive social behaviors.'' However, my reading of Piaget, especially his 1932 book on moral judgment, indicates that prosocial behaviors in infants do not present any particular problem for his theory. Piaget's theory is a theory of cognition, not behavior. Similar behaviors may stem from quite different cognitions. Thus, children may behave ''prosocially'' (by, for example, helping others) for quite different reasons. Piaget has characterized the social cognition of the young child as ''egocentric.'' By this Piaget meant that young children have *cognitive* problems differentiating their points of view from that of others, not that young children are *behaviorally* selfish. Although Piaget was far from clear about the dynamics of egocentricity, he was explicit in claiming that this quality could cause young children to view events from the most salient perspective, even when it originates from others. Thus, egocentricity may give rise to either ''selfish'' or ''prosocial'' behaviors, depending on which perspective is most powerful. A young child who offers his sad mother a teddy bear for consolation is behaving both egocentrically and prosocially. The authors of both chapters acknowledge these points in one way or another but do not explore their implications for a revision in the position popularly (but I think incorrectly) imputed to Piaget.

The issue of egocentricity relates to the issue of the nature of altruistic behavior. If a little girl helps her brother because she has failed to distinguish between his perspective and her's, the helping behavior really ought not be considered altruistic (at least in motive). Looked at in this way, a prerequisite for altruistic behavior would be the ability to distinguish between self and other and to take the role of the other as a separate object. This and related points are developed well by Bridgeman.

The fifth and sixth chapters of this volume take up where chapters 3 and 4 leave off: The children involved tend to be older (from about 3–11) years, and the focus of the second set of chapters is on cognitive structures and processes rather than behavior.

The notion that role-taking mediates altruism has been around for a long time. Looked at quickly, it seems eminently plausible. Therefore, it came as a surprise to many investigators when a number of studies failed to support the expected relationship. In 1981 Cristine Russell and I examined the research on the relationship between role-taking and altruism in an attempt to find out why it contained inconsistent results. We found a host of methodological and conceptual problems. Focusing on tests of affective role-taking, Smith, Leinbach, Stewart, and Blackwell (Chapter 5) find the same thing.

The central problems with most "role-taking" tests is that they do not supply any insight into the cognitive processes that children employ when they take the tests. Rather, the tests are scored on the basis of the conclusions that the children reach. As pointed out by Smith et al., however, different children may arrive at the same answer (e.g., a girl in a picture feels sad) (a) through projection; (b) simply reading her facial expression off of the picture; or (c) normative inference—by inferring how she must feel from the situation; and so on. Creating incongruities between situational cues and facial expressions does not solve this problem.

Consider Borke's test of perspective-taking for example. Children are told stories and shown pictures of children whose facial expressions match the outcome of stories (e.g., receives a toy and smiles). What can you infer if the child correctly identifies the emotion the character is expressing? You do not have to possess any role-taking ability to be able to infer that a smile on a cartoon character's face signifies that the character is happy. You simply have to read it off of the picture. Making the child's face sad in a happy situation does not help much either. You are only creating an unnatural, incongruent juxtaposition. If the child orients either to facial or situational cues, you have no basis for inferring why. It is dangerous to label these orientations "empathic" and "projective," respectively, because the child may arrive at the same conclusion (e.g. "she feels happy") in a variety of ways. In my view, the most useful information available from a test such as this is the child's spontaneous verbalization of how he or she is construing the problem, or, as in the Smith et al. study, an indication of the child's ability to synthesize two sources of information (the girl being chased by a tiger is happy "because she can run faster than the tiger"), and even this is not necessarily perspective-taking.

In a 1982 study, Lucy LeMare examined eight of the most popular tests of role-taking, including Borke's. Although she found that Borke's test failed to relate meaningfully to the other tests in her 6–12-year-old sample, there were tests that did appear to supply valid tests of role-taking ability. Tests created by Selman (1976) and Feffer and Gourevitch (1960), for example, fared quite well. What these tests have in common is the potential to reveal the structure of role-taking processes that the child is employing. The conclusions the child reaches are irrelevant in these tests. It is the (role-taking) processes through which the child reaches the conclusion that are scored. (A similar problem limits the test of values employed by Sibulkin in Chapter 6 of this volume)

If you don't employ a valid measure of role-taking, you cannot expect to find a meaningful relationship between it and prosocial behavior. In addition, you ought not necessarily expect to find a relationship between role-taking and altruism even if you do employ a valid test! As Turiel (1978) has made clear, role-taking is an information-gathering tool. It is one of several ways to obtain knowledge about others' inner qualities (what they are perceiving, thinking, feeling, etc.). Prosocial behavior involves assisting others. Why should the ability to understand what another is thinking or feeling generate the motivation to assist him or her? In most situations, there is not really any reason to expect it to. As Cristine Russell and I have argued (Krebs & Russell, 1981), the circumstances under which role-taking ought to relate to prosocial behavior are really quite constrained: Role-taking is a necessary but not sufficient condition for a prosocial response in circumstances where role-taking is the only means through which an observer can infer that another wants or needs help. Although knowing that another wants or needs help generally is a prerequisite for helping (and indeed, it may generate the motivation to help), it does not by any means guarantee that the individual will help. Other motives such as self-interest, fear, or embarrassment may interfere.

When you think of the relationships that actually are investigated in studies, the most surprising result is that so many of the studies obtain positive findings (see Underwood & Moore, 1982). Why should a child's ability to say that a smiling girl in a picture receiving a present is "happy" have anything to do with whether the child actually comforts someone who bangs her knee in real life? In order for role-taking abilities to mediate behavior, they must be activated in a situation, give rise to the motive to help, and supersede other conflicting self-interested motives.

In addition to an examination of the relationship between perspective-taking and prosocial behavior, Smith *et al.* examined the relationship between a situational manipulation—verbal exhortation—and prosocial behavior. I have been quite critical of some of the conclusions drawn by investigators who have manipulated situational variables (see Krebs, 1978, 1982a, 1982b). Smith *et al.* summarize some of the problems with research in this area nicely in the introduction to their study: "When children are placed in a relatively unusual situation with an unfamiliar adult who specifies what behavior is expected, the safest course of action is to do what one is told. These criticisms seem especially potent when applied to the experimental study of the effects of instructions or other verbal communications on the prosocial behavior of children." Smith *et al.* go on to point out that one of the most problematic features of many studies on the effects of verbal exhortation and modeling on prosocial behavior is their reliance on the standard donation to charity paradigm.

One of the purposes of the study that Smith *et al.* go on to describe is to minimize demand characteristics. Their method of minimization was to create as natural an experimental context as possible and to assess the types of prosocial behavior normally displayed by 4–5-year-old children. The care that these investigators took to increase the ecological validity of their dependent measures is laudatory.

Smith *et al.* found that verbal exhortations from adults (such as, "When I play with you, I want you to help," and "Jenny doesn't have any candy kisses. If you share your candy kisses, then she'll have some too") have a rather profound positive effect on the frequency of prosocial behavior displayed by 4–5-year-old children, and that this effect is not specific to the immediate situation—it prevailed after a week, in the presence of unfamiliar adults. The effects observed by these investigators were really quite powerful. There can be no doubt that one of the most effective ways of inducing children to do what you want them to do is put them in a novel setting with unfamiliar adults who indicate either directly or indirectly that they expect them to behave in a particular manner. Indeed, the classic studies of Milgram show that adults too are extremely susceptible to demands from authorities. There is, however, some question about the extent to which behaviors that are evoked in one context will generalize to other contexts. This question concerns the extent to which investigations such as the one we are discussing are most appropriately considered studies on socialization or social influence. Given that strange adults can induce compliance in young children quite easily, can we infer that the techniques they employ would be valuable to parents and other familiar adults as methods of inducing internalized standards that supply general guides to prosocial behavior?

On the positive side, Smith *et al.* found that children who were induced by two adults to increase the frequency of particular prosocial behaviors in an initial "social influence" session also displayed more of these types of behavior in a follow up session with two different adults. In addition, these children also displayed more comforting behavior, even though it had not been evoked in the social influence session. On the negative side, it must be pointed out that the follow up session was remarkably similar to the social influence session, with two strange adults in the same room verbalizing the same sorts of needs; and that the entire experience (i.e., the three experimental sessions) was undoubtedly unprecedented in these young children's lives. The investigators explained their failure to find any difference between power-assertive and inductive exhortations as follows: "It is not clear that the subjective meaning of the experimental manipulations . . . differed for the two treatment groups." It is possible that the reason why there was no difference was because even a mild inductive exhortation is enough to instill a powerful sense of demand in young children in the "strong" situations created for the purpose of experimental research (see Snyder & Ickes, in press). It would be interesting to determine the extent to which the behaviors evoked by the adults generalized to subsequent interactions between the children and their parents or playmates in everyday life over time. Hopefully, Smith *et al.* and other investigators will test the generality of such effects in subsequent research.

Many of the issues raised by Smith *et al.* in Chapter 5 also pertain to the study described by Sibulkin in Chapter 6. Instead of role-taking, Sibulkin investigated the effect of the value "considerateness" on prosocial behavior. As with the cognitive measure employed by Smith *et al.*, there are some questions about the extent to which the measure of values employed by Sibulkin was valid. Furthermore, we can question the expectation that the value of considerateness should mediate prosocial behavior.

Consider the actual operations assessed by the test of considerateness. Children were asked to choose between four children whom they would prefer to be like; for example, Debbie, who keeps her room neat, or Mary, who helps out other kids who cannot do something. When subjects replied "Mary," the experimenter inferred that they valued considerateness more than cleanliness. However, in analysing her findings, Sibulkin found that children's tendency to endorse active statements of the value considerateness, such as the one associated with Mary, was negatively correlated with their tendency to endorse passive statements of the same value, such as "Barbara does not say mean things to hurt other kids' feelings." Teacher and peer ratings of which subjects were like the people described in the phrases followed the same pattern. What, then, can we conclude about the extent to which the test assessed the value of considerateness?

To Sibulkin's credit, she digs into her data in search of an explanation. She concludes that considerateness may be motivated either by active assertiveness, especially among friends, or obedience to authority. This explanation is very insightful; I would carry its implications further. To me it indicates that our (adult or social scientist) view that children possess general "values" such as "considerateness" may be misguided. What some of the children seem to value, instead, is the same sort of thing valued by the younger children in Chapter 3—being one of the kids who helps other kids rather than being one of the kids who needs help—that is, *being competent*. Other children seem to value *being good*—obeying rules, and not getting in trouble.

Forced-choice tests like those used by Smith *et al.* and Sibulkin have two limitations—they constrain the alternatives a subject can give, and they fail to obtain information about the cognitive processes that produce the choices that subjects make (and, thus, what the choices mean to the subjects). What Sibulkin might be picking up in her results is a division between Piaget's heteronomous moral orientation (or Kohlberg's Stage 1), and Piaget's autonomous moral orientation (or Kohlberg's Stage 2). Sibulkin's speculations about reciprocity, which is a defining characteristic of the latter orientation, supports this possibility. It is interesting to wonder what Sibulkin would have found if she had interviewed the kids, asked them what sorts of people they liked and would want to be like and why. Although this method does not produce the types of results that are easily quantified, it does permit an investigator to obtain a more representative indication of how children view the world.

As concerns the relationship between values and prosocial behavior, the care with which Sibulkin matched appropriate levels is laudable. Too often investigators give subjects tests of a broad cognitive orientation—such as how highly they value freedom or equality, or their level of moral development—and assess the relationship between scores on these tests and particular behaviors in one, highly specific situation. Taking guidance from refinements in theoretical expectations about the relationship between attitudes and behavior (see Ajzen & Fishbein, 1977), investigators would seem well-advised to match general measures of prescriptive cognitions with general measures of behavior, and measures of more specific cognitive processes with more specific measures of behavior. Wisely, Sibulkin uses the same types of questions to ask her subjects' classmates and teachers to name the people who value various things as she used to ask her subjects to assess their own values.

As it turned out, there was little relationship between the extent to which children ranked the values of considerateness high in the hierarchy of values presented to them and the extent to which they were viewed by others as engaging in related behaviors, at least on an item-to-item basis. This does not, in my opinion, mean that there is no relationship between values and behavior. Indeed, values should be more closely aligned with behavior than other cognitive processes, such as role-taking, because they are more prescriptive. However, in order to get at this relationship, you must get at the child's values from the child's perspective, and, as indicated, forced-choice tests are not very well-equipped to perform this task.

As a way of consolidating some of the points I have been making about the ambiguity of content or conclusions and the importance of getting at the structure of underlying cognition, consider Smetana's study, reported by Smetana, Bridgeman, and Turiel in Chapter 7. These investigators began by classifying events in pictures as representing either moral, social conventional, or personal issues according to their own (as opposed to their subjects') criteria. They then showed the pictures to subjects and asked them to rank them for ''rightness or wrongness.'' Here they are meeting their subjects halfway—they are supplying the events and the categories (rightness–wrongness) but permitting their subjects to define the correlation. Then they release their subjects and ask them to justify their rankings. These investigators find that their subjects distinguish between domains in much the same way as they do: The subjects tend to rank the ''moral'' items presented by the experimenters as most right or wrong, ''conventional'' items as intermediately right or wrong, and ''personal'' items as least right or wrong.

Ranking events supplies only a relatively superficial indication of their meaning. Smetana et al. delve deeper into the cognitive structures of their subjects by asking them to justify their rankings. The justifications given by the subjects support the assumption that subjects construe events in the three domains differently. I say ''support'' rather than ''establish'' because, as is always necessarily the case, the investigators, in effect, construed the subjects' constructions—that is, they coded the justifications in accordance with their (or, more precisely, Nucci's, 1981) criteria of moral, conventional, and personal. (As Chapter 8, by Bill Puka, shows, there is considerable controversy about where the boundaries circumscribing the moral domain should be drawn.) Note that of the several criteria for classification in each of the three domains, only some served as a source of distinction for the subjects.

An important contention made by the authors of Chapter 7 is that people distinguish among moral, conventional, and personal issues, as these authors have defined them, regardless of their age. Even though few significant age differences were found in this study, and even though a number of other studies have failed to find age differences (see Turiel, 1978, Nucci, 1981), I nonetheless question this contention. If people develop the ability to distinguish between domains, we would expect a steady increase in the number of "correct" classifications from the fifth grade to college in the present study and a decrease in "incorrect" classifications. I think there is some support for this expectation. College students ranked 13–28% more of the events correctly than fifth grade students in $\frac{5}{8}$ rankings (see Tables 7.2 and 7.3). College students also made fewer incorrect classifications than fifth graders on $\frac{7}{12}$ rankings. In addition, when subjects were asked to sort items in accordance with whether they were right or wrong, or a person's own business, the fifth graders made the most "mistakes." I cannot help but suspect that if younger children had been tested, they would have classified even more items incorrectly (i.e., revealed an even greater inability to distinguish between domains) than the fifth graders.

The central issue addressed by Smetana et al. concerns the conceptual status of prosocial behavior. The evidence they present indicates that prosocial acts are not necessarily moral acts—that is, that the construct of prosocial behavior may be construed in either moral, conventional, or personal terms. I agree unequivocally with this contention. I have argued that prosocial behavior is an ambiguous construct and that a prosocial behavior or event (for example, "sharing your lunch with a child who has none") may be moral or immoral, altruistic or selfish, conventional or nonconventional, and so on, depending on the motives and intentions underlying the behavior. For example, the act might be moral if the child engaged in it because he or she felt that people should do unto others as you would have them do unto you; conventional if the motive was to obey a school rule; and personal if the motive was to get rid of an undesirable sandwich (see Krebs, 1978, 1982a, 1982b).

The focus of Smetana et al.'s concern is prosocial behavior. The conceptual status of altruism is a more complex matter. The question here is whether a truely altruistic behavior can be conceptualized in any way other than as an aspect of morality: If you construe an event in conventional or personal terms, must it be nonaltruistic by definition? I must acknowledge that my position on this matter has been somewhat unclear. Because Smetana et al. distinguish between moral and conventional domains and because "conventional reasoning" may be employed to support behaviors that are construed as altruistic by the conventional reasoner ("You should help others at your expense because there is a social norm or convention that says so"), they conclude that issues involving altruism need not necessarily fall in the domain of morality. However, because I tend to view "conventional reasoning" as undifferentiated moral reasoning, I am inclined to view issues involving altruism as moral issues (even though the reasoning employed to support them is impure or confounded moral reasoning).

A great deal of the confusion surrounding the construct of altruism can be dissipated by recognizing that it may be construed both as a moral *issue*—something to be reasoned about, and as a principle or *standard* of morality. In early versions of Kohlberg's scoring manual, altruism was listed as a moral issue. In recent versions it has been removed from the list of moral issues and is treated more as an aspect of structure—a *standard* or morality. In retrospect I think I have confused these functions. As a moral issue altruism concerns our obligation to treat others generously. People may take any of a number of positions (pro- or antialtruism) on this issue and support it in any number of ways. As a principle of moral reasoning, altruism may assume any number of forms. One might, for example, argue that "it is always right to give more than you get" or "everyone is obliged to maximize the good, which entails behaving altruistically on many occasions." What I have argued in the past is that in the sample of moral reasoning tapped by Kohlberg's test, the tendency to employ a principle of altruism as one's primary standard of morality peaks at Stage 3 and that this type of standard or principle is not a very lofty one (see Krebs, 1982a). In Chapter 8 Bill Puka attempts to rescue altruism from the grip of nice-but-naive Stage 3 moral reasoning, and to reconstrue it in Stage 6+ terms.

Puka's arguments may be a little difficult for the nonphilosopher, so I will attempt to summarize them. There are two opposing traditions in ethical philosophy—those that define morality deontologically, in terms of absolute standards of the *right,* and those that define morality teleologically, in terms of the *good.* The difference between these traditions can be exemplified by asking yourself whether you think it is morally correct to violate an ideal standard (the *right*) such as keeping promises, in order to maximize the net benefit or *good* to others. (For example, is it morally acceptable to lie in order to save face for someone else?) Much of the work of ethical philosophers consists in advancing arguments for one position and against the other, or constructing compromise positions such as rule (*right*)–utilitarianism (*good*). (For example, "You should abide by moral rules that, on balance, maximize the net benefit to all.")

Kohlberg's test of moral judgment is scored in accordance with a deontological ethical position in which justice is the paramount principle of morality. There is an intrinsic incompatibility between the principle of altruism and the principle of justice: "Inasmuch as the idea of altruism means giving more than one's share, or giving more than one 'should', it entails a violation of the balance of reciprocity that defines justice [Krebs, 1982c, p. 73]." It is primarily for this reason that altruism does not fare very well when viewed from the standards of morality adopted by Kohlberg.

Puka explains why the principle of justice reigns supreme in the moral reasoning of people who take Kohlberg's test by pointing out that, in effect, the content of Kohlberg's test is biased toward justice. The dilemmas it contains involve issues related to decisions involving justice, such as how to divide resources, etc. However, suggests Puka, if you ask people to resolve moral conflicts involving other moral issues—say, for example, the amount of time one ought to allot to his or her career, as opposed to his or her mate, children, or hobby—you might well end up with structures of reasoning in which principles of justice fare less well. The point here is that the questions that Kohlberg asks on his test limit, to a great extent, the answers that he can get. Puka then sets out to sketch the parameters of an ethical theory in which the principle of altruism supersedes the principle of justice.

In order to establish his position, Puka ultimately must establish that a moral theory based on justice fails to supply a sufficient guide for all moral conduct, and he must show how a moral theory based on altruism can do a better job. What, then, is wrong with justice? Puka points out that the essence of justice involves respecting individuals as equal and autonomous beings, and, necessary as this notion is in morality, it suffers two limitations:

1. It is irrelevant to questions such as "What sort of obligation do I have to better myself?" and "Should I spend my time helping the poor or building my business?"—which, suggests Puka, fall in the moral domain.
2. Principles of justice are neutral with respect to a number of values. Giving each his due means respecting his or her values, goals, and desires, whatever they are—as long as they do not perpetrate injustice.

One obvious alternative—one that has been tried by other philosophers—is to abandon justice and substitute another principle, such as love (a construct that Puka uses interchangeably with altruism). Puka summarizes some of the past philosophical arguments that have been adduced in support of the primacy of altruism and notes that they contain lethal deficiencies. In particular, he argues that utilitarianism (a teleological principle that focuses on maximizing the good) is problematic because (*a*) it defines as immoral any activity that does not seek to maximize the good; (*b*) it fails to supply a way of rank ordering different kinds of good; and (*c*) it does not indicate how the good that it maximized should be divided—that is, it permits a few to reap the benefits contributed by many.

Having established that both justice and altruism are inadequate in themselves as primary moral principles, Puka seeks to construct a hybrid structure consisting of the best of both. More particularly, he tries to fatten up the principle of justice with a principle of the good and control the permissability of coercing people to maximize the good with a principle of justice that obliges them to respect others as equals.

What emerges is the following four-level hierarchy:

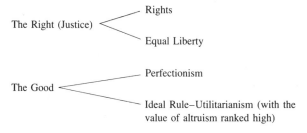

The Right (Justice) — Rights
— Equal Liberty

The Good — Perfectionism
— Ideal Rule–Utilitarianism (with the value of altruism ranked high)

According to Puka, all four levels are needed to supply a full justification of altruism; and the hierarchy is necessary in order to resolve the inevitable conflicts between principles.

The questions we must ask about the moral robe stitched together by Puka are whether the thread will hold (whether he has successfully integrated the various layers), whether the garment is overadorned or incomplete (whether it is parsimonious and encompassing), and whether anyone will ever wear it (whether it corresponds to high forms of natural moral reasoning). As concerns the first question, Puka admits that he really has only tacked together a rough pattern—that many of the details have not been specified. In particular, he has not specified the rights people should be granted or the ideals they ought to pursue; nor has he indicated why altruism is a more virtuous dimension of perfectionism than other qualities. In order to construct a hierarchy such as the one constructed by Puka, you must ensure that it does not contain any inherent incompatibilities and that the principles employed to resolve conflicts between levels work in all relevant situations. Although Puka's arguments for the necessity of retaining both a principle of the right and a principle of the good (to supplement and counterbalance one another) are compelling, he does not supply a full justification for ranking the right above the good or, indeed, for the hierarchy as a whole.

The key to altruistic motivation in Puka's scheme is perfectionism. Puka feels that he needs a principle of perfectionism to solve the problem of infringing on individual liberty in order to maximize the good or exalting individual liberty to the point where nothing good gets accomplished. The question he must answer is why bettering oneself necessarily entails behaving altruistically. He argues that principles of perfectionism will direct individuals to follow a course of moral development that will instill in them the disposition to accept the principles of perfectionism as their own. Therefore, they will not have to be compelled to behave altruistically from the outside (i.e., be morally obliged to do good), and because they will want to behave altruistically, this behavior will not entail a violation of their liberty. The central question here is a psychological one—how can a set of principles instill in individuals the disposition to believe in them; how can an "ought" prescription generate an "is" condition. At a philosophical level, I wonder whether the tasks that are undertaken by perfectionism in Puka's model could be accomplished by the ideal in ideal rule–utilitarianism, thus enabling Puka to cut the layer of perfectionism from his scheme.

In summary, Puka sets out to outline a high-level "in principle" philosophical justification for the argument that behaving in a truely altruistic manner entails fulfilling the highest standards of morality. In the process he exposes the deficiencies of an unbuttressed principle of justice and makes it clear that Kohlberg's test assesses only part of the domain of morality. Although he does not fully develop his case for the assumption that we have a moral obligation to better ourselves, I sense that this assumption is valid and significant; however, I am not completely convinced that it will supply a bridge to altruism. Although sincere altruism may be laudable, I would argue that we are morally obligated to behave altruistically only when it follows from a principle of the good (e.g., maximizes the net welfare of people) *or* from a principle of the right (e.g., do not make special concessions for the person in your position simply because it is you). If people abided by principles such as these, there would be a lot more altruism in the world than there is now, and in my opinion, plenty enough for most purposes.

# REFERENCES

Ajzen, I., & Fishbein, M. Attitude–behavior relations: A theoretical analysis and review of empirical research. *Psychological Bulletin,* 1977, *84,* 888–918.

Feffer, M. H., & Gourevitch, V. Cognitive aspects of role-taking in children. *Journal of Personality,* 1960, *28,* 383–396.

Krebs, D. L. A cognitive-developmental approach to altruism. In L. Wispé (Ed.), *Altruism, sympathy, and helping.* New York: Academic Press, 1978.

Krebs, D. L. Altruism: A rational approach. In N. Eisenberg (Ed.), *The development of prosocial behavior.* New York: Academic Press, 1982. (a)

Krebs, D. L. Psychological approaches to altruism: An evaluation. *Ethics,* 1982, *92,* 147–158. (b)

Krebs, D. L. Prosocial behavior, equity, and justice. In J. Greenberg & R. C. Cohen (Eds.), *Equity and justice in social behaviors.* New York: Academic Press, 1982. (c)

Krebs, D. L., & Russell, C. Role-taking and altruism: When you put yourself in the shoes of another, will they carry you to their owner's aid? In J. P. Rushton & R. M. Sorrentino (Eds.), *Altruism and helping behavior: Social, personality and developmental perspectives.* Hillsdale, N. J.: Erlbaum, 1981.

LeMare, L. On the construct validity of role-taking. Paper presented at the 43rd Annual Meeting of the Canadian Psychological Association, Montreal, Quebec, 1982.

Nucci, L. The development of personal constructs: A domain distinct from moral or societal concepts. *Child Development,* 1981, *52,* 114–121.

Piaget, J. *The moral judgement of the child.* London: Routledge & Kegan Paul, 1932.

Selman, R. Social–cognitive understanding: A guide to educational and clinical practice. In T. Lickona (Ed.), *Moral development and behavior.* New York: Holt Rinehart & Winston, 1976.

Snyder, M., & Ickes, W. Personality and social behavior. In G. Lindzey & E. Aronson (Eds.), *The handbook of social psychology* (3rd ed.) Reading, Mass.: Addison–Wesley, in press.

Turiel, E. Social regulations and domains of social concepts. In W. Damon (Ed.), *New directions for child development: Social cognition.* San Francisco: Jossey–Bass, 1978.

Underwood, B., & Moore, B. Perspective-taking and altruism. *Psychological Bulletin,* 1982, *91,* 141–173.

# CROSS-CULTURAL APPROACHES TO PROSOCIAL DEVELOPMENT

# The Genesis of Prosocial Behavior[1]

## BEATRICE BLYTH WHITING

It has become commonplace to affirm that women are the more nurturant sex, that they are more likely to be responsive to the individuals who share their daily lives, and more willing to assume responsibility for the emotional well-being of these individuals (Chodorow, 1978; Gilligan, 1977, 1982; Miller, 1976). Comprehensive reviews of the evidence for these generalizations have been compiled by numerous authors (Maccoby & Jacklin, 1974). It is beyond the scope of this chapter to review the theories that have been advanced to explain the gender differences that have been found in nurturant, responsive, and responsible behavior, behaviors we include in our definition of prosocial behavior. In exploring the relative contribution of nature and nurture, psychologists have searched for early manifestations of these behaviors in American and European children (see Hartup, in press, for review). As these studies may be confounding cultural with biological and socialization variables (Ember, 1981), their findings should be scrutinized in the light of evidence from the study of the behavior of children growing up in parts of the world that are not dominated by cultural beliefs, values, and social practices of the Western world.

To understand human development we must expand our horizons beyond the

[1]This chapter is a summary of the collaborative research of the author, Carolyn Edwards, Carol Ember, Gerald Erchak, Sara Harkness, Ruth Munroe, R. L. Munroe, Susan Seymour, Charles Super, and Thomas Weisner. The pooling of the observational data and the comparative analysis has been possible by a grant from the Ford Foundation. Lawrence Baldwin and Martha Wenger have helped with the analysis of the data. The findings of the project will appear in a collaborative volume entitled: *The Company They Keep: The Genesis of Gender Role Behavior,* by Beatrice Whiting, Carolyn Edwards, C. Ember, G. Erchak, S. Harkness, R. Munroe, R. L. Munroe, S. Seymour, C. Super, and T. Weisner.

THE NATURE OF PROSOCIAL DEVELOPMENT

confines of Western societies and study the behavior of children in cultures that differ from our own. It is difficult to identify the environmental factors that influence development if there is, comparatively speaking, no variation in the economic and social structures of the sample families and no major difference in the cultural beliefs, values, and practices of the individuals responsible for socialization. As a result of studying societies that do not differ radically on these dimensions, we tend to attribute either too much or too little to environmental factors.

Anthropologists tend to emphasize the difference in experience and search for the social and cultural variables associated with the differences. Cross-cultural psychologists have tended to emphasize similarities and attribute them to biological maturational variables (Kagan, 1981). There is need for both groups of social scientists to adopt a more multi-variant model. When we find differences across cultures, we must attempt both to identify the possible economic, social structural, or cultural conditions associated with the differences and, wherever possible, add these variables to our analysis of the genesis of gender differences. When we find similarities in the behavior of young boys and girls, we must ask to what extent they may be attributed to the similarity of the experiences of young children regardless of culture. Cross-cultural studies can contribute these perspectives to the study of the genesis of gender role behavior.

We have reviewed our cross-cultural data on gender differences in the prosocial behavior of children 2–12 years of age in an attempt to assess the relative contribution of nature and nurture to its development. Our cross-cultural research was designed to analyze gender differences in the social behavior of boys and girls who have grown up in societies that provide learning environments that are different from those of children raised in the postindustrial countries of the Western world. A group of us has pooled the observational data collected in Africa, India, the Philippines, Okinawa, Mexico, and the United States. This chapter summarizes our findings on gender differences in prosocial behavior and our theory as to its genesis.

*Prosocial behavior* is defined here to include nurturance (those behaviors in which the actor was judged to have the intention of meeting the perceived needs of another) and *prosocial dominance* (those behaviors in which the actor was judged to have the intention of changing the behavior of another to meet the social rules of the society and to ensure the welfare of the family). The essence and prototype of prosocial behavior is what has been traditionally called *maternal* or *parental behavior,* a term used here with the recognition that both males and females, and adults and children may behave in maternal ways.

Current theories of the genesis of prosocial behavior have focused on three explanatory systems (Edwards & Whiting, 1980): (*a*) the biological model that points to constitutional, usually hormonal, factors; (*b*) the cognitive-developmental model that stresses stages in the development of behavior associated with maturation; and (*c*) the socialization model. The biological model gains importance as the technology for studying neural and hormonal development improves, but to date biological variables are difficult to measure. The cognitive-developmental model has emphasized the interaction between the organism and experience, but up until very recently (see Berry, 1981; Edwards, 1981; Price Williams, 1975, 1981, for reviews) researchers have neglected to specify the environmental variables. The socialization model has been restricted in its research, overly concerned with the role of the mother during the early years. With a few notable exceptions (Hartup, 1976, in press; Konner, 1975; Lamb, 1978), it has neglected the role of peers and the influence of task performance and play activities on shaping behavior.

Our theory accepts the importance of the cognitive-developmental model, in particular two of its tenets:

1. The child's development of concepts of gender constancy, around the ages of 3 and 4, forms the basis for identification with the same-sex parent, older siblings, and peers. The child now attends to and imitates their behavior.
2. The second important cognitive development is the growing ability of children to take the point of view of the companions with whom they interact frequently. This ability is associated with patterns of reciprocal interaction rewarding to both actors in a dyad.

We are not adverse to biological explanations, particularly those based on differences in hormonal profiles of male and female children, but we believe that until more research is done in this area we should proceed to concentrate on research relevant to the other models.

In particular, we believe that the socialization model has been too restricted because it has concentrated on the observed interaction of mothers, teachers, and more rarely, fathers, to the neglect of interaction with children, and second because it has neglected the analysis of the indirect techniques of socializers, in particular their role in assigning children to different settings where they engage in different activities. In general, these settings are determined by the environmental and cultural milieu in which the adults and children live. Individual socializers have little opportunity to assign children to settings that vary from the normative patterns. Thus in the United States society, there is a law that all children between the ages of 6 and 16 must attend school. These settings prescribe the choices of individuals with whom a child will interact. Preferred marriage and residential rules also limit the choice of companions. Since the mean size of families is small (2.3 in the 1980 census), few children will have the opportunity, once they have acquired gender constancy, to interact with infants. As schools and playground are predominately age-graded, few children will have the experience of interacting with children more than 1 or 2 years older or younger. As families are predominately nuclear or single parent, children will have little daily interaction with adults other than parents and teachers.

The degree to which these environmental factors shape the learning experiences of children has received little attention because they are shared by the majority of children in our society and therefore do not lend themselves to psychological studies that analyze the antecedents of individual differences. Those families that do not conform to the norm are considered deviant by the members of the society and, so labeled, have characteristics that confound the learning environment variables.

Thus, as noted by J. Whiting (1954), weaning at the age of 2 may have quite a different influence on children when this is the cultural norm than it has in societies like our own where the norm for weaning is younger. Members of the family and community may consider the 2-year-old who is still nursing "spoiled," and the mother overly indulgent. As a consequence they may consciously or unconsciously punish them for deviance from the norm.

By looking at the social behavior of children brought up in societies that provide different normative learning environments, we can explore the effects of variations in socialization that are difficult to study in any one society. We can note the features of the environment that are invariant across cultures, dictated by those biological characteristics of humans that are universal and by the universal social imperatives (Goldschmidt, 1959). We can attempt to evaluate the contributions of nature and nurture to the genesis of gender role behavior in general and, in this chapter, of prosocial behavior.

Our data confirm the generalizations about gender differences in prosocial behavior. In our cross-cultural sample mothers score proportionately higher than fathers[2] or children. Girls, overall, score proportionately higher than boys. Our findings on the effect of age and caretaking experience, however, indicate that we need a multivariant model of the genesis of prosocial behavior.

## MODEL OF THE GENESIS OF PROSOCIAL BEHAVIOR

We start with the assumption, in accord with the sociobiologists, that, from a phylogenetic perspective, maternal behavior has as a motivating force the desire of individuals to reproduce themselves. To this end parents invest in their offspring with the goal of raising them to maturity. To reach this goal, parents and their surrogates must act in nonegoistical ways, putting aside immediate self-gratification for the welfare of another human being.

A viable offspring must not only be physically healthy but must also be an acceptable member of a social group. To produce this offspring, parents must transmit the customs, values, and beliefs—the culture of their social group. Although the details of the socialization process and the content of culture differ from one society to another and within a society from one mother to another, the similarities are striking. In our model these similarities are due to the interaction between phylogenetic and universal sociocultural requirements. Individuals must be reproductively successful, and the societies to which they belong must have viable rules and practices governing the process of socialization that are learned and transmitted from generation to generation. For these reasons, parental behavior in

---

[2]It is interesting to note that in those cultures that expect fathers to play an active role in the socialization of young children, they are more prosocial in their behavior than fathers who are not expected to take responsibility for the social behavior of their children in the early years. Sub-Saharan African fathers, in general, are not expected to play this role.

the early years consists primarily of nurturance and prosocial dominance, the latter behavior in the service of teaching the rules and values of the society.

Parental behavior in all societies is geared to the developmental age of the offspring. In the earliest years of an infant's life the physical well-being of the child is paramount, and nurturance predominates in parental behavior. The infant, due to its physical characteristics, elicits nurturance (Lorenz, 1971). During the preverbal state successful nurturance requires that the caretaker be capable of judging and satisfying the *needs* of the infant. We use the term *needs* here in the true sense of the word, those things essential for physical survival, including food, oxygen, and temperature control; protection from noxious environmental elements and disease; relief from fright and anxiety through physical contact; and both stimulation and rest. In most of the world, especially in the Third World where infant mortality is high, the focal concern of parents in infancy is physical survival, meeting these universal basic needs.

With age, the child develops wants (desires) as well as needs. These are the products of social living and are shared by the majority of members of a society. Nurturant behavior will include acts judged to have the goal of satisfying these wants. Although differing in content from society to society, these wants can be categorized into a transcultural typology. In our model we include in the trans-cultural list the desire for responsiveness from the physical and social environment—included here is the desire for social interaction and stimulation; the desire for predictability, reassurance, physical and verbal comfort (including physical contact); the desire for emotional support, approval, and self-esteem; and at various times the desire for autonomy and freedom to explore the physical and social world (B. Whiting, 1980).

In many respects, the experience of both infants and toddlers is similar across societies. By their very nature they elicit similar responses from the individuals with whom they spend time. In response to the development of the child, caretaker behavior changes, and the sequence of changes in outline looks similar the world over. The infant elicits nurturance; the toddler, prosocial dominance. When the infant begins to talk and is no longer a lap child but a toddler, parental investment requires a set of caretaking behaviors that are different from those appropriate for infants. The proportion of prosocial dominance increases as parental figures seek to protect the child who is not yet able to understand danger. They limit the mobility of the child, teaching it not to wander too far from parental figures and not to approach or handle dangerous animals, plants, or objects. They teach the toddler the control of bodily functions.

Following the inculcation of physical etiquette comes the teaching of appropriate social behavior, approved patterns of social interaction with adults and with younger, older, and same-aged children. The admonitions in this domain predominate in the content of prosocial behavior around the ages of 3 and 4.

Thus, although the details of the content of prosocial vary from society to society, during the early years of a child's life, the domains of behavior that are the focus of the parental demands are similar. The universal physical and cognitive characteristics of children, and universal social imperatives lead to similar socialization practices across cultures, and within cultures across genders.

There are, however, also major important differences in the experiences of girls and boys in different cultures that result in gender differences in prosocial behavior. There are marked differences across societies in the settings girls and boys frequent, in the age and sex of their daily companions, and in the activities in which they engage. The power of socializers in shaping gender differences in social behavior lies in their assignment of girls and boys to different settings, occupied by casts of characters differing in age and gender composition, and offering the occupants different types of activities. Girls more often than boys are in the company, interacting with, and/or in charge of infants and toddlers. More frequently than boys they are with parental figures who model prosocial behavior. They are more frequently working, whereas boys have more opportunity to play.

In sum, our model for the genesis of prosocial behavior posits that the gender differences between the prosocial behavior of girls and boys is in part attributed to biology, in part due to an interaction between biology and the universal necessity for socializing infants and toddlers who share physical and cognitive characteristics regardless of the society into which they are born. Sociocultural factors are important in the genesis of gender differences in prosocial behavior. Factors such as rules of residence, marriage forms, size of families, the division of labor by sex, and cultural beliefs and values will determine the settings that individuals frequent; they will determine who will spend time interacting with infants and toddlers and who will be responsible for their care. Individuals who are assigned their care and are frequently in their company will be more prosocial in their behavior than children who do not have this experience.

The data from which this model has been derived is presented next.

## METHODOLOGY

### Sample

Our sample consists of records of the behavior of girls and boys 2–12 years of age observed during the 1950s by the field teams of the Six Culture Study: by John and Ann Fischer in Orchard Town, United States (1966); by Robert LeVine and Barbara LeVine in Nyansongo in western Kenya (1966); by Thomas and Hatsumi Maretzki in Taira, Okinawa (1966); by Leigh Minturn in Khalapur, India (1966); by William and Corinne Nydegger in Tarong, the Philippines (1966); and by A. K. and Romaine Romney in Juxtluhuaca, Mexico (1966) (See also B. Whiting, & Whiting, 1975). The children were observed in naturally occurring settings on an average of 18 times for 5-min periods, and their interactions with others were recorded in running paragraphs and coded into interacts that specified the age of the actor and the age grade of the alter (i.e., the recipient or target of the social behavior). (See B. Whiting & Whiting, 1975, for methodology.)

Six additional samples were collected in Kenya during the 1960s and 1970s under the auspices of the Child Development Research Unit, directed by John and Beatrice Whiting. These samples were collected in western Kenya by Sara Harkness and Charles Super among Kipsigis-speaking families in the communities of Chapalungu and Oli; by Carol Ember among Luo speakers in Oyugis; by Thomas Weisner among Abaluya-speakers both in the rural community of Kisa and in Kariboangi, a housing estate in Nairobi. The author collected samples of children's behavior in the Kikuyu village of Ngeca. A Liberian sample was collected by Gerald Erchak in Kien-Taa. Susan Seymour made observations of mother–child dyads in two districts of Bhubaneswar, Orissa, India. The observations made in Africa were of longer duration than those collected in the Six Culture Study—some 15 min in duration, others 30 min. The number of hours of observation vary across the samples from 45 min to 360 min per child. In these samples, both sex and the actual age rather than the age grade of the alter were recorded (see Edwards & Whiting, 1980, for detailed description methodology).

The number of children in each sample varies from 20 to 140. In the Six Culture Study, 24 children (12 girls and 12 boys) between the ages of 3 and 10 were observed. In the more recent samples, each field researcher designed an independent study. All field workers, however, shared a common method for selecting samples and observing behavior. In choosing the sample of families, they attempted to find 20–40 families who knew each other and who were likely to share beliefs, values, and socialization practices (See J. Whiting, 1966, for description of Primary Sampling Unit). The observational techniques were the same, and the behavior was coded in a similar transcultural format (Edwards & Whiting, 1980; B. Whiting, 1968).

## Observing and Coding

The majority of the observations were made in the family compound. The observers, educated members of the child's culture, focused on one child, recording in sequence all interaction between the child and the individuals present in the setting. By associating with the families over a year or more, these observers were able to make repeated observations without unduly disturbing ongoing activities and could identify the cast of characters who interacted with the focal child. After the initial training period, observers were not rotated as it was found that behavior was more self-conscious if a variety of observers were introduced to the settings. Children were also more apt to seek to interact with the observer if different individuals appeared on consecutive days.

Since both the behavior of the sample child and the children with whom she or he interacted were recorded in sequence, the number of children whose behavior could be analyzed varied across the samples depending on the consistency of the cast of characters who appeared in the child's daily life. As one would expect, these were most frequently siblings, half-siblings, and courtyard cousins.

In the Six-Culture Study, all coding of the interaction was done at the Laboratory of Human Development at Harvard University. The detailed specification of the behaviors to be coded in the transcultural categories was discussed with the field workers (see B. Whiting & Whiting, 1975, for the description of the methodology). In the new studies an attempt was made to have all observations both recorded and coded by the local assistants, who, attuned to the subtleties of linguistic and body language communications, were better able to judge intention than observers or coders from the United States.

## Social Behavior Defined

The transcultural code distinguishes between egoistic and nonegoistic behavior (B. Whiting, 1968, 1980). The former includes those acts (*mands*) judged to have the intention of changing the behavior of another to satisfy the actor's own desires or wants without consideration for the needs or goals of the alter. These mands include simple requests for help, food and material goods, support, approval, and privileges, behaviors frequently classified as dependent; ego-dominant mands; and agonistic mands that employ coercive techniques of persuasion. Nonegoistic behavior includes prosocial behavior as previously defined. Sociable behavior includes mands that have the intention of eliciting friendly exchanges.

A more detailed description is needed of the two behaviors that we have included in our definition of prosocial behavior. Nurturance is defined as all those helping and supporting behaviors offered to an individual who is perceived by the actor to be in a state of need. On a mundane level, the observer of nurturant behavior records an individual's responsiveness to the succorant demands of alters or acts anticipating what she or he judges to be alter's needs and desires. The nurturant acts include offering food, material goods, emotional comfort, support and approval, and rights and privileges when the actor controls resources the other individual needs or wants. Thus a young child who attempts to distract a crying baby by offering it food or a toy, or by attempting to make it smile, is judged to act nurturantly to the baby; a child nurtures a friend who is encountering difficulty by helping him to carry a heavy basket, a nurturing mother or child caretaker smiles approval at the 3-year-old who is attempting to sweep the yard or sends the small child who is harassed by his or her siblings on an errand usually assigned to older children. A nurturant child responds to the requests of others for help.

Prosocial dominance is defined as all those attempts to change the behavior of an alter that are judged by the observer to have the intent of ensuring that the alter behaves in a socially approved way and does not lose the support of the social group. It includes suggestions and commands intended to influence an alter to obey the rules of etiquette, refrain from acts that are dangerous to his or her physical well-being, or from acts that are culturally proscribed, and to perform those acts that are required as the expected contribution of the alter to the family and community work: "Say good morning to your auntie." "Wash your hands before you eat." "Don't interrupt your father.'' ''Pick up your toys.'' ''It is time to change the tether on the goat.'' ''This pan is not clean; wash it again.'' ''It is your turn to set the table.'' ''Don't walk too close to the bull.'' ''Be careful that the baby doesn't fall.'' ''If you tie the baby this way, it will not slip off your back.'' ''Look both ways before you cross the street.''

The essence and prototype of nurturance and prosocial dominance is what has been traditionally called *maternal behavior,* a term used here with the recognition that both males and females, adults and children may behave in maternal ways. Young children who have only just learned the rules of propriety are often severe critics of the deviant behavior of their peers and prone to prosocial dominance. ''You should take turns on the slide.'' ''Your socks don't match.'' ''You did not feed the chickens.'' In societies that assign the care of younger siblings to children, this prosocial behavior is approved by the elders. Since in most of the nonindustrialized countries, children around 8 years of age act as child nurses, prosocial behavior is expected, rewarded, and practiced in childhood. As a member of an extended family and/or an interdependent community, concern for others and concern for acceptance by one's social group is inculcated; children are trained to be responsible members of their family and kin group.

## Dyad Types

All coded social behavior consists of interactions between individuals. The members of a dyad may be adult and child, or children of the same or opposite sex, of the same age, or of 1 or more years apart in age. In pooling the data, we found it best to work with dyad types rather than individual dyads. In naturally occuring settings, one must take interaction as it occurs, with whomever is in the child's environment at the particular time the observation is made. Although in all the samples the majority of observations were made in the home or family compound of the focal child, in the large extended courtyard of Khalpur, India, the large polygynous homesteads of Kenya, and the shared yards of Tarong hamlets in the Philippines, there may be 20 or more individuals with whom a sample child may interact. Thus frequencies of interaction of the same individuals in a dyadic pair are often too low to permit the use of individual dyad scores. Dyad types were compiled by combining actors and alters by sex and age grade. The age grades include adults, infants (younger than 2 years of age), toddlers (2–3-year-olds), yard children (4–5-year-olds), school-aged or neighborhood children (6–12-year-olds).[3]

No dyad type was included in the analysis if the frequency was less than 30 interacts. The range of interacts for a dyad type is from 30 to 500; the number of individual dyads in a dyad type, from 4 to 63. Whenever possible the dyads specify the age grade of the children, both actors and alters. In some comparisons where

---

[3]It should be noted that it is often difficult in societies that do not record births to be sure of the day and month of a child's birth. For this reasons we have not attempted to define the sex–age grades by months.

frequencies are low, dyads are based on the sex and relative age of actors and alters, that is, older girl or boy to same or opposite sex girl or boy one or more years younger or older, etc.

For each dyad type the proportion of nurturance and prosocial dominance was computed by dividing the sum of their frequencies by the total frequency of all the coded social behavior summed for the dyad type.

## GENDER AND AGE DIFFERENCES IN CHILDREN'S INTERACTION WITH INFANTS AND TODDLERS

In many of the societies that we have studied, the task of socializing offspring is shared by the mother, father, adult kin, and older siblings and cousins. Although in the early years of life, in all of our samples, the mother is the major caretaker, in some societies, as young as 4–6-month-old infants may be entrusted to older siblings who play a major role in their care. Girls are favored over boys but if there is no girl of the appropriate age, boys may be called upon.[4]

Our data includes "spot" observations made in a sample of six societies. Children were observed during the daylight hours to ascertain where they spent their time. Their companions and their work and play activities were recorded. (For description of the methodology, see Munroe & Munroe, 1971; Rogoff, 1978). The sample included children in a pastoral community in Peru, children in two villages in eastern Guatemala, three samples of children from our sub-Saharan African communities, and a sample from Claremont, California.[5]

In all the samples, girls were observed caring for children and in the company of younger children more frequently than boys. They also spent more time with adult females than their male peers.

In the 12 societies where we have observed children's behavior, we also have data on their daily routines and the work assigned to them. In all the samples girls interact with young children more frequently than boys. The percentage of interacts between children and 0–2-year-olds is greater for girls than for boys. In addition, there are cultural differences in the amount of interaction. Boys 7–10 seldom interact with either infants or toddlers in 7 of the 12 societies. In industrial societies with schools and in societies where women spend less time outside the home or

[4]Sibling order determines in large part the selection of child nurses. In sub-Saharan Africa and other societies where the mother depends on the help of child nurses—the societies where women have heavy workloads and there are no adult women available to help them (B. Whiting & Whiting, 1975; B. Whiting, C. Edwards, C. Ember, G. Erchak, S. Harkness, R. Munroe, R. L. Munroe, S. Seymour, C. Super, T. Weisner, in press)—mothers prefer children who are older than 5 but younger than 10 or the age at which they can help in the agricultural or animal-husbandry pursuits of the family.

[5]The observations were made by Ralph and Charlene Bolton in Peru; by Sara Nerlove in Guatemala and Nyansongo, Kenya; by R. L. Munroe and Ruth Munroe in two villages in Kenya, Vihiga, and Ngeca. In addition, we have data from another village in Guatemala, San Pedro, collected by Barbara Rogoff (1981).

have other adults in residence to help in child care, girls and boys interact with infants and toddlers far less frequently than in societies, like those in our African samples, where women are responsible for raising the food for their children. In the United States samples, interaction of the children with infants and toddlers is very infrequent.

In the role of child nurse, girls and boys are called upon to learn and practice prosocial behavior. In this role there is intrinsic reinforcement for modeling the prosocial behavior of the mother, observing and copying those behaviors that keep the infant or toddler safe and happy; caring for an unhappy child is an unpleasant task. Since girls interact with infants and toddlers more frequently than boys do, they have more practice in prosocial type behavior. Since they are around female adults more frequently than boys they have more opportunity to observe and copy prosocial behavior. We will therefore expect girls to have higher proportion scores for prosocial type behavior than boys.

## NURTURANCE

Our data cannot speak directly as to the innate, gender-linked components of prosocial behavior, as our earliest observations are of 2–3 year-old girls and boys who have already experienced differential socialization. We do not have sufficient observations of children of this age grade to quantify our findings in more than one or two of the societies, but the case material does not suggest gender differences in the prosocial behavior of toddlers.[6] At this age we have been able to observe nurturance: toddlers offering objects, food, and friendly attention to infants when the goal of their behavior was judged to be the satisfaction of the toddler's perception of the infant's needs and wants.

Our findings suggest that the important determinant of nurturant behavior in both adults and children is the ability of infants to elicit these types of behaviors. In arguing that there are certain characteristics of infants that trigger the release of nurturing-type behavior, Lorenz (1971) lists as among the important babyish features ''a relatively large head, predominance of the brain capsule, large and low-lying eyes, bulging cheek region, short and thick extremities, a springy elastic consistency, and clumsy movements [p. 154].'' In the Six-Culture Study, we found that the highest percentage of observed nurturance was to infants 0–2 years of age. We rank ordered (according to their observed frequency) six types of behaviors[7] of the sample children to infants. Nurturance to 0–2 year olds ranked highest, number 1, on the scale whereas nurturance to peers ranked 5, and to adults, 4 (B. Whiting & Whiting, 1975, p. 158).

---

[6]In our analysis of the social interaction of mothers with sons and daughters as measured in our studies, we found few robust differences attributable to gender (B. Whiting, C. Edwards, C. Ember, G. Erchak, S. Harkness, R. Munroe, R. L. Munroe, S. Seymour, C. Super, & T. Weisner, in press).

[7]The six types of behavior included nurturant, aggressive, prosocial, sociable, dominant–dependent, intimate dependent.

A more detailed analysis is possible with the data collected during the 1960s and 1970s in sub-Saharan Africa. In this sample we have separated infants 0–18 months from toddlers 2–3 years of age. We have contrasted the proportion of acts judged to be nurturant in five dyad types: children to (a) infants; (b) children more than 3 years younger than the actor; (c) children 1 or 2 years older or younger than the actor; (d) children 3 or more years older than the actor; and (e) mothers. Table 9.1 presents this data. It can be seen that, in all the samples, children are proportionately more nurturant to infants and children more than 3 years younger than themselves.

The released responses triggered by the infant are not the only important antecedent to nurturant behavior. Physical and cognitive maturation and experience in caretaking are also important. Older children are more nurturant than younger children; 2- and 3-year-olds are not as successful in nurturing infants as older children. Young children vary between attempts to elicit sociable responses from infants, especially smiles and laughter, attempts to be nurturant, and agonistic behavior. Detailed analysis of the behavior observations (Wenger, 1976) suggests that 3- and 4-year-olds, in their responsiveness to infants, frequently misperceive the infant's wants and needs or do not have the resources to meet them and are, therefore, unsuccessful in their attempts to nurture. Frustrated by the infant's crying and unable to persevere in their attempts, they may become agonistic and strike out at the infant. Sometimes in their desire to play and elicit friendly responses they overstimulate the infant and cause crying or discomfort that they are then unable to quiet. Frustrated, they become impatient and aggressive, shaking, punching or slapping the infant in exasperation. Thus their profile of behavior is nurturing, sociable, and agonistic. With age, child nurses learn not to overstimulate the infant. The proportion of sociability decreases; agonistic behavior decreases; and nurturing behavior becomes more consistent.

**TABLE 9.1**

*Percentage of Nurturance by Dyad Type*

|  | Kpelle | Chap | Oli | Kisa | Kariobangi | Ngeca |
|---|---|---|---|---|---|---|
| 1. Children to infants | 36 | 39 | 31 | 37 | 38 | 33 |
| 2. Children to child more than 3 years younger | 14 | 13 | 15 | 13 | 17 | 13 |
| 3. Children to adjacent-aged child | 7 | 5 | 8 | 3 | 6 | 6 |
| 4. Children to children more than 3 years older | 8 | 3 | 2 | 3 | 4 | 3 |
| 5. Children to mothers | 2 | 7 | 3 | 3 | 4 | 2 |
| Total number of acts to infants | 182 | 43 | 165 | 46 | 239 | 270 |

In the analysis of the behavior of a sample of Ngeca children collected by the author in 1968–1970 and 1972–1973 (Wenger 1976; Wenger & Whiting, 1979), a comparison of the rates of *nurturance, sociability, aggressive dominance,* and *prosocial dominance* was made of three age grades of children to 2-year-olds. The mean rate of these behaviors was computed for 3–4-year-olds, 5–7-year-olds, and 8–10-year-olds. Nurturance was found to increase linearly, significantly between the youngest (3–4) and oldest (8–10) age grades ($p < .007$). Sociability and aggressive dominance decrease most between the age grades of 3–4 and 5–7, the differences between the youngest (3–4) and oldest (8–10) age grades significant at the .01 level for sociability and the .05 level for aggressive dominance. Prosocial dominance does not change significantly. This pattern replicates in the other samples where there is sufficient interaction to make the analysis possible, primarily in the sub-Saharan African samples where children from 5 on serve as child nurses.

These findings suggest a cognitive-developmental increase in impulse control, an increased ability to take the perspective of another, and hence the ability to intuit the needs and wants of another individual, developmental changes that have been hypothesized and documented by psychologists (Selman, 1976; White, 1970). These changes in behavioral profile are associated with more experience interacting with infants, especially in the role of child nurse. Since there are insufficient data on the interaction of children with infants in those societies where children do not serve as child nurses, it is impossible at present to determine the relative contribution of maturation and caretaking experience.

That mothers recognize the change in the capacity of children as they grow older is reflected in their preference for child nurses around 8 years of age. In many of the preindustrial societies and the later developing countries, mothers prefer 6–8-year-olds, and, if they have both boys and girls of approximately this age, they choose the girls. Just why mothers prefer this age rather than older children is an interesting question. It may well be that in these societies where women work outside the house in subsistence activities and depend heavily on children's help, older children can contribute to the economic activities that require physical strength. It appears also from our observations, however, that the younger child nurses are more willing to engage in activities that interest infants and toddlers, perhaps better able to intuit their wants since they have more recently been of the age grade. The girls of 6, 7, and 8 seem more desirous than adolescents of modeling their mothers' behavior, less interested than the older girls and adolescents in establishing their own identity. The older girls are more interested in entering into the adult world where they will have their own babies. Younger child nurses are less frustrated than the older children who have been granted the privilege of frequenting settings at a distance from the homestead where they can engage in activities not supervised by adults.

The preference for female rather than male child caretakers raises unanswerable questions. Do mothers prefer girls because they recognize some innate and gender-linked capacity in girls that make them more responsive to infants than boys? Do they recognize that there is a tendency for girls to be more interested in babies? (See Berman, Abplanalf, Cooper, Mansfield, & Shields, 1975; Berman & Goodman,

1981; Berman, Monda, & Meyercough, 1977; Melson & Fogel, 1982; for discussion of gender differences in interest in babies.) Or do they consider it inappropriate for male children to play the caretaker role? The latter is not the case in societies where women are important in subsistence agriculture. The Kenyan mothers who were in the fields 4 or 5 hrs a day used sons as well as daughters as child nurses. Tarong mothers in the Philippines (Nydegger & Nydegger, 1966), a society in which fathers help with the care of infants and young children, train their sons as well as their daughters to care for younger siblings. As can be seen in Table 9.2, boys in these societies are nurturant to infants, more nurturant in one of the Kenyan groups, Nyansongo, very similar in two of the others, Oli and Ngeca, and similar in Tarong, in the Philippines. The greatest gender difference in nurturance is in Juxtlahuaca, Mexico, a society in which there is a marked division of labor by sex. Women only help in agricultural work seasonally, and men do not care for infants. In all societies, however, girls interact with infants more frequently than boys.

Overall girls score higher than boys in nurturance in all dyadic interaction. If one compares the proportion of nurturant behavior of girls and boys in 14 dyad types—girls and boys to mothers, to infants (0–2), to younger same- and opposite-sex children, to older same- and opposite-sex children, and to same- and opposite-sex children of the same grade—overall, in 15 samples, girls behave more nurturantly than boys (Edwards & Whiting, 1980). Girls are more nurturant than boys in 64% of the 73 comparisons; significantly more nurturant in 11 (15%); boys were significantly more nurturant in 2 (3%). Eight of the significant differences are of girls to children younger than the actor—three to infants, four to younger girls, and one to younger boys. One of the significant differences is of girls to older girls, and two of older girls (7–10) to older girls of the same age grade, suggesting the generalization of nurturant behavior from younger to older children.

Our data do not preclude an innate preprogramming for nurturance in females that makes them more apt students of responsive nurturance, biologically tuned to

**TABLE 9.2**

*Sex Differences in the Nurturance of Girls and Boys to Infants (0–18 Months)*

|  | Number of cases girls | Proportion of nurturance | Number of cases boys | Proportion of nurturance | Difference |
|---|---|---|---|---|---|
| Kpelle | 6 | 41 | 3 | 30 | G+ n.s. |
| Oli | 10 | 32 | 8 | 29 | G+ n.s. |
| Kisa-Kariobangi | 14 | 34 | 6 | 16 | G+** |
| Ngeca | 17 | 34 | 6 | 31 | G+ n.s. |
| Nyansongo | 6 | 49 | 4 | 60 | B+ n.s. |
| Tarong | 5 | 42 | 4 | 47 | B+ n.s. |
| Juxtluhuaca | 6 | 63 | 8 | 27 | G* |

*Significant at the .05 level.
**Significant at the .01 level.

respond to an infant's cries.[8] Nor can we dismiss the importance of the girl's perception of gender identity with the mother who models nurturant and responsive behavior. Our model must be multivariant, including biological and cognitive–developmental variables, but the experience of caring for infants must be stressed as it affords both motivation for modeling prosocial behavior and practice in behaviors that are nurturant.

In our society few children have this opportunity. In the Orchard Town, United States, sample, only 3% of children's interaction was with infants, in comparison with 21–27% in the four other societies in the Six Culture sample, societies where children were expected to care for infants. Because of the low frequency of interaction, it is not possible to compare the behavior of Orchard Town girls to infants with the behavior of girls to infants in other samples. We can compare the mean proportion of nurturant behavior of 7–10-year-old Orchard Town girls to younger same-sex children. Of the total of five societies where the comparison can be made, Orchard Town girls have the lowest proportion of nurturance. In interaction with children of the same age grade, 3–6-year-old Orchard Town girls rank fourth in the five society comparison.

## PROSOCIAL DOMINANCE

The second component of prosocial or maternal-type behavior, prosocial dominance, is elicited by children younger than the actor, but toddlers rather than infants. Table 9.3 presents the proportion of prosocial dominance in four of the sub-Saharan samples. The proportions are computed for four age grades of children: children to those more than 3 years younger; to those 1 or 2 years younger; to those 1 or 2 years older; and to those more than 3 years older. (Infants 0–18 months have not been included in younger children.) It can be seen that children younger than the actor receive the greatest amount of prosocial domiance, especially children more than 3 years younger. Younger children rarely try to prosocially dominate their elders. When child actors are separated into age grades, the highest scores that we have recorded for Kpelle, Oli, and Ngeca are for 8–12-year-olds to toddlers. Mothers score highest of all actors.

As noted earlier the caretaker of a toddler must protect the child from dangers not yet perceived by the 2- and 3-year-olds. In our society this age grade is often referred to as the *terrible two's*. The desire to explore the physical and social world has earned them this epithet. Unaware of the dangers of the environment and the rights and privileges of others, they unwittingly embark on foolhardy physical and social adventures. The role of the caretaker is to protect them from harm and instruct them in appropriate behavior. Toddlers consequently elicit a higher proportion of prosocial dominance than infants.

[8]See Hoffman (1977) for a discussion of sex differences in empathy.

**TABLE 9.3**

*Proportion of Prosocial Dominance by Dyad Type[a]*
*(Sub-Saharan Sample)*

| Dyad type | Kpelle | Chapalungu | Oli | Ngeca |
|---|---|---|---|---|
| Mothers to toddlers | | | | |
| (2–3 years of age) | 45 | — | 32 | 51 |
| 8–12-year-olds to tod- | | | | |
| dlers (2–3) | 26.8 | — | 26 | 21 |
| To children more than 3 | | | | |
| years younger than | | | | |
| the actor | 23 | 7 | 12.6 | 20.8 |
| To children 1 or 2 years | | | | |
| younger than the | | | | |
| actor | 15.6 | 8 | 10.3 | 10.1 |
| To children 1 or 2 years | | | | |
| older than the actor | 12.8 | 4 | 2.8 | 4.4 |
| To children 3 or more | | | | |
| years older than the | | | | |
| actor | 3 | 2 | 2 | 3.8 |

[a]No dyad is included with less than 30 interacts.

Since we have found that young girls, especially girls 5 and over are in the company of younger children more frequently than boys, they have more practice in prosocial dominance as well as in nurturance. They are also more frequently in the presence of their mothers who serve as a model for prosocial dominance as well as for nurturance.

It is not surprising, therefore, to find that girls are more prosocially dominant than boys. The frequency of prosocial dominance increases as children reach the age when they are expected to spend time supervising toddlers. Girls develop a style of controlling the toddler that assumes they know what is best for the welfare of the child. Boys are more apt to command in a manner that the observers judged to be egoistically motivated. They more frequently used agonistic styles, particularly insulting styles.

Table 9.4 presents the percentage of the dominance of girls and boys of three age grades that was judged to be prosocial. It can be seen that in all comparisons girls score proportionately higher in prosocial dominance. They become more prosocially dominant with age, especially as they reach the age when they are expected to be responsible for toddlers. Mothers score highest in their proportion of prosocial dominance. Girls become increasingly like their mothers, more so than their male peers. In some cases older girls are more restrictive than their mothers, perhaps because they have just learned the rules themselves, perhaps out of frustration at caring for toddlers who demand constant supervision.

Table 9.5 presents the proportion of dominance by older boys and girls in the sub-

**TABLE 9.4**

*Gender and Age Differences of the Style of Dominance to Toddlers:
The Proportion of Dominance That Is Prosocial*

|               | Kpelle | | Oli | | Ngeca | |
|---------------|-------|------|-------|------|-------|------|
| Age of actor  | Girls | Boys | Girls | Boys | Girls | Boys |
| 4–5 years     | .44 | .22 | .29 | .21 | .22 | .19 |
| 6–7 years     | .74 | .29 | .26 | .25 | .50 | .48 |
| 8–12 years    | —   | —   | .70 | .30 | .49 | .46 |
| Mothers       | .69 |     | .65 |     | .98 |     |

Saharan sample that is prosocial dominance to children more than 3 years younger. It can be seen that girls are consistently more prosocially dominant.

The comparison is difficult in the Six Culture data as 2-year-olds have been combined with infants. Table 9.6 presents the proportion of all dominance that is prosocial. It can be seen that gender differences hold for the 7–10-year-olds to younger children, but the findings are ambiguous in the interaction of children to the 0–2 age grade.

Carol Ember's (1970, 1973) research among the Luo of western Kenya lends support to the theory of the importance of experience in the genesis of prosocial behavior. In 1968–1969, she observed and recorded the social behavior of 28 children ranging in age from $7\frac{1}{2}$ to 16 years of age. She also interviewed 56 children about the type of tasks they considered the domain of men and women and, using the list for probes, interviewed the children individually about the work they performed. This information was checked with the parents of each child. Tasks considered "feminine" included fetching and carrying wood and water, food preparation, cooking, house cleaning, and child tending, etc. The boys were scored as to the amount of "feminine" work they did.

Boys who performed a high amount of such work were compared with boys who did very little. The proportions of five types of behaviors in interaction with chil-

**TABLE 9.5**

*Percentage of Dominance That Is Prosocial Dominance
(Sub-Saharan Sample)*

|            | Older girls to girls and boys 3 years younger (mean age 8.2) | Older boys to girls and boys 3 years younger (mean age 8.5) |
|------------|------|------|
| Kpelle     | .68 | .30 |
| Chapalungu | .32 | .18 |
| Oli        | .35 | .30 |
| Ngeca      | .56 | .54 |

**TABLE 9.6**
*Percentage of Dominance that Is Prosocial—Six Culture Sample[a]*

| Age grade of actor | Nyansongo | | Tarong | | Juxtluhuaca | | Taira | | Khalapur | | Orchard Town | |
|---|---|---|---|---|---|---|---|---|---|---|---|---|
| | Girls | Boys | Girls | Boys | Girls | Boys | Girls | Boys | Girls | Boys | Girls | Boys |
| 3–6 to infants (0–2)[b] | .65 | .45 | .61 | .40 | .55 | .56 | | | | | | |
| 7–10 years to infants (0–2) | .82 | — | .69 | .71 | .66 | .92 | | | | | | |
| 7–10 years to boys and girls 3–6 years | .90 | .70 | .59 | .42 | .64 | .60 | .55 | .51 | .39 | .15 | .64 | .33 |
| Mothers to 3–6-year-old boys and girls | .90 | | .84 | | .71 | | | | .24 | | .73 | |

[a]No dyad is included with less than 30 interacts.

[b]In the Six Culture sample toddlers 2 years of age were classed with infants. Most of the *prosocial dominance* coded for this age grade (0–2) is to 2-year-olds.

dren other than infants were contrasted for these two samples and a sample of girls. Boys high on ''feminine'' work were significantly more prosocially dominant than boys low on ''feminine'' work. Both groups of boys scored lower than girls. The $F$ value of the linear regression was significant at the .01 level, $F = 11.67$ for all comparisons of boys who did more ''feminine'' work in general; $F = 18$ for those boys who did more ''feminine'' work inside the home (Ember, 1973, p. 431).

Ember did not find significant differences in the amount of nurturant behavior of boys and girls. There were, however, differences in the predicted direction; girls scored higher than boys, and boys who did ''feminine'' work scored higher than boys who did not. However as in the case of our findings, the gender differences in nurturance were not robust.

There is evidence that an individual's prosocial style generalizes across alters. In analyzing the Six Culture data we found that individual children who scored above the mean in prosocial dominance to infants (0–2 years of age) were significantly above the mean in prosocial dominance to peers and adults (B. Whiting & Whiting, 1975, p. 163). These findings suggest that individuals have styles of behavior that generalize across dyad types, perhaps styles that can be considered personality characteristics.

In sum, it is our hypothesis that experience plays an important role in the genesis of the prosocial dominant style, in particular the experience of interacting with younger children and spending time in the presence of and interacting with the mother. As noted earlier our data show that, as early as 5 years of age, girls spend more time with younger children and adult women. Prosocial dominant behavior is elicited by younger children and modeled after the observed behavior of the mother. It is also experienced interacting with the mother, being the recipient of her prosocial dominance. The evidence for the role of experience in this type of prosocial behavior is stronger than that for nurturance.

## CONCLUSION

People who are prosocial assume that they are responsible for the well-being of others. If an individual is perceived to be in a state of need or to have unsatisfied but socially approved desires, the prosocial actor attempts to satisfy these needs and wants. If the individual is unable or does not ask for help, support, affection, approval, food, material goods or rights and privileges, the prosocial actor may intuit the needs and desires of the individual and attempt to satisfy them. Intuition is of prime importance in the care of the preverbal child.

The motivation to be responsive to the needs and desires of an infant, in our opinion, is the best candidate for preprogramming—an innate response to the physical characteristics of infants. If the infant has been part of one's body, the motivation to be responsively nurturant must be especially strong.

There is no doubt that with the maturation of physical and cognitive skills, particularly with the development of increased impulse control, the actor is better able to intuit and satisfy the needs of another. With maturation the actor has increased cognitive and physical skills. However, as in other domains, experience is essential to the development of responsive and nurturant skills. Interacting with younger children, interacting with the mother, being entrusted with and sharing with her the care of younger children not only increases the understanding of the maternal role, but also increases the motivation to attend to and imitate the mother's behavior. The actor develops habits of responsive nurturance. There is evidence, directional but not significant, that these habits of nurturance generalize to others, such that children who have had these experiences are more nurturant than their same-sex peers to other children and to their mothers.

Since girls are in the presence of younger children and adult females more than boys and since girls perceive themselves to be of the same gender as their mothers who give birth to and in all our societies are the primary caretakers of young children, girls will be more nurturant than boys. On the other hand, as infants and young children elicit nurturance and as boys may have the experience of interacting with them and caring for them, boys will also develop habits of nurturance.

If nurturance is preprogrammed in females, girls will find it easier to learn nurturance than boys. Since there are cognitive-developmental and direct experiential variables that are involved in the genesis of nurturance, we cannot as yet separate the unique contribution of biology.

The evidence for a biological base for prosocial dominance is far more dubious. There is no doubt that prosocial dominance by caretakers is essential for the survival of toddlers and young children and may be in response to the perception that a child must be socialized into an acceptable member of the society into which it is born. However, this perception involves cognitive maturity and social learning.

Since female children associate more frequently with toddlers and their caretakers, we will expect girls to form stronger habits of prosocial dominance. Our evidence for the generalization of prosocial dominance is more robust than that for nurturance. Since prosocial dominance implies a feeling of responsibility for the behavior of others, we will expect girls and women to be more concerned with the well-being and with the appropriate behavior of others. The conscious justification for prosocial dominance will be the genuine concern for others and the well-being of the social group.

The generalization of the habit of prosocial dominance, however, may lead to the assumption of responsibility in domains where it is inappropriate. As a style of dominance it may be used by children in interaction with older and stronger individuals who refuse to comply with the actor's egoistic wishes (Lubin & Whiting, 1977). In our observations we have noted that young girls, when boys refuse to comply to their demands or when boys harass them, frequently retaliate with prosocial dominance rather than retaliatory agonistic behavior. Adult women interacting outside the domestic domain may also use this style as a technique for persuasion.

It should be noted that consciously nurturant behavior may also lead to inappropriate behavior. The overly nurturant caretaker may be misinterpreting the wants of another, perhaps influenced by the desire to control. Much has been written about the overprotective mother who is the model of this type of prosocial behavior.

In reviewing the early treatises on female characteristics, it is our opinion that prosocial behavior has been denigrated. Too little attention has been given to its importance for the survival of a healthy society. Responsiveness is frequently denigrated and labeled *compliance*. Behavior that has the goal of caring for others, having concern for others, can too easily be seen as dependent, field dependent, or conventional. Sometimes the reader of this literature wonders whether the interpretations are not influenced by male researchers' and authors' aversion to the prosocial dominance of their mothers. There is no doubt that the prototype of these behaviors is maternal behavior, behavior essential for the survival of the young and their success as members of a society that remains viable.

If our theory is correct, as fathers become more involved in the care of infants and toddlers, they will become more prosocial in their behavior, more tolerant of the behavior that thwarted their childhood wishes. Allowed the caretaker's role, they will be better able to take the perspective of the individuals who were responsible for their early socialization.

## ACKNOWLEDGMENTS

The thoughtful criticisms of Carolyn Edwards and Carol Dweck were particularly helpful in writing this chapter.

# REFERENCES

Berman, P. W., Abplanalf, J., Cooper, P., Mansfield, P., & Shields, S. Sex differences in attraction to infants: Do they occur? *Sex Roles*, 1975, *1*, 311–318.

Berman, P. W., & Goodman, V. Sex differences in children's responses to babies and caretaking instructions. Paper presented at Annual Meeting of American Psychological Association, Los Angeles, 1981.

Berman, P. W., Monda, L. P., & Meyercough, R. P. Sex differences in young children's responses to an infant: An observation within a day care setting. *Child Development*, 1977, *48*, 711–715.

Berry, J. N. Comparative study of psychological differentiation. In R. H. Munroe, R. L. Munroe, & B. B. Whiting (Eds.), *Handbook of cross-cultural human development*. New York: Garland STPM Press, 1981.

Chodorow, N. *The reproduction of mothering*. Berkeley: University of California Press. 1978.

Edwards, C. P. The comparative study of the development of moral judgment and reasoning. In R. H. Munroe, R. L. Munroe, & B. B. Whiting (Eds.), *Handbook of cross-cultural development*. New York: Garland STPM Press, 1981.

Edwards, C. P., & Whiting, B. B. Differential socialization of girls and boys in light of cross cultural research. *New Directions for Child Development–Anthropological Perspectives on Child Development*, 1980, *8*, 45–57.

Ember, C. "Feminine" task assignment and its effect on the social behavior of boys. Paper presented at the 69th Annual Meeting of the American Anthropological Association, San Diego, 1970.

Ember, C. Feminine task assignment and social behavior of boys. *Ethos*, 1973, *1*, 424–439.

Ember, C. A cross-cultural perspective on sex differences. In R. H. Munroe, R. L. Munroe, & B. B. Whiting (Eds.), *Handbook of cross-cultural human development*. New York: Garland STPM Press, 1981.

Fischer, J. L., & Fischer, A. *The New Englanders of Orchard Town, U.S.A.* New York: Wiley, 1966.

Gilligan, C. In a different voice: Women's conceptions of self and morality. *Harvard Educational Review*, 1977, *47*(4), 481–517.

Gilligan, C. *In a different voice:Psychological theory and women's development*. Cambridge: Harvard University Press, 1982.

Goldschmidt, W. *Man's way*. New York: Holt Rinehart & Winston, 1959.

Hartup, W. W. Cross-age versus same-age peer interaction: Ethological and cross-cultural perspectives. In V. L. Allen (Ed.), *Children as teachers*. New York: Academic Press, 1976.

Hartup, W. W. Peer system. In P. Mussen, *Carmichael's manual of child psychology*. New York: Wiley, in press.

Hoffman, M. L. Sex differences in empathy and related behaviors. *Psychological Bulletin*, 1977, *84*, 712–722.

Kagan, J. Universals in human development. In R. H. Munroe, R. L. Munroe, & B. B. Whiting (Eds.), *Handbook of cross-cultural human development*. New York: Garland STPM Press, 1981.

Konner, M. Relation between infants and juveniles in comparative perspective. In M. Lewis & L. A. Rosenblum (Eds.), *Friendship and peer relations*. New York: Wiley, 1975.

Lamb, M. E. The development of sibling relations in infancy: A short-term longitudinal study. *Child Development*, 1978, *49*, 1189–1196.

LeVine, R., & LeVine-Lloyd, B. *Nyansongo: A Gusi community in Kenya*. New York: Wiley, 1966.

Lorenz, K. *Studies in human and animal behavior*. Cambridge, Mass.: Harvard University Press, 1971.

Lubin, D., & Whiting, B. B. Learning techniques of persuasion: An analysis of sequences of interaction. Paper presented at the biennial meeting of the Society for Research in Child Development, New Orleans, 1977.

Maccoby, E., & Jacklin, C. *The psychology of sex differences*. Stanford, Calif.: Stanford University Press, 1974.

Maretzki, T. W., & Maretzki, H. *Taira: An Okinawan village*. New York: Wiley, 1966.

Melson, G. F., & Fogel, A. Young children's interest in unfamiliar infants. *Child Development*, 1982, *53*(3), 693–700.

Miller, J. *Toward a new psychology of women.* Boston: Beacon Press, 1976.

Minturn, L., & Hitchcock, J. T. *The Rajputs of Khalapur, India.* New York: Wiley, 1966.

Munroe, R. L., & Munroe, R. Household density and infant care in an East African society. *Journal of Social Psychology,* 1971, *83,* 3–13.

Nydegger, W. F., & Nydegger, C. *Tarong: An Ilocos barrio in the Philippines.* New York: Wiley, 1966.

Price Williams, D. R. *Explorations in cross-cultural psychology.* San Francisco: Chandler & Sharp, 1975.

Price Williams, D. R. Concrete and formal operations. In R. H. Munroe, R. L. Munroe, & B. B. Whiting (Eds.), *Handbook for cross-cultural human development.* New York: Garland STPM Press, 1981.

Rogoff, B. Spot observations. *Quarterly Newsletter of the Institute for Comparative Human Development,* 1978, *2,* 2.

Rogoff, B. Adults and peers as agents of socialization. *Ethos,* 1981, *9*(1), 18–36.

Romney, A. K., & Romney, R. *The Mixtecans of Juxtlahuaca, Mexico.* New York: Wiley, 1966.

Selman, R. L. A developmental approach to interpersonal and cultural awareness in young children. In T. C. Hennessy (Ed.), *Values and human development.* New York: Paulist Press, 1976.

Wenger, M. Child–toddler social interaction in an East African community. Unpublished qualifying paper, Harvard Graduate School of Education, 1976.

Wenger, M., & Whiting, B. B. Studying the context of children's socialization: Sibling caretakers in a rural community in Kenya. Paper presented at the second Congress of the Instituto de Psiquitria y Medicine Psicosomatica, Mexico City, 1979.

White, S. A. Some general outlines of the matrix of developmental changes between 5 and 7 years. *Bulletin of the Orton Society,* 1970, *20,* 41–57.

Whiting, B. B. (Ed.). *Six cultures: Studies of child rearing.* New York: Wiley, 1963.

Whiting, B. B. Transcultural code for social interaction. Unpublished manuscript, 1968.

Whiting, B. B. Culture and social behavior: A model for the development of social behavior. *Ethos,* 1980, *8*(2), 95–116.

Whiting, B. B., Edwards, C. P., Ember, C., Erchak, G., Harkness, S., Munroe, R., Munroe, R. L., Seymour, S., Super, C., and Weisner, T. *The company they keep: The genesis of gender role behavior.* (In process).

Whiting, B. B., & Whiting, J. W. M. *Children of six cultures A psycho-cultural study.* Cambridge, Mass.: Harvard University Press, 1975.

Whiting, J. W. M. The cross-cultural method. In G. Lindzey (Ed.), *Handbook of social psychology* (Vol. 2). Cambridge, Mass.: Addison–Wesley, 1954.

Whiting, J. W. M., Child, I. L., Lambert, W. W., & the field teams of the Six Culture Series. *Field guide for the study of socialization.* New York: Wiley, 1966.

# The Cultural Context
# of Prosocial Development:
# An Ecological Model

## NANCY B. GRAVES and THEODORE D. GRAVES

## INTRODUCTION

> Some of my friends and I have a question for you. We want to know whether, in other
> civilizations that are not bound by the competitive ethic like the Americans, children still
> have that built-in little tune that they just know, they're born with, that little tune of "*Nyaa,*
> *nyaa, nya-nyaa, nyaa. I'm* bigger than you are," or "*I'm* better than *you* are; *I've* got one
> and *you* don't!" Just seems that they all know that automatically around here, even though
> we try so hard to discourage it. We were wondering if maybe this is universal, or if it's just
> the result of our "evil" society over here.

This young mother's lament was sent to us in 1975 while we were spending a
year on the tiny island of Aitutaki in the middle of the South Pacific. We were not
there specifically to study prosocial development. Rather, we had come with a more
general interest in the impact of Western industrial society and market economy on
island life, on the personality and interpersonal relations of these Polynesian people,
and on their motivation to migrate to New Zealand. Our speciality as psychological
anthropologists has been research on the adaptation of migrant families from traditional societies to life in cities of the Western world. In each of the areas where we
have worked—the American Southwest, East Africa, and now the South Pacific—
we have also spent time in the rural home communities from which people were
emigrating.

This cross-cultural exposure, however, has made us aware of strong contrasts
between the course of prosocial development in traditional non-Western communities and in the Western urban societies that generated most of our theories of

243

THE NATURE OF PROSOCIAL DEVELOPMENT

human development. Although modern urban children seldom feel their work is necessary to the functioning of the family, in small subsistence economies children, almost from infancy, are contributing parts of a collectivity, combining their efforts with those of siblings, cousins, parents, and other older relatives and neighbors toward common family and community goals.

This was true on Aitutaki, one of 15 islands in the Cook group, a self-governing protectorate of New Zealand with cultural affinities to their neighbors to the east, the Tahitians of the Society Islands. We selected this island for intensive anthropological study not only because it exemplifies the finest of traditional Polynesian life, but because, within its 7-mile perimeter and population of 2500, it contains a full range of variation from extended families cooperatively engaged in fishing and subsistence agriculture to highly Westernized teachers, doctors, clerks, and business people. Thus it serves as a stage on which the economic, social, and psychological changes of the last 300 years in the West are being reenacted within a few decades.

As we have measured and recorded the changes occurring in island life over the last few years, we have begun to understand the way in which the prosocial behavior that island children display from infancy emerges from the total social and cultural context within which they are raised. As this context shifts in the direction of modern, Western institutional structures and traditional interdependencies are lost, Aitutaki children's behavior is becoming more similar to the pattern of prosocial development in the West. In this chapter we will trace the correlates of continuity and change in prosocial behavior among these Polynesian islanders, both adults and children.

## THEORETICAL ORIENTATION

Much of the theoretical discussion regarding the development of prosocial behavior has revolved around an issue endemic to social science: How much weight should be given to intrapersonal factors (e.g., personality, cognitive development, skills, affective states), and how much to situational or environmental factors (e.g., cultural values, social norms, parental socialization, situational pressures). This is Allport's "inside or outside the skin" problem (cf. Allport, 1955; Barker, Gump, Friesen, & Willems, 1970; Kanfer, 1979). Although at some level there is recognition that both types of factors must play a role, specific theory and research efforts have tended to emphasize one or the other of two basic orientations: the relativistic *enculturation* position or the more universalistic *individual development* position.

The enculturation model is represented by many ethnographic studies of non-Western cultures. In its most extreme form it claims, unlike comparative research such as the Six Cultures Study, that "culture has such a profound effect that developmental sequences from one culture to another cannot be compared [B. Whiting & J. Whiting, 1975, p. 174]." Other more subtle formulations of this focus would include social reinforcement theory (e.g., Bandura & Walters, 1963) and values research that emphasizes deliberate socialization of cultural or class (subcultural) norms by parents (e.g., Inkeles, 1955; Levine, 1973).

Proponents of the importance of intrapersonal processes would include those taking a cognitive developmental stand (e.g., Flavell, Botkin, Fry, Wright, & Jarvis, 1968; Kohlberg, 1964, 1969; Piaget, 1932, 1950; Selman, 1976; Turiel, 1969). Essentially, this view holds that infants are adualistic at birth, centered in self-survival and that prosocial tendencies gradually develop through maturation of internal structures. Although a process of *negotiation* with their social environment (particularly with peers) for the mutual advantage of each individual is usually believed to be required for the proper development of prosocial behavior, if the requisite cognitive structures have not yet emerged, social influences are unlikely to have much impact.

These contrasting points of view are curiously alike, however, in that both are a product of the individualistic orientation common to most social scientists raised in modern, industrial societies of the Western world. The prevalence of a cultural ethos of "self-contained individualism [Sampson, 1977, p. 769]" in social science theory and research has recently drawn comment from a number of sources (cf. Hogan, 1975; Kanfer, 1979; Sampson, 1977). From this Western perspective, human beings are typically seen as having a self-centered, egocentric perspective until either they are properly socialized into a more sociocentric stance for the good of society (enculturation theory) or their cognitive structures develop sufficiently for them to take the perspective of others and see the personal advantage of altruism and cooperation (cognitive developmental theory). As Bar-Tal (1976) noted, both the above approaches assume that individuals "*have to learn* altruistic behavior because human beings are innately motivated by self-interest [and] are by nature utilitarian, although they behave altruistically in rare events [p. 50 italics added]."

The impasse between these competing but similarly individualistic theoretical world views can be dissolved if one steps back and considers individuals as *inseparable* parts of their social group, sociocentric from the beginning, yet influencing the group through the way in which their unique characteristics are integrated into the whole. We can refer to this alternative theoretical position as an *ecological model* of prosocial development. We cease to focus exclusively on either the influence of the environment *upon* individuals or the negotiations *between* individuals and their environment. Instead, they are seen as parts of a structural whole or, as Jerome Bruner (1971) phrased it, a "people-in-the-world unity [p. 27]." Such an approach "requires that the person be viewed at the psychological level as a component of the complex system of which he or she is a part [Kanfer, 1979, p. 231]."

This shift in perspective is more than simply going up one level of abstraction. It results in fundamental changes in ideas about the nature of learning and development of prosocial behavior. Now, as Bronfenbrenner (1976) points out, our concern is with the "degree of 'fit', of mutual interdepedency, between the organism and its surround [p. 5]." Theorists taking this orientation appear to agree on the following points:

1. *Both* altruistic or empathetic *and* self-aggrandizing or aggressive tendencies exist as potentials in human beings from birth (Borke, 1978; Hoffman, 1975). The original adualistic state of the infant is seen as sociocentric rather than egocentric; that is, "man has evolved as a social species; infants . . . are preadapted to an ordinary expectable social environment. . . . thus children are social from the beginning [Stayton, Hogan, & Ainsworth, 1971, p. 1059]."
2. At the same time, behavior lifted out of the context of its ecological system cannot be taken as evidence for universal, abstract stages of moral development within human beings as a species. Although both prosocial and self-aggrandizing behavior arise spontaneously in early years, more complex prosocial behavior (as well as the cultural values and norms which support such behavior) arises as an *emergent* of a system that requires interdependence between persons in daily interaction.

Once such an ecological stance is taken a number of logical correlatives follow. First, all behavior is seen as *contextual,* not simply interactive. Seeing prosocial behavior as an emergent requires the recognition of *reciprocal causation* or mutual arising, ruling out unilinear explanations. This also resolves the awkward problem of accounting for what is often termed *structural effects,* as when the atmosphere of the group affects individual perceptions. In addition, all intrapersonal characteristics of the individual will have to be interpreted in terms of their meaning for group functioning.

The *balance* of egoistic and prosocial behavior in any particular society will vary between societies and may be in flux within a given society. Societies can therefore be classified by their relative emphasis on group or individual goals in daily life, with the more technologically complex, industrialized, mass-market societies stressing individualistic, competitive tendencies (thus providing the mobile units needed during the beginnings and expansion of industrialization; cf. Stone, 1975; Toffler, 1980), whereas simpler, subsistence-level economies with kin-based social organizations are more apt to emphasize group-oriented, cooperative behavior. Since there is continual balancing and change within any ecosystem, one strategy for the generation of theory as to the way in which prosocial behavior develops is to study those societies or subgroups undergoing major social change. Within such societies there should be subsystems existing side by side with differing emphases on prosocial and self-aggrandizing tendencies. An alternative strategy is to implement naturalistic experiments within a subcultural setting and chart changes in prosocial behavior as they develop over time.

In our cross-cultural research on the development and display of prosocial behavior, we have tried both strategies within the framework of an ecological orientation. Three complementary types of methodology will be illustrated. The traditional anthropological method of controlled comparison is used when we compare the prosocial behavior of Cook Islands children with that of New Zealand children from a European cultural background or when we compare the behavior of Cook Islands children raised within nuclear or extended families, and town or country environments. We have used a correlational design to examine the structural and background experiential correlates of prosocial behavior among both adults and children in Aitutaki, Cook Islands. Finally, we will briefly describe our current field experiment designed to discover the behavioral effects of restructuring the learning environment among American and New Zealand school children from differing cultural backgrounds.

In this work we have employed a variety of data-gathering techniques: participant observation, systematic observations amenable to quantitative analysis, interviews, questionnaires, and various psychological tests and measures. These techniques obviously vary in their replicability and generalizability, but the ecological approach requires a broader coverage than the usual program of systematic theory verification. Certain aspects of the picture are emerging in great detail, while others are still vague and their general outlines are inferential. Nevertheless, by employing a range of interdisciplinary methods within a variety of samples, we hope to produce a convergence of data to illumine the problem as a whole.

## THE DEVELOPMENT OF PROSOCIAL BEHAVIOR
## WITHIN A POLYNESIAN ISLAND SETTING

Soon after we arrived in Aitutaki and settled into our village home with four of our six children, it became apparent to us that our Polynesian neighbors expended little effort explicitly training children in prosocial behavior. As soon as they could toddle, most children seemed eager to be involved in the busy round of family and neighborhood activities, which they were allowed to join as they became physically capable.

We were particularly struck by the rarity of object attachment, parallel play, "private speech" monologues, or other manifestations of "egocentrism" that characterize early developmental stages in the West. Instead, children from traditional families appear to have a strong group orientation from infancy, which is continuously reinforced in dozens of ways: They are raised in large families by a variety of caretakers; they attend and participate in most family and community affairs; they are sent with food or goods to share with other people; they take the family's contribution to the front of the church on Sunday; and they learn to work, drum, and dance on the perimeter of groups to which their older siblings, cousins, or parents belong. When they grow up and leave the island to migrate to New Zealand (as we found over 80% were doing by the age of 23; T. Graves & N. Graves, 1976), they usually live with relatives in the city who exhort them to "remember the name of your island" and bring honor upon it.

This high degree of group participation and identification and the many manifestations of prosocial behavior that flow from it, we came to recognize, has its roots in the economic, social, and psychological interdependencies fostered by their subsistence economy. With Western influence, however, these interdependencies are breaking down, and with them are passing the need for and support of the high level of sociocentric behavior that has characterized island life.

Traditionally, for example, a fisherman who catches more than his family can eat that day will ''store the surplus in his neighbor's belly.'' Then he and his family can count on a constant supply of fresh fish through gifts from others in return. Thus a network of mutual obligation, caring, and concern is formed throughout the village. (Anthropologists will recognize that this networking is enhanced by the Polynesian system of bilateral kinship.) With the advent of electricity, however (which only came to Aitutaki in 1964, but was being used by 90% of the households a decade later), freezers became popular. Now, a family's surplus can be stored at home, and the need for networks of food redistribution diminishes. The same process has occurred with the introduction of sheet metal roofing, which eliminates the periodic need for communal thatching parties; commercial beer, which can be bought a few bottles at a time, replacing the large batches of home brew; tractors rented from the agriculture department plowing individual fields which earlier would have been worked by labor exchange groups; outboard motors reducing the need for communal fishing by extending the range of individual boats, and so forth. People can now ''afford'' to quarrel with their neighbors, and the social skills that had developed to prevent, deflect, or resolve such quarrels atrophy or are never learned.

Underlying all these changes is the dramatic growth in a cash economy on the island since World War II. As more and more men are shifting from a subsistence economy to wage work (less than 10% in 1945, about 60% by 1975; see T. Graves & N. Graves, 1976), their neighbors report ''he's fishing in the shops these days.'' Furthermore, low wages and high prices make the ''cost'' of generosity greater, just as the appeal of material possessions, now within their grasp, increases. Some islanders see these economic changes as the growth of an un-Christian, selfish materialism, whereas others welcome the opportunity to escape what they see as unreasonable obligations imposed on them by family and community.

Our understanding of the interconnections within this process of change grew during 6 months of participant observation. We then began the task of documentation, using several more formal procedures for measuring various aspects of prosocial behavior. These included systematic observations of preschool children in the homes, a reward allocation task and the Madsen Cooperation Board administered in the schools, and interviews with the fathers and mothers of the children we had been observing or testing, including a modified version of the reward allocation task.

## Prosocial Development in the Home

Twenty-eight girls and 21 boys between the ages of 5 and 6, who would be entering school the following year, were each observed in their homes or surrounding environs during four 45-min sessions, two during the mornings and two in the afternoons. The observers were five native Aitutakian female teachers on holiday who were trained by the investigators. Upon entering the setting, the observer recorded everyone present, the activities they were engaged in, and the relationship they had to the target child. This placed all subsequent action within its social context, which was updated throughout the observation period as activities shifted and people came and went.

Using a structured, narrative procedure developed in the field, observers then recorded the target child's behavior in "action units." Each act included the verb or *action,* the *initiator* of the action, the *responder* (either the target child or another in the environment if the act was interpersonal), and *modifiers* of the action (including adjectives, adverbs, and expressions of affect). After translation, the "action units" in each protocol were postcoded into a variety of categories. In addition to our own categories concerning the social make-up of the environment and the "chore opportunities" within it, we also scored the protocols for categories used in the Six Cultures Study (B. Whiting & J. Whiting, 1975): "altruism" (offering or giving help, offering or giving support, and suggesting responsible behavior to others); "egoism" (asking for help or support, seeking attention, and seeking dominance or competing); and "mands" (commands, demands, or requests made to or by the target child; for more detail see B. Whiting, 1980, p. 108–109). Protocols were scored by two coders with a reliability range of between .84 and 1.0, and differences were then resolved through discussion and agreement.

Since we were interested in the effects of modern structural changes on prosocial behavior, we divided our sample of children by two major dimensions: nuclear or extended family household structure and rural or town residence. Each cell contained at least five boys and five girls. This four-cell division resulted in a "most traditional" category of *rural* children raised in *extended* families ($N = 12$) and a "most modern" category of *town* children raised in *nuclear* families ($N = 10$). The other two cells, rural–nuclear ($N = 17$) and town–extended ($N = 10$) were intermediate in degree of modernization.

First, we looked at the social context of behavior in the home environment (see Table 10.1). We assumed that a major determinant of children's interaction patterns would be the *persons present* in their immediate environment. As B. Whiting (1980) noted, "The power of settings is in the cast of characters who frequent the settings [p. 112]." Although we found no substantial differences between families with different degrees of modernization as to the *number* of persons present (all averaged between 4.5 and 5.1, and boys and girls had identical averages of 4.8), they did differ sharply in the *category* of persons available to the child. The most traditional children (extended–rural families) had more extended kin and few nonrelatives around, whereas the most modern children (nuclear–town families) had few wider kin and many conjugal family members and nonrelatives present.

Both the modernization variables, family structure and family location, are responsible for these differences in the children's social environment. For example, with respect to whether the *mother* was present at any time during an observation period, the significant factor was extended versus nuclear family structure ($\chi^2 = 20.76$, $p < .001$, see Table 10.2). Over half the time when observers visited rural

**TABLE 10.1**

*Type of Persons Present during Home Observations*

*Percentage of those present who were
nuclear family members*

| Family type | Location | |
|---|---|---|
| | Rural | Town |
| Extended | 39% | 31% |
| Nuclear | 72% | 52% |

*Percentage of those present who were
extended family members*

| Family type | Location | |
|---|---|---|
| | Rural | Town |
| Extended | 49% | 49% |
| Nuclear | 19% | 14% |

*Percentage of those present who were
nonrelated persons*

| Family type | Location | |
|---|---|---|
| | Rural | Town |
| Extended | 11% | 19% |
| Nuclear | 8% | 34% |

extended families, the mother was *absent* throughout the observation period, and the child was interacting with other caretakers. By contrast, this was true only 15% of the time in town–nuclear families observed.

Town versus rural residence had only a small and nonsignificant relationship to mother's presence, but it was the major factor in whether *nonrelatives* were present ($\chi^2 = 30.25$, $p < .001$, see Table 10.3). Such unrelated persons were present

**TABLE 10.2**

*Percentage of Observation Sessions
with Mother Present*

| Family type | Location | |
|---|---|---|
| | Rural | Town |
| Extended | 47% | 52% |
| Nuclear | 78% | 85% |

**TABLE 10.3**
*Percentage of Observation Sessions*
*with Nonrelative Present*

| Family type | Location | |
|---|---|---|
| | Rural | Town |
| Extended | 21% | 49% |
| Nuclear | 25% | 78% |

during less than a quarter of the observations among rural–extended families, but over three-quarters of the observations in town–nuclear families.

As anticipated the type of persons *present* appears largely responsible for the social categories of person *interacted with* by the target child. Thus we found that the largest proportion of *social acts* by traditional children (47%) were with extended kin and only secondarily with nuclear kin (39%) whereas they seldom interacted with nonfamily persons (7%). Modern children showed the opposite pattern, interacting with nuclear family members (55%) and unrelated persons (31%) most.

These differences in personnel and resulting interaction mean that traditional children are surrounded by and must learn to relate to a wide and varied circle of relatives, many of whom have authority over them (including older siblings and cousins). This group provides them with their sense of identity and belonging. Modern children, by contrast, are learning to *differentiate* themselves from others through their participation in a smaller, more exclusive family group and frequent contact with persons not belonging to this group. This could also provide them with less sense of social *interdependence* than is experienced by traditional children. Furthermore, nonrelatives are not directly responsible for the children's behavior, and therefore may not as often promote the prosocial acts required within the family for cohesive functioning.

Within the limits set by the personnel present, children's learning experience is further shaped differentially by who *they* choose to interact with, who chooses to interact with *them,* and *what form* that interaction takes. First, in rural extended families preschool girls were interacting with adults at a far higher rate than preschool boys: 34 acts per hour for girls compared with only 9 per hour for boys. Instead, boys were spending more of their time in play groups interacting with their peers.

Second, we discovered that the *type* of interaction between children and adults in traditional homes was very different for boys and girls. For girls, almost a quarter of their interaction with adults involved *mands:* commands, demands, or requests directed toward the target child. By contrast, only 11% of adult interaction for boys involved such mands. Thus girls were having far more practice than boys in meeting the needs of adults, whereas the boys were often playing outside the arenas within which adults were working. In town settings, however, boys and girls did not differ in the number of mands they received from either adults or children.

Finally, when we looked into the *content* of the children's behavior, we found that in the traditional context girls were performing useful chores for the household at the rate of over 8 per hour, whereas boys were doing only about 1. So traditional girls were receiving a great deal of experience in contributing useful work to the family group, whereas boys were seldom called away from their play groups to perform chores. Again, in town boys and girls are not much different, although girls continue to do more chores than boys: 2.6 per hour compared to 1.8 for town boys.

These differences between boys and girls are related to three things: the *number* of chores available to be done in the country as compared to town that are at a level 5-year-olds could be expected to handle; cultural values concerning the *appropriateness* of these tasks for boys or girls; and *how many other* eligible children are around to do them.

Rural environments in general provide more opportunities than town environments for children to help the family. Traditionally, men do more of the fishing, planting and maintenance of food crops, and gathering, husking and processing of coconuts, while women are expected to maintain the home, prepare food and clothing, and care for infants. Preschool boys are not considered old enough to participate in the men's work, whereas common and easy household tasks, such as collecting leaves and rubbish, keeping the fire going, running errands, washing dishes, sweeping, and a variety of child-care activities are usually performed by girls, if any are available. All of these except errands, fall under the sex-role division of labor. For example, although preschool boys *could* care for babies and seem to enjoy them, we found only 8 of the 21 boys ever did so during our observations, whereas 24 of the 28 girls in our sample did so ($\chi^2 = 12.0, p < .01$). These patterns parallel those found in other cross-cultural studies (B. Whiting & Edwards, 1973; Ember, 1973).

Thus circumstances in traditional families create a situation where cooperative behavior directed toward family goals is learned earlier for girls than boys, except in cases of "underwomaning" of the setting. This "underwomaning," however, is more likely to occur in nuclear than in extended families. Consequently, the boys whom we observed in nuclear households actually performed *more* chores than those in extended households: 2.7 per hr compared with 1.3 per hr.

*All* children, however, experience a radical reduction in the number of chores available to them when their families move to town: The mean number of "chore opportunities" for town–nuclear children was only 5.5 compared to 17.9 for rural–extended children. The result of this is not only fewer family contributions and less responsibility for the preschooler, but also lower maternal expectations for them, and therefore, fewer adult-directed learning experiences.[1] In addition, there

---

[1] See N. Graves (1971) and the section by N. Graves in T. Graves and N. Graves (1978) for similar results among urbanizing Spanish Americans in the southwestern United States and urbanizing Baganda families in Kampala, Uganda.

are more attractions outside the home—nearby friends and town amusements—to tempt the child from family work. "Wandering" was cited by town mothers as a major problem with children this age.

These differences have important implications for the development of prosocial behavior. It is clear from our observations that supportive and helpful behavior, as well as suggestions to others that they behave responsibly (the behaviors categorized as "altruism" in the Whitings' scoring system), often occurred in conjunction with family work around the home. Thus we found that being given responsible tasks promoted altruistic acts. Because much of this help is given in situations where others are involved in the work as well, chores also promote cooperative behavior involving coordination of effort.

As a result, when we examine the data for *altruism,* we find that in extended families in rural settings girls displayed the most altruistic behavior, 24% of all their acts, and there were sharp differences between boys and girls (see Table 10.4). Conversely, in modern, nuclear families in town, boys and girls are similarly *low* in altruistic behavior: between 5% and 8% of their acts.

Boys and girls also differed in the *type* of prosocial behavior they displayed. Boys acted altruistically mainly in relation to their *playmates,* for example, by sharing toys and food, but most of the girls' altruism took the form of responsible behavior in conjunction with family chores. Thus girls are learning to be cooperative within a hierarchical system of family responsibility, whereas boys are learning altruism in an egalitarian peer situation.

Boys and girls also differed sharply in *egoism,* as indexed by acts of asking for help and support, or performing boastfully or competitively. In general, boys were about twice as egoistic as girls, and neither boys nor girls differed greatly from one family type or setting to another. We therefore tentatively conclude that modernization does not affect this kind of behavior at this age and that it is more related to sex differences in assertiveness.

Contrary to the Whitings' suggestion in their Six Cultures Study, however, egoism does not seem to us to be the opposite leg of the prosocial dimension. Rather, we believe from our observations that the opposite of prosocial behavior is *individualistic* behavior, which in our study involves playing on one's own, often without others or ignoring their presence (as in parallel play), and often with one's attention on objects—things rather than people. Here the important ecological determinant in our study was town residence. Whereas children from extended or nuclear

**TABLE 10.4**
*Percentage of All Acts Categorized as Altruistic*

| Location | Extended | | Nuclear | |
|---|---|---|---|---|
| | Girls | Boys | Girls | Boys |
| Rural | 24% | 8% | 12% | 16% |
| Town | 14% | 10% | 5% | 8% |

families did not differ in the amount of such nonsocial, solitary behavior, fully *half* of all the acts by town children were nonsocial, as compared to less than a third for the rural children. This probably reflects the dispersion of the family and the relative paucity of cooperative joint tasks in town, as well as an increase in interesting modern objects in the child's environment.

## Prosocial Behavior in the Schools

The island's three primary schools provided settings within which formal measures of various types of prosocial behavior could be administered. We designed a *Reward Allocation Task* intended to capture within a single standardized procedure the many opportunities that islanders encounter in daily life to distribute valued resources among self and others. Building on earlier work by Kagan and Madsen (1972), our task is simpler in format but more complex in content. In pretesting we found it suitable for use with children as young as 5, yet it retained the interest of well-educated adults. Thus we could use it among school children of all ages, as well as with their parents.

Our procedure involved each subject in choosing one from each of nine pairs of cards on which different numbers of pennies are placed for both the chooser and an observing child of the same age and sex. (For details of format and administration, see N. Graves & T. Graves, 1978.) These choices make it possible to examine the relative strength of four motives: *"rivalry"* (either maximizing own gain relative to other or minimizing other's gain in absolute terms); *"generosity"* (either maximizing other's gain in absolute terms or maximizing it relative to own gain); *"equalization"* (attempting to equate both own and other's gain either on a particular trial or over the 9 trials); and *"self-maximization"* (attempting to maximize own gain regardless of other).

Although Kagan and Madsen treated their own procedure as if each choice were an independent event, we found that subjects usually appeared to develop a general strategy across all nine choice pairs. Because of the way the task is designed, however, the pursuit of any strategy involves trade-offs, and most subjects compromised somewhat. Subjects who made rivalrous choices on at least six of the nine choice pairs have been classified as *rivalrous;* those who made such choices three or less times were classified as *generous;* and those with intermediate scores of 4 or 5 were classified as *equalizers.* Each subject also received a "self-maximization" score, which is independent of the other three strategies.

We tested 261 boys and 212 girls on this procedure, virtually all the children in the first three grades (United States K–2), Grade 5 (United States Grade 4), and Forms I and II (United States Grades 6 and 7). After returning to New Zealand, we also tested 48 boys and 39 girls from an inner city and a rural school in the greater Auckland area.

A comparison between the behavior of 5–8-year-olds in the Cook Islands with the similar aged children in New Zealand is presented in Figure 10.1. Among New

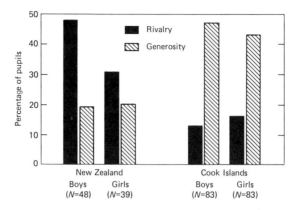

**FIGURE 10.1.** Cultural differences on the Reward Allocation Task.

Zealand children 44% of the boys and 31% of the girls were classified as "rivalrous" on this procedure. (This sex difference was not statistically significant, although it may reflect early sex-role differences in socialization to rivalry.) By contrast, only about 14% of the Cook Islands children were rivalrous, whereas 45% were generous. Only 18% of the New Zealand children were generous. These differences are highly significant statistically. On an item-by-item analysis these cultural differences were relatively small for the pretest and first few trials, when children were still developing their strategies, but, on Trial 3 and from Trial 5 on all differences are highly significant ($p < .01$ on 2-tailed $\chi^2$ tests).

Interestingly, both culture groups were almost identical in their self-maximization scores: The average child, whether Cook Islander or New Zealander, chose the self-maximizing option about three-quarters of the time it was offered. As a result, choosers in both groups averaged the same amount of money for themselves. The difference between the two groups, therefore, is not in *how much* they were willing to sacrifice their own interests, but *for what purpose* they would do so. Cook Islands children frequently gave up some of their possible earnings so that the other child would receive *more* money; New Zealand children sacrificed so that the other would receive *less*. Consequently, the observing child received 18¢ on the average in Aitutaki (1.3¢ *more* than the choosing child), whereas the observing child received only 15.7¢ on the average in New Zealand (.9¢ *less* than the choosing child). This difference is also highly significant statistically ($p < .001$ on a 2-tailed $t$ test).

Since the children in both societies were only beginning school, it seems likely that these dramatic contrasts in behavior are a result of the two distinct cultural contexts rather than differences in education or cognitive capacity. Furthermore, the behavior of neither group fits an egocentric stage model. If these young children were unable to consider the gains and losses of the observing child, they should simply have self-maximized whenever possible. In fact, only about a quarter of the children in both culture groups self-maximized all the time; the rest made calculated decisions at some time to take a personal loss in order to achieve some social purpose. For Cook Islanders this purpose was usually to give the other child as much or more than they received themselves; for New Zealand children this purpose was frequently to insure that the other child received *less*. The situation was perceived as a chance to ''win'' more than someone else, and this was explicitly stated by many of the New Zealand children or displayed nonverbally by a triumphant grin as a rivalrous choice was made. By contrast, among the Cook Islands children, choices that involved taking more than the observing child often produced embarrassment, displayed by hesitation to choose, downcast eyes, or hands to face.

The school system in Aitutaki, though predominantly staffed by native Aitutakians, is imported from New Zealand and reflects modern, Western value systems and norms of interaction. During their primary years, Cook Islands children must not only master academic skills and learn English (first taught systematically in Grade 3), but they must also learn new interpersonal behavior. The new setting requires the suppression of help-giving under most circumstances, rewards are individually distributed rather than shared by a group, and children must vie for these rewards by ''doing better'' than their peers. Furthermore, authority is vested in a single adult, the teacher, rather than among peers, siblings, cousins, and a wide variety of adults. Given the sharp contrast between behavioral expectations within this context and traditional island homes, the adjustment for many children takes time. Some prefer the style of interaction common in their home environment or see no advantage from adopting the behavior required by the schools and so are slow or resistant to change.

As can be seen in Figure 10.2, our cross-sectional sample of Aitutaki school children at different grade levels reveals a striking change in interpersonal behavior the longer they have been in school. In fact, by Form I and II (ages 12 to 13), the Cook Islands children are displaying about as much rivalry as New Zealand children

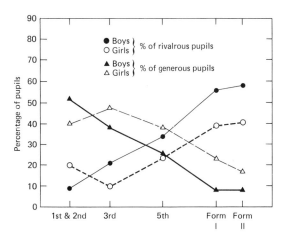

**FIGURE 10.2.** Development of rivalry in Aitutaki children. Grade level: First and second, $N = 56$ boys, 49 girls; third, $N = 31$ boys, 39 girls; fifth, $N = 56$ boys, 38 girls; Form 1, $N = 48$ boys, 46 girls; Form 2, $N = 74$ boys, 47 girls.

in the first three grades, and a statistically significant sex difference has also now appeared. Overall differences between the younger and older children are all highly significant, of course, as well as on seven of the nine individual items.

Again we found that the younger and older Cook Islands children do *not* differ in the frequency with which they selected the self-maximizing options; more of the older children had now learned to sacrifice for a competitive advantage rather than out of generosity. Thus the typical prosocial developmental path in the West has been *reversed* in Aitutaki as children learn new rivalrous and individualistic patterns.

This conclusion is further supported by an examination of the *correlates* of rivalry and generosity among the older children. Those boys and girls who lived in Western *nuclear* families were far more likely to be rivalrous (67%) than those from more traditional families (34%). Furthermore, those who received high marks (above the median) and conformed best to the school's dress standard (an index of their general conformity to school expectations, which was unrelated to their family's socioeconomic position) were also significantly more rivalrous and less generous. In fact, among the 22 children in our oldest school sample who were low on *both* of these indexes of conformity to school expectations, only 23% were rivalrous, and 50% were *generous*. This strongly suggests that an *identification* with the school as a Western institution that would prepare them for a life away from their home island was necessary for them to adopt a style of interpersonal behavior at variance with what many were experiencing in their home and village. Transfer of prosocial behavior between settings thus may be affected by a variety of personal aspirations and expectations.

Our general conclusions concerning the development of prosocial behavior on Aitutaki are given further support from data gathered on the Madsen Cooperation Board. We chose this 4-person task because it requires coordination of effort within a group without necessarily involving much verbal problem solving. This type of spontaneous small group cooperation takes place in many physical tasks on the island from packing bananas to fishing with a net or preparing a feast. Since the cross-cultural use of this instrument is already well-documented (N. Graves & T. Graves, 1978; Kagan & Madsen, 1971; Madsen, 1967; Madsen & Shapira, 1970; Miller, 1973; Miller & Thomas, 1972; Shapira & Madsen, 1969; Somerlad & Bellingham, 1972; Thomas, 1975), we will not go into detail here. Our procedure followed that of Thomas (1975), providing no initial "cooperative set" in the instructions. (See N. Graves & T. Graves, 1978.)

Over 2 successive years, 152 seventh grade Aitutaki children (88 boys and 64 girls, ages 11–13) were tested in same-sex groups of four on this instrument. Since the results from these 2 years did not differ, they have been combined here. Our criterion for successful cooperation was the same as Thomas's: over four 1-min trials, at least three of the four group members had to receive a reward within a single trial.

Of these groups 45% achieved cooperation, a rate not substantially higher than the 33% cooperative among rural Maori school children tested by Thomas in New

Zealand,[2] but this high rate of successful cooperation differs sharply from the success rate he reported among both urban Maoris (8%) and white New Zealand children (12%).

Again, a correlational analysis adds weight to our conclusion that this level of cooperation among Cook Islands children is an emergent from their traditional cultural milieu. The *major* determinant of success or failure on the coop board was the number of children in the group of four who came from traditional extended families ($r = .56$). Only about a third of the children in "successful" groups came from Western-style nuclear families, whereas almost two-thirds of the unsuccessful children were from nuclear families. Our observations of their performance on this task revealed that the major determinant of success or failure was not good leadership, but good *membership* behavior (N. Graves & T. Graves, 1978, p. 131); children from nuclear families had apparently not learned these group membership skills as well as those from more traditional families. The second most important determinant of cooperative success or failure was the number of children in the four-person group who were rivalrous on the Reward Allocation Task ($r = -.26$). Over 60% of the unsuccessful children were rivalrous, compared to only about 40% of the successful children. Having two or more highly rivalrous children on the team created a strong barrier to successful cooperation. No other variables in our study made a significant contribution to success or failure on this procedure.

## Prosocial Behavior among Adults

Data from interviews with a sample of 147 parents (80 men and 67 women) of children we have been testing or observing provides further evidence concerning the influence of modernization on prosocial behavior. At the end of our interviews, parents were also administered the Reward Allocation Task. Since they were usually interviewed in their homes, norms of hospitality toward guests and solidarity toward family members precluded the use of a real person in the role of "receiver." Consequently, subjects were instructed to "imagine" that another man or woman was sitting across the table from them, where an empty chair and jar were placed. Otherwise the procedure was identical.

Adults quickly recognized the metaphor for life that this task provided. As one old fisherman observed, "That's what we do when sharing the fish. The one who shares gets the least, because he just gives the big ones to the others and the small ones to himself. Otherwise the people will talk about him, saying he takes all the big ones for himself."

The results from this study, reported at length elsewhere (N. Graves & T. Graves, 1978), further reinforce our conclusion that prosocial behavior is signifi-

[2]In Thomas's study children were given six trials, but only 9% became cooperative after Trial 4. In order to make our results directly comparable, we obtained his permission to rescore his original data. Thus figures reported here differ slightly from his 1975 article.

cantly related to the degree to which persons are part of a traditional, interdependent or a modern, competitive economic and social system. Men who lived in remote areas of the island as part of an extended family, who were engaged in traditional planting and fishing activities, who had less than average formal education, and who had never been to New Zealand had a consistently low probability of behaving in a rivalrous manner on the Reward Allocation Task. By contrast, men who headed nuclear families; who were involved in the wage economy, particularly in skilled, professional, or managerial positions; who had more than average formal education; and who had been to New Zealand at least once, had a consistently high probability of behaving in a rivalrous manner on this task. Women displayed a basically similar pattern of results.

These findings support the interpretation often suggested in the literature on altruism (Munroe & Munroe, 1975, 1977; B. Whiting & J. Whiting, 1975; J. Whiting & B. Whiting, 1973) that Western formal schooling is not supportive to prosocial behavior. In fact, the nine Cook Islands teachers we tested were the most rivalrous occupational group on the island: two-thirds were rivalrous and none were generous.

## SUMMARY

Our work on a modernizing island in the South Pacific, along with insights from contrasting New Zealand data, points up the importance of ecological context in the emergence of prosocial behavior among both children and adults. In observing preschool children in both rural and town settings from traditional extended families and modern nuclear families, we found that these changes in the social make-up of the home and its wider community setting led town–nuclear children to experience less interaction with their extended kin group, their group of identification, more consolidation with the conjugal family group, and more contact with nonrelatives, lower rates of chore performance, and less altruistic behavior. At the same time their rate of individualistic behavior, as measured by nonsocial self- or object-oriented acts, was higher. In 1974–1975, when the study was conducted, a minority of the children were in the most modern category, but, as the society undergoes structural change in that direction, it is not surprising that cooperative village work is declining, and increasing numbers of young people are either leaving the island or refusing to join in village work crews.

A further lesson was learned from the observation data about the structure of prosocial development in traditional settings. Two alternative routes to the learning of prosocial behavior appear to be available, one more commonly experienced by girls, the other by boys. The first is a hierarchical path of being incorporated with elders into meaningful cooperative work around the home while also learning nurturance toward younger, more dependent family members. Preschool girls enter on this path sooner than preschool boys in the traditional environment: performing more chores; receiving more mands from adults; and behaving more altruistically in terms of giving help, support, and responsible suggestions to others. For girls, involvement in this path to learning prosocial behavior is reduced both by nuclear family structure and town residence.

Preschool boys experience this first path only if their setting is "under-womaned," although after the age of 8 or 9, they will begin to participate in cooperative work groups when they are taken with the men to fish, plant, or gather coconuts. Instead, they start first on the second path of prosocial development: that of egalitarian peer group play. Thus, although preschool boys' altruism is low when measured by indicators that tap the first route, no boy–girl differences appeared in children during the first three grades of school when altruism was measured by a reward allocation task involving peers. This indicates a need for careful choice of measures to include both paths of prosocial development.

Interestingly, these alternative styles of prosocial behavior are reflected in the adaptive coping strategies of Pacific Islands immigrants in New Zealand (N. Graves & T. Graves, 1977; T. Graves & N. Graves, 1980). Polynesians (including indigenous Maoris) in the city of Auckland displayed mainly group-oriented strategies whereas New Zealanders from a European background more often preferred an individualistic strategy (self-reliance), relying on the resources of their nuclear family or formal institutions in the society. The two types of group-oriented strategies corresponded to our two prosocial development paths: *kin reliance,* involving reciprocal obligations to and support from extended kin in a hierarchical, age-graded system; and *peer reliance,* egalitarian exchange relationships with friends of the same generation. More men than women chose the latter as a major adaptive strategy.

In addition to the home, the school is another microsetting that provides a structure that can facilitate or inhibit the emergence of prosocial behavior. In a society where the individualistic ethic and self-reliant adaptive strategies predominate, young New Zealand children showed a high proportion of rivalrous acts in a reward allocation task with peers. Conversely, in a society where the traditional ethic is one of interdependence and the most common traditional adaptations were group oriented, Aitutaki children in the first three grades of school exhibit a pattern of high generosity, and low rivalry. The school setting, however, is structured according to New Zealand norms of individual work and competition toward personal goals, and discourages helping others toward a common goal. Thus we saw more Aitutaki children becoming rivalrous with each year in school. Among both children and adults in this changing society, however, those with the most traditional backgrounds were the most cooperative and altruistic.

## IMPLICATIONS FOR RESEARCH

Our research has suggested to us the importance of intervention in the school environment if prosocial development and academic learning are to go hand in hand. Although children from individualistic backgrounds fit well into the structural demands of the conventional classroom, those from settings that emphasize cooperative interdependence and peer reliance either learn to drop their adaptation for a more isolated and competitive one, or they fare poorly in school. They have few, if any, opportunities to learn cooperatively in groups, as they would prefer.

There are no inherent reasons why individualism and academic learning should be linked, other than historical circumstance, and the effectiveness of cooperative learning groups for improving performance and promoting positive attitudes towards school, classmates, and self has now been amply demonstrated (Aronson, Blaney, Stephen, & Sikes, 1978; Aronson & Osherow, 1980; Johnson & Johnson, 1979; Sharan, Hare, & Webb, 1980; Slavin, 1978, 1980; Slavin & DeVries, 1979; Weigel, Wiser, & Cook, 1975; Ziegler, 1981). We have therefore set out to develop a program of cooperative learning that will embody an ecological approach to the total context of the classroom. A demonstration project, involving rural and urban schools in both the United States and New Zealand, is underway to create *analogs* in the classroom for the structural conditions present in traditional cooperative environments like those on Aitutaki. During the pilot years (1981–1982), teachers worked with the investigators to develop locally appropriate activities that will implement a series of graduated principles important to the cooperative environment. These activities prepare the ground for the growth of cooperative behavior by providing the following contextual features:

1. A basis for a *common bond* within the classroom as a whole through creating a class *identity,* giving each child a role, functions, and a *sense of belonging,* and occasions for *unity experiences* with the group

2. A *variety of personnel*— both younger and older persons incorporated into the classroom, lay persons as well as professionals, and relatives wherever possible

3. Changing the style of social interaction by providing students with *opportunities to direct others* as well as being directed by them, to participate in their own planning of activities and discipline, by providing *group* in addition to individual *rewards* and emphasizing *intrinsic rewards* of group activities and moving toward *a mixture of cooperative, competitive and individualistic activities*

4. *Concrete and tangible tasks* where children can realize their contribution to group goals within the classroom, the school, and the wider community.

In the spring of 1982, teachers began implementing a varied series of cooperative small-group techniques for learning academic subjects, which have been graduated according to the level of skill in prosocial, cooperative behaviors that each appears to require. We will compare: (*a*) the degree to which teachers implement the groundwork of context-restructuring just outlined; (*b*) the degree of implementation of the small-group academic techniques with or without this preparatory work; and (*c*) a group of teachers, as control comparisons, who do not change their teaching styles or add any cooperative techniques. Children from minority cultures having traditional structures facilitating prosocial behavior will be compared with children from majority, Anglo-Saxon backgrounds and long-term urban experience. All children will be monitored through observation of prosocial behavior and periodic written measures of self-esteem, academic performance, and sociometric measures to chart the development of prosocial behavior and its effect on personal and social characteristics within and between classrooms using different techniques. The final year of the study (1982–1983) is a demonstration year since contextual change techniques and measures will have been pretested and most teachers trained with a year of experience.

Our holistic, ecological approach to the development of prosocial behavior leaves us with no illusions that restructuring a few classrooms will, by itself, lead to lasting changes in cooperative behavior, but society as a whole is also changing. The vast majority of available jobs are now in the tertiary sector where social skills are of great importance (Cohen, 1973; Shallcrass, 1974). The average person from a Western background raised in a small, nuclear family in town has few opportunities to acquire these social skills, and growing numbers of adults are turning to various forms of "human relations" training to compensate for this cultural deficit. Our work in the schools will provide some compensatory education for these children, while helping children from more traditional backgrounds to retain and utilize the prosocial behavior they have learned at home. As we come to recognize that we are interdependent inhabitants of a tiny planetary island in a vast cosmic sea, the lessons that the Polynesian experience has to offer will become increasingly relevant to us all.

## REFERENCES

Allport, F. H. *Theories of perception and the concept of structure.* New York: Wiley, 1955.

Aronson, E., Blaney, N., Stephan, C., Sikes, J., & Snapp, M. *The jigsaw classroom.* Beverly Hills: Sage, 1978.

Aronson, E., & Osherow, N. Cooperation, prosocial behavior and academic performance. In L. Bickman (Ed.), *Applied social psychology annual* (Vol. 1). Beverly Hills: Sage, 1980.

Bandura, A., & Walters, R. H. *Social learning and personality development.* New York: Holt Rinehart & Winston, 1963.

Bar-Tal, D. *Prosocial behavior: Theory and research.* Washington, D.C.: Hemisphere, 1976.

Barker, R. G., Gump, P. V., Friesen, W. V., & Willems, E. P. The ecological environment: Student participation in non-class settings. In M. B. Miles & W. W. Charters, Jr. (Eds.), *Learning in social settings: New readings in the social psychology of education.* Boston: Allyn & Bacon, 1970.

Borke, H. Piaget's view of social interaction and the theoretical construct of empathy. In L. S. Siegel & C. J. Brainerd (Eds.), *Alternatives to Piaget: Critical essays on the theory.* New York: Academic Press, 1978.

Bronfenbrenner, U. The experimental ecology of human development. Unpublished manuscript, Cornell University, 1976.

Bruner, J. S. Culture and cognitive growth. In J. S. Bruner (Ed.), *The relevance of education.* London: Allen & Unwin, 1971.

Cohen, R. School reorganization and learning: An approach to assessing the direction of school change. In S. T. Kimball & J. H. Burnett (Eds.), *Symposium on learning and culture, proceedings 1972 annual spring meeting, Ethnological Society.* Seattle: University of Washington Press, 1973.

Ember, C. R. Feminine task assignment and social behavior of boys. *Ethos, 1,* 1973, *1,* 424–439.

Flavell, J., Botkin, P., Fry, C., Wright, J., & Jarvis, P. *The development of role-taking and communications skills in children.* New York: Wiley, 1968.

Graves, N. B. City, country, and child rearing: A tricultural study of mother–child relationships in varying environments. Doctoral dissertation, University of Colorado, 1971. *Dissertation Abstracts,* 1972, *32*B(No. 4), p. 1969. (University Microfilms No. 71-25, 828).

Graves, N. B., & Graves, T. D. Preferred adaptive strategies: An approach to understanding New Zealand's multicultural workforce. *New Zealand Journal of Industrial Relations,* 1977, *2*(3), 81–90.

Graves, N. B., and & Graves, T. D. The impact of modernization on the personality of a Polynesian people. *Human Organization,* 1978, *37,* 157–162.

Graves, T. D., & Graves, N. B. Demographic changes in the Cook Islands: Perception and reality. Or, where have all the *mapu* gone? *The Journal of the Polynesian Society,* 1976, *85*(4), 447–461.

Graves, T. D., & Graves, N. B. Evolving strategies in the study of culture change. In G. L. Spindler (Ed.), *The making of psychological anthropology.* Berkeley: University of California Press, 1978.

Graves, T. D., & Graves, N. B. Kinship ties and the preferred adaptive strategies of urban migrants. In S. Beckerman & L. Cordell (Eds.), *The versatility of kinship.* New York: Academic Press, 1980.

Hoffman, M. L. Developmental synthesis of affect and cognition and its implications for altruistic motivation. *Developmental Psychology,* 1975, *11*(5), 607–622.

Hogan, R. Theoretical egocentrism and the problem of compliance. *American Psychologist,* 1975, *30,* 533–540.

Inkeles, A. Social change and social character: The role of parental mediation. *Journal of Social Issues,* 1955, *11,* 12–23.

Johnson, D. W., & Johnson, R. The instructional use of cooperative, competitive and individualistic goal structures. In H. J. Walberg (Ed.), *Educational environments and effects: Evaluation, policy and productivity.* Berkeley, Calif.: McCutchan, 1979.

Kagan, S., & Madsen, M. C. Cooperation and competition of Mexican, Mexican-American, and Anglo-American children of two ages under four instructional sets. *Developmental Psychology,* 1971, *5,* 32–39.

Kagan, S., & Madsen, M. C. Rivalry in Anglo-American and Mexican children of two ages. *Journal of Personality and Social Psychology,* 1972, *24,* 214–220.

Kanfer, F. H. Personal control, social control, and altruism: Can society survive the age of individualism? *American Psychologist,* 1979, *34*(3), 231–239.

Kohlberg, L. Development of moral character and moral ideology. In M. L. Hoffman & L. W. Hoffman (Eds.), *Child development research.* New York: Russell Sage, 1964.

Kohlberg, L. Stage and sequence: The cognitive-developmental approach to socialization. In D. Goslin (Ed.), *Handbook of socialization theory and research.* New York: Rand McNally, 1969.

Levine, R. *Culture, behavior, and personality: An introduction to the comparative study of psychological adaptation.* Chicago: Aldine, 1973.

Madsen, M. C. Cooperative and competitive motivation of children in three Mexican subcultures. *Psychology Reports,* 1967, *20,* 1307–1320.

Madsen, M. C., & Shapira, A. Cooperative and competitive behavior of urban Afro-American, Anglo-American and Mexican village children. *Developmental Psychology,* 1970, *3,* 16–20.

Miller, A. Integration and acculturation of cooperative behavior among Blackfoot Indian and non-Indian Canadian children. *Journal of Cross-cultural Psychology,* 1973, *4,* 374–380.

Miller, A. G., & Thomas, R. Cooperation and competition among Blackfoot Indian and urban Canadian children. *Child Development,* 1972, *43,* 1104–1110.

Munroe, R. L., & Munroe, R. H. *Cross-cultural human development.* Monterey, Calif.: Brookskole, 1975.

Munroe, R. L., & Munroe, R. H. Cooperation and competition among East African and American children. *Journal of Social Psychology,* 1977, *101*(1), 145–146.

Piaget, J. *The moral judgment of the child.* London: Kegan Paul, 1932.

Piaget, J. *The psychology of intelligence.* New York: Harcourt & Brace, 1950.

Sampson, E. E. Psychology and the American ideal. *Journal of Personality and Social Psychology,* 1977, *35*(11), 767–782.

Selman, R. L. Social-cognitive understanding: A guide to educational and clinical practice. In T. Lickona (Ed.), *Moral development and behavior*. New York: Holt Rinehart & Winston, 1976.

Shallcrass, J. Ultimately politics and power. *NZ Listener,* March 2, 1974, 29.

Shapira, A., & Madsen, M. C. Cooperative and competitive behavior of kibbutz and urban children in Israel. *Child Development,* 1969, *40,* 609–617.

Sharan, S., Hare, P., Webb, C. D., & Hertz-Lazarowitz, R. *Cooperation in education: Proceedings, first international conference on cooperation in education. Tel-Aviv, Israel, July 1979.* Provo, Utah: Brigham Young University Press, 1980.

Slavin, R. E. *Using student team learning.* Baltimore, Maryland: Johns Hopkins University Center for Social Organization of Schools, 1978.

Slavin, R. Cooperative learning in teams: State of the art. *Educational Psychologist,* 1980, *15*(2), 93–111.

Slavin, R. E., & DeVries, D. L. Learning in teams. In H. J. Walberg (Ed.), *Educational environments and effects: Evaluation, policy, and productivity.* Berkeley, Calif.: McCutchan, 1979.

Sommerlad, E. A., & Bellingham, W. P. Cooperation–competition: A comparison of Australian–European and Aboriginal school children. *Journal of Cross-cultural Psychology,* 1972, *3,* 149–157.

Stayton, D., Hogan, R., & Ainsworth, M. D. S. Infant obedience and maternal behavior: The origins of socialization reconsidered. *Child Development,* 1971, *42,* 1057–1069.

Stone, L. The rise of the nuclear family in early modern England: The patriarchal stage. In C. E. Rosenberg (Ed.), *The family in history.* Philadelphia: University of Pennsylvania Press, 1975.

Thomas, D. R. Cooperation and competition among Polynesian and European children. *Child Development,* 1975, *46,* 948–953.

Toffler, A. *The third wave.* New York: Morrow, 1980.

Turiel, E. Developmental processes in the child's moral thinking. In P. H. Mussen, J. Langer, & M. Covington (Eds.), *Trends and issues in developmental psychology.* New York: Holt Rinehart & Winston, 1969.

Weigel, R. H., Wiser, P. L., & Cook, S. W. Impact of cooperative learning experiences on cross-ethnic relations and attitudes. *Journal of Social Issues,* 1975, *31*(1), 219–245.

Whiting, B. B. Culture and social behavior: A model for the development of social behavior. *Ethos,* 1980, *8*(2), 95–116.

Whiting, B. B., & Edwards, C. P. A cross-cultural analysis of sex differences in the behavior of children aged three through 11. *The Journal of Social Psychology,* 1973, *91,* 171–188.

Whiting, B. B., & Whiting, J. W. M. *Children of six cultures: A psycho-cultural analysis.* Cambridge, Mass.: Harvard University Press, 1975.

Whiting, J. W. M., & Whiting, B. B. Altruistic and egoistic behavior in six cultures. In L. Nader & T. W. Maretzki (Eds.), *Cultural illness and health.* Washington, D.C.: American Anthropological Association, 1973.

Ziegler, S. The effectiveness of cooperative learning teams for increasing cross-ethnic friendship: Additional evidences. *Human Organization,* 1981, *40*(3), 264–267.

# Commentary and Critique: Cross-Cultural Approaches to Prosocial Development

**DENNIS KREBS**

Psychological research on prosocial behavior is more narrow and limited than the typical investigator is willing to acknowledge: most of it employs North American children or college students as subjects; it is cast in a laboratory context; and it sets as its goal the examination of the effect of a constricted sample of independent variables on a constricted sample of behaviors. Although defended by researchers such as Rushton (1980), I believe that the ecological validity of most research on prosocial behavior is severely limited (see Krebs, 1982a, 1982b; Krebs & Miller, in press). The cross-cultural research presented in this section supplies a refreshing change from laboratory research. N. and T. Graves and B. Whiting report observations of children and adults engaging in the prosocial behaviors of their choice in the natural contexts of their everyday lives. These observations draw attention to a number of parameters of prosocial behavior that have largely remained beyond the purview of laboratory research. Particularly notable are age-appropriate behaviors, sex differences, dyad types, family differences, and cultural differences.

## Age Appropriate Behaviors

In their tendency to investigate the effect of independent variables on one type of prosocial behavior, most laboratory experiments are insensitive to the tendency of children of different ages to engage in different types of prosocial behavior. Infants display their prosocial proclivities mainly through smiles and signs of recognition (see Chapters 3 and 4). In the "terrible two's" children insist on doing things

THE NATURE OF PROSOCIAL DEVELOPMENT

themselves, and may well impose their unrefined attempts to assist others on their caretakers. Still older children may assume significant responsibility for household chores. There is a world of difference between observing children (and adults) engaging in prosocial behaviors appropriate to their age and examining the effect of various experimental manipulations on the frequency of one, often arbitrarily-selected type of behavior on children of different ages.

## Sex Differences

Both B. Whiting and H. and T. Graves draw attention to the fact that because the social roles of males and females—girls and boys as well as mothers and fathers—differ significantly in all known cultures, the number and types of prosocial behaviors that males and females display also tend to differ. The authors of Chapters 9 and 10 report that females typically engage in more prosocial behavior than males. The role of mother is more nurturant than the role of father in all cultures studied. Girls are socialized in a different manner from boys. In Aitutaki, for example, girls are required to do more household tasks than boys, especially those that involve the care of younger children. This does not mean, however, that there are no cultures in which boys behave nurturantly, or that they do not display prosocial behavior in other ways. Boys take care of infants in societies where mothers are needed for help in agriculture, and boys assume caretaking responsibilities when social groups are "underwomaned." In addition, even though the girls of Aitutaki engage in nurturant behaviors at a younger age than boys, the boys tend to even up the score around the age of 9–10, when they became physically able to participate in activities defined as masculine.

## Dyad Types

In attending to the type of dyad in which prosocial exchanges occur, B. Whiting points to the significance of the match between helper and recipient. Some experimental studies have varied the nature of the recipient (for example, friend versus stranger); however most of them are insensitive to the tendency of children and adults to treat people differently depending on whether they are old or young, male or female, sibling or parent. The research on the elderly reviewed in Chapter 12 supplies an additional exemplification of this point.

## Family Differences

A principle that emerges with great force in both Chapters 9 and 10 is that the preponderance of prosocial behavior displayed by children and adults is directed toward members of their families. (Stewart & Smith make the same point in Chapter

12). In spite of the significance of kin in sociological, anthropological, and socio-biological theory, few psychological experiments have employed relatives as subjects. In Chapter 11, Brown and Solomon voice concern about the growing self-centeredness of American youth. Cross-cultural research suggests that a primary villain is dissolution of large, extended families and the growth of urbanization. Growing up in a family or community in which it is necessary to perform prosocial tasks (such as helping to care for younger siblings) emerges as the single most significant determinant of prosocial behavior, especially in females.

## Cultural Differences

The most general message delivered in Chapters 9 and 10 is that people who grow up in different cultures may adopt different styles of prosocial behavior. This message is significant less as an indictment of the samples of subjects typically employed in psychological research as it is an indication that the behavior of individuals should be considered in the context of their social environment. In both the research of B. Whiting and the Graveses, the Western world emerges as singularly unconducive to prosocial behavior. Both sets of studies suggest that the primary reason for this is the absence of small communities in which prosocial behavior by children is adaptive.

Although not featured explicitly by either of the authors of the cross-cultural studies, the notion of *role* may supply the most parsimonious account of the prosocial behavior observed. In the early chapters of this volume we saw that North American children model their parents' behavior from an early age—for example, they copy their mothers' house-cleaning behavior. In the present section we see that children, especially girls, in nonindustrial societies also model the prosocial behavior of their parents, particularly by taking care of younger siblings. The difference is that because of the structure of industrialized societies, the role-modeled prosocial behavior of Western children is nonfunctional or even dysfunctional; whereas the behavior of the children from nonindustrial societies serves a useful purpose. When children are needed to help in a community—when this is part of their social role—they help. The role assessed by many psychological experiments may primarily be that of a good subject. In order to get at the prosocial influence of social roles, one must sample subjects' behavior in its natural context. Stewart and Smith supply an example of this strategy in the final chapter.

Another characteristic of the nonindustrial communities discussed in Chapters 9 and 10—one that is closely related to the notion of role—is their tightly knit, first-order system of reciprocity. Trivers emphasizes the biological adaptiveness of reciprocal helping. Reciprocity is institutionalized in the social roles of nonindustrialized societies, where there is wide-scale repeated contact between individuals who are familiar to one another (many of whom are kin). In contrast, the network of social relatives in industrial societies tends to be much more individualized.

## THE GENERALITY OF ROLE-RELATED PROSOCIAL BEHAVIOR
## AND THE VALIDITY OF PSYCHOLOGICAL TESTS

With the authors of studies on North American infants, the authors of the cross-cultural studies suggest or assume that early role-related experience with prosocial behavior will instill in children prosocial motives or habits that will generalize to other contexts. The Graveses tested this assumption on Aitutaki children by giving them a reward allocation task patterned after that of Kagan and Madsen (1972). They found that trends in the behavior of the children on this task paralleled trends in their naturalistic social behavior: Girls tended to be more generous than boys; children from Aitutaki were substantially more generous than children from New Zealand; the longer the Aitutaki children were in Western-oriented schools, the less prosocial they became, especially if they adapted well to school; and children from nuclear families (the more Westernized children) were less generous than children from extended families. The children's behavior on the Madsen Cooperation Board paralleled these trends.

Although I have been critical of the ecological validity of laboratory studies on prosocial behavior, the correspondence between the naturalistic and nonnaturatlistic measures observed by N. and T. Graves is encouraging. It is important, however, to note that the laboratory measures were patterned after behaviors typical in the culture; and they were viewed in that manner by the subjects. That the reward allocation and cooperation tasks proved to be appropriate analogues for distributive and cooperative behavior probably was due at least in part to the fact that they involved actual (or in the case of adults, imagined), ecologically representative types of social interaction—a feature not shared by many laboratory measures of prosocial behavior.


## BIOLOGY AND CULTURE

One of the difficult questions that emerges about the sex differences in prosocial behavior reported in the present section concerns its source: Is it "preprogrammed" or is it instilled by socialization? Although not featured in the biological chapters of this volume, sociobiologists have drawn attention to the significance of the fact that the females of most species make a significantly greater investment in their offspring than males (see Barash, 1979). Males may generate millions of reproductive cells, whereas females produce significantly fewer (in the human case, about one per month). In parallel with this basic biological difference between the sexes, sociobiologists argue that it is more adaptive genetically for females than for males to invest in a small number of high-quality offspring. The differential physical investment made by females than males during pregnancy is thought to support this biologically based sex difference.

It is important to note that biological support for feminine nurturance does not entail evidence against the possibility that males also inherit dispositions to nurture the young; in fact Lorenz and others suggest that the evidence indicates that they do. Clearly, there is less sexual dymorphism in the human species than in most other primate species and much greater flexibility in sex-role behavior. Human males typically do not father children willy-nilly and then abandon them. As pointed out by Lovejoy (1981) in a recent review of the evidence on human evolution, cooperative divisions of labor between pair-bonded males and females involving a heavy investment by both in a small number of offspring may have been instrumental in the differentiation of the human species. The evidence does not suggest that males are not biologically predisposed to behave nurturantly toward infants; it suggests only that they are somewhat less strongly or reliably predisposed than females.

In addition, sociobiologists do not deny that cultural traditions may support or suppress biologically based inclinations and, thus, may reverse biologically based sex differences. Males were better adapted biologically to hunt and defend than females in our evolutionary past, and females were better adapted for childrearing (although as indicated, each sex can perform both tasks). For this reason, it makes sense that boys would engage in "egaltarian peer group play" and that men would go off to work in almost all cultures, whereas girls would tend to stay home and help their mothers around the house. This division of labor is adaptive because it entails an optimal match between biological capacities and ecological necessities. One result is that in most cultures young girls end up with more experience than young boys with activities we call prosocial. This experience evokes and reinforces biological dispositions toward nurturance, with the result that females typically display significantly more nurturant behavior than males. The males, however, may assume the nurturant role and females may assume relatively nonnurturant roles if for any reason the traditional division of labor is not maximally adaptive. There appears to be a tendency in our own society toward a decrease in traditional sex differences in nurturance.

An organically interactive conception of the relationship between biology and culture is consistent with the ecological model of the relationship between the person and the situation presented by the Graveses. It directs our attention to the overall fit between component parts of the whole—a perspective poorly accommodated by the particularistic and mechanistic methodologies employed in most laboratory research. The question here becomes more how everything fits together in mutually interacting systems than how a change in one variable causes a change in another. Consistent with the findings from research on young children reported in the early chapters, individuals possess dispositions to behave both prosocially and antisocially—altruistically and egoistically. All social systems evoke and support both types of behavior. However, different people (males versus females; children versus adults) may put it all together in different ways in different social systems. Anthropological research supplies an indication of some of the ways biological and cultural, personal and situational factors merge in social systems that are conducive or nonconducive to prosocial behavior. The last chapters of this volume supply an indication of how these factors merge in our own society—employing children in school and the elderly as cases in point.

# REFERENCES

Barash, D. *Sociobiology and behavior.* New York: Elsevier, 1979.

Kagan, S., & Madsen, M. C. Rivalry in Anglo-American and Mexican children of two ages. *Journal of Personality and Social Psychology,* 1972, *24,* 214–220.

Krebs, D. L. Altruism: A rational approach. In N. Eisenberg (Ed.), *The development of prosocial behavior.* New York: Academic Press, 1982. (a)

Krebs, D. L. Psychological approaches to altruism: An evaluation. *Ethics,* 1982, *92,* 147–158. (b)

Krebs, D. L., & Miller, D. Altruism and aggression. In G. Lindzey & E. Aronson (Eds.), *The handbook of social psychology* (3rd ed.). Reading, Mass.: Addison–Wesley, in press.

Lovejoy, C. O. The origin of man. *Science,* 1981, *211,* 341–350.

Rushton, J. P. *Altruism, socialization, and society.* Englewood Cliffs, N.J.: Prentice–Hall, 1980.

# APPLIED APPROACHES
# TO PROSOCIAL DEVELOPMENT

# A Model for Prosocial Learning: An In-Progress Field Study

## DYKE BROWN and DANIEL SOLOMON

## INTRODUCTION

The following chapter describes an effort to translate research knowledge about prosocial development into a comprehensive demonstration project. This project, called the *Child Development Project,* began implementation in the fall of 1982 in several elementary schools in the San Francisco Bay Area and will assess effects on prosocial behavior and attitudes over a 5-year period.

The two parts of this chapter describe two phases in the genesis of this project: an initial, extensive exploration of current knowledge and potential applications undertaken by Dyke Brown and a subsequent development and implementation of a specific project plan by the Developmental Studies Center.

The initial exploration of prosocial research was made possible by the William and Flora Hewlett Foundation. During the 1950s, Dyke Brown was responsible for the Ford Foundation's Public Affairs and Youth Development programs and became convinced of the importance of prosocial development for the successful functioning of our democratic system. He left the Foundation in 1963 to establish the Athenian School in Danville, California, one purpose of which was to foster adolescent involvement in public affairs and community service. After 12 years he (along with many others) concluded that adolescents were becoming more self-preoccupied rather than less, and that whatever factors were contributing to this self-centeredness were operative long before adolescence.

Dr. Roger Heyns, president of the Hewlett Foundation, shared his concern. As a result, Mr. Brown spent a year as the foundation's consultant exploring existing

273

knowledge of prosocial development. He interviewed leading research scholars and studied significant research findings. The results were reported to the foundation in July, 1979, together with recommendations for action stemming from the researchers' findings and views. The report was received favorably by the foundation, which then asked Mr. Brown to see whether its recommendations could be implemented. After checking their feasibility with numerous teachers, school administrators, and parents, Mr. Brown sought an organization qualified to integrate research findings, to translate them into specific school curricula, to implement a comprehensive program, and to measure its effects. The first result was a planning grant in April, 1980, to the Developmental Studies Center. Dr. Solomon joined the center shortly thereafter and took a major role in the development of a plan for the total project. Funding for the project was awarded by the foundation to the Developmental Studies Center in November, 1980.

The first part of this chapter is primarily a summary of Dyke Brown's 1979 report to the foundation. It describes his investigation of prosocial research and the implications of current knowledge for school and preschool practices that might enhance prosocial behaviors. Except where specifically indicated with citations of publications, the comments and conclusions in this part of the chapter are based on conversations and interviews. In the second part of the chapter, Daniel Solomon, Director of Research for the project, describes the plans for program implementation, measurement, and evaluation, along with the major theoretical rationale and empirical support.

## THE INITIAL INQUIRY

In mid-1978, I (Dyke Brown) became a consultant to the Hewlett Foundation in Palo Alto to do two things. First, I was to find out what we know about how caring, sharing, and helping—with their accompanying sense of responsibility—take shape in young Americans (I use the researchers' term *prosocial* for this). The negative social condition underlying the inquiry can be described in various ways:

—as a decline in moral standards, erosion of values, deterioration of trust
—as selfishness, hedonism, self-indulgence, pursuit of pleasure, narcissism
—as a lack of a sense of social responsibility, misuse of power for personal or political ends, irresponsible use of personal freedom

A key element throughout is behavior that reflects excessive concern for self and inadequate concern for others. The second goal was to find out if there are ways (existing or possible) through which prosocial attitudes and behavior could be better fostered in our young.

Prosocial attitudes and behavior are important in our society, because they provide the foundation for:

1. *Helpfulness, caring, and service to others,* from family, friends and neighbors to the less fortunate generally.

2. *Observance of law and respect for the rights of others.* These things depend primarily on the way people feel and behave; laws work well only if most people want to act in a decent and law-abiding manner. Much antisocial behavior—lying, stealing, cheating, aggression, irresponsibility—are in part a consequence of inadequate concern for others.

3. *Good citizenship, social responsibility*—and leadership in public and business affairs. At their root, these desirable behaviors depend upon a reasonable concern for the well-being of others, achieved through the successful functioning of democratic processes and our economic system.

4. The quality of *relations between persons:* spouses, friends, etc. A person handicapped by a limited capacity to care or share faces obstacles in establishing durable close relations with others.

The first step was to learn what our leading research scholars in several disciplines (developmental, clinical, and social psychology; pediatrics; child psychoanalysis; psychiatry; the child-care professions; sociology; anthropology; and education), know (or suspect) about how prosocial qualities develop. This was done by talking to them and by reading their research papers and books.

The second step concerned implementation: Are there existing programs that reflect the foregoing knowledge? Can new and better ways be devised to put into practice what we already know?

When I reported what I had learned to the foundation in July, 1979, I summed up the researchers' views as follows: We do not know as much as we would like to know about prosocial development, but we know a great deal more than we take advantage of in our current practices.

## Some Shared Observations about Character, Its Development, and Relevant Trends in American Society

Nearly everyone with whom I talked agreed on a number of points.

First, a person's character is primarily shaped by culture (i.e., parents and family, teachers, peers, television, etc.); thus, character is not immutably fixed in any of us by our genes. Second, genes may have a small effect on character and temperament, but the range of potential development in individual humans is so great that cultural factors are overriding and are the primary determinants of character (including prosocial). Paul Mussen, director of the Institute of Human Development at the University of California at Berkeley, and his coauthor, Professor Nancy Eisenberg-Berg, say that there is no evidence to support the notion that specific genes determine altruistic or other prosocial behavior. Socially adaptive cooperative and altruistic behaviors, they say, are the products of social learning and not biological evolution (Mussen & Eisenberg-Berg, 1977).

E. O. Wilson, the eminent Harvard biologist identified with the view that links character and behavior with the genes, does not appear to take a contrary view. He has recently summarized his thinking in *On Human Nature* (Wilson, 1978). His views[1] are reflected in the following summary:

> *On aggression:* Human aggression is innate, but aggression is an ill-defined array of different responses to different situations (p. 101). Particular forms of aggression are not inherited but are shaped by the necessities of the environment and the history of cultural evolution within the group [p. 114].
>
> *On altruism:* Wilson believes that the form and intensity of altruistic acts are to a large extent culturally determined and that human social evolution is obviously more cultural than genetic (p. 153). Wilson feels it is fortunate we are not programmed altruists like the bees, so that we do not lay down our lives willy-nilly for others. Since this is clearly a culturally implanted trait, it is (unlike the bees) modifiable. He states that since the altruistic impulse is so powerful, it is fortunate that it is mostly soft (i.e., not blind, but based on reciprocity). He believes that humans have "a flawed capacity for a social contract, mammalian in its limitations, combined with a perpetually renewing, optimistic cynicism with which rational people can accomplish a great deal [p. 164]." His book ends with a chapter entitled "Hope" [p. 195].

Similarly, J. Z. Young, an influential British biologist, believes that, from the enormous number of possible brain pathways that each infant inherits, humans select through social learning the ones that fit their culture and needs. Childhood learning and culturally transmitted elements thus give us our particular conception of morals, rights, and duties (Young, 1978).

Some cultures promote the development of primarily prosocial persons; others promote egocentric persons. The Hopi culture, for example, yields persons who are helpful, cooperative, noncompetitive, unaggressive, and concerned about the welfare, rights, and feelings of others. On the island of New Guinea, Margaret Mead (1935) found two tribes at opposite ends of the spectrum: the Arapesh, who were cooperative, generous, loving, and unaggressive; and the Mundugamor, who were aggressive, ruthless, and lacking in gentleness and cooperation. American culture is generally regarded as lying at the individualistic end of the continuum (i.e., as egocentric, achievement-oriented, competitive, self-assertive—even aggressive). Many of the accomplishments of Americans stem from these values. Although kindness, fairness, and helping are also respected American values, the behavioral balance appears to be well in the other direction.

Cultures change, and individual character often changes as a result. Thus, when the Ik of Uganda (described by Colin Turnbull, 1972) lost their hunting grounds, their laws, mores, and customs disintegrated. They broke into small, ruthless bands concerned only with survival. Caring for others, even mates and children, disappeared, and scheming, stealing, and even killing became "normal."

There is widespread concern in the United States over an apparent decline in standards and values, an increase in self-centeredness and self-indulgence, and an insufficient sense of social responsibility.[2] In the last decade or two, American

---

[1]Not all scientists agree with Wilson's views—for example, see Stephen Jay Gould (1977, 1978).

[2]Although I have not seen any validating empirical research, one finds numerous references to the "me" generation in social commentaries—as, for example, in Lasch (1978).

young people are regarded as having become more self-oriented and less concerned with other persons and the community. Almost all the research scholars I talked with remarked on the greater self-orientation and "privatism" of today's young; and many of them describe American society as a whole in these terms.

Almost everyone with whom I talked felt that we ought to do something to help increase the prosocial balance in the character of our young. America, it is felt, faces a serious problem in achieving a proper balance between personal freedom and social concern and responsibility. Some of them feel the problem is of great importance and urgency. Jerome Kagan, for example, suggested that 50 of the most influential school superintendents in the United States should be brought together for a conference to plan what schools can do to build better character and values in American young people. They should, he feels, take steps to celebrate character and to raise consciousness of values within schools (by prizes, changes in the moral atmosphere, etc.)—accompanied, if possible, by a television and media blitz. Robert Coles has done extensive fieldwork interviewing and writing about American children (cf. his five-volume *Children of Crisis* [1977], especially Vol. 5). He feels that American children are being deprived of the values they need for living by parents and adults who fail to transmit their own values and by media and peers that treat all values as relative. Without the values they need, children become self-centered and preoccupied with themselves and their feelings. He believes action is urgently needed. William Kessen, Chairman of the Psychology Department at Yale, feels that the increasing self-orientation in the United States since World War II is a serious problem and one about which we should do something.

Between research results and informed insights, scholars believe we have a significant body of understanding concerning the development of character—including prosocial attitudes and behavior. The behavioral sciences have generated substantial new knowledge in the last 25 years, and we are only beginning to make use of it. Clearly, more research is needed, but, even in 50 years' time, scholars believe we will not have a complete knowledge of character development—which in any event changes as the acts of history change. The problem is real and current, and we are not taking enough advantage of what we now know in our current practices—in parenting, infant and day-care centers, nursery schools and kindergartens, and grade schools through elementary and high school.

Researchers and others believe that present conditions are favorable for constructive improvements in our practices. People generally are concerned about standards and values, especially those of young people. The foregoing concern is reflected in new programs by schools, churches, and other organizations dealing directly with values. Although public education has tended to shy away from ethical questions because of the separation of church and state, concern over moral behavior (including aggression) is leading educators to review the school's role in this regard. Under Willson Riles' guidance, the California Legislature amended the Education Code in September, 1977, to state its belief that the schools should (among other things) assist each pupil to become a contributing and responsible member of society and to develop esteem of self and others (and) personal and social responsibility. Schools can apply for planning grants to develop a 3-year school improvement plan, which must include the foregoing elements (among others). Independent evaluations of progress under these plans are to be made to the legislature and governor. Other states have taken similar action.

Public interest is further underscored by widespread concern with trends in family conditions and family structures. For example, there is much discussion of the increasing numbers of children of divorce and children in one-parent families.[3] There is also widespread interest in natural childbirth and in ways to improve parenting practices. New parent education programs have recently been undertaken in a number of states, for example: the Minnesota Early Learning Design (MELD); a program in the Santa Barbara County schools, in conjunction with the American Association of University Women; a program by the Junior League of the East Bay in Alameda and Contra Costa counties, California; a March of Dimes' program in "parenthood education"; and many others.

Increases in the numbers of working mothers have caused parallel increases in the numbers of children, of all ages, who spend significant amounts of time in day-care or comparable settings. This creates concerns but also opportunities for incorporating positive elements in the programs of such centers. The practice of putting preschool children in such centers will probably continue to grow. Over half of United States women are now working (up from 30% in 1960); 58% of women with school-age children are in the work force, and 41% of mothers with children too young to attend school. It is generally expected that United States women's labor force participation will continue to increase. The proportion is currently comparable to that in England and France, lower than that in Japan and several Scandinavian nations.

There are few if any institutions presently devoting their efforts to understanding the development of prosocial character in terms of our present knowledge about it and using that knowledge to help improve practices (in schools, day-care centers, parenting). There does not appear to be any foundation or other source providing funds for translating what is known into improved practices.

On the other hand, a number of persons, although recognizing that change may be taking place in American character, believe that the change occurs in response to basic forces that are beyond our capacity to alter to any extent. In this view, there are strong internal cultural dynamics—television, affluence, wars, weakened families, peer pressures, greater family mobility, use of political power for personal ends, etc.—that carry American society and personality before them like a flood and may easily overwhelm any contrary tendencies. As one researcher put it, "until the adult world is visibly dealing more honestly with problems that impact the future (such as energy, technology, the environment, etc.), it is not realistic to expect small efforts to redirect the socialization of the young to have much effect. . . .

---

[3]The U.S. Bureau of the Census (1979) has released figures on 1970–1978 showing a sharp increase not only in the rate of divorce, but also in the number of families headed by women with no husbands at home and in the number of children living with only one parent.

Schooling and parenting depend radically on the social context in and to which children are being reared.'' Even those more optimistic about our ability to foster prosocial attributes recognize that there are powerful contrary forces that cannot be avoided and from which children cannot be wholly insulated.

Questions have been raised concerning the compatibility of prosocial tendencies with general personal competence. Is a prosocial, caring person unable to function effectively in our society, a kind of well-meaning, but incompetent, "do-gooder?" Mussen and Eisenberg-Berg's (1977) survey of the research concludes that children and adults who are most responsible and competent are also most likely to be considerate, helpful, and generous to others. Myron Woolman's view[4] is that pro-social skills are as necessary for survival in the modern world as ''the three R's''; in his view, the ethical anchor is not altruism but enlightened self-interest. Prosocial behaviors produce greater social rewards than do conflicts and are necessary in working with others to advance and to achieve mutually rewarding goals. Professor Diana Baumrind, at the University of California, Berkeley, has similar views: She believes that it is the balanced combination of caring and competence that character-izes persons who are effective in social behavior. Research on successful business managers reaches a similar conclusion: High achieving managers show substantial concern for people as well as production, whereas moderate and low-achieving managers do not (Hall, 1976). Thus, development of competence and reasonable capacity to compete is not only compatible with prosocial development; the two qualities in balanced combination yield more effective persons. The opposite of a prosocial inclination (or caring about others) might be described not as competitive-ness but as selfishness, self-centered individualism, greed (or doing what one wants regardless of others). In sports, as in business management, the best competitors are the players who cooperate well with each other on a team.

## Some Things Researchers Believe We Know about Prosocial Development

Most scholars with whom I talked agree with the following statements (which are somewhat random because an integrated body of knowledge about character devel-opment does not yet exist). These statements do not represent a comprehensive summary of all that is known in this area but are meant to describe some of the conclusions that seemed relevant to this inquiry.

In biological or genetic terms, all human beings (except those born with serious physical or mental impairment) have the potential of becoming caring and responsi-ble persons. The underlying bases of prosocial versus egocentric character begin to take shape soon after birth; important developments occur throughout childhood and adolescence, and changes can still occur in adult years. Some researchers regard the first several years of life as very important; others attach particular importance to

[4]Letter to Dyke Brown of May 1, 1979.

periods during childhood or adolescence; no one rules out any of these years as being irrelevant to prosocial development.

There may be some consistent and durable general traits or predispositions (e.g., empathy, the ability to see things through the eyes of another person, etc.) involved in prosocial behavior. In the United States (and many other countries) parents are, and are likely to continue to be, the primary agents shaping a child's character; their actions will have a determining effect on their child's personality, character, and competence (even though we do very little to educate people to assume their roles as parents). There is no "built-in" mechanism that ensures "natural" character growth in a child in modern society. Thus, there is no validity to the belief held by some that children do or should simply grow and develop, with a minimum of parental intervention. Whether they intend it or not, parents' actions, inactions, and example inevitably shape the child.

Next to parents, teachers are probably the most important adults in the process whereby children acquire their egocentric or prosocial characteristics: they are rapidly being joined in this role by the persons who care for children in the parents' absence (in the home, in infant and day-care centers, etc.). Although, as indicated previously, public schools have shied away from teaching ethics and moral values, their practices and atmosphere play a role in transmitting attitudes and behavior. The potentialities of schools and child-care centers for fostering behavioral characteristics desired by most Americans—honesty, work, cooperation, helping, etc.—are only beginning to be examined.

Peers and peer groups play an important role in the development of children's attitudes, standards, and values. Where parental transmission of values is weak (as in permissive or indifferent parenting), peer influence is often greater. The media, especially television, play an important role in the development of attitudes, behavior and values in children. Kagan, Siegel and others feel that caring behavior in children (or its absence) can be much influenced by the media, especially television.

Interaction from birth onward with a loving caretaker (usually the mother)[5] is essential for the healthy development of a child—physically, mentally, and in human feelings (which are basic to later caring and kindness). Considerable research documents the negative consequences of the absence of continuing interaction with an affectionate caretaker. Among other deficiencies, children acquire a reduced capacity to feel for other humans. Interesting lines of current research by Professor Mary Ainsworth (1977) in Virginia; Professor Alan L. Sroufe (1978) in Minnesota; and Dr. Marian Radke-Yarrow and colleagues (Zahn-Waxler, Radke-Yarrow, & King, 1977) at the National Institute of Mental Health (NIMH) suggest that the character of the infant's attachment to the mother may be fundamental in its further development, including its prosocial development. The more securely attached infants, for example, show more prosocial characteristics at 2, 3, and 4 years of age.

---

[5]Wherever "mother" is used, it is shorthand for "primary caretaker," which could be the mother, father, or parent surrogate.

A loving caretaker may impede social and cognitive development by immediately fulfilling all of a child's demands, no matter how unreasonable. If children are taught that the world revolves exclusively around them and that they can insist on having their own way, they will be predisposed to operate in a self-centered fashion in all of their subsequent interpersonal relationships, according to Dr. Burton White, who has studied infants since 1965 at the Harvard Graduate School of Education's Preschool Project. White believes that a child's primary social orientation is established by age 2 and is hard to change after 3. Others see change and development as continuing and as not necessarily totally conditioned by prior experiences in early years.

The most effective parents are those who are loving but firm with their children from the early years on. Diana Baumrind's research at the University of California, Berkeley, Institute of Human Development finds that "permissive parents" are less successful than "authoritative parents" in developing social responsibility and independence in their children.

One of the important probable sources of prosocial behavior is *empathy*—experiencing another's emotional state. Empathy is found in very young children, according to Dr. Marian Radke-Yarrow at NIMH (Zahn-Waxler, Radke-Yarrow, & King, 1977). A child of 14 months who sees a 6-month-old baby crying is observed to have tears well in her eyes, to cry, and to look to the mother. At 12–16 months, patting or touching the victim begins, and, at 18 months, offering cookies and toys.

Emphasis on their egocentrism has blunted our awareness of children's sensitivity to roles, according to Jerome Bruner, a leading authority on cognitive development (now Professor of Psychology at Oxford University, formerly at Harvard). Quite young children can take another's position when giving instructions on simple tasks, he reports, and 4-year-olds can clearly understand a partner's point of view in conversation (Bruner, 1978). Burton White also finds signs of a child's ability to see something from the perspective of another child at age 3, and he thinks it may underlie later caring behavior.

Although research on the learning of empathy is only just beginning, Marian Radke-Yarrow (Yarrow, Scott, & Waxler, 1973) has found that nursery school children display more helping behavior than controls after watching a teacher looking at pictures of a child or animal in trouble and hearing her helpful comments (e.g., of a boy falling, "hope he isn't hurt, I'll pick him up") and later watching the teacher actually be helpful or sympathetic (e.g., to another adult who bumps her head picking up toys). She has concluded from her research that a child's empathy, if it is to develop fully, must be trained by its mother through interaction, just as is the case with its cognitive development. Children learn a great many things by example and by imitating the behavior of parents and adults. This is one of the reasons why television is important. Adult "modeling" is an important source of prosocial attitudes and behavior. Most researchers, led by Albert Bandura at Stanford, believe that the most important thing parents can do (more important than punishing or not punishing) is to be a model of the positive values in which they believe. Actually seeing another's signs of distress or pleasure is important in encouraging helping behavior, and sympathy is greater for persons felt to be closer—family, friends, persons "like me."

Role-taking is one way of increasing prosocial behavior. Kindergarten children become more helpful after putting themselves in (*a*) the role of a person needing help (e.g., trying to carry a chair that is too heavy); and (*b*) the role of the person trying to give the help (one of the findings of Professor Ervin Staub [1975], University of Massachusetts, who has done extensive research on helping).

Moralizing alone probably does little to increase prosocial behavior. Bryan (1970) conducted a series of experiments showing that what an adult *says* is much less important than what the adult *does* as an influence on children's subsequent donating behavior. Knowledge of what adults generally value as responsible and caring behavior may not be sufficient, in itself, to control what a child actually does in specific situations.

Children who are given responsibility tend to behave more responsibly. Staub (1979) found that children in kindergarten and the first grade who were given responsibility for a child in another room were more likely to try to help him when in distress than those who were not given such responsibility.

As children grow older, become more aware generally and better able to form concepts, their way of thinking about moral issues and motives changes. Although there has been considerable research on modes and levels of moral thinking, especially by Professor Lawrence Kohlberg at Harvard (e.g., Kohlberg, 1976), carrying forward Piaget's ground-breaking work in the early 1930s (Piaget, 1965), the relation between moral cognition and prosocial behavior is not clearly delineated.

Children who are given rewarding responses (e.g., praise) for cooperative or sharing behavior increase their cooperative and sharing behavior, and, conversely, children whose selfish responses (e.g., not giving help when needed) are disapproved tend to behave less selfishly (Mussen & Eisenberg-Berg, 1977). Dr. Gerald Patterson (1979) and the Oregon Social Learning Center have had considerable success over a period of years in modifying aggressive and self-centered behavior in families with difficult younger children. The same techniques of rewards and disapprovals seem relevant to family and school efforts to enhance prosocial behavior.

Participating in helping activities (such as making toys for others) or teaching such activities to others increases prosocial behavior; this is enhanced when its positive consequences are explained to and thought about by the children (Staub, 1975). Professor Urie Bronfenbrenner (1970) describes how children in the Soviet Union are trained from very young ages in helping behavior, in school and in the community. School children are given responsibility at an early age for younger schoolmates, whom they are expected to help with homework and other problems. The children appear in consequence to develop a sense of consideration and responsibility for others.

A child who has developed optimism, confidence, and positive self-esteem is more likely to behave in prosocial ways than one who is depressed or insecure (Mussen & Eisenberg-Berg, 1977).

In examining prosocial development, it is instructive to look at other cultures in which children and adults reflect more prosocial characteristics than Americans. Professors John and Beatrice Whiting of Harvard are recognized for their preeminent research on child rearing in six different cultures over the last 25 years (Whiting & Whiting, 1975). The children involved were from 3–6 and 7–11 years of age, in villages in the Phillipines, India, Okinawa, Kenya, Mexico, and a town in New England. The most nurturant children were found to be those in the villages of Kenya, Mexico, and the Phillipines. Beatrice Whiting (1978) explains the lower development of nurturant qualities in young Americans (who scored lowest of all six cultures on altruistic behavior), as follows:

> One aspect of socialization in the U.S. that is peculiar when compared with other cultures (especially nonindustrial countries) is the long hours of schooling, with the enforced confinement of children with same-aged peers. . . . Interaction with same-aged peers involves a competitive and mildly aggressive type of sociability, often not conducive to protracted intimacy [p. 218].
>
> In most of the cultures of the world, eight- to ten-year-olds are the primary surrogate caretakers of infants and toddlers [p. 219].
>
> It is caring for and associating with these young children that encourages responsibility and responsible nurturance [p. 225].
>
> To take a lesson from tribal societies, we need to encourage the young to feel responsible for siblings and younger community members, to feel responsible for the welfare of the social group, to interact in nonschool settings in work that is focused on the welfare of the group. We need more cross-age grouping of children, less same-age peer interaction, more young caretakers of infants [p. 226].

The Whitings draw attention to the fact that children in the nurturant cultures were expected to help their parents by doing economic chores and caring for younger siblings.

## Researchers' Ideas about Ways of Fostering Prosocial Development

The foregoing has described our understanding of prosocial development and the context in which it now goes on in American society. This section moves ahead to various ideas of researchers about what can and should be done about it.

### PARENTS, FAMILY, GRANDPARENTS, PARENT SURROGATES

Several researchers favored parent education efforts to enhance parent effectiveness, although they recognized that efforts to get inside families and change parents' behavior have not been very successful. Although Jerome Kagan's priority is kindergarten through fifth grade, he would also set up parent education groups modeled after Alcoholics Anonymous, as the only type of adult education that has in fact modified adult behavior. Parents with children from birth to 5 years of age would commit themselves to participate with the group over a period of time in improving their effectiveness as parents. The group would have a resource person and could be based at a public school. Kagan hopes they would come to regard the school as the community center that the church used to be—a neutral rallying place concerned with everyone's children. Control groups would be set up for comparison, and researchers would measure change and try to identify its determinants.

William Kessen also believes that the first several years of school are priority years. He feels that parents are bewildered by the multiplicity of "expert" views on childrearing. As a result, they are paralyzed and do not know where to turn for good answers. In their uncertainty they are reluctant to impose their standards on their children—which only confuses the child and enhances his self-centeredness. Kessen would emphasize "parent empowerment" in parent education: They must be disabused of the notion that there are any real "experts," he says, and be made to realize that their values and moral feelings are as right as anyone's and must be continuously communicated to their growing children—using their own judgment and speaking out with conviction when they feel it. He also feels that parents (mothers especially) feel isolated, especially in the suburbs and very much *need* other parents to talk to and share with—hence the value of Kagan's idea, involving group support. Kessen would make service (e.g., helping around the house) an absolute "must" within the family. Kessen is not overly optimistic that such efforts will succeed, because he believes parents at their best have difficulty off-setting the effects of television and the general culture.

Urie Bronfenbrenner at Cornell places strong emphasis on each child's having a continuing interaction with a loving caretaker—one who really cares—from birth through high school. He would develop ways to support parents in this role, including supplementing them (since so many now work) with other caring adults—volunteers as well as paid persons (such as day-care staff, teachers, etc.). Robert Coles at Harvard feels very strongly about the need for parents, grandparents, and teachers to communicate their values clearly and forcefully to children.

## SCHOOL AND PRESCHOOL

Jerome Kagan's national priority would be the public schools: kindergarten through fifth grade, starting with his aforementioned idea to bring together a large group of influential school superintendents to plan how to build better character and values within their schools—for example, by recognizing and honoring good character, by changing the moral atmosphere of the school, by giving prizes for outstanding moral behavior (rewarding it equally if not more than academic accomplishments), etc.

Kagan would also find a specific community in which to demonstrate an exemplary program on "the celebration of character" over a 5-year period, with another "control" community against which to measure it (on such matters as grades, juvenile delinquency, vandalism, etc.). Parents would be closely involved in the experiment, character would be the focal issue at school assemblies, etc.

Kessen believes that the first several years of schooling are crucial for prosocial development. American children at age 4 have, in his view, a normal and natural amount of self-centeredness; but by the time they are 8, they have deeply implanted in them (by the schools and television) a somewhat excessive ego-centered achievement orientation—hence the critical importance of kindergarten through third grade. Kessen believes we should try out a curriculum in kindergarten through third grade built around cooperative learning; he thinks it would be worth it, even if some traditional learning of reading, etc., was delayed—and it might even enhance such learning.

Psychologist Myron Woolman, director of the Institute of Educational Research in Washington, D.C., conducted an experimental preschool center in Vineland, New Jersey, as a part of the public school system, working with 109 4- and 5-year-old children (mostly Puerto Rican and black) of migrant workers, for 5 years in the early 1970s. Its goal was to get these "culturally deprived" children up to New Jersey public school levels when they entered first grade after a year or so. It succeeded, as documented by a subsequent evaluation summarized by Irving Lazar (1977). The program was based on the assumption that in learning, as in play and other activities, children's efforts and self-image are considerably affected by interactions with peers. Hence, the children worked in pairs; one could not progress (e.g., to the next "higher" table of six) unless his partner did also; and if one failed, each had to do the work again. It was therefore in the interest of each child to help his partner, which they did. When children advanced to a certain point, they could become "monitors" and help other children for 20% of their time. The play area contained large blocks and toys that required the cooperative efforts of at least two children for them to function.

Lazar's (1977) evaluation of the children's later performance in grade school found the results "quite impressive" because they indicated that, having had such an early interaction program, high-risk children were able to meet the minimal school requirement as well as the general school population, which contained both middle- and lower-class children. Although the goal of the program was to improve academic performance, the method involved children helping and sharing in order to learn. Their social behavior also improved as a part of this type of cooperative learning process, which is quite different from traditional learning approaches, which are more individualistic and competitive.

Psychologist Elliot Aronson at the University of California at Santa Cruz, found comparable results in a similar experiment in Austin, Texas, with fifth graders in seven elementary schools, and this was repeated by Robert Geffner in Watsonville, California, schools. The program started from a belief that desegregated classrooms were not, as had been hoped, overcoming prejudice and improving black performance; in fact, the opposite was occurring, in part because blacks felt even less competent in mixed classrooms based on traditional competition. Aronson's hypothesis was that interdependent learning environments would establish the conditions necessary for the increase in self-esteem and academic performance and the decrease in prejudice expected from desegregation.

Accordingly, students were placed in six-person "jigsaw" learning groups, with the lesson divided into six written parts such that each student had only one part. The student's job was to learn and teach this part of the material to the others in the group. Consequently, children learned that competitive behavior did not work; success depended on students paying attention to and learning from each other—with the role of teacher played by black students as well as white. The jigsaw classes met for one period per day, 3 days per week, for 6 weeks. There were also three control classes, using traditional teaching.

White children, both high and low performers, did just as well in jigsaw groups as in traditional classes. Black students did better. Of equal importance, the self-esteem of all jigsaw students (both white and black) increased more than for controls, and jigsaw students increased more than controls in both their liking for school and for group-mates (within and across ethnic boundaries).

People who work together in an interdependent fashion increase their ability to take one another's perspectives. Further experiments by Aronson's colleague, Diane Bridgeman (1981), show that fifth-grade students, after 8 weeks of jigsaw cooperative learning, were better able to take the roles of others and put themselves in a bystander's position than were students from control classrooms. A number of factors appeared to be involved in achieving these results. Although the processes of modeling and imitation had some role, the more important determinant seemed to be that effective functioning in a cooperative venture *requires* role-taking. Aronson further concludes that jigsaw groups work even if used for as little as 20% of a child's classroom time and that they are not incompatible with competitive learning or individually guided learning—all can coexist.

Professor David W. Johnson in educational psychology at the University of Minnesota and Professor Roger T. Johnson in elementary education at the same institution summarized the varying effects of competitive, cooperative, and individualistic types of curricula and learning, including their own research on cooperative learning among fourth graders. Johnson and Johnson (1974) concluded that "the use of cooperative goal structures within learning situations may be crucial to cognitive development of students, the reduction of egocentrism necessary for social development, ability to communicate effectively, empathy, and autonomous moral judgment based upon mutual reciprocity and justice [p. 222]."

Professors John and Beatrice Whiting, who carried out the long-term cross-cultural research on child rearing in six cultures described earlier, believe two things very strongly: First, ways should be developed, both inside and outside school, for older children to associate with and care for younger children—for the reasons previously set out. Second, same-age groupings in schools should be enlarged to increase the age spread of classes, thereby reducing the competitiveness and aggressiveness that (they feel) are inherent in same-age groupings. This agrees with the views of many child development specialists. Professor Urie Bronfenbrenner at

Cornell and Professor Willard Hartup at Minnesota both agree with the Whitings' views of same-age grouping. Hartup drew attention to new proposals in Scandinavia for "sibling day-care centers," to increase the age-spread of the children in such centers from the usual 3–7 years (youngsters there start regular school at 7 years of age).

Professor Brewster Smith at Santa Cruz recommends offering instruction to adolescents on "baby-sitting" and related child care. He believes that it would have an appeal similar to that of driver education and also would be seen as helpful for earning money. Learning about parenting and child psychology and development could be a natural part of such a course. Professor Alberta Siegel of the Stanford Medical School believes the Red Cross could teach baby-sitters much as they do life guards, with appropriate certificates upon course completion—and parents could be encouraged to hire only certified baby-sitters.

Professor Irving Lazar at Cornell would incorporate experimental elements designed to foster prosocial development in 100 or so Head Start programs, with controls to measure the effectiveness of each. Basically, he would give religious or other groups, with precepts about how to develop caring and prosocial attitudes, opportunity to try their approaches in separate programs—Catholics, Episcopalians, Jewish groups, etc. He would like to see one in which the sole criterion for hiring would be warmth and affection of staff for children.

Kessen (1975) at Yale is the source of an important idea that comes from the visit of 13 social scientists to children's institutions in China in 1973 plus his reflections since that time (Kessen, 1978). The group asked the Chinese why China, which spent so much on agricultural research, spent almost nothing for research on children. They never got much of an answer and not much interest in the question— only the uniform Chinese belief, reflected in practice, that children all develop in much the same way, ways that are well known to all Chinese. Kessen's eventual conclusions about this are as follows: A thousand years of tradition has produced Chinese adults and children with "a shared sense of what a child is" and how a child should behave at any place or time. Because of this common belief, which is made manifest in the conduct of adults with children and among children themselves, children behave the way everyone expects them to behave. Why do Chinese children, whether four or five years old or fourteen months, sit quietly in a semicircle around their teacher, with no one jumping up, shoving or speaking out of turn? Why would Chinese kindergartners watch a new mechanical pingpong game closely but patiently at a distance, when a European child in the class breaks through them to lunge at the toy? Because, says Kessen, of the stability or consistency of expectations that all Chinese have about children, to which expectations the children conform. "The shock to American observers is to see how smoothly and without symptoms Chinese children meet the expectations of adults and become socially adept, calm, dutiful school children who amaze the Western visitor [Kessen, 1978 p. 31]." By contrast, expectations in America about children are bewildering in their variety, says Kessen. In response, children behave one way for parents, another for the kindergarten teacher, another for the dance or swimming teacher, another for friends, another for store clerks, another for ''uncomprehending grandparents [p. 31].'' Children are defined by the people they meet. Hence ''the contemporary child is a crazy quilt of expectations [Kessen, 1978, p. 31].''

The expectations that a society has for its children have an important effect on how they develop. Urie Bronfenbrenner's work on Soviet children stresses the uniform character of adult expectations in Russia and the way in which groups of children are involved in support of adult expectations (Bronfenbrenner, 1970). This contrasts with the United States, where there is a large variety of expectations, some of which reflect the divergent values and attitudes of peers, popular songs, the media, etc.—as well as those of teachers and parents. *Diversity* of expectations by itself—quite apart from content—contributes to a youngster's feeling that all values are relative and one may pick and choose among them. If there is peer or media support for attractive values that conflict with those of parents and teachers, children will be affected by it. Bronfenbrenner describes this process at some length.

One conclusion that might be drawn from this is that children would be more likely to become and behave as their parents wish them to if a relatively greater stability or consistency of expectations existed for them. If it were possible to strengthen the parents' role and confidence in transmitting their standards and values to their children and if the child's other experiences (in school, in watching television, etc.) could, insofar as is practical, involve parallel and reinforcing standards from other persons, the prospects might be greater that children would assimilate parental values, standards, and behavior—including their expectations that the child be a helping and responsible person.

## TELEVISION AND THE MEDIA

Concern about television and its effects on children was widespread among the persons with whom I talked. Although the research is limited, ever since Professor Albert Bandura of Stanford's pioneering research in the early 1960s and subsequent replications by others, it seems clear that television plays an important role in socializing the young—through the process of ''modeling'' or observational learning described earlier. Mussen and Eisenberg-Berg (1977), in commenting on this and on the fact that children and adolescents spend more time watching television than any other activity except sleep, say, ''It is therefore quite possible that television viewing may have greater impact on children's lives than school does [p. 102].''

As already indicated, one of the important ways in which children learn attitudes and behaviors is through watching and imitating others—especially parents. This form of observational learning goes on in a child when images are portrayed (on television, film, etc.), not just when he sees real-life behavior—in fact, a child is not always aware of the difference between the two. Young children—from the age of 2 or 3 on—observe such images for considerable amounts of time. During years that are regarded as important in the development of prosocial (or egocentric) attitudes and behavior, children observe a large quantity of behavior on television.

This occurs *before* reading has become a channel for learning, so that there is during those years no diverting competition from the written word, except to the extent they are read to. Even so, the moving colored images with sound are directly experienced by the child, with all the power that visual action (as contrasted with action described in words) carries.

Research by Stein and Freidrich (1973) indicates that nursery school children who have television "diets" of prosocial programs (for example, Mister Roger's Neighborhood, which portrays cooperation, sharing, sympathy, control of aggression, etc.) increase their prosocial behavior. Mussen and Eisenberg-Berg (1977), after summarizing the research, state that the overwhelming weight of the evidence supports the hypothesis that exposure to television programs that model prosocial behavior enhances children's prosocial tendencies and, conversely, that there is indisputable evidence that aggressive behaviors are directly acquired from television programs and retained.

Professor Alberta Siegel (1974) of Stanford, a member of the United States Surgeon General's Scientific Advisory Committee on Television and Social Behavior, states: "Despite their inability to separate fact from fancy, we permit young children to spend one-third of their waking hours in a world of conflict, violence, mayhem and murder, with endless opportunities to learn antisocial behavior but very limited opportunities to learn prosocial behavior [p. 23]." Further, she points out:

> A horde of untutored savages arrives in our midst annually; these are our infants, who come among us knowing nothing of our language, our culture, our values. . . . Twenty years are all we have to civilize these barbarians. . . . The child starts life totally ignorant of . . . decency, gentleness, compassion, sympathy, kindness. . . . The human infant . . . emerges from essentially the same gene pool [and] he learns in the same way that children of hunting and gathering nomads learned, through observation and immitation. . . . How may we adapt the modern media of communication to the continuing task of civilizing oncoming generations [p. 23]?"

## Conclusions and Recommendations

Few of the persons with whom I talked questioned the importance of the balance between prosocial and egocentric behavior; it goes to the heart of the values that makes ours a decent society. The biggest question is: Can we do anything about it? The leading researchers believe we can—that we have enough usable knowledge to do much better than we are now doing. Conditions for trying to use that knowledge are good: parents and adults generally are concerned about the decline in values, standards of behavior and social responsibility. So are many teachers and others in education. The domains of these two groups—the home and the school—are key areas for trying to use what we know.

In spite of the concerns of researchers, parents, teachers, some elected officials, etc., none of them alone seems able to do much to affect the situation. Few are in strategic positions to bring about constructive change. In this kind of situation a demonstration project could play a catalytic role, by bringing the parts together to translate what we know into practical new approaches. To this end I have outlined briefly what seem to me to be the more promising beginning points. They are described in general terms only, since they represent places to start making the further investigations or analyses that would necessarily precede any action.

## AGES $2\frac{1}{2}$–14 YEARS

The most promising place for a project to begin is with children $2\frac{1}{2}$ years (or thereabouts) to ages 13 or 14, for the following reasons:

1. It includes the ages regarded by a number of researchers as most important for prosocial development.
2. It is a more practical age level for a demonstration than, say, from birth to $2\frac{1}{2}$, since there are existing institutions (elementary schools, nursery schools, day-care centers, etc.) that provide a framework in which to work and through which successful demonstrations could in time be extended.

My suggestions, which derive from the exploration described in the preceding pages, include the following:

1. Involving children from about age 6 on with responsibilities for caring for younger children, under adult supervision. This could be carried out in a nearby nursery school or day-care center or in the kindergarten or lower grades of an elementary school. The responsibilities could range from playing and physical care to games and acting as tutors, teachers' assistants in regular classes, etc. The Collegiate School in New York City has recently had a successful course in which boys ages 10–11 diapered, fed, and cared for small babies.
2. Using "cooperative learning"—learning that requires that children work with each other in order to master a lesson—as a regular part of the curriculum. Competitive learning would continue to exist (e.g., in certain courses or in games), but it might be between groups or teams, as well as between individuals.
3. Involving children in structured programs of activities for helping others (such as doing useful work around the school or in a nearby park or playground (e.g., gardening, painting, cleaning up, etc.); making toys or other things for others; visiting shut-ins, older persons, or persons in nursing homes or hospitals; etc.
4. Mixing the ages of students at various levels from $2\frac{1}{2}$ years on, and, ultimately, through adolescence.
5. Involving children in regular practice in role playing in situations involving persons in need of help, in distress, etc. (undertaking the roles of "helper" and of "victim," to experience the feelings of each).
6. Involving children in home chores on a regular basis with the approval and cooperation of their parents.
7. Involving an entire elementary school in a regular program to recognize and

reward caring, helping, responsibility, and other prosocial behavior by the school's children in and outside the school and home.

8. Providing children with opportunities to see adult models who exhibit prosocial qualities in their behavior, not only in real life (through hearing such persons describe what they do, watching newspapers for examples of such persons, drawing attention to how persons in the community help others, etc.), but also in stories, films, television, etc. Parent cooperation could help in identifying examples and in monitoring television viewing to emphasize prosocial programs and minimize their opposite.

9. Providing training in the development of empathy (e.g., giving nursery school and kindergarten children opportunities to see examples of persons and animals in distress and hear adults both comment on how to help them and display actual helping behavior to them).

10. Incorporating a number of the preceding elements into a single comprehensive program. The argument against "mixing" several new elements is that although the researchers can evaluate the overall effort, they would be unable to determine which new elements were causing what. The argument in favor of a combination program stems from skepticism about whether anything can, in the face of all the ongoing cultural forces in American society, have an appreciable effect on prosocial development. Thus the first hurdle (in this view) would be to provide concrete evidence that measurable prosocial development can be fostered. The best conditions for this would include *saturation* and *continuity* in the child's development (over a period of perhaps 5–10 years). This may be necessary to create a sufficiently strong and unified "sense of expectation" around children in a demonstration program, with a variety of different elements, each of which in different ways communicates prosocial expectations. If the results of such a combination program were nil, presumably there would be no point in trying programs with individual new elements. If the converse were true, then demonstrations involving separate new elements could be undertaken to identify the causal factors with particularity and to determine whether significant results could be secured more simply.

## BIRTH TO AGE $2\frac{1}{2}$ YEARS

Although I believe this is an extremely important period, I would initially defer activities focused on parents and their babies during the first $2\frac{1}{2}$ years of life. Reasons for this are: Our knowledge is meager, even though it is in a period of rapid increase. Furthermore, the knowledge that does exist bears mainly on overall healthy development, although increasing attention is being given in research to how empathy develops, as a precursor of prosocial behavior. In addition, what we do know would be difficult to get incorporated into improved parent behavior. There are few existing sets of institutions through which to work (comparable to schools, preschools and day-care centers for children $3\frac{1}{2}$ and older). Books and words are hardly enough—it takes "seeing" (e.g., through films or television), and it also probably requires an observer to watch and advise a willing parent in the process of caring for a child. Even so, parenting "style" may be very much "set" by the personal chemistry involved and difficult to change. On the other hand, new developments in parent education very much bear watching, especially if research yields reliable data on the early development of prosocial antecedents.

## ADOLESCENTS (AGES 13 OR 14 ON) AND MORAL COGNITION

It may be difficult to foster prosocial attributes in adolescents unless a good foundation has been previously laid down. On the other hand, adolescence may well be a period of potentially significant prosocial growth—or, at least, reinforce-ment—for all youngsters, in particular those who have benefited from a good prosocial foundation in childhood.

A minimal approach would involve waiting until one had a good sample of preadolescents with a solid prosocial foundation. Prosocial high school programs could then be started for two groups of students, one prosocially prepared and one not. Baselines could be established for each and measurements made of further prosocial development. A control group of each type should be included, which would receive no further prosocial program. This kind of experiment would be necessary to show whether early prosocial development persists through adoles-cence with no further support or whether reinforcement during adolescence is necessary.

## THE PROJECT PLAN[6]

The Developmental Studies Center, with financial assistance from the William and Flora Hewlett Foundation, has undertaken a $7\frac{1}{2}$-year project to ascertain whether a comprehensive, longitudinal school- and home-based program directed at children from the ages of 3–9 or 10, can effectively foster responsibility, helping, and cooperation. (The age span of the project has been set for practical reasons only, with full recognition of the likely importance to prosocial development of experi-ence before age 3 and after age 9 or 10.) The project will not encourage children to ignore their own needs and desires, but rather will help them to develop ways of attending to, and accommodating, *both* their own needs and those of others.

Dyke Brown's suggestions for possible program components provided the start-

[6]The development of the plan summarized in this section was a group activity. Eric Schaps is project director and was instrumental in the initial formulation and the various revisions of the plan. Nancy Eisenberg played a very important role in the initial formulation of the plan, as did Joel Moskowitz. Extremely thorough and helpful reactions to an early statement of the plan were provided by Marilynn Brewer, Daniel Koretz, Martin Hoffman, Paul Mussen, Marian Radke-Yarrow, Doreen Spilton, and Ervin Staub. Contributions to later elaborations and refinements of the initial plan have been made by members of the project staff, including Victor Battistich, Carole Cooper, Pat Tuck, Judith Solomon, Wendy Ritchey, and Marilyn Watson.

ing point for the planning of this project. In developing the plan, however, an independent assessment of the relevant literature was made. A basic strategic decision in the formulation of this project has been to attempt to maximize the possibility of producing and demonstrating socially significant effects on children's prosocial behavior and on those internal processes (motives, values, cognitive skills) believed to underly such behavior. Many social and educational demonstration projects have failed to show clear and lasting effects. Such failures have in some instances had profound impacts on policy and on further efforts to explore particular areas. Yet, because such demonstrations have often been brief, narrowly focused, and weakly or inconsistently delivered, it can be argued that few of the evaluations have constituted fair and reasonable tests of the effects of the programs.

The first priority of the project, then, is to show that it is possible to create and deliver a program that can produce clear and long-lasting effects on children's prosocial behavior and related internal processes. This seems most likely to be accomplished by a complex program containing several components. Demonstrating that a small set of strong interventions can produce meaningful and enduring effects on prosocial outcomes seems an essential step toward stimulating wider interest in this field. After such effects have been demonstrated, it will then be reasonable to try to isolate and compare the relative impacts of the various interventions and their combinations. This maximizing decision has implications for various features of the program delivery and evaluation designs.

First, it suggests that the program should consist of a combination of those components that are best supported by prior research and theory and that are also mutually consistent and coherent. It further implies that the program should begin as early in childhood as is feasible and should extend over a long time span. It also suggests that the sample should be relatively homogeneous (to minimize within-group variance); that measurement should be intensive and specific; and that a comprehensive set of outcome and mediating variables should be assessed, representing the broad range of behaviors and internal processes thought to be either direct or indirect products of any or all of the program components. A broad-gauged assessment strategy will also permit the representation and understanding of the complex behavior and internal processes with which this project is concerned. It will further serve to elucidate the relevance of the several theoretical perspectives that are being exploited in the development of the project plan.

## Varieties and Determinants of Children's Prosocial Behavior

Before presenting the plan for this project, it may be useful to provide a framework for viewing the broad domain of prosocial behavior and its determinants (see Figure 11.1). A wide variety of prosocial forms of behavior have been identified and studied. These can be conceptualized in terms of the expectations an individual has that a given act will result in benefits versus costs to other(s) and benefits versus

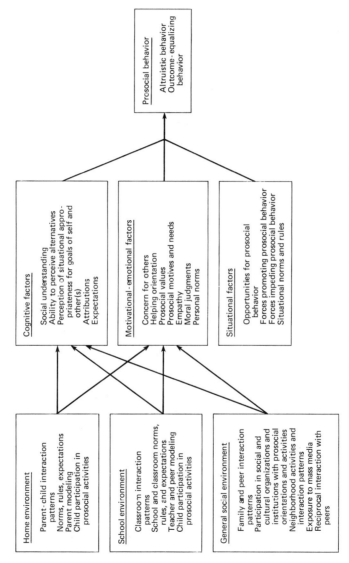

**FIGURE 11.1.** Suggested determinants of prosocial behavior.

costs to the self. Acts that are expected to benefit other(s) with no gain, or at some cost, to the self, are termed *altruistic* (these include donating, some types of sharing, rescuing, defending). Certain behaviors are oriented toward *equalizing the outcomes,* whether they be costs or benefits, between the self and the other(s). These include compromising, cooperating, and some forms of negotiating. Finally, some behaviors are intended to produce gains for the self with concomitant or resultant costs or losses for others. These include competitive behaviors and some forms of egoistic behavior (other forms might involve no costs *or* gains for others).

Toward the goal of helping to develop individuals who are able to achieve an effective balance between acting on behalf of others and on behalf of self, some emphasis will be placed on outcome-equalizing forms of behavior (cooperating, compromising, etc.). Several of the interventions and the measurements will also focus on certain altruistic behaviors (taking responsibility for others, helping, donating).

Three general classes of factors are considered essential for eliciting prosocial behaviors in individuals—cognitive, motivational, and situational factors. The individual must have the cognitive capacity to perceive the need for an act and to understand what that act should be, as well as the motivation to perform the act; the situation must allow or promote the performance of the act. All three classes of factors must be present to some degree, but the particular balance between them may vary. Great strength in one may overcome weakness in another; thus a strong motive may impel an individual to perform a prosocial act even in a situation in which the act is discouraged.

Among the *cognitive factors* determining prosocial behavior, perhaps the most crucial is the level of role-taking ability. This refers to the individual's ability to perceive and understand the situation as the other person perceives and understands it. This would seem to be a necessary condition for an accurate determination of the need of another person, and of ways to help meet it. Also important, particularly for the outcome-equalizing forms of behavior, is the ability to conceive of alternate types of appropriate and relevant actions and to conceive of ways to compromise and achieve some of the goals of several persons. A related cognitive skill is that of perceiving which situations are appropriate for pursuing goals of the self and which for pursuing goals of others. An individual who is able to make distinctions of this sort can achieve both self- and other-oriented goals by pursuing each in its appropriate situation (as well as both in some situations). An individual's belief that a prosocial act is likely to be effective (or that his/her acts in general are) would also seem a necessary condition for performing that act. Similarly, an individual's beliefs that his/her prosocial acts are self-directed and are produced for internal, prosocial reasons will probably promote further prosocial acts.

A number of *motivational–emotional* factors are also considered important in the production of prosocial behavior. These include an individual's concern with the needs and welfare of others, a general helping orientation, and values concerning helping, sharing, reciprocating, cooperating, and compromising. The individual's empathic capacity is judged to be a crucial determinant of certain kinds of altruistic behaviors. This may be one aspect of role-taking, referring to affectively experiencing (not just cognitively apprehending) the other person's emotional state. It has been suggested that role-taking has both cognitive and affective components and that both are probably necessary for many types of prosocial behavior.

Important *situational factors* in the production of prosocial behaviors include the presence of a need or opportunity for prosocial behavior, the presence of factors or forces promoting or encouraging prosocial behavior (e.g., classroom tasks in which small-group interaction and cooperation are allowed and supported), the presence of factors or forces impeding or discouraging prosocial behavior (e.g., classroom tasks that are competitive—"zero-sum"—so that one's gain is another's loss), and situational norms and rules with relevance to particular forms of prosocial behavior.

A guiding assumption of this project is that many of the internal factors (cognitive and emotional-motivational) listed earlier can be influenced, during the course of child development, by introducing changes into the child's environment, particularly the home and school settings. In order to help children to develop dispositions that will be internal and generalized, not simply responsive to specific situational pressures, the proposed program will seek to produce long-lasting influences on prosocial responding through an intermediate effect on cognitive and motivational factors.

The theoretical base for this project is eclectic, as indicated earlier, but not indiscriminate. Each of the proposed program components is supported not only by empirical evidence, but also by plausible mechanisms suggested by one or more theories. It is our position that any or all plausible mechanisms may be operating; we do not, at this point, wish to rule any of them out. Thus, in justifying and explaining the expected effects of the various program components, we have drawn on cognitive and affective mediating theories, social learning theory, theories of small-group processes and influences, theories of cognitive and social development, and several others.

## Description of the Program

The program will be long-term and comprehensive. It will: (*a*) begin in early childhood (3-year-olds in one group, 5-year-olds in another); (*b*) be given to the same children for a period of 5 years; (*c*) consist of a set of complementary elements, each clearly supported by social science research and theory; (*d*) be appropriate to the developmental levels and skills of the children at each age level; and (*e*) be provided in the children's normal school and home environments.

Six elementary schools in the San Francisco Bay Area are involved in the project. In cooperation with school administrators, teachers, and parents, a "prosocial" program is being developed and provided in three of the schools, together with a related home program. The other three (nonprogram) schools constitute a comparison group that will provide important information about the types and levels of prosocial behavior and related characteristics to be expected in the absence of a special prosocial program. These latter schools are receiving additional services relevant to their educational programs, as well as periodic reports based on their own data.

Elementary schools that are similar with respect to turnover rate, size, and socio-economic status and whose staffs and administrators expressed definite interest in participating were chosen for the project. Each selected school was randomly assigned to either the prosocial development program or the comparison group.

The program is being implemented at all grade levels in the participating schools, with particular emphasis on two longitudinal "cohorts." The first cohort will receive the program for 5 years, beginning in kindergarten and continuing through the fourth grade. The second cohort will begin with 3-year-olds, in play groups and other preschool settings. This group will begin a year after the first cohort, and will be followed for 4 years, through first grade. Parents of 3-year-olds living in the districts of the elementary schools involved in the program will be recruited for this second cohort. The preschool program will be conveyed through parent discussion groups, a parent "network," cooperative play groups, and a set of project-run preschool demonstration classes. Parents of the children in both cohorts will be encouraged to provide a complementary set of program-related activities in their homes.

The program activities began in the fall of the 1982–1983 school year. Until then, the project was in a developmental phase, during which many of the details were worked out, including specific program activities, training procedures and schedules, and research procedures and instruments. The advice, consultation, and participation of parents, teachers, and school administrators have been essential in the selection and/or development of each of the activities. Although we expect that many refinements and alterations will be made during the course of the project, the major directions and elements of the elementary school program and evaluation procedures have been determined and are now underway. These will be described later. (The preschool program is less well-developed at this writing but will include appropriate versions of the same components.)

## THE ELEMENTARY SCHOOL AND HOME PROGRAM

Some parts of the school program will be provided to children in their individual classrooms; other parts will be "school-wide." Each program component is expected to influence one or more specific prosocial or antisocial behaviors (e.g., helping, sharing, cooperating, compromising, aggressing, teasing, destroying property), and/or one or more related motives or skills (e.g., the inclination to be helpful; the ability to understand the other person's perception of a situation, or to experience some part of the other person's feelings). Following are brief descriptions of the major program components:

*Participation in Prosocial Activities.*   Evidence obtained in cross-cultural research (Whiting & Whiting, 1975) and in laboratory studies (Staub, 1975) indicates that children can learn to behave prosocially through actual participation in proso-cial activities. Children who are induced to help others or are given responsibility for others in the home subsequently exhibit prosocial behavior, possibly because they have received intrinsic or extrinsic rewards for performing such behaviors and/or have come to think of themselves as "helping" people. Routine perfor-mance of such activities may also help develop a group normative structure (e.g., in classroom or school), and normative expectations supporting this type of behavior. Among the activities that are included under this component are (a) cross-age tutoring; (b) giving children responsibilities to care for and work and play with younger children; (c) giving children regular "chores" to be responsible for; (d) involving children in other helping activities; and (e) school and community service activities.

*Cooperative Group Activities.* Organizing children into cooperative learning and activity groups has been shown to yield positive effects on children's academic achievement, self-esteem, liking of peers, role-taking capacities, empathy, and subsequent cooperative behavior (Aronson, Bridgeman, & Geffner, 1978; Bridge-man, 1981; Johnson & Johnson, 1978; Johnson, Maruyama, Johnson, Nelson, & Skon, 1981; Kimbrough, 1978; Sharan & Sharan, 1976; Slavin, 1980). The tech-niques include instituting general norms encouraging cooperation on tasks, using cooperative learning procedures and materials in appropriate academic courses, devising and implementing games in which children must cooperate to succeed, and introducing tasks requiring that children take turns and each play a productive role. In a sense, these procedures are similar to the participation interventions discussed earlier because children appear to learn about cooperation and other aspects of positive peer interactions by actually acting cooperatively. Cooperative participa-tion probably helps children to acquire certain social skills involved in cooperation, including the ability to work toward common goals, to attend to others' needs, and to role-take (Bridgeman, 1981).

Cooperative learning approaches now in use employ various methods and formats (e.g., one involves within-group cooperation and between-group competition, while another has no competition of any kind). There are advantages and disadvan-tages to each approach; several are being used for this project. In addition to these relatively formal group activities, opportunities will be provided for children to interact in relatively unstructured small group settings that allow or require a certain amount of interpersonal bargaining and negotiating. Youniss (1980) has made a strong argument, derived from the work of Piaget and H. S. Sullivan, for the crucial importance of children's interacting and negotiating with status equals (i.e., other children) for the development of social understanding, role-taking, and cooperative skills and inclinations.

Parents are also being encouraged to undertake cooperative family activities with their children.

*Modeling.* Children often imitate the behavior of those around them who, thereby, intentionally or unintentionally, act as "models" for those children. There is evidence that "modeling" is an effective method for enhancing positive social behavior, at least over the short term. The likelihood of behaving positively increases, in both children and adults, after viewing another person doing so (cf. Mussen & Eisenberg-Berg, 1977; Rushton, 1976, 1980; Staub, 1978, 1979). With children, modeling is most effective if the model is nurturant, has an ongoing relationship with the child (who thereby may be more motivated to attend and imitate), and engages in real-life prosocial behaviors (Mussen & Eisenberg-Berg, 1977; Yarrow, Scott, & Waxler, 1973). In this project teachers are being encouraged to model positive behaviors in their ongoing everyday activities. Situations in which children witness other adults or peers performing helping behaviors are also arranged. Prosocial behavior is often recognized when it occurs among children and is brought to the attention of others in the classroom groups; this should help to promote the development of prosocial norms and expectations in these groups. Audiovisual and curricular materials that provide examples of prosocial behavior are also being introduced in the classroom.

*Training in Social Understanding.*    There is some evidence, not unequivocal (see Kurdek, 1978; Mussen & Eisenberg-Berg, 1977; Rushton, 1980; Staub, 1978), that the acquisition of social understanding (including role-taking skills) is basic to prosocial behavior. Understanding of others' thoughts, feelings, perceptions, and/or needs would seem a necessary condition for eliciting behavior that responds to those needs. Understanding would be an insufficient determinant in itself, however; without an accompanying helping or cooperative orientation, accurate perception of the other's perspective could easily lead to exploitative and manipulative behavior.

As indicated earlier, role-taking abilities are a component of empathic responding. Some evidence exists (primarily anecdotal and naturalistic) that empathy relates to prosocial behavior (Eisenberg-Berg, 1979; Hoffman, 1976; Murphy, 1937; Radke-Yarrow & Zahn-Waxler, 1980). In addition, a few studies have reported success in promoting positive social behaviors through the use of interventions designed to enhance role-taking and empathy (Feshbach, 1978; Ianotti, 1978; Mussen & Eisenberg-Berg, 1977; Staub, 1971).

Role-playing activities in which children act out and discuss others' perspectives in various situations can be effective in promoting the development of role-taking skills and of empathy. Therefore, some forms of role playing are being used in the project. Additional training in empathy may also be provided (e.g., presenting examples of persons or animals in distress and showing the responses of concerned adults or children to that distress).

*Positive Discipline.*    "Positive discipline" refers to several aspects of the adult–child relationship, including clear communication of norms and expectations; use of minimal force by adults; appropriate levels of child autonomy and participation in and influence on decisions; an adult orientation toward analyzing and understanding children's motives and behaviors; and the use of "induction" (explaining and discussing with children the effects of their actions on others). Major emphases are given to helping parents feel comfortable with clearly expressing and enforcing important values, standards, and norms; with their establishing understanding and sympathetic relationships with their children; and with inductive techniques. There is some evidence that the use of induction facilitates the development of prosocial behavior (Dlugokinski & Firestone, 1974; Hoffman, 1970, 1977; Hoffman & Saltz-stein, 1967; Staub, 1979; Zahn-Waxler, Radke-Yarrow, & King, 1979). Similar effects are expected for the other aspects of positive discipline, through an intermediate effect on interpersonal understanding, acquisition, and internalization of values and the development of self-control.

PARTICIPATION OF PARENTS, TEACHERS, AND OTHER SCHOOL STAFF
IN PROGRAM ACTIVITIES

A primary goal of this project is to determine whether it is possible to have a significant impact on children's prosocial development in the context of existing institutions—that is, elementary schools and homes. Most (perhaps all) of the program will therefore be provided by adults with whom children normally have much contact—parents, teachers, and other school staff members. As previously mentioned, these same adults have had important roles in determining the content and form of the various program activities. Input from participants is an essential element of all workshops and other training activities that are offered, whether they involve school staff, parents, or both. The involvement of school personnel and parents began during the developmental phase and will continue throughout the program phase of the project.

## Expected Effects of Proposed Interventions on Cognitive and Motivational Factors

As the foregoing discussion indicates, each of the proposed program components is expected to have an effect on one or more of the internal factors considered to underlie prosocial behavior. These expected relationships are shown in Table 11.1 and will be briefly summarized here.

The child's participation in prosocial activities (including cooperative groups and other groups) probably results in learning of new skills and competencies (e.g., skills in negotiation, cooperation, compromising, and performance of actual helping activities) that can be applied in subsequent social interactions. Participation in cooperative and other group activities may also influence role-taking and empathy (Bridgeman, 1981). Furthermore, actual performance of positive behaviors may change the individuals' attributions and expectancies regarding themselves (i.e., they may be more likely to view themselves as prosocial persons once they have performed prosocial behaviors). Finally, while participating in a prosocial activity the individual may receive personal and social rewards for this behavior. These

**TABLE 11.1**

*Hypothesized Influences of Suggested Interventions*

| Interventions | Processes influenced by intervention | | | | | |
|---|---|---|---|---|---|---|
| | Cognitive | | | Motivational–emotional | | |
| | Social understanding | Skill in compromising, cooperating, negotiating | Self-attributions, expectancies | Motives, needs | Values, moral judgments, norms | Empathy |
| Participation in proso-cial activities | | X | X | X | X | |
| Structured, cooperative group activities | X | X | X | X | X | X |
| Cooperative atmo-sphere and norms | X | X | X | X | X | X |
| Modeling | X | X | | X | X | |
| Training in social un-derstanding | X | X | | | | X |
| Positive discipline | X | | | X | X | X |
| Prosocial media and materials | X | | | | X | |

rewards may induce the child to attend to, value, and perhaps internalize norms relating to positive behaviors. Thus, induced performance of positive behaviors may eventually result in values and motives consistent with these behaviors.

A general cooperative atmosphere and normative structure may help the child to develop norms, expectations, and values concerning helping and cooperation. Repeated and routine cooperation should prompt the child to attend to, be concerned about, and try to accommodate to the needs and values of others.

Although it is not entirely clear how modeling procedures produce their effects, it is likely that children learn skills and develop competencies by observing a model's prosocial actions. Modeling may also present children with norms that they may adopt. If the model is a powerful, nurturant, and loved individual, the child should be especially likely to emulate or identify with the model and internalize the values and motives associated with the modeled prosocial act.

Training in social understanding and empathic responding should facilitate not only children's social understanding and vicarious affective responding, but also their skills and inclinations with respect to cooperating, compromising, and negotiating because understanding and emotionally experiencing the other person's perspective should enhance awareness of and responsiveness to that person's goals.

Positive discipline may have effects on several of the internal determinants of prosocial behavior. Inductive techniques that point out the consequences of the child's behavior for others probably enhance the likelihood of prosocial responding by inducing the child to empathize and role-take. Furthermore, when inductions and other aspects of "positive discipline" contain information clarifying socializers' values (in the context of a warm and valued relationship), children may be better able and more motivated to adopt those values. Finally, a variety of other motives and cognitive skills may be enhanced by the use of positive discipline, for example, the ability to understand the consequences of a behavior and the alternatives to a given course of action (Hoffman, 1970, 1977).

Some research (cf. Staub, 1979) has demonstrated short-term effects of prosocial television content on children's prosocial behavior. Effects of other media and effects on the various internal factors have not yet been investigated, to our knowledge. However, it seems plausible that the clear and consistent communication of prosocial themes would influence children's values and norms concerning the welfare of others, and would also help them to understand and appreciate the views and perspectives of others.

## EVALUATION OF THE PROGRAM

The evaluation of this program will be designed to answer four major questions:

1. Is the intended program actually being carried out?
2. Is the program having the expected effects on prosocial and antisocial behavior, motives, etc.?
3. Are there other factors in the school or home settings, not part of the prosocial program, that are having effects on prosocial behavior, motives, etc.?
4. Is the program having positive effects on academic achievement?

*Program Verification.*   It makes little sense to attempt to assess the effects of a program until it has been established that the program is actually being implemented. Assessing how well and how fully the various aspects of the program are being provided is therefore a basic evaluation activity, and is taking place in all program settings—play groups, elementary schools and homes.

Each participating focal classroom (i.e., containing the longitudinal cohort children) is visited by trained observers on numerous occasions, totaling about 20 hr each year. These observations focus on the frequency and adequacy of provision of each of the program components and on general aspects of classroom atmosphere and teacher–student interaction (information relevant for answering Question 3). Further information about the classroom program and classroom practices is obtained through interviews and questionnaires given to teachers. Information on how well the school-wide aspects of the prosocial program are being provided will come from informal observations made in nonclassroom school settings (playgrounds, lunchrooms, assemblies) and from interviews with administrative staff and teachers.

Information about the provision of the home-based components of the prosocial program is being obtained from parent interviews and questionnaires; these may be supplemented by some structured observations of parent–child interaction and of program-related home activities for a portion of the sample. The parent interviews and questionnaires also ask about those aspects of their current and earlier relationships with their children that are expected to relate to the development of prosocial inclinations and behaviors.

*Assessment of Prosocial Outcomes.* Prosocial behavior, motives, values, skills, and feelings are being assessed for children in each of the two longitudinal cohorts in both sets of elementary schools (prosocial program and comparison) during each year of their project involvement. We also conducted a "cross-sectional" assessment of children in grades K, 2, 4, and 6 in each participating elementary school in the spring before the first year of the program. This was done to provide an additional basis for comparison and an additional fund of relevant developmental data.

Most of the data on children are being obtained through observations and interviews. Tasks designed to elicit various types of prosocial behavior have been adapted from prior research (e.g., Kimbrough, 1978; Pepitone, 1980; Solomon, Ali, Kfir, Houlihan, & Yaeger, 1972) and, in some cases, newly developed. Some of these tasks are administered to each child individually, and some are administered to small groups of children. Each child spends about 1 hr per year in these experimental tasks. Children are also observed in some natural school settings, primarily playgrounds during recess. The observations in the structured tasks and in the natural settings focus on such behaviors as dividing and sharing resources, cooperating, compromising, negotiating, helping others, aggressing, teasing, destroying property, etc.

Each child is interviewed for about 1 hr each year (divided into two half-hour sessions for kindergarteners). In these interviews, children are asked questions about various hypothetical situations. From their responses (including reasons given to explain or justify the initial responses), the researchers assess prosocial motives and values and related cognitive skills and perceptions. The major assessment of social understanding is made by showing children short sequences from a film ("Our Vines Have Tender Grapes") and asking them questions about the motives, intentions, and feelings of the characters. Empathy is assessed through analysis of children's facial expressions and postures, videotaped as they watch the film. These film stimuli were originally used to assess social understanding by Flapan (1968). Other aspects of the interview have either been newly developed or adapted from prior research (e.g., Eisenberg-Berg, 1979).

The prosocial program is expected to make a positive contribution to academic progress as well as to prosocial outcomes. It is important to verify whether this has occurred. For these assessments, data from achievement tests administered routinely by the schools are being acquired. For an overview of the variables to be assessed and the procedures to be used in assessing them, see Table 11.2.

**TABLE 11.2**
*Summary of Data Collection Activities*

| Methods | Types of variables to be measured |
| --- | --- |
| *Program monitoring and process data* | |
| Classroom observations | Program implementation |
| | Classroom atmosphere and dynamics |
| | Teacher–student interaction |
| Interviews with teachers | Program implementation |
| Teacher questionnaires | Program implementation |
| | Individual child program participation |
| School-level observation | School-level program implementation |
| Interviews with principals and other school staff | Program implementation |
| Interviews with parents | Program implementation in home |
| | Relevant aspects of home environment |
| | Child-rearing attitudes and values |
| *Assessment of prosocial and related variables* | |
| Observations of children in individual and small-group settings | Prosocial behavior |
| Class-level and school-level observations | Class-level and school-level prosocial behavior |
| Child interviews | Cognitions, motives, values, empathy, role-taking |
| Child questionnaires | Cognitions, motives, values |
| Parent interviews | Child prosocial behavior |
| Parent questionnaires, ratings, $Q$-sorts | Child prosocial behavior and personality |

SIGNIFICANCE OF THIS PROJECT

It is hoped and anticipated that the results of this project will have implications for educational policymakers, administrators and teachers, parents and children, researchers and practitioners.

Impact on policymakers and administrators will of course be greatest if the project is successful in demonstrating that prosocial outcomes can be enhanced through a comprehensive program and that it is possible to achieve a healthy, adaptive balance between children's self- and other-oriented tendencies while at the same time maintaining or improving their academic performance. Such findings, if widely and clearly disseminated, could contribute to a shift in educational priorities. The particular practices employed in this demonstration could also be adopted, as appropriate, in schools, teacher-training programs, parent workshops, etc.

The ultimate hope is that this project will shed light on how the prosocial–egoistic balance develops in a young person, will demonstrate some specific ways in which to foster the development of an optimal balance, and will produce substantial information that can be used to extend and broaden the realization of this goal.

## REFERENCES

Ainsworth, M. Social development in the first year of life: Maternal influences on infant–mother attachment. In J. M. Tanner (Ed.), *Developments in psychiatric research: Essays based on the Sir Geoffrey Vickers Lectures of the Mental Health Foundation*. London: Hodder & Staughton, 1977.

Aronson, E., Bridgeman, D., & Geffner, R. Interdependent interactions and prosocial behavior. *Journal of Research and Development in Education*, 1978, *12*, 16–27.

Bridgeman, D. L. Enhanced role taking through cooperative interdependence: A field study. *Child Development*, 1981, *52*, 1231–1238.

Bronfenbrenner, U. *Two worlds of childhood: U.S. and U.S.S.R.* New York: Russel Sage, 1970.

Bruner, J. S. Learning the mother tongue. *Human Nature*, 1978, *1*(9), 42–49.

Bryan, J. H. Children's reactions to helpers. In J. R. Maccaulay & L. Berkowitz (Eds.), *Altruism and helping behavior*. New York: Academic Press, 1970.

Coles, R. *Children of crisis* (Vol. 5). *The privileged ones: The well-off and the rich in America*. Boston: Little Brown, 1977.

Dlugokinski, E. L., & Firestone, I. J. Other-centeredness and susceptibility to charitable appeals: Effects of perceived discipline. *Developmental Psychology*, 1974, *10*, 21–88.

Eisenberg-Berg, N. The development of children's prosocial moral judgment. *Developmental Psychology*, 1979, *15*, 128–137.

Feshbach, N. D. Studies on empathic behavior in children. In B. A. Maher (Ed.), *Progress in experimental personality research* (Vol. 8). New York: Academic Press, 1978.

Flapan, D. *Children's understanding of social interaction*. New York: Teachers College Press, 1968.

Gould, S. J. *Ever since Darwin*. New York: Norton, 1977.

Gould, S. J. Review of "On Human Nature" by E. O. Wilson, *Human Nature*, 1978, *1*(10), 20.

Hall, J. To achieve or not: The manager's choice. *California Management Review*, 1976, *17*.

Hoffman, M. L. Moral development. In P. H. Mussen (Ed.), *Carmichael's manual of child development* (Vol. 2). New York: Wiley, 1970.

Hoffman, M. L. Empathy, role-taking, guilt, and development of altruistic motives. In T. Lickona (Ed.), *Moral development and behavior: Theory, research and social issues*. New York: Holt Rinehart & Winston, 1976.

Hoffman, M. L. Moral internalization: Current theory and research. In L. Berkowitz (Ed.), *Advances in experimental social psychology* (Vol. 10). New York: Academic Press, 1977.

Hoffman, M. L., & Saltzstein, H. D. Parent discipline and the child's moral development. *Journal of Personality and Social Psychology*, 1967, *5*, 45–57.

Ianotti, R. J. Effect of role-taking experiences on role-taking, empathy, altruism, and aggression. *Developmental Psychology*, 1978, *14*, 119–124.

Johnson, D. W., & Johnson, R. T. Instructional goal structure: Cooperative, competitive, or individualistic. *Review of Educational Research*, 1974, *44*, 213–240.

Johnson, D. W., & Johnson, R. T. Cooperative, competitive, and individualistic learning. *Journal of Research and Development in Education*, 1978, *12*, 3–15.

Johnson, D. W., Maruyama, G., Johnson, R., Nelson, D., & Skon, L. Effects of cooperative, competitive, and individualistic learning experiences on achievement: A meta-analysis. *Psychological Bulletin*, 1981, *89*, 47–62.

Kessen, W. (Ed.), *Childhood in China*. New Haven, Conn.: Yale University Press, 1975.

Kessen, W. The Chinese paradox. *Yale Alumni Magazine*, 1978, *41*, 29–33.

Kimbrough, J. The socialization of collective behavior in preschool black children. Final report to the Administration for Children, Youth, and Families. Office of Human Development Services, U.S. Department of Health, Education, and Welfare, 1978.

Kohlberg, L. Moral stages and moralization: The cognitive-developmental approach. In T. Lickona (Ed.), *Moral development and behavior: Theory, research and social issues*. New York: Holt Rinehart & Winston, 1976.

Kurdek, L. A. Perspective taking as the cognitive basis of children's moral development: A review of the literature. *Merrill–Palmer Quarterly*, 1978, *24*, 3–27.

Lasch, C. *The cult of narcissism*. New York: Marrow, 1978.

Lazar, I. The persistence of pre-school effects. Report from the Consortium on Development Continuity, Yale University, 1977.

Mead, M. *Sex and temperament in three primitive societies*. New York: Morrow, 1935.

Murphy, L. B. *Social behavior and child personality: An exploratory study of some roots of sympathy*. New York: Columbia University Press, 1937.

Mussen, P. H., & Eisenberg-Berg, N. *Roots of caring, sharing, and helping*. San Francisco: Freeman, 1977.

Patterson, G. *Living with Children: New Methods for Parents and Teachers*. Champaign, Il.: Research Press, 1979.

Pepitone, E. A. *Children in cooperation and competition: Toward a developmental social psychology*. Lexington, Mass.: Lexington Books, 1980.

Piaget, J. *The moral judgment of the child*. New York: Macmillan, 1965.

Radke-Yarrow, M., & Zahn-Waxler, C. Roots, motives, and patterning in children's prosocial behavior. Paper presented at the International Conference on the Development and Maintenance of Prosocial Behavior. Warsaw, 1980.

Rushton, J. P. Socialization and the altruistic behavior of children. *Psychological Bulletin*, 1976, *83*, 898–913.

Rushton, J. P. *Altruism, socialization, and society*. Englewood Cliffs, N.J.: Prentice-Hall, 1980.

Sharan, S., & Sharan, Y. *Small-group teaching*. Englewood Cliffs, N.J.: Educational Technology Publications, 1976.

Siegel, A. E. The great brain robbery. *Johns Hopkins Magazine*, 1974, *25*, 19–23.

Slavin, R. E. Cooperative learning in teams: State of the art. *Educational Psychologist*, 1980, *15*, 93–111.

Solomon, D., Ali, F., Kfir, D., Houlihan, K., & Yaeger, J. The development of democratic values and behavior among Mexican-American children. *Child Development*, 1972, *43*, 625–638.

Sroufe, A. L. Attachment and the roots of competence. *Human Nature*, 1978, *1*(10), 50–57.

Staub, E. The use of role playing and induction in children's learning of helping and sharing behavior. *Child Development*, 1971, *42*, 805–817.

Staub, E. To rear a prosocial child: Reasoning, learning by doing, and learning by teaching others. In D. DePalma & J. Folley (Eds.), *Moral development: Current theory and research*. Hillsdale, N.J.: Erlbaum, 1975.

Staub, E. *Positive social behavior and morality* (Vol. 1). *Social and personal influences*. New York: Academic Press, 1978.

Staub, E. *Positive social behavior and morality* (Vol. 2). *Socialization and development*. New York: Academic Press, 1979.

Stein, A. H., & Friedrich, L. K. Aggressive and prosocial television programs and the natural behavior of preschool children. *Monographs of the Society for Research in Child Development*, 1973, *38*, whole no. 151.

Turnbull, C. *The mountain people*. New York: Simon & Schuster, 1972.

U.S. Bureau of the Census. Martial status and living arrangements. *Current Population Reports*. Series P-20. Washington, D.C.: Department of Commerce, 1979.

Whiting, B. B. The dependency hang-up and experiments in alternative life styles. In J. M. Yinger & S. J. Cutler (Eds.), *Major social issues: A multidisciplinary view*. New York: Free Press, 1978.

Whiting, B. B., & Whiting, J. W. M. *Children of six cultures: A psycho-cultural analysis.* Cambridge, Mass.: Harvard University Press, 1975.

Wilson, E. O. *On human nature.* Cambridge, Mass.: Harvard University Press, 1978.

Yarrow, M. R., Scott, P. M., & Waxler, C. Z. Learning concern for others. *Developmental Psychology,* 1973, *8,* 240–260.

Young, C. Z. *Programs of the brain.* London: Oxford University Press, 1978.

Youniss, J. *Parents and peers in social development: A Sullivan–Piaget Perspective.* Chicago: University of Chicago Press, 1980.

Zahn-Waxler, C., Radke-Yarrow, M., & King, R. A. The impact of the affective environment on young children. Paper presented at meeting of Society for Research in Child Development, New Orleans, La., 1977.

Zahn-Waxler, C., Radke-Yarrow, M. R., & King, R. A. Child rearing and children's prosocial initiations towards victims of distress. *Child Development,* 1979, *50,* 319–330.

# Prosocial Behavior
# for and by Older Persons[1]

BARBARA J. STEWART and CATHLEEN L. SMITH

## INTRODUCTION

This is a chapter about services rendered and received. Our concern in these pages is prosocial behavior for and by older persons. Following Staub (1978), we define prosocial behavior as behavior that benefits others. Our focus is on an area we have found to be an especially rich source of research on adult prosocial behavior: social gerontology. Many recent social gerontological studies have focused on prosocial behavior as it occurs for and by older persons. Interestingly, these studies have not used the label *prosocial behavior,* although that is precisely what is being examined.

During the course of our research on children's prosocial behavior described elsewhere in this volume, one of us was also involved in two research projects at the Institute on Aging at Portland State University. One project was a longitudinal study of 400 frail (i.e., extremely poor and debilitated) older persons, and the other was an investigation of the attitudes and behaviors of service providers who deliver services to older clients. One of the benefits of being involved in separate research activities simultaneously is that concepts and findings in one area often trigger a new perspective regarding research in another area. Such a situation occurred here. The helping, sharing, teaching, and comforting behaviors we studied in children

[1]Research by the first author included in this chapter was supported by a contract from the Social Security Administration (SSA-PMB-74-275) and by a research grant from the Administration on Aging (AoA grant No. 90-A-1006), both of which were awarded to the Institute on Aging, Portland State University, Portland, Oregon.

were found to have counterparts in social interactions involving older adults. For example, it became apparent that one of the major reasons some of the unusually frail persons in our longitudinal study were able to maintain themselves at home rather than enter nursing homes was because of family, friends, neighbors, and formal service providers who helped with housework, shopping, and transportation and who served as confidants to the disabled older person.

Our informal observations of help and comfort on behalf of frail elderly led to a more systematic examination of the existing research in social gerontology regarding prosocial behavior for and by older persons. In general, this research concerns older persons as recipients of prosocial behavior from others, especially middle-aged adults; studies examining positive forms of social behavior by older persons are somewhat less common. The major social gerontological research findings regarding adult prosocial behavior are focused on those older persons who have needs, the extent of their needs, the degree to which these needs are met through prosocial acts, and, generally, who exhibits the prosocial behavior. Much less information exists on personal characteristics and motivation of those who behave prosocially. Furthermore, there is limited information on the reactions of older persons to the receipt of such care.

The descriptions of prosocial behavior in the gerontological literature concentrate primarily on: those older persons who have the most obvious need for prosocial responses from others, such as those who are sick and need medical assistance; those who have mobility limitations and need help in activities of daily living (e.g., dressing, shopping, cooking); those who have become widowed and need legal, financial, and emotional support; and those who are unusually poor and require supplementary income, housing, and nutritional aid. Persons who respond prosocially to meet these needs include the informal network of family, friends, and neighbors on the one hand, and formal service providers (paid and volunteer) in public and private agencies, on the other.

Our review of social gerontological research regarding prosocial behavior begins with the informal support systems of older persons as we examine the prosocial behavior of family, friends, and neighbors. We move next to a consideration of professional caregivers and the formal support system, where we include some original data on the attitudes and behavior of individuals who provide services to older persons. We then present the more limited information on prosocial behavior by older persons. We conclude by offering a few reflections on a life-span perspective of prosocial development.

## PROSOCIAL BEHAVIOR TOWARD OLDER PERSONS

### Informal Support Systems:
### Family, Friends, and Neighbors

The informal support systems or natural helping networks of older persons—family, friends, and neighbors—are a current and major concern in social gerontological research. Research regarding the nature of family life for older persons has been reviewed by Shanas (1968), Troll (1971), and Sussman (1976), and information concerning the social networks of the elderly has been summarized by Lowenthal and Robinson (1976).

## HELPING BEHAVIOR TOWARD SICK AND DISABLED ELDERLY

Regardless of age, older persons in this country wish to remain independent and self-sufficient for as long as possible. However, as they become unable to provide for themselves, older persons turn first to family members, particularly their children, for help (Cicerelli, 1981; Robinson & Thurnher, 1979; Shanas, 1980; Weeks & Cuellar, 1981). Although it is often asserted that the elderly in this country have been abandoned by their families, the evidence suggests otherwise. In particular, provision of help to those older persons who are sick and disabled seems to be largely the province of a spouse or child. For example, using a 1975 national probability sample of 5775 persons aged 65 and over, Shanas (1979) found twice as many older persons who were bedfast or housebound residing in the community as were residing in institutions. In other words, in 1975 the majority of the sick and frail elderly in American were living in their own homes or in the homes of family members rather than in institutions or group homes. (At any given time, approximately 5–6% of older persons are institutionalized, and 10% of the noninstitutionalized elderly are chronically bedfast or housebound.) Of interest here are the caretakers for those sick and frail aged living in the community. Shanas found that chronically bedfast persons were helped most in housework, meal preparation, and shopping by a spouse (38%, 44%, and 30%, respectively), by a child (40%, 36%, and 62%), and by paid helpers (20%, 18%, and 8%). Approximately one-fourth of Shanas's total sample (excluding those who were chronically bedfast) had been temporarily ill (confined to bed) at least once during the previous year. Two-thirds of the ill men were taken care of by their wives and approximately 15% by children. In contrast, women, who were more likely to have been widowed, were most often cared for during their temporary illness by a child. Of these ill women, 41% mentioned children, 25% mentioned spouse, and 20% mentioned relatives or nonrelatives outside the household as providing help. Although 10% of the elderly men reported receiving no help during illness, two to three times as many women received no help with housework, meal prepration, or shopping when they were ill.

Institutionalization is generally viewed by the elderly as undesirable (Sussman, 1976) and is less likely to occur for those ill or housebound older persons who are cared for by a spouse or child. This buffer against institutionalization was dramatically illustrated by S. Brody, Poulshock, and Masciocchi (1978) in their examination of chronically ill elderly, some of whom were in private or public nursing homes and others who were community residents served by a home health agency. Contrary to what might be expected, the chronically ill elderly in private nursing homes did *not* score significantly worse on functional disability than those residing in the community. The two groups differed, instead, in their marital and family status. Those still residing in the community were living with a spouse and/or children (67%) or with other relatives (34%); in contrast, older persons in the private nursing home had never married (42.9%), were widowed (47.6%), or divorced (4.8%). Only 4.8% of the nursing home elderly were married. The majority (68%) of the moderately impaired private nursing home residents had no children. It appears that the presence of a spouse and/or children is an important deterrent to institutionalization for chronically impaired older persons who remain in the community.

## GENDER AND CAREGIVING

The current focus on informal support systems and family of older persons as alternatives to institutionalization has called attention to the disproportionate number of women who serve as caregivers in this capacity (E. Brody, 1981). Indeed, it has been asserted (Brody, 1981) that the ''natural or informal support system'' and ''family'' are ''euphemisms for adult daughters (and daughters-in-law), who are the true alternatives [p. 474].'' As might be expected, the extra pressures on adult daughters depend in part on the age of the elderly parent . E. Brody (1981) examined the life-style and caregiving preferences of three generations of women (i.e., noninstitutionalized elderly grandmothers, their middle-aged daughters, and the young adult granddaughters) in the Philadelphia area. We focus here on the middle-aged daughters and their elderly mothers. Approximately half of the daughters reported that they helped their mother on instrumental tasks (e.g., shopping and other errands, personal care, household maintenance tasks). Similar to trends in the population at large, the majority of these middle-aged women were in the work force. Interestingly, however, the amount of help given was not highly related to the daughter's employment status but was strongly associated with her age (and the age of the older mother), ranging from an average of 3 hr of help per week by those 40–49 years to 22.7 hr by the 60-year and over adult daughter.

Although as E. Brody and others (e.g., Horowitz, 1981; Lurie, 1981; Shanas, 1968) have documented, women are the principal caregivers of the aging family member, men are also involved in prosocial behavior toward the elderly. In one of the few studies that systematically examined the effect of caregiver gender, Horowitz (1981) found that sons undertook the role of primary caregiver to an older parent by default (i.e., when they were only children or in male-only sibling networks). In tasks such as financial management, financial assistance, dealing with bureaucratic organizations, and providing emotional support (defined as giving advice or talking to the parent when he or she was upset or depressed), sons and daughters who were primary caregivers were equally likely to report helping. However, sons were significantly less likely than daughters to report providing assistance with transportation, household chores, shopping, meal preparation, and personal care. Furthermore, sons indicated spending considerably less time than daughters in caring for their older parents and were more likely to involve their spouse in the caregiving activities.

In a 5-year longitudinal study of normative life transitions in middle-aged adults,

Robinson and Thurnher (1979) indicated, in some contrast to other research, that men were as likely to report helping an older parent as women. However, women were more often than men involved in providing complete care. Compared to women, men seemed to distance themselves physically and emotionally from their parents more easily, to experience less guilt, and to accept more readily the fact that they did not have the power to make their parents happier. Both husband and physicians were likely to advise the adult daughter not to become too emotionally involved with her mother. Over the 5 years, men provided instrumental and economic help but were less likely than women to feel responsible for the emotional well-being of the parent.

Recent evidence suggests that the amount of help rendered by adult sons and daughters may depend upon the sex of the aging parent. In a large-scale study in a midwestern city examining patterns of help-giving by adult children to elderly parents, Cicerelli (1981) found that daughters reported more service provision to elderly mothers than did sons. However, no gender difference in reported help to fathers was noted (perhaps, we would suggest, because elderly fathers are likely to be cared for by their wives).

OTHER PREDICTORS OF HELP-GIVING

There is only limited information on factors other than gender that are associated with provision of care to an elderly relative. Robinson and Thurnher (1979) noted that geographical proximity to the aging parent is associated with help-giving. Differences in educational level or socioeconomic status (Archbold, 1981; Cicerelli, 1981), as well as ethnic background and migration experience (Weeks & Cuellar, 1981) also influence the role family members play in the helping networks of older parents. Cicerelli (1981) found that the two most important predictors of the adult child's self-report of current provision of services to both mothers and fathers were attachment behaviors (defined as living close to parents and seeing or telephoning them frequently) and perceived dependency of the parent. A path analysis showed that filial obligation (the adult child's sense of duty and responsibility) and feelings of closeness and affection for the parent had indirect effects on the child's present helping through their effects on attachment behaviors. The amount of conflict in the history of interaction with the parent did not predict current helping.

It should be noted that the older parents in Cicerelli's (1981) study were generally neither sick nor disabled and were perceived by their offspring as needing little present help. (Indeed, the levels of help the middle-aged children reported were quite low, with most saying they gave no or only occasional help to their parents in 16 service areas. In fact, only in the service area of "psychological support—listening to problems, giving understanding and affection, etc. [Cicerelli, 1981, p. 66]" did more than a third of the adult children report providing some regular help.) However, most adult children felt a considerable commitment to help in the future, when the older parent would be in greater need. These acknowledgements of future commitment to help were related most strongly to the amounts of help the adult child currently provided, as well as, once again, the level of attachment behaviors he or she currently displayed.

## COSTS OF CAREGIVING

Caregiving to older persons, although having obvious benefits, is also accompanied by various costs to the caregiver. Although some forms of help may be physically tiring (e.g., lifting the older person, helping with bathing) or unpleasant (e.g., taking care of bowel and bladder accidents), it seems that the major costs are the restrictions on personal time and the changes in life-style that accompany caregiving to a sick or disabled elderly relative. In their examination of caretaking for aged parents, Robinson and Thurnher (1979) found a significant negative relationship between reported helping of a parent and morale of the caregiver. Changes in relationships with parents were twice as likely to be negative rather than positive over the 5 years of their study. Negative portrayals of parents were related both to perceived mental deterioration of the parent and to the confinement and life-style infringements experienced by the adult child as a result of caretaking. Robinson and Thurnher concluded that adult children attempt to delay their parents' institutionalization as long as possible, but at considerable costs to themselves.

Similar findings regarding the costs to adult children of caregiving for elderly parents were obtained by Cicirelli (1981); in this study, amount of services provided to both mothers and fathers was a significant predictor of the level of personal strain (e.g., feeling physically worn out, emotionally exhausted, tied down) in adult children. Provision of services to fathers was also a significant predictor of negative feelings (e.g., frustration, irritation, impatience) in the child. Other research (Horowitz & Shindelman, 1980) also identifies restrictions on personal time and freedom as major problems of family members who care for an elderly relative.

Not unexpectedly, there is some suggestion that women are more negatively affected than men by their caregiving activities toward older relatives. Robinson and Thurnher (1979) reported that women were more likely than men to characterize caring for a parent as oppressive. Similarly, even after controlling for daughters' more extensive involvement in service provision, Horowitz (1981) found that daughters experienced caregiving as substantially more stressful than did sons.

Suggestions for relieving burdens of caregiving for both the adult child and the older parent have been presented by Crossman, London, and Barry (1981) and Robinson and Thurnher (1979). Families with elderly members are urged to take advantage of available community resources such as in-home meals and housekeeping services; respite services are recommended as especially effective in providing relief to the caretaker for a few hours up to a few days or even more. Zarit, Reever, and Bach-Peterson (1980) indicated that when relatives other than the primary caregiver make more visits to the impaired older person, the feelings of burden by the caregiver are less. Furthermore, if the caregiver's spouse is supportive of the help-giving role, regardless of whether actual assistance is provided, the impact of caregiving is perceived as less severe (Horowitz & Shindelman, 1980). Finally, daughters who identify their parents' needed services and then manage their provision by others suffer fewer emotional costs than daughters who provide direct care to older parents (Archbold, 1981).

## FRIENDS AND NEIGHBORS AS SUPPORT
## FOR THE ELDERLY

Friends and neighbors are sometimes an overlooked source of support for older persons (Cantor, 1979). In her study of elderly residents of inner New York City, Cantor found that 37% had at least one nonrelated "functional" friend (a friend seen at least monthly or through telephone contact at least weekly). Furthermore, 53% of the respondents had at least one "functional" neighbor; that is, a neighbor whom the respondent knew well and who provided or received from the older person at least one kind of "instrumental" (e.g., help when ill, help with shopping) or "affective" (e.g., visits, eating together) help. Although some willingness to call on neighbors for some kinds of help was expressed, older persons reported they would first choose family to give them help regarding health-related tasks, financial matters, daily living–housekeeping tasks, and discussion of family problems. To provide relief from loneliness, however, the proportions of respondents choosing kin and friends were roughly the same. For all kinds of help, formal organizations were the least preferred source of support. Cantor interpreted her findings as consistent with a "hierarchical-compensatory model [p. 453]" of support systems in which kin (mainly children) are generally seen as the most desirable support givers, followed by significant others (friends and relatives), and finally by formal organizations.

The views of the older person regarding the limitations of the friendship network are apparently shared by the adult child. Cicerelli (1981) found that adult children perceived themselves as being the major providers of needed services to their parents. Although friends and neighbors were acknowledged as sources of psychological support, they were seen as casual sources of help having relatively limited and supplementary usefulness.

## MORALE OF THE ELDERLY AND INTERACTION
## WITH FAMILY AND FRIENDS

It is clear that help given to older persons by family members may be quite extensive and that neighbors and friends may also provide important aid. It is also well-established that caregiving is most often done by middle-aged women and is frequently burdensome to the caregiver, especially when the older person is ill, disabled, or mentally deteriorated. Although family caregiving is crucial in postponing or preventing institutionalization of the older person, we have not yet discussed other consequences for the elderly of the provision of such care. Considered particularly important are effects on morale, life satisfaction, and related constructs, perhaps the most common outcome variables in social gerontological research (see the review by Larson, 1978). Is morale of the elderly related to contact with family members, who remain the most important (and most preferred) sources of help, especially in time of need, and/or with friends, to whom older persons often turn to provide relief from loneliness?

Interestingly, the literature to date seems to suggest that although interactions with friends and the presence of a spouse are often positively related to feelings of well-being, contacts with one's children and siblings are generally unrelated, or sometimes even negatively related, to morale (Creecy & Wright, 1979; Edwards & Klemmack, 1973; Larson, 1978; Lee, 1979; Lee & Ihinger-Tallman, 1980). For example, Lee's (1979) examination of married persons aged 60 years and over indicated that interactions with children (as measured by number of children, interaction with most frequently seen child, total visits, and total calls) had small negative correlations with morale. The number of letters received from children was uncorrelated with morale. Lee proposed that generational differences, as well as lack of common interests and values, may have contributed to the absence of a positive relationship between morale of the older person and contact with children. However, even interactions between older persons and their siblings (i.e., persons of approximately the same generation and age) are not positively correlated with morale of the older person (Lee & Ihinger-Tallman, 1980).

Unfortunately, the prosocial aspects of contact between the elderly and their families or friends have generally not been the primary focus in studies of the subjective well-being of older persons. For our purposes here, it is clearly not enough to attempt to relate contact and morale without specifying what form the contact takes, the motivations of the family members for increased contact, and the qualitative nature of the interaction with the older person. For example, contact can provide benefits to the older person (and thus fit the definition of prosocial behavior), or serve primarily the needs of other family members. Contact can disrupt the life-style and daily activities of the older person, or can help to provide an element of continuity in his or her life. Unfortunately, the research to date provides little information about the effects on morale of the elderly of these various kinds of contact with family. However, two case studies from the longitudinal investigation of frail elderly mentioned in the introduction illustrate how an increased amount of contact with family can have quite different impacts on morale. In this study elderly individuals were interviewed three times over a 2-year period; in each interview questions regarding the older person's life satisfaction were included. In cases where the older person died before the study would be completed, interviews with family members and acquaintances helped to provide a picture of the circumstances surrounding the death.

The first case study (White & Wagner, 1978) describes an elderly person who was functioning well and who expressed a high level of life satisfaction at the time of the initial interview. However, over the course of the study her morale declined, at least in part because of interactions with family members. Mrs. Smith was 85 at the first interview, living alone in her small, well-kept home of 30 years. Although she needed help to get out to do her errands, she could be seen nearly every day working in her yard, in which she took great pride. Her husband and only son were dead; her family consisted of a daughter-in-law (who took her grocery shopping every week), a granddaughter and her husband, and two teenage great-grand-children. Her next door neighbor, Sarah, was middle-aged, and, as Mrs. Smith's closest friend and companion, frequently prepared meals for Mrs. Smith, drove her to the doctor, ran errands, and assisted in lawn mowing. Every morning Mrs. Smith raised a window blind in her kitchen by 8 A.M. to signal that she was fine; on a few occasions when the blind was not raised, Sarah would go to her home and check on her. Sarah viewed Mrs. Smith as a good friend who offered much to their relationship, frequently invited Mrs. Smith to family gatherings, and kept her hedge cut between their houses so Mrs. Smith could sit in her own living room and watch Sarah's grandchildren play.

A few months after the first interview Mrs. Smith's granddaughter, who was to inherit the house after Mrs. Smith's death, felt her own housing was inadequate and consequently with her husband, teenaged children, and two large dogs moved into Mrs. Smith's home. Sarah, the neighbor, stated that Mrs. Smith's decline began with this event. After several months of the new arrangement, during which Mrs. Smith's peaceful existence was disrupted and her garden destroyed by the dogs, she asked her granddaughter's family to leave. Her relationship with her family was strained after the move and visits were less frequent, occurring only on special occasions. On one such occasion, a few months before Mrs. Smith's death, her granddaughter's family visited on Mother's Day and brought a pizza, which Mrs. Smith could not eat. Mrs. Smith was very depressed at their lack of consideration for her ("The pizza said it all," she told Sarah in tears).

Sarah awoke one day to find the window shade still down and after Mrs. Smith did not answer the door, Sarah called the granddaughter, who refused to allow her to break a window to gain entrance to the house. The police would not intervene. An hour and a half later, a family member came with the keys; Mrs. Smith was hospitalized and died 2 hrs later of a stroke. Her granddaughter's family moved into her house the next week.

The second case study (Tissue, 1981), presented in less detail, illustrates that increased contact with family can sometimes have positive outcomes. Mrs. Kemp, 80, was healthy and active at the first interview; she saw her children, neighbors, and friends regularly. She went to the grocery store, bank, and church at least weekly, sometimes driving her own car. However, by the time the study ended 2 years later, Mrs. Kemp had developed both heart problems and cancer. She could get out only with help and no longer drove her car. Over the course of the study, her contact with children, grandchildren, neighbors, and friends increased; these persons provided her with the necessary assistance so that she could continue many of her regular activities. In contrast to other persons whose health worsened over time and who experienced concomitant declines in morale, Mrs. Kemp exhibited a positive change in life satisfaction over the 2 years (moving from an average level of morale at the first interview to a level of morale at the third interview that was higher than would have been statistically predicted). She reported that although her health was declining, her level of activities was maintained, primarily due to the support of her family and friends.

Thus, although positive correlations do not generally exist between morale of the elderly and contact with family, we suspect that the qualitative nature of the family interaction, the motivations of family members for increased contact, and the extent to which the contact involves prosocial behavior that provides some continuity in the older person's life can be critical for the older person's sense of well-being. Unfortunately, however, we know of no direct evidence that receiving help from family members actually improves the morale of older persons. In fact, there is a suggestion in at least one study of *negative* relationship between receipt of services from one's family and the older person's mental health. Lurie (1981) has recently reported some preliminary data showing that the more services provided to an older parent by a daughter both before and after the parent's hospitalization, the more depressed was the older person. This relationship remained even after controlling for the marital status and self-perceived physical health of the older recipient.

THE INFORMAL SUPPORT SYSTEM: CONCLUSIONS

We have reviewed evidence from the social gerontological literature concerning the "natural helping" of the elderly by persons in their informal support system. References to prosocial behavior in this literature most often take the form of descriptions of caregiving by family members, although the prosocial behavior of friends and neighbors has also been examined. Much of the available information concerning prosocial behavior toward the elderly involves descriptions of care to the impaired older person. Fewer data exist regarding the incidence or form of prosocial behavior toward physically healthy and psychologically sound older adults, although as we shall see, these are precisely those older persons who are identified as engaging in (rather than receiving) prosocial behavior.

What is evident is that the help given to the ill or disabled elderly by family is extensive, critical in postponing or preventing institutionalization, and often viewed as burdensome by the caregiver. Although some forms of help in and of themselves may be upsetting or tiring, it is mainly the confinement and restrictions on the caregiver's time and activities that are associated with feelings of stress. What is also evident is that it is women, particularly those who are middle-aged or aging themselves, who are the principal caregivers to older family members, whether a spouse, their parents, the spouse's parents, or other relatives. (It is also the case that, of those older persons who are in need and do not receive help, women outnumber men.) When men do take part in caregiving (for example, to a parent), there is a suggestion that they have a more limited time and task commitment than women and are less likely to view the situation as burdensome. Unfortunately, however, there are few systematic data regarding how men and women differentially accomplish or experience their caregiving roles.

Nor do we know much about the determinants of this kind of prosocial behavior or the motivation underlying these helping acts. It would seem important to begin to identify person variables other than gender, including personality characteristics and cognitive processes, that influence individual family members to assume more or less care of their elderly relatives. The extent to which the taking care of an aged parent is accompanied or mediated by empathy or more advanced stages of moral reasoning, for example, rather than feelings of obligation or expectations of return (e.g., through bequests from the older person) has not yet been adequately examined, although the obligatory nature of parent caregiving, at least, has been questioned (Cicerelli, 1981; see also Hess & Waring, 1978). How do caregivers view their prosocial behavior? What reasons do they offer for engaging in the caregiving activities? Information on the attitudes of caregivers and the attributions they make regarding their own prosocial behavior would be useful in beginning to explore the factors associated with a caregiving commitment.

Research also needs to be directed at examining the impact on older persons of the prosocial behavior they receive. Although contact with family members per se is not generally associated with higher morale in the elderly, the qualitative nature of the contact rather than the sheer amount of it has rarely been assessed. As a result, we have little information concerning the relationship between subjective well-being of the elderly and the amount or kind of prosocial behavior they receive from others or the manner in which such help is delivered. We do know that declines in health of older persons are accompanied by declines in their life satisfaction (Tissue, 1981). The lack of a positive relationship between morale of the elderly and their contact with children and siblings may thus be a function of the fact that such contact tends to increase at times when the older person has become ill or disabled (Lee, 1979). However, data that show a link at such times between receipt of services and depression in the older person must be interpreted with caution. Receipt of prosocial behavior may indeed produce lower morale if, for example, the older person is uncomfortable in such a dependent position or feels unable to reciprocate. Conversely, low morale or depression in the older person may itself elicit more helping from family members. Cicerelli's (1981) data cited earlier, for example, would suggest that when adult children become aware of their parents' needs through frequent telephone conversations and visits, they respond with increased service provision.

The social psychological literature on recipient reactions to help (Fisher, De-Paulo, & Nadler, 1981; Fisher, Nadler, & Whitcher-Alagna, 1982) would also seem to be of some relevance to an analysis of the relationship between elderly morale and caregiving by family members. This literature suggests, for example, that help should be more positively evaluated by the recipient when it is voluntary and offered freely by the helper rather than requested by the person in need. Moreover, help will be evaluated as evidencing care and concern to the extent that it is seen by the recipient as motivated by positive intentions and costly to the help-giver (although costly help may also be avoided). These same characteristics of helpers and helping situations, however, have also been found to elicit feelings of obligation and attempts to reciprocate by the person helped. Thus, if circumstances are such that opportunities for reciprocity are limited and the older person is uncomfortable in such a dependent position, if help must be actively sought, if older persons sense that they are a burden to the caregiver or if the caregiver engages in negative behaviors in addition to the helpful activities, lowered morale may be the result of receipt of such care.

Finally, we might comment on the methodology used in most social gerontological research. The dearth of information on the qualitative nature of social interactions with the elderly may be a function of the almost exclusive use of questionnaires and/or structured interviews. Such survey techniques may be inadequate to produce data, for example, on the affective components of individual's lives (Masciocchi, Patrizi, & Brody, 1981). Reliance on self-report methodologies may be particularly problematic when one is dealing with socially desirable (rather than neutral) activities, such as the prosocial behavior evidenced in caring for an elderly relative. Thus, direct observation of caregiver and recipient behavior may be necessary to supplement information obtained from questionnaires or in-depth interviews.

## Formal Support Systems

During the last decade in the United States, formal services have been an increasing source of support for older persons having special needs (see Beattie, 1976, for an overview of social services to the aging); this increase can be traced to federal legislation enacted by the United States Congress. In the late 1960s, for example, the federal government expanded social services to the aging through Title I (Old Age Assistance) of the Social Security Act. In 1973, the Comprehensive Service Amendments to the Older Americans Act of 1965 were passed. This 1973 federal legislation has resulted in the establishment of approximately 600 Area Agencies on Aging (AAA) across the country. The designated purpose of the AAAs was to develop comprehensive and coordinated delivery systems of social services for Americans aged 60 years and older. Targeted services included health care (outpatient/home and inpatient), recreation, continuing education, homemaking, counseling, transportation, nutrition, and housing. These services may be more familiar under names such as Meals on Wheels, Loaves and Fishes, friendly visitors, visiting nurses, and senior centers. Because federal funding has increased the availability of such services, there have been concomitant increases in the number of persons delivering these services and in their utilization by older persons.

At the outset, then, it appears that the recent increase in formal service provision for the elderly has been markedly influenced by actions at the federal government level. One might speculate that the initiation of such legislation might have been due, in part, to prosocial values of the initiators. However, Estes (1979) has suggested that both economic and political benefits for the benefactors underlie the activities of those who initiate and implement such legislation. Indeed, according to Estes, the term *helping* in reference to services for the elderly conceals the actual power relationships that exist between those who control the services and those older persons who must submit to authority in order to obtain benefits. From this point of view, formal service strategies may contribute to the perception of the aged as dependent and limit the opportunities for older persons to reciprocate for services received.

Formal services for the aged do not usually supplant, but rather supplement, the help given by members of informal helping networks. Formal service providers must then cooperate with the older persons' informal networks in providing care. Research regarding such cooperative efforts (Froland, Pancoast, Chapman, & Kimboko, 1981) has resulted in guidelines for the promotion of partnerships between formal service providers and informal helping networks in support of the elderly and others who may require help. Important bases for the success of these partnerships have been found to include: viewing the recipient of help as having strengths and resources as well as problems and needs; recognizing that an enduring network of social relationships is important for the recipient; maintaining equality of status among professional and informal caregivers; and balancing informal and formal caregiving roles and responsibilities.

Individuals who work in social service agencies include both paid and volunteer service providers, with many of the latter group being older persons themselves. In the following sections, we concentrate on these service providers and attempt to identify some of the factors related to the prosocial nature of their work. Two important types of formal care to older persons, care given in institutions and care given to terminally ill persons, do not receive emphasis here but have been addressed in detail by others (e.g., Glasscote, Beigel, Butterfield, Clark, Cox, Elpers, Gudeman, Gurel, Lewis, Miles, Raybin, Reifler, & Vito, 1976; Kalish, 1976; Koff, 1980; Schulz, 1978; Tobin & Lieberman, 1976).

## A STUDY OF ATTITUDES AND BEHAVIOR OF SERVICE PROVIDERS

Individuals whose work is of a general prosocial nature may differ markedly in *how* they proceed to deliver the care they provide. In any examination of formal service provision, it is thus important to differentiate between the actual provision of a prosocial service per se and the manner or style in which this service is provided. This distinction was highlighted in the Client Relations study, a research project on service provider attitudes and behavior recently completed at the Institute on Aging at Portland State University. A questionnaire assessing general attitudes toward older clients and toward their jobs was mailed to a random sample of 530 service providers whose work involved direct provision of services to older persons. A response rate of 81% ($N = 428$) was obtained. A later stage of the study involved behavioral observations of 51 service providers (32 in-home nursing personnel and 19 outreach workers employed by senior centers and social service agencies) who had previously completed the general attitudes questionnaire, either as part of the original random sample or as part of a supplemental sample included to compensate for subject loss due primarily to job turnover. Of the 51 service providers, 45 were observed providing services in the homes of three of their older clients; the remainder were observed with two of their older clients, for a total of 147 observed service encounters. Trained observers used a time-sampling procedure and 28 behavior categories to classify behaviors occurring in a 10-min segment of each service encounter. Following the service encounter, client evaluations of the encounter were obtained in a structured private interview. In addition, service provider attitudes regarding that specific older client were assessed using some of the same items that were included on the earlier general attitude questionnaire.

A primary question for the Client Relations project was whether attitudes of the caregivers toward their older clientele in general, toward their jobs, and toward the specific older clients with whom they were observed were predictive of their behavior during the service delivery encounter. A further question concerned whether client evaluations assessed following the observed encounter would be related to service provider attitudes and behavior. Nine global attitude scales (based on the general attitude questionnaire and the specific attitude assessment that followed the observed service encounters) were constructed and validated by Petersen (1981); the behavioral observation scales were validated by Behn (1980). Correlational analyses were employed to determine the interrelationships among service provider attitudes, service provider behaviors, and client evaluations (Stewart, Petersen, & Behn, 1980, 1981). Overall, the statistically significant ($p < .05$) service provider attitude–behavior correlations were in the mid-.20s to mid-.40s range, similar to the general level of attitude–behavior correlations currently found in the social psychological literature.

*Service Provision as Prosocial Behavior.* Of the 28 behaviors coded during the service delivery encounter, seven categories were most directly connected to the actual provision of services to the older clients, and might be considered prosocial in nature. These behaviors were: *attending* (listening to or paraphrasing the older person); *complying* (fulfilling the older person's request or command); *describing problems* (describing or clarifying the older person's present problem); *proposing solutions* (teaching or advising the older person); *questioning* (phrasing statements as questions); and *volunteering help* (offering help where personal effort was involved). Also assessed were *normative* behaviors, that is, behaviors regularly performed when providing a service (such as giving medication or taking a person's temperature, both of which are "normative" for a nurse or aide). When these behaviors were correlated with the nine attitude measures, only 6% of the 63 possible correlations were statistically significant at $p < .05$. These results suggest that there was no linear relationship between expressed attitudes of caregivers and the frequency of these seven behaviors most directly involved in actual service provision. If attitudes do mediate the prosocial acts of service providers, such mediation was not evidenced by increased levels of the seven service provision behaviors described here.

*The Qualitative Nature of Service Provision as Prosocial Behavior.* Other behaviors exhibited by service providers had less to do with provision of actual prosocial services to the elderly than with the style of service delivery. In particular, a nucleus of four behaviors—laughing, supportive statements, interrupting, and complaining—was identified by Behn (1980) in her factor analysis of the behavior scales as forming a "friendly" factor. This cluster of behaviors was described by Behn as characterizing caregivers who were active, friendly, supportive, and who interacted with their older clients in a way that allowed for mutuality. Although *supportive statements* (expressions of approval or praise) and *laughter* seem obvious "friendly" behaviors, their juxtaposition with interruptions and complaints requires further explanation. These latter behaviors, although originally conceptualized as rude and negative, were interpreted by Behn as representing the service provider's active participation in the interaction (*interruptions*) and his or her requests from the client for sympathy regarding an outside or personal problem (*complaints*).

When these four behaviors reflecting the qualitative nature or style of service delivery were correlated with the nine attitude scales, 28% of the 36 possible correlations were statistically significant at $p < .05$. Although no clear pattern of correlations emerged between attitudes of service providers and the number of complaints they made during service delivery, attitudes were significantly correlated with the other three "friendly" behaviors in conceptually meaningful ways. Service providers who laughed frequently during the service encounter were more likely to perceive the older person for whom they were caring as having positive (e.g., appreciative, pleasant, socially contributing) but not negative (e.g., hostile, rejecting) characteristics. Those service providers who more often interrupted their older clients described them as having more positive characteristics and expressed higher levels of enjoyment regarding their older clientele in general. Making supportive statements was unmistakably the behavior most strongly related to attitudes; it was significantly correlated with six of the nine attitude scales. Caregivers who made more supportive statements to their older clients during service delivery were more likely to describe their job as having positive but not negative qualities and to express enjoyment with their work. They were also less likely to describe their older clientele in general as hostile or rejecting. When partial correlations controlling for service type (i.e., in-home nursing personnel versus outreach workers) were computed, the relationships between service provider attitudes and style of service delivery generally remained significant. (The absolute values of the correlations just referred to ranged from .24 to .38, were significant at $p < .05$ to $p < .01$, and were computed for $N = 51$ service providers.)

The importance of the qualitative nature of the service encounter rather than the delivery of services per se was also found in the data regarding client satisfaction with the service interaction. Higher levels of satisfaction in the older person could be traced to higher levels of laughing ($r = .57; p < .001$), interrupting ($r = .45; p < .001$), and supportive statements ($r = .42; p < .001$) by the caregiver during service delivery (Stewart, Petersen, & Behn, 1980). Importantly, supportive statements, laughing, and interruptions by the service provider were also correlated with these same behaviors in the older person ($r = .31, .57,$ and $.61$, respectively; $p < .001$); apparently, friendly behaviors of service providers tend to be accompanied by the same behaviors from their older clients. Again, however, the frequency of caregiver behaviors more closely associated with actual provision of services (e.g., "normative" behaviors, volunteering help, fulfilling requests, proposing solutions) was found to be unrelated to the older person's professed satisfaction with the service interaction. Apparently, it is not the frequency of prosocial service in and of itself that is associated with satisfaction in the older client, but what we might call the *positive "affective tone"* of the interaction (i.e., the fact that such service is delivered in a positive, mutually interactive, and supportive context).

*Service Delivery to Unpleasant Older Clients.*   How does a person who has chosen to work in a prosocial occupation behave with an older client who possesses unpleasant characteristics? (Older clients identified as unpleasant were characterized by service providers as refusing to help themselves, having given up on life, having serious emotional problems, and as being uncooperative, ungrateful, hostile, angry, overly demanding, and chronic complainers.) Recall that service providers were just as likely to deliver actual services of a prosocial nature (e.g., help, attention, or advice) to older persons whom they viewed less positively. However, they were less likely to laugh, interrupt, or furnish supportive statements to these disliked clients. Were these "friendly" responses replaced by more negative behaviors that may also accompany formal caregiving?

In addition to the behaviors described earlier, observers coded the frequency of several other service provider behaviors during the service delivery encounter. These behaviors included *disregarding* (behaviors that appeared to dehumanize or objectify the client, such as talking or making judgments about the older person without including him or her in the evaluation); *ignoring* (failing to respond when a verbal response was clearly called for); *not tracking* (failing to maintain eye contact with the older person while he or she was speaking); and *nervous behavior* (e.g., scratching, leg swings, holding arms tightly folded, directing posture away from the client). Surprisingly, service providers who described their older clientele and their job as having more negative characteristics were actually less likely than service providers with more positive attitudes to disregard their older clients during service delivery ($r = -.25$ and $-.29$, respectively; $p < .05$). Similarly, the less positively service providers described their jobs and the older clients with whom they were observed, the less likely they were to ignore those clients during the service encounter ($r = .35$ and $.41$, respectively; $p < .01$). However, service providers who felt less positive about their older clientele, their jobs, and the specific older persons with whom they were observed engaged in more nervous behavior in the service provision context ($r = -.49$, $-.35$, and $-.35$, respectively; $p < .01$), and had less eye contact ($r = -.24$ and $-.28$, respectively; $p < .05$) than did service providers expressing more positive affect.

In summary, the more negatively a service provider viewed one or more components of the service provision situation (i.e., older clientele in general, the job conditions, a specific older client), the less likely that he or she displayed negative behaviors such as disregarding or ignoring the older client during the service encounter. Nor were disliked clients less likely to receive actual services of a prosocial nature, such as help, attention, or advice. However, there is some suggestion of a more subtle nonverbal form of avoidance. In dealing with disliked older clients, service providers displayed less eye contact, increased nervous behavior, and fewer instances of laughter, interruptions, and supportive statements. Apparently, service providers may go out of their way to avoid negative behavior with clients whom they like less, but what we have called the qualitative nature or affective tone of service provision is influenced nonetheless.

REACTIONS OF OLDER PERSONS TO THE RECEIPT
OF FORMAL SERVICES

The definition of prosocial behavior we have adopted specifies a positive impact on the recipient of the positive act. Does the receipt of a formal service in and of itself produce benefits for the older person? The temptation might be to conclude that because some needed or desirable service is provided, the accrual of benefits to the older person is rather automatic. One might even envisage that the benefits from receiving a service carry over to the more general psychological and physical well-being of the recipient. Evidence to the contrary is suggested by results obtained by Schulz (1976) in a field experiment involving visitations by undergraduate students to elderly residents of a retirement home. Visiting patterns to older persons are of special interest to gerontologists, who believe that visits serve as "affective help [Cantor, 1979, p. 449]" in fulfilling emotional needs and providing relief from loneliness. In the formal service system, one of the main roles of volunteers is to visit older persons in their homes or in institutional settings such as nursing homes or hospitals. In the Schulz study, some of the elderly subjects could determine for themselves both the frequency and duration of the visits (controllable visits). Other subjects were informed when they would be visited and how long the visit would last but could not control these events (predictable visits). A third visitation group was visited on a random schedule, and a fourth group received no visits. A methodology by which older persons were yoked across the three visit conditions allowed the duration and frequency of visits for individuals in the predictable and random visit conditions to be made equivalent to those received by the elderly who controlled their visits.

All three groups of visited elderly reported equal enjoyment of the visits. However, the random visit group showed no significant advantage over the no-visit group on more generalized measures of activity level, physical health, and psychological status; visitation did not, in itself, produce generalized positive effects. In contrast, both the predictable and controllable visit groups were significantly superior to the random and no-visit groups on these measures.

Field experiments with older persons, such as the one just described, are a rarity in the current gerontological literature. Consequently the follow-up study examining the long-term effects of the intervention (Schulz & Hanusa, 1978) provides an especially valuable perspective regarding research on prosocial behavior toward older persons. An examination of the health and psychological status of the four groups at 24, 30, and 42 months after termination of the original study revealed that the generalized effects of the controllable and predictable visit conditions were temporary. These two groups exhibited substantial declines in health and psychological status after completion of the study, in contrast to the random visit and no-visit groups which displayed a stable pattern over time.

Schulz and Hanusa's discussion of ethical implications of these follow-up findings has particular relevance for research on prosocial behavior. If some kind of prosocial intervention is employed in a field experiment, researchers must consider the possible negative outcomes of withdrawing that intervention and devise ways of insuring, insofar as possible, that such negative outcomes are minimized, for example, by transferring the intervention (or some form thereof) to the older persons' ongoing social environment.

## THE FORMAL SUPPORT SYSTEM: CONCLUSIONS

Discussion of prosocial behavior for older persons would be incomplete without acknowledgement of the help the elderly receive from formal services. In this country at this time, it is not enough to speak of the support given to the elderly by their family and friends; formal caregivers play a critical role in providing a wide range of services to older persons. Research on these formal support services has yielded several important insights into the nature of, factors associated with, and reactions of older recipients to prosocial behavior in formal help-giving settings. For example, it appears that prosocial behavior by professional helpers must be conceptualized to include not only the actual provision of prosocial services but the qualitative nature of the service delivery. In the Client Relations study, provision of services per se was unrelated to the attitudes of the helpers or the satisfaction of those served. Instead, the qualitative nature or "affective tone" of the service delivery (i.e., the number of "friendly" behaviors) emerged as crucial when relationships with service provider attitudes or client satisfaction were examined.

We do not mean to imply that the absolute level of help provided to the elderly is unimportant or that attitudes of the caregiver or the older person are always unrelated to the provision of services per se. The failure in the Client Relations study to find a relationship between attitudes of service providers or client satisfaction and objective service provision behaviors such as help or advice may have been a function of the sample of caregivers, who were probably more homogeneous on these latter behaviors than people in general. These individuals had in fact made a choice to enter work involving care of the elderly. Furthermore, presumably, they must have delivered a certain minimal level of service in order to keep their jobs. That they took their caregiving role seriously was suggested by their behavior in dealing with disliked clients, with whom deliberate or overt negative behaviors were actually less likely. We suspect that the attitudes of a more heterogeneous group of persons (including those whose work does not routinely involve helping others and, most probably, those who are part of informal helping networks) might be more strongly associated with those behaviors necessary for providing even basic care. However, just as we stressed the necessity for examining the qualitative nature of the helping relationships as well as the specific amount of help given among family members, friends, and neighbors, the data presented here would also suggest the importance of such an analysis where behavior in formal help-giving contexts is at issue.

If prosocial behavior to the elderly involves supportive companionship in addition to objective helping, it is also apparently necessary for the older person to be able to look forward to or predict the service in order for broader outcomes of the prosocial act to be realized. The results of the Schulz (1976) study would suggest that a positive event (in this case, friendly visits to older persons) will have generalized positive effects (e.g., increased physical and psychological well-being of the person visited) only to the extent that the affected individual is able to predict the helpful intervention. However, the generalized benefits may not endure once the predictable positive event is discontinued (Schulz & Hanusa, 1978). Unfortunately, we do not yet know whether or to what extent factors other than predictability contribute to generalized effects of formal service provision, and we have no information on those aspects of prosocial interventions that promote longer lasting positive changes in older individuals in need.

## PROSOCIAL BEHAVIOR BY OLDER PERSONS

Prosocial behavior by older persons has received less attention than prosocial behavior on their behalf. Nonetheless, it is very clear in the existing social gerontological literature that helping, advising, sharing with, and comforting family and friends, as well as caring for others in the role of service volunteer are not uncommon behaviors for older persons.

### Prosocial Behavior by Older Persons toward Family, Friends, and Neighbors

Older persons report themselves as helpful to their children and grandchildren (L. Harris & Associates, Inc., 1975). When asked how they help their younger family members, a national sample of persons 65 years and over reported that they give gifts (90%); help out when someone is ill (68%); take care of grandchildren (54%); help out with money (45%); shop or run errands (34%); and fix things around their houses or keep house for them (26%). As might be expected, 65–69-year-olds were more likely to provide such aid than those 80 or over; however, even among this oldest subgroup, substantial numbers of persons reported helping their younger family members (e.g., 86% give gifts; 57% help out when someone is ill; 38% give financial help; and 34% take care of grandchildren). Although older persons with higher incomes were more likely to report giving gifts and helping out with money, income level appeared to have a nonlinear relationship with other forms of helping. For example, similar proportions of older persons with incomes less than $7,000 and more than $15,000 reported helping out with illness, caring for grandchildren, and shopping; however, both of these groups actually reported less helping on these tasks than those with incomes between $7,000 and $15,000.

The reciprocity of support between many older persons and their neighbors has also been documented. More than a fifth of the older respondents in Cantor's (1979) study of inner New York City residents indicated that they and their neighbors helped each other "a lot;" an additional 40% reported helping each other in emergencies (38% reported not helping one another at all). Of those who reported helping each other in emergencies or more often, nearly two-thirds indicated that neighbors helped them when they were ill, and, in turn, nearly two-thirds helped their neighbors during illness. Roughly similar percentages reported giving and receiving affective help (e.g., visits).

Prosocial behavior in the form of sharing can be seen in the bequests older persons make to family members, friends, and neighbors. There is substantial evidence for well-established norms of generational transfer according to notions of distributive justice and exchanges of care, service, and material goods between members of the older and middle generations (Sussman, 1976). For example, in cases where the older parent required special care, the pattern of distribution to particular children is based at least in part upon the older benefactor's perception of the services each has rendered. Sibling members of the middle generation likewise agree that the sibling who has shown the greatest amount of service to the elderly parent should receive the major portion of the inheritance upon the parent's death.

Although family members continue to be the primary recipients of this form of sharing, Rosenfeld (1979) has suggested that the pattern of bequests may be changing such that nonfamily members may be inheriting more from wills than they have in the past. Rosenfeld found that residents of a retirement community left more of their estates to friends (12%) and to organizations (16%) than did older persons in a residential community or a long-term geriatric ward at a local hospital (5% and 6%, respectively, to friends; 4% and 6%, respectively, to organizations). Rosenfeld describes one widow who willed her home to two neighbors to share equally, with an additional amount to one of the neighbors in appreciation for her many kindnesses. Another woman specified that the proceeds from the sale of her home be divided among three neighbors who cared for her in her home rather than allow her to be put into a nursing home. Rosenfeld predicts that, as older persons acquire more power and status in groups outside the family and complete parental obligations earlier in the life cycle (e.g., paying for children's college or helping with the down payment for a house), there will be increased opportunities for bequests outside the family.

What factors are associated with prosocial behavior in the elderly? Evidence from a number of studies indicates a relationship between helping or sharing with others (or the perception that one does so) and better morale or self-concept in older persons. For example, Mancini (1980) found higher morale scores for older persons who perceived themselves as more often providing help to their friends when they were sick, understanding their friends' problems, likes, dislikes, feelings, and providing good company for their friends. Similarly, Midlarsky and Kahana (1981a) found that residents of a retirement community who exhibited altruistic attitudes on an internally consistent altruism scale had better self-concepts and perceived health than those with less altruistic attitudes.

In one of the few field experiments examining prosocial behavior by older persons, Trimakis and Nicolay (1974) investigated the relationship between the self-concept of women tenants in a low-income senior housing project and their pledges to donate winnings from a lottery (to an entertainment fund that would benefit everyone in the building) under various experimentally induced social influence conditions. Unfortunately, the "positive" versus "negative" social influence conditions in this study varied not only with respect to references to differing group norms of altruism (i.e., senior citizens are generous versus senior citizens usually keep any money offered to them), but also with respect to the public versus private nature of the woman's choice to share. Although it was reported that women with high self-concept scores contributed more money than women with middle or low self-concept scores, a significant interaction between self-concept and influence condition showed that women with high self-concept scores were more generous only under "positive" social influence.

There is also some suggestion of improvement in self-concept as a *result* of prosocial responses by older persons. The idea that helping benefits the helper (perhaps more than those who are helped) has been elucidated by Riessman (1976) in the "helper-therapy principle [p. 41]." He cites specific benefits for helpers that include feeling less dependent and more socially useful. Midlarsky and Kahana (1981a, 1981b) have recently proposed a similar conceptual model regarding prosocial behavior by the elderly. It emphasizes that helping by older persons may be a useful coping strategy in terms of adjustment during later life and predicts that older helpers should experience positive outcomes with regard to morale, competence, and self-esteem. Finally, in her interviews and participant observation with 50 older adults, Wentowski (1981) found that opportunities to engage in prosocial behavior (and, especially, to reciprocate for past favors done for oneself) were important for maintaining the older persons' helping networks as well as for preserving their self-esteem.

It is of interest to compare the self-perceptions of older persons concerning how they spend their time (including amount of time spent on prosocial activities) with the perception of the elderly by the general public. According to the L. Harris and Associates, Inc. (1975) survey, when asked how much time they spend at various activities, 27% of persons over 65 reported that they spend "a lot of time" caring for younger or older members of the family; 47% indicated spending a "lot of time" socializing with friends. These percentages agreed roughly with the percentage of the general public (aged 18–64) who described "most people over 65" as spending "a lot of time" caring for younger or older family members (23%) and socializing with friends (52%). However, the general public also viewed older persons as spending "a lot of time" watching television (67%), sitting and thinking

(62%), sleeping (39%), and just doing nothing (35%), whereas the actual percentage of persons 65 and over who reported spending ''a lot of time'' on these activities was approximately half of the general public perception of them.

Thus, although the general public does tend to agree with older persons regarding the social contributions of the latter, this picture may be overwhelmed by their more predominant view of the elderly as passive, inactive, and uninvolved. Although the public may indeed be laboring under an inaccurate stereotype, it is also the case that it may be difficult for older persons to admit that they spend ''a lot of time'' watching television or just doing nothing. Direct observation of their behavior would begin to clarify the discrepancy between perceptions of the general public and older persons themselves.

## The Older Person as Service Volunteer

Older persons may also engage in prosocial behavior by participating in volunteer service activities. In the Client Relations study described earlier, the mean age for the total sample ($N = 428$) was 43.6 years, whereas for volunteers ($N = 39$) it was 68.9 years (Petersen, 1981), suggesting that volunteers who provide services to the elderly tend to be older themselves. Payne (1977) cites estimates that 14–22% of those over 65 have done volunteer work recently and with some regularity. The L. Harris and Associates, Inc. (1975) report found voluntarism less frequent among those 80 and over (10%) than among those 65–69 years (28%) and 70–75 years (20%). An additional tenth of each of these three older age groups, however, indicated that, although they did not do volunteer work currently, they would like to. Older volunteers were most often found working in hospitals and clinics; in programs for the emotionally ill; as drivers for the aged, ill or handicapped; in programs giving away food, clothing, and other household items; in social support services such as friendly visiting to the homebound; and in family-, youth-, and children-oriented services such as programs for foster children.

Not only do some older persons volunteer, a substantial number of others endorse prosocial values and active involvement in community affairs. When asked what makes a useful member of one's community, three attributes were mentioned most often by those 65 and over (L. Harris and Associates, Inc., 1975): helping and serving others (50%); taking part in community activities, politics, and organizations (43%),; and being a good neighbor or citizen (34%). Interestingly, the self-perceptions of those 65 and over were predominantly positive, with 40% viewing themselves as very useful and 39% as somewhat useful members of their own community. In contrast, 18–64 years olds were less likely to view themselves as very useful (29%), and more likely to describe themselves as somewhat useful (55%), members of their communities.

What characterizes the older person who does volunteer? In the L. Harris and Associates, Inc. (1975) survey, older persons identified as volunteers included a disproportionately high number of high school and college graduates, employed persons, and persons with annual incomes greater than \$7,000. Sex differences were not great, however, with 23% of older women and 20% of older men reporting service as volunteers. Past participation patterns in organizations also distinguish older adult volunteers from nonvolunteers (Dye, Goodman, Roth, Bley, & Jensen, 1973). Among regular participants in the recreational program of a community center, those who also participated in the center's Volunteer Service Program had been more active in organizations in the past in terms of number of memberships, involvement in service-oriented organizations, and frequency of attendance at organization meetings. In addition to expressing a greater enjoyment derived from their participation in these past organizations, the volunteers had less free time available and fewer difficulties in finding activities to fill this time than the nonvolunteers. The two groups did not differ, however, with respect to their needs for succorance, nurturance, or affiliation.

Although the participation of older persons in volunteer work has been documented and some characteristics of older volunteers identified, only a few studies address the motivation for volunteering or its benefits to the older volunteer. In Ward's (1979) recent examination of the meaning of voluntary associations to individuals 60 and over, older persons who participated in any charity or volunteer work did not exhibit higher life satisfaction scores than those who did no charity or volunteer work. Nor did voluntary membership in groups per se appear to be motivated primarily by concern for others, although prosocial reasons were endorsed by some of the older respondents. When individuals who belonged to one or more groups were asked to choose three statements that best described their own reasons for joining groups, the two reasons regarding help to others ("I like it because I like to do things that will be of benefit to society" and "I get to help other people") ranked fifth and sixth, being chosen by 30% and 23%, respectively. (The most frequently endorsed reason [73%] was that group membership brought the older person into contact with friends.) Helping others was more often mentioned as a reason for group membership by group leaders, persons who participated in volunteer or charity work, and those who were involved in active group participation (e.g., discussions, shows, bazzaars, telephoning) rather than in social, recreational, and travel activities. Despite the connection between reported prosocial reasons for joining groups and participation in groups involved in helping others, endorsing the reason of helping others was not correlated with life satisfaction after controlling for health, income, education, and occupation.

In contrast, other research suggests the importance for the older person of a professed prosocial motivation. Fengler and Goodrich (1980) asked a small sample of older disabled men who had participated in a sheltered workshop program 1 year or more why they had done so. On a scale of 1–6 where 6 was "very important," three factors had an average rating over 5: getting out of the house ($\bar{X} = 5.2$); being with others ($\bar{X} = 5.1$); and being able to help others ($\bar{X} = 5.1$). Fengler and Goodrich suggested that volunteering provided the older disabled men with a new understanding of their own capabilities and usefulness. Monk and Cryns (1974) likewise proposed that doing things for others through volunteering may reflect successful resolution of Ericksen's proposed crisis of integrity versus despair during the last stage of the life cycle.

Payne (1977) based her theoretical approach to volunteering among the elderly on Kuypers and Bengtson's (1973) social reconstruction theory of aging, which holds that older persons' social competence and sense of worth are diminished insofar as society deprives them of useful roles. She emphasized that meaningful volunteer work can provide older persons with an opportunity to "restructure" their skills into age-appropriate roles, thereby providing some continuity in their social contributions as well as reducing their dependence on family members for social–psychological support. Using data from a sample of 68 men and women who volunteer one or more times a week to illustrate her model, she reported that those items on the Volunteer Satisfaction test receiving the highest level of endorsement were "thanks from the recipients for helping them" and "the personal satisfaction of helping others." A particularly interesting observation was that men, for whom the direct delivery of service was usually a new experience, found such direct service to people more satisfying than did women, who had typically been involved in more service delivery in the past. In contrast, women were adding dimensions to their volunteering by combining new instrumental roles with prior expressive service roles.

In order for volunteering by older persons to be classed as prosocial behavior, benefits to the recipients of the voluntary service must be demonstrated. Although such effects have rarely been studied, there are hints that they are substantial. For example, in an evaluation of a "foster grandparent" program in which impoverished elderly were employed part-time to provide personal relationships with institutionalized children (Saltz, 1973), it was found that the children so treated had significantly higher IQ scores than did children in a similar institution without the extra personal attention. These effects on IQ were interpreted as resulting from the affective quality of the interactions between the older persons and the children rather than from the increase in quantity of stimulation per se.

## Implications for Further Research

Although information is limited, pockets of research findings concerning prosocial behavior by older persons exist in the gerontological literatures on family and other social networks, inheritance transfers, and voluntarism. Prosocial behavior by older persons is rather well documented, but the antecedents, correlates, and outcomes of such behavior for either the older helper or the persons who are helped remain largely unexplored. Although some attempts at linking elderly morale or self-concept with cognitive variables such as altruistic attitudes or prosocial self-perceptions have demonstrated such connections (Mancini, 1980; Midlarsky & Kahana, 1981a), others have not (Ward, 1979), and relationships with actual prosocial behavior, only rarely assessed (Trimakis & Nicolay, 1974), remain unclarified. Nevertheless, an emphasis on the positive outcomes for older persons of active involvement in various kinds of prosocial behavior is apparent in recent theoretical conceptualizations regarding the elderly (Midlarsky & Kahana, 1981a, 1981b; Payne, 1977) and represents a needed antidote to a literature otherwise heavily weighted with references to older persons as recipients, rather than performers, of prosocial behavior.

## TOWARD A LIFE-SPAN PERSPECTIVE ON PROSOCIAL DEVELOPMENT

At the current time, there is no integrated conceptualization of prosocial behavior across the life span; neither existing theories nor empirical studies directly address the issue of the development of prosocial behavior in this larger sense. The literature reviewed earlier in this chapter does, however, point to critical questions to be posed in future life-span examinations of prosocial behavior. In this closing section we describe three important concerns such research would need to address: the definition and measurement of prosocial behavior; the development of prosocial behavior; and prosocial behavior in the future.

### The Definition and Measurement of Prosocial Behavior

At the forefront lies the important task of operationalizing the construct of prosocial behavior so as to allow for its examination across an individual's life span. Earlier in this chapter we borrowed Staub's (1978) definition of prosocial behavior as any behavior that benefits another person. Straightforward as this definition may seem, the specification of the domain of observable behaviors related to the construct of prosocial behavior, especially from a life-span perspective, is not a simple task. When one focuses on older adults either as perpetrators or recipients of prosocial behavior, the kinds of responses highlighted include helping and comforting during illness and disability, sharing material possessions, and providing various kinds of aid in volunteer settings. However, is the frequency of household help an adult child performs for an older parent conceptually comparable to the frequency with which a young child helps a parent with household tasks? Furthermore, in a three-generation family, is the comforting given by a middle-aged female qualitatively the same when the recipient is her college-aged child, her same-aged sibling, or her older parent? Does the pattern of correlations among various types of prosocial behavior (e.g., helping, sharing, comforting) change across the life span and/or differ for various birth cohorts? Answers to such questions will both clarify the meaning of prosocial behavior from a life-span perspective and aid in directing the longitudinal analysis of such behavior.

Furthermore, such investigations regarding the nature of prosocial behavior will aid in determining the dimensionality of positive social responses. Our review of caregiving for older adults suggests that there are at least two strong and distinct dimensions—one instrumental and the other affective—that must be measured if a complete picture of prosocial behavior is to be obtained. Although the instrumental aspects of prosocial behavior are well-studied by both developmental and social psychologists, the qualitative nature of the helping activities (what we have termed *the affective tone of the service encounter*) has received considerably less research attention. The verbal statements or nonverbal cues that accompany overt helping behavior in natural settings may convey to the recipient messages either congruent or dissonant with the instrumental help he or she is receiving. We know from the Client Relations study reviewed earlier, for example, that helping behaviors by formal caregivers may be accompanied by ''friendly'' verbal and nonverbal behaviors that are better predictors of the helper's attitudes about caregiving and the recipient's satisfaction with the service encounter than is the instrumental help itself. We strongly suspect that the qualitative nature, or affective tone, of service delivery will prove exceedingly important in an analysis of prosocial behavior in informal networks. However, direct evidence for this proposition, with reference either to the informal networks of older adults or of persons of other ages, is at present lacking.

Although the definition of prosocial behavior we are endorsing does not incorporate the prerequisite of altruistic intent, it does insist that a prosocial act produce benefits for the recipient. Such a requirement would then disqualify as prosocial a behavior such as that illustrated earlier in this chapter in the incident of bringing a pizza to an elderly grandmother. Evaluating the beneficial nature of a presumed prosocial act, however, is not simple and would be best accomplished by using multiple criteria, including, but not limited to, the reactions of the person served. Indeed, behaviors that are commonly assumed to be prosocial may produce both benefits and costs to the recipient; for example, an older person may temporarily benefit from an especially helpful service provider or relative, and yet this ''overservicing'' may foster a state of dependence that is actually deleterious to the older person. In addition, he or she may feel uncomfortable because of an inability to reciprocate for the services rendered. The ''mixed blessing'' involved in the receipt of aid (Fisher, DePaulo, & Nadler, 1981; Fisher, Nadler, & Whitcher-Alagna, 1982) seems to have special relevance where the recipients are older persons needing extensive care. To understand the underpinnings of the various reactions to being cared for at the end of one's life, developmental psychologists may want to begin to measure the costs as well as the benefits of prosocial behavior for recipients at all points of the life course.

## The Development of Prosocial Behavior

Our examination of prosocial behavior for and by older persons suggests several important issues concerning the development, from a life-span perspective, of positive social responses. We are struck, for example, with the rather profound gender difference that is apparent in the current social gerontological literature: Women are the primary caregivers for the older generation, which, because of gender differences in mortality, itself includes a larger proportion of women than men. Recent data involving a much younger cohort (present-day toddlers) hint that patterns of socialization that promote women as caregivers (and women as cared for) may not be limited to those cohorts that are presently studied by social gerontologists. Fagot (1978) found that parents give little girls more positive responses than little boys when they try to help adults with tasks as well as when they ask for help themselves. Boys' help, in contrast, is discouraged by parents, and their requests for help more likely to be met with negative responses. Whether the major role of women as caregivers to elderly relatives can be traced in part to childhood reinforcement patterns (which are, of course, subject to modification in succeeding generations) is the kind of question a life-span perspective on prosocial behavior would begin to answer.

The gender difference so prominent in the literature on prosocial behavior by and for the elderly is related to yet another important life-span issue: that of the stability of prosocial behavior. Stability questions can refer to intraindividual stability through time (e.g., "Did the elderly woman now caring for her neighbor show similar concern for her classmates as a schoolgirl?") or to the stability for a given group through time (e.g., "Does the frequency of prosocial behavior by women remain the same, increase, or decrease with age?"). Similar questions might be addressed regarding the stability of those cognitive processes (including the attitudes and self-perceptions discussed in this chapter) that may mediate the frequency of assistance as well as the quality of care provided to individuals in need. Questions such as those just posed necessitate longitudinal data from several cohorts for their resolution, and unfortunately such data do not presently exist.

The emphasis in the social gerontological literature on prosocial behavior for older persons calls attention to the need in life-span research for a focus on the recipient, as well as the performer, of positive social responses. Although some data are available on stimulus characteristics of persons who are more or less likely to be helped (see Staub, 1978, for a review), there is little systematic work on this topic and almost none that examines characteristics of help seekers of varying ages. In two of three recent field experiments, Weinberger (1981) found that older help seekers (in their 70s or 80s) were consistently more likely to be assisted by a stranger than were those adults who were middle-aged (in their 40s) or young (in their 20s). Based on findings from a fourth experiment, where judges rated pictures of young, middle-aged, and old help seekers, Weinberger concluded that the latter received more assistance because they were seen more negatively than young and middle-aged adults on physical dimensions (e.g., healthy, strong, rugged, fast) but more positively on dimensions having to do with personal approachability (e.g., friendly, relaxed, warm, safe, courteous). Further research should begin to clarify other characteristics of persons of various ages that increase the likelihood of their receiving help.

From a life-span perspective on the development of prosocial behavior, the help given by adult children to disabled aging parents is of particular interest. Baltes and Nesselroade (1979) have emphasized that the complexity of life-span development can only be accounted for by a multiple interactive causal system that includes three sets of influences: normative age-graded influences (e.g., biological maturation); normative history-graded influences (e.g., the 1930s economic depression in the United States); and nonnormative influences (e.g., divorce, death of a spouse). According to Baltes, Cornelius, and Nesselroade (1979), nonnormative influences on development may increase in relative importance in adulthood and old age and within cohorts would "tend to be the primary agents for producing interindividual differences in developmental change [p. 82]." We suggest here that having an older parent requiring extensive care is one of the critical nonnormative influences on prosocial development for many adults, at least in this country.

The prosocial behavior involved in caring for an aging parent may be considered from several theoretical perspectives. The relationships among family members have been characterized as "communal," in which benefits are bestowed in response to needs; such relationships are distinguished from "exchange" relationships, where benefits are given in expectation of receiving benefits in the future or in response to having obtained benefits in the past (Clark & Mills, 1979). However, exchange notions are often invoked by gerontologists to explain relationships among family members (e.g., Bengston & Cutler, 1976; Blau, 1973; Hendricks & Hendricks, 1981; Sussman, 1976; Wentowski, 1981; Williamson, Munley, & Evans, 1980). It has been suggested, for example, that there is an intrinsic and reciprocal relationship between parent caring and child rearing; that is, in parent caring the imbalance in the exchange of help that now favors the older parent is a kind of reversal of the earlier process whereby the parent had cared for the dependent infant and child (Cicerrelli, 1981). Although acceptance by both adult children and elderly parents of the dependency of the latter has been cited as an example of "filial maturity [p. 57]" (Blenkner, 1965), the evidence reviewed here of the considerable costs associated with provision of services to an aging parent (and the hints of costs as well as to the recipient of such care) suggests more of a "filial crisis" than a mature acceptance of the need for prosocial responses by all parties concerned.

On the other hand, we would predict that if the elderly parent has modeled mature filial behavior in relation to the adult child's grandparents, if the services to the older person are rendered in a manner we might characterize as "supportive companionship," if the older person is valued for his or her contributions however reduced they may be, then the probability of caregiving as "communal" behavior will be increased. Clearly, there are varying degrees between truly communal help and help that is given begrudgingly or not at all. From a life-span perspective, caring for parents at the end of their lives seems to us to be an especially fruitful arena for an examination of the styles and substance of naturally occurring prosocial behavior.

## The Future of Prosocial Behavior

Although important, a systematic analysis of the way in which prosocial behavior for and by older persons is linked to cohort and time-of-measurement factors has not been undertaken in this review. The birth cohort to which one belongs provides a common core of experiences (e.g., a world war, a period of economic depression, educational opportunities) that may in turn be related to prosocial attitudes and behaviors. Likewise, events connected with the time of measurement during which prosocial behaviors are assessed may influence the frequency and nature of that behavior for some portion of the population experiencing these time-of-measurement events, as, for example, when a study of helping behaviors is undertaken during a national crisis or natural disaster.

The needs of older persons for various kinds of help will inevitably continue in the future. Not only do older persons need help, but they also benefit from it, as illustrated by the reduced risk of institutionalization when family support exists. However, it is likely that changing societal characteristics, such as general economic conditions, increased female participation in the work force, and reduced fertility resulting in fewer children, are altering and will continue to alter the nature of caregiving options for older persons (E. Brody, 1981; Treas, 1977). Demographic data from the U.S. Bureau of the Census (1976) indicate that the aged dependency ratio (i.e., the ratio of the number of persons aged 65 and over to the number of persons of working age, 15–64 years) was .07 in 1900 and .18 in 1975 but is projected to be nearly .29 by 2030 when the "baby boom" generation will have moved into old age. It appears, then, that there will be a proportionately smaller class of workers who can contribute financially through private donations or through taxes to support formal helping programs for the elderly. Furthermore, fewer offspring will exist to provide care, and working women may find it more difficult to participate in the complete levels of care they have displayed in the past.

One might optimistically anticipate a greater sharing of caregiving tasks by men and women and perhaps, especially for men, a heightened sense of personal reward due to direct caregiving (such as Payne, 1977, found for her older male volunteers). One might look forward to an increase in prosocial behavior from friends, older volunteers, and family members other than children in order to meet the needs of the future elderly. Finally, one might hope that prosocial values will be expressed not only at the individual level, but also at the larger system level (Nikelly, 1981) and that public and private funding agencies will respond to the needs and preferences of older persons by allocating resources in a manner that preserves both the independence and self-esteem of the elderly.

## ACKNOWLEDGMENTS

We are grateful to Pat Archbold, John Bond, Leonard Cain, Nancy Chapman, Michael DeShane, Mary Driver Leinbach, Marilyn Petersen, and Richard Schulz for their comments and insights.

## REFERENCES

Archbold, P. G. Impact of parent-caring on women. Paper presented at the XII International Congress of Gerontology, Hamburg, July 1981.

Baltes, P. B., Cornelius, S. W., & Nesselrode, J. R. Cohort effects in developmental psychology. In J. R. Nesselroade & P. B. Baltes (Eds.), *Longitudinal research in the study of behavior and development.* New York: Academic Press, 1979.

Baltes, P. B., & Nesselroade, J. R. History and rationale of longitudinal research. In J. R. Nesselroade & P. B. Baltes (Eds.), *Longitudinal research in the study of behavior and development.* New York: Academic Press, 1979.

Beattie, W. M., Jr. Aging and the social services. In R. H. Binstock & E. Shanas (Eds.), *Handbook of aging and the social sciences.* New York: Van Nostrand–Reinhold, 1976.

Behn, J. D. An observational study of service provider/client dyadic interactions. Unpublished doctoral dissertation, Portland State University, 1980.

Bengtson, V. L., & Cutler, N. E. Generations and intergenerational relations: Perspectives on age groups and social change. In R. H. Binstock & E. Shanas (Eds.), *Handbook of aging and the social sciences.* New York: Van Nostrand–Reinhold, 1976.

Blenkner, M. Social work and family relationships in later life with some thoughts on filial maturity. In E. Shanas and G. Streib (Eds.), *Social structure and the family: Generational relations.* Englewood Cliffs, New Jersey: Prentice–Hall, 1965.

Blau, Z. S. *Old age in a changing society.* New York: Franklin Watts, 1973.

Brody, E. "Women in the middle" and family help to older people. *The Gerontologist,* 1981, *21,* 471–480.

Brody, S. J., Poulshock, S. W., & Masciocchi, C. F. The family caring unit: A major consideration in the long-term support system. *The Gerontologist,* 1978, *18,* 556–561.

Cantor, M. H. Neighbors and friends: An overlooked resource in the informal support system. *Research on Aging,* 1979, *1,* 434–463.

Cicirelli, V. G. *Helping elderly parents: The role of adult children.* Boston: Auburn House, 1981.

Clark, M. S., & Mills, J. Interpersonal attraction in exchange and communal relationships. *Journal of Personality and Social Psychology,* 1979, *37,* 12–24.

Creecy, R. F., & Wright, R. Morale and informal activity with friends among black and white elderly. *The Gerontologist,* 1979, *19,* 544–547.

Crossman, L., London, C., & Barry, C. Older women caring for disabled spouses: A model for supportive services. *The Gerontologist,* 1981, *21,* 464–470.

Dye, D., Goodman, M., Roth, W., Bley, N., & Jenson, K. The older adult volunteer compared to the nonvolunteer. *The Gerontologist,* 1973, *13,* 215–218.

Edwards, J., & Klemmack, D. Correlates of life satisfaction: A re-examination. *Journal of Gerontology,* 1973, *28,* 484–492.

Estes, C. L. *The aging enterprise.* San Francisco: Jossey–Bass, 1979.

Fagot, B. The influence of sex of child on parental reactions to toddler children. *Child Development,* 1978, *49,* 459–465.

Fengler, A. P., & Goodrich, N. Money isn't everything: Opportunities for elderly handicapped men in a sheltered workshop. *The Gerontologist,* 1980, *20,* 636–641.

Fisher, J. D., DePaulo, B. M., & Nadler, A. Extending altruism beyond the altruistic act: The mixed effects of aid on the help recipient. In J. P. Rushton & R. M. Sorrentino (Eds.), *Altruism and helping behavior.* Hillsdale, N.J.: Erlbaum, 1981.

Fisher, J. D., Nadler, A., & Whitcher-Alagna, S. Recipient reactions to aid. *Psychological Bulletin,* 1982, *91,* 27–54.

Froland, C., Pancoast, D. L., Chapman, N. J., & Kimboko, P. J. *Helping networks and human services.* Beverly Hills: Sage, 1981.

Glasscote, R., Beigel, A., Butterfield, A., Jr., Clark, E., Cox, B., Elpers, R., Gudeman, J. E., Gurel,

L., Lewis, R., Miles, D., Raybin, J., Reifler, C., & Vito, E. *Old folks at homes: A field study of nursing and board-and-care homes*. Washington, D.C.: American Psychiatric Association, 1976.

L. Harris, & Associates, Inc. *The myth and reality of aging in America*. Washington, D.C.: The National Council on the Aging, 1975.

Hendricks, J., & Hendricks, C. D. *Aging in mass society: Myths and realities* (2nd ed.). Cambridge, Mass.: Winthrop, 1981.

Hess, B. B., & Waring, J. M. Parent and child in later life: Rethinking the relationship. In R. M. Lerner & G. B. Spanier (Eds.), *Child influences on marital and family interaction: A life-span perspective*. New York: Academic Press, 1978.

Horowitz, A. Sons and daughters as caregivers to older parents: Differences in role performance and consequences. Paper presented at the meeting of the Gerontological Society of America, Toronto, November 1981.

Horowitz, A., & Shindelman, L. The impact of caring for an elderly relative. Paper presented at the meeting of the Gerontological Society of America, San Diego, November 1980.

Kalish, R. A. Death and dying in a social context. In R. H. Binstock & E. Shanas (Eds.), *Handbook of aging and the social sciences*. New York: Van Nostrand Reinhold, 1976.

Koff, T. H. *Hospice: A caring community*. Cambridge, Mass.: Winthrop, 1980.

Kuypers, J. A., & Bengtson, V. L. Social breakdown and competence: A model of normal aging. *Human Development*, 1973, *16*, 181–201.

Larson, R. Thirty years of research on the subjective well-being of older Americans. *Journal of Gerontology*, 1978, *33*, 109–125.

Lee, G. R. Children and the elderly: Interaction and morale. *Research on Aging*, 1979, *1*, 335–360.

Lee, G. R., & Ihinger-Tallman, M. Sibling interaction and morale: The effects of family relations on older people. *Research on Aging*, 1980, *2*, 367–391.

Lowenthal, M. F., & Robinson, B. Social networks and isolation. In R. H. Binstock & E. Shanas (Eds.), *Handbook of aging and the social sciences*. New York: Van Nostrand Reinhold, 1976.

Lurie, E. E. Formal and informal supports in the post-hospital period. Paper presented at the meeting of the Gerontological Society of America, Toronto, October 1981.

Mancini, J. A. Friend interaction, competence, and morale in old age. *Research on Aging*, 1980, *2*, 416–431.

Masciocchi, C., Patrizi, P., & Brody, S. J. Limitations of surveys in explaining placement and disability of elderly. *The Gerontologist*, 1981, *21*, 139. (Abstract)

Midlarsky, E., & Kahana, E. Altruism and helping among the elderly: An alternative to helplessness? Paper presented at the meeting of the American Psychological Association, Los Angeles, August 1981. (a)

Midlarsky, E., & Kahana, E. Altruism in the aged: An alternative to helplessness. *The Gerontologist*, 1981, *21*, 218–219. (Abstract) (b)

Monk, A., & Cryns, A. G. Predictors of voluntaristic intent among the aged. *The Gerontologist*, 1974, *14*, 425–429.

Nikelly, A. Society and psychology: A contradiction of goals. *APA Monitor*, 1981, *12*, 16.

Payne, B. P. The older volunteer: Social role continuity and development. *The Gerontologist*, 1977, *17*, 355–361.

Petersen, M. The assessment of service provider attitudes toward older clients in an urban social service system. Unpublished doctoral dissertation, Portland State University, 1981.

Riessman, F. How does self-help work? *Social Policy*, 1976, *7*, 41–45.

Robinson, B., & Thurnher, M. Taking care of aged parents: A family cycle transition. *The Gerontologist*, 1979, *19*, 586–593.

Rosenfeld, J. P. Bequests from resident to resident: Inheritance in a retirement community. *The Gerontologist*, 1979, *19*, 594–600.

Saltz, R. Effects of part time "mothering" on IQ and SQ of young institutionalized children. *Child Development*, 1973, *9*, 166–170.

Schulz, R. Effects of control and predictability on the physical and psychological well-being of the institutionalized aged. *Journal of Personality and Social Psychology,* 1976, *33,* 563–573.

Schulz, R. *The psychology of death, dying, and bereavement.* Reading, Mass.: Addison–Wesley, 1978.

Schulz, R., & Hanusa, B. H. Long-term effects of control and predictability-enhancing interventions: Findings and ethical issues. *Journal of Personality and Social Psychology,* 1978, *36,* 1194–1201.

Shanas, E. The family and social class. In E. Shanas, P. Townsend, D. Wedderburn, H. Friis, P. Milhøj, & J. Stehouwer, *Old people in three industrial societies.* New York: Atherton Press, 1968.

Shanas, E. The family as a social support system in old age. *The Gerontologist,* 1979, *19,* 169–174.

Shanas, E. Older people and their families: The new pioneers. *Journal of Marriage and the Family,* 1980, *42,* 9–15.

Staub, E. *Positive social behavior and morality* (Vol. 1). New York: Academic Press, 1978.

Stewart, B. J., Petersen, M., & Behn, J. D. Service provider attitudes as predictors of provider and older client behavior in a service delivery encounter. Unpublished research, Portland State University, 1981.

Stewart, B. J., Petersen, M., & Behm, J. D. Service provider attitudes as predictors of provider and older client behavior in a service delivery encounter. Unpublished research, Portland State University, 1981.

Sussman, M. B. The family life of old people. In R. H. Binstock & E. Shanas (Eds.), *Handbook of aging and the social sciences.* New York: Van Nostrand–Reinhold, 1976.

Tissue, R. An analysis of environmental, social and personal dimensions and their relationship to psychological well-being in late life. Unpublished doctoral dissertation, Portland State University, 1981.

Tobin, S. S., & Lieberman, M. A. *Last home for the aged.* San Francisco: Jossey–Bass, 1976.

Treas, J. Family support systems for the aged: Some social and demographic considerations. *The Gerontologist,* 1977, *17,* 487–491.

Trimakis, K. A., & Nicolay, R. C. Self-concept and altruism in old age. *Journal of Gerontology,* 1974, *29,* 434–439.

Troll, L. E. The family of later life: A decade review. *Journal of Marriage and the Family,* 1971, *33,* 263–290.

U.S. Bureau of the Census. *Demographic aspects of aging and the older population in the United States.* (Current Population Reports, Series P-23, No. 59). Washington, D.C.: U.S. Government Printing Office, 1976.

Ward, R. A. The meaning of voluntary association participation to older people. *Journal of Gerontology,* 1979, *34,* 438–445.

Weeks, J. R., & Cuellar, J. B. The role of family members in the helping networks of older people. *The Gerontologist,* 1981, *21,* 388–394.

Weinberger, A. Responses to old people who ask for help. *Research on Aging,* 1981, *3,* 345–368.

Wentowski, G. J. Reciprocity and the coping strategies of older people: Cultural dimensions of network building. *The Gerontologist,* 1981, *21,* 600–609.

White, D., & Wagner, D. Selected case histories from three outcome groups: Deceased, institutionalized, and continued self-maintenance. In J. E. O'Brien & R. Alexander (Eds.), *A longitudinal study of a high-risk urban elderly population: An analysis of the environmental, social, economic and personal aspects of everyday life.* Final report for Social Security Administration Contract SSA-PMB-74-275, 1978.

Williamson, J. B., Munley, A., & Evans, L. *Aging and society: An introduction to social gerontology.* New York: Holt, 1980.

Zarit, S. H., Reever, K. E., & Bach-Peterson, J. Relatives of the impaired elderly: Correlates of feelings of burden. *The Gerontologist,* 1980, *20,* 649–655.

# Commentary and Critique: Applied Approaches to Prosocial Development

**DENNIS KREBS**

There is a feeling of tragedy in the Graveses' description of the westernization of the people of Aitutaki. It is as though the original splendor of these island people has been corrupted by the modern world. Indeed, the Graveses outline of a program to set up cooperative learning environments in the United States and New Zealand patterned after the prosocial environment of traditional Aitutaki.

The authors of Chapter 11 share the Graveses sense of dismay about the decline of prosocial behavior in the Western world. Brown and Solomon suggest that the youth of America is becoming increasingly selfish, irresponsible, and immoral, and they too set out to develop a program to combat these trends. To this end, Dyke Brown spent a year investigating the relevant research literature on the development of prosocial behavior. The first part of Chapter 11 describes, in point form, the results of this investigation. These findings are valuable in two respects: (*a*) in their capacity to stimulate thought about a wide variety of issues associated with the development of prosocial behavior; and (*b*) as a source of ideas for those who seek to develop interventions designed to foster the growth of prosocial behavior.

Some of Brown's findings support points made in earlier chapters of the present volume: Prosocial dispositions mainfest themselves early in the lives of infants; role-taking is an important determinant of some kinds of prosocial behavior; adults can influence the behavior of children through exhortation and modeling; giving children responsibility for the care of others fosters prosocial development; and the structure of the family and culture may guide the course of children's social development. Other conclusions reached by Brown, however, run counter to positions advanced in the present volume. For example, Campbell and Trivers would not

THE NATURE OF PROSOCIAL DEVELOPMENT

concur that "a person's character is primarily shaped by culture;" rather, they would argue that biological and cultural factors are inseparable in the determination of character; and the results of Sibulkin's study call into question the assumption that children do not possess prosocial values.

Before considering the program derived in part from Dyke Brown's findings, I would like to issue a number of general cautions about the development and implementation of intervention programs. First, I believe that it is important to establish clearly that a program is needed. In the present case the program is intended to combat an ostensible "decline in standards and values, an increase in self-centeredness and self-indulgence and an insufficient sense of social responsibility" in American children. However, Brown acknowledges in a footnote that he has "not seen any validating empirical research" to support the assumption that this state of affairs exists. When I compare the behavior of my daughters and their friends to the behavior of my friends and me when we were in high school, the younger generation doesn't really fare that poorly.

Second, one might well question the negative value attached to Western individualism. I do not want to go on record as promoting selfishness—altruism is one of the qualities I value most in people; however, the work of both the anthropologists and sociobiologists who have contributed to this volume shows that individuals in various social systems develop patterns of behavior that are adaptive—culturally and biologically. The type of prosocial cooperation that characterizes societies such as traditional Aitutaki may be dysfunctional in Western society. To quote Dyke Brown, we must be careful not to cultivate "a prosocial, caring person (who is) unable to function effectively in our society, a kind of well-meaning, but incompentent 'do-gooder'." The onus is on the intervener to identify clearly the costs involved in individualism and to demonstrate that these costs can be reduced through more prosocial systems. Research such as that of Aronson, Bridgeman, and Geffer (1978), showing that cooperative "jigsaw" classrooms promote efficient learning and high self-esteem in students, supplies a good model.

A third general point that should be raised about the recommendations for socialization made in Chapter 11 relates to the type of prosocial behavior the authors seek to cultivate. For example, should we teach our children to put the interest of others before their own, or should we teach them that the most effective way of promoting their own interest is, in a manner outlined by Campbell and Trivers at a biological level, by forming networks of cooperation and reciprocity? The research summarized by Dyke Brown favors the latter; however the matter is more complex than a life-style polarity between selfishness and altruism, competition and cooperation. Each of these modes of interaction is adaptive in particular circumstances. When you are running a relay race, you had better be prepared to cooperate; however, when running the 100-yard dash, you have little choice but to go it alone.

To summarize the orienting points I have been attempting to make: first, We must be careful not to assume that there is a problem where no problem exists. Second, if we establish that there is a problem, we should recognize that it may have developed for a purpose. And third, in an effort to implement improvements, we should take care not to deprive the individuals in an adequately functioning system of the resources they need to cope. Of course, we have to start somewhere. One clear value of the projects proposed by the Graveses and by Brown and Solomon lies in their capacity to advance our knowledge about the effects of various systems of learning. If the effects of the interventions are desirable, they may supply a model for implementing wide-scale salutary social change.

The project outlined by Daniel Solomon has a number of laudatory features. The project seeks to "achieve an effective balance between acting on behalf of others and acting on behalf of self," thus implicitly acknowledging the dangers of dysfunctional altruism. There is a recognition that long-term changes in behaviour must be mediated by deep-seated changes in internal cognitive, motivational, and emotional factors. The investigators recognize that prosocial behavior results from an interaction between internal, person-specific processes and characteristics of situations (see Krebs & Miller, in press). Unlike the transitory interventions imposed by most experimental research, the interventions involved in the project described by Solomon are "long-term and comprehensive." If you want to change childrens' social *orientation* in a significant way, you must be prepared to implement a massive change in their lives. Particularly impressive in this respect is the length of the intervention (5 years), the number of children involved, and the changes implemented in both home and school environments (in and out of the classroom).

Finally, although some of the interventions that will be employed are still somewhat tentative pending confrontation with the practical limitations the program is bound to encounter, the types of intervention that are included have been derived from the most promising research—the sort of role-related helping described by B. Whiting and N. and T. Graves in Chapters 9 and 10; the cooperative groups that have proven successful in the research of Aronson *et al.* (1978) and Bridgeman (1981); modeling; training in role-taking and empathy; and induction.

The focus of the content of Chapter 11 is on the independent variables that foster prosocial development. Although this focus is understandable in the early stages, the investigators ultimately will have to come to terms with the difficulties in evaluating outcomes. The 2 hr per year allocated for experimental testing of each child may not be enough. Interviews are notoriously susceptible to a variety of confounds. Although the natural behavior of the children undoubtedly supplies the most valid indication of the effect of the interventions, reliable coding systems will have to be developed or adapted for this purpose. It is difficult to see how "prosocial motives and values, related cognitive skills and perceptions, social understanding and empathy" can be assessed adequately during 1 hr of interviewing each year, and, as indicated in the commentary following Section II, there are a number of difficulties with existing tests of role-taking.

By way of conclusion, it should be emphasized that no study of this magnitude has ever been launched in the investigation of prosocial behavior, and, in view of the multiplicity of methods and range of interventions, the prognosis for large-scale change seems quite positive indeed. If conducted with appropriate care, this program undoubtedly will serve as a model for others in the future.

The final chapter in this volume, coauthored by Barbara Stewart and Cathleen Smith, supplies an appropriate summary, integration, and extension of the ideas and observations presented in several of the earlier chapters. In a nicely symmetrical way, this chapter is organized around what family and friends, on the one hand, and service providers, on the other, can do for the elderly, and what the elderly can do in return.

The approach described by Stewart and Smith in Chapter 12 and the approach described in the earlier chapters on cross-cultural research have a great deal in common. In both types of investigation the structure of helping behavior in social systems as a whole is examined. In both cases systems of helping embedded in networks of social relations are of interest, as opposed, for example, to specific responses to specific experimental manipulations. Interestingly, the approaches adopted in these two sets of investigation give rise to quite similar findings—in particular, findings relating to the significance of familial role relations and the disproportionate amount of assistance rendered by females. The central differences between the two approaches stem from the absence of a comparison culture and the almost exclusive reliance on interview data in research on the elderly.

It is interesting to note that whereas prosocial behavior tends to be institutionalized almost exclusively in sex roles and family and community relations in nonindustrial societies, it tends in addition to be institutionalized on a societal level in America. In industrialized social systems, specialized professional helpers supplement the informal systems of assistance. Stewart and Smith describe a set of investigations on one such professional helping role—"service provider" to the elderly. The results demonstrate clearly the value of distinguishing between social roles and the individuals who occupy them. A measure of the attitudes of service workers did not correlate significantly with role-related helping behavior—the individuals in question behaved in a manner appropriate to their role, regardless of how they felt about the elderly. Indeed, service workers who disliked particular clients appeared to bend over backward to behave attentively toward them. However, when it came to the style with which the services were delivered, the workers with the more positive attitudes adopted a significantly more positive affective tone.

The evidence presented by Stewart and Smith showing that offspring perform a great deal of service for their elderly parents is, on the face of it, somewhat problematic for sociobiological theory. If the ultimate reason why parents help children is in order to propagate replicas of their genes, why should children help parents who are no longer able to propagate their genes? Natural selection is a merciless process. Inasmuch as it affects the disposition to help others, it would seem that it should lead to the extinction of the disposition to assist those who can no longer enhance the helper's genetic fitness.

Faced with evidence of genetically nonadaptive assistance to the elderly, a sociobiologist might offer one (or more) of three types of explanation. He or she might (a) argue, as Campbell does about altruism in general, that helping the elderly is a culturally induced behavior that runs counter to biologically based selfishness; (b) establish that this type of assistance is reinforced through reciprocity; or (c) demonstrate that it is anomalous—an overgeneralization from behavior that was adaptive in our evolutionary past (see the commentary following Section I).

The first alternative will appeal to most. It corresponds most closely to the sense we have of responsibility for the aged, and it endows the helping rendered with the most dignity. However, there also is some support in Chapter 12 for the second defense, namely, that biologically based dispositions to assist the elderly developed and are preserved through reciprocity. As Stewart and Smith show, the elderly make more contributions to the younger generations than is commonly assumed—they give gifts, help care for their sons and daughters when they are ill, babysit their grandchildren, and render financial assistance. Indeed, there seems to be a disheartening tendency for offspring to develop increasingly negative feelings toward their elderly parents as the parents reach an age where they are less and less able to reciprocate. But, of course, the elderly often have an ultimate ace in the hole: control over their wills. It is interesting, from a sociobiological perspective, to note the extent to which individuals tend to pass on their money to those to whom they have passed on their genes (although, as revealed by Stewart and Smith, there are some signs that this is beginning to change). In addition, there appears to be a positive relationship between the amount of assistance rendered by an offspring and the amount of money bequeathed to him or her.

Another notable finding reported by Stewart and Smith is that the elderly who receive the most assistance tend to feel the worst about themselves. This trend, of course, could reflect the tendency for those who receive the most help to need the most help; however it also could reflect both a tendency for helpers to begrudge unreciprocated assistance and reluctance on the part of the elderly to accept it.

Although there is something distasteful about the notion that individuals help mainly or only when it pays off for them in return, reciprocal helping is, in many respects, more dignified than more pure altruism. Research on recipients' reactions to assistance (see Fisher, Nadler, & Whitcher-Alagna, 1982) demonstrates that helping others may be a somewhat sinister way of cementing your power over them, cultivating dependency, and elevating your status. One of the problems with altruism as a principle of morality is that giving others more than their share and doing favors that cannot be repaid is intrinsically inequitable (see Krebs, 1982). What recipients gain in material benefits, they often pay for in self-respect. Helping people who can help themselves and rendering assistance that cannot be reciprocated is, in some contexts, among the most demeaning of activities. This principle applies not only to the elderly, but also to children and adults, and members of the opposite sex. Our children teach us to stop doing things for them, especially during the second year of their lives and during puberty. They do not want help; they want independence. Feminists are teaching us that doing things for women may be a subtle way of preserving the masculine advantage in interpersonal relations. As Stewart and Smith point out, one of the most salutary things you can do for the elderly is to preserve their opportunity to continue making contributions to family and society and to give them ample opportunity to reciprocate the help they receive.

## REFERENCES

Aronson, E., Bridgeman, D., & Geffer, R. Interdependent interactions and prosocial behavior. *Journal of Research and Development in Education,* 1978, *12,* 16–27.

Bridgeman, D. L. Enhanced role taking through cooperative interdependence: A field study. *Child Development,* 1981, *52,* 1231–1238.

Fisher, J. D., Nadler, A., & Whitcher-Alagna, S. Recipient reactions to aid. *Psychological Bulletin,* 1982, *91,* 27–54.

Krebs, D. L. Prosocial behavior, equity, and justice. In J. Greenberg & R. L. Cohen (Eds.), *Equity and justice in social behavior.* New York: Academic Press, 1982.

Krebs, D. L., & Miller, D. Altruism and aggression. In G. Lindzey & E. Aronson (Eds.), *The handbook of social psychology* (3rd ed.). Reading, Mass.: Addison–Wesley, in press.

# Afterword

**DENNIS KREBS**

The central goal of this volume is to offer an interdisciplinary perspective on prosocial behavior by juxtaposing chapters from a variety of disciplines. One of the values of such an arrangement is its capacity to feature the strengths and limitations of the methods of investigation employed in different areas of specialization. Because the preponderance of research on prosocial behavior is experimental in nature, chapters exemplifying the limitations of this approach are particularly useful.

Foremost among the limitations of the experimental approach is the necessity of extracting behaviors from their natural context. Observing individuals naturalistically makes it clear that most of the prosocial behaviors in which they engage are inextricably bound with the context in which the behaviors occur. Bridgeman found that the context in which interactions between parents and children occur exert a significant influence on the form of their prosocial behavior. The Graveses insist that we must consider individuals "as *inseparable* parts of their social group," and they quote Kanfer who notes that an ecological or systems approach "requires that the person be viewed at the psychological level as a component of the complex system of which he or she is a part." The authors of Section IV attend in a variety of ways to the significance of the national, academic, community, and home contexts that support and inhibit altruistic behavior.

In addition to the intrinsic limitations of the experimental approach, there are a number of problems with the way in which it is customarily employed to investigate prosocial behavior. First, the use of operational definitions has tended to discourage the pursuit of the kind of conceptual clarification of the construct implicit in the writings of Campbell and Puka. Clearly, the same type of behavior—donating to charity, for example—may stem from a wide variety of motives and may serve any number of purposes, and, equally clearly, the motives and purposes of an act contribute significantly to its conceptual status. Few observers would be willing to endow an act of donating to charity with the label ''altruistic'' when its purpose was to reduce income taxes or create a false impression.

Second, experimental research on prosocial behavior has tended to employ conveniently located subject samples, especially students. The extension of subject samples to nonhuman animals, babies, the children of other cultures, and the elderly in various chapters of this volume is refreshing.

Third, in almost all experimental research the prosocial behaviors that are assessed are directed toward strangers. Implicit in the sociobiological, developmental, anthropological, and geriatric chapters of this volume is the observation that the preponderance of prosocial behavior in all societies is directed toward members of one's family.

It is interesting to note that the prosocial behavior of parents toward children has evoked little attention in the chapters of this volume, even though, according to evolutionary theory, it should be the most powerful and deeply ingrained of all types. Apparently, it is so common and obvious that we take it for granted. What is featured in both the developmental and geriatric research is the (reciprocal) helping that very young children and middle-aged adults bestow on their parents. This type of helping is significant because, although directed toward relatives, it does not obviously foster inclusive fitness, and, therefore, is not supported by biologically based dispositions in the same way as parent–offspring helping. Trivers has published an insightful analysis of the sociobiology of sibling conflict, but no one, to my knowledge, has explored offspring–parent helping in the same manner.

A final limitation of experimental research on prosocial behavior is the rather constricted domain of responses examined. The types of prosocial behavior that have been most thoroughly investigated (donating to charity, bystander intervention) are quite unrepresentative of the types of prosocial behavior in which most people engage in their everyday lives. The studies on babies in their homes, the cross-cultural research, and the research on the elderly supply more ecologically valid samples of behavior.

In drawing attention to the limitations of experimental research on prosocial behavior, I do not want to imply that they cannot be counteracted or that the experimental approach is without merit. As indicated in the cross-cultural research of the Graveses, experimental measures may well supplement naturalistic observations, and, holistic systems approaches are not well-equipped to specify the components of systems that exert the most significant causal effects. Considering the complementarity between experimental and ecological approaches, it would seem most sensible to begin with the latter, sketching out in broad strokes the domain to be investigated, and to follow it up by specifying the details in selected areas with the former. It is interesting that, in the field of psychology, the opposite trend has occurred.

Viewing prosocial behavior in terms of the systems of which it is a part supplies a useful perspective on two of the most contentious issues in the history of social thought—the relationship between the person and the situation and the relationship between nature and nurture. As concerns the former, the sociobiological, naturalistic, cross-cultural, and survey research contained in this volume demonstrates the reciprocal and dynamic nature of the interaction between people and situations. Individuals react to the demands of situations (as is so clearly demonstrated in experimental research) and also select, influence, and construe situations in terms of their inner qualities, especially their cognitive, information-processing abilities. As demonstrated by Smith, Leinbach, Stewart, and Blackwell in Chapter 5 and Smetana, Bridgeman, and Turiel in Chapter 7, developmental differences in cognitive abilities such as perspective-taking and conventional reasoning give rise to significantly different interpretations or constructions of situations, and these differences in turn mediate differences in the form of their prosocial behavior.

Viewing individuals as parts of ecological and social systems leads to a recognition of the interacting influence of nature and nurture on both altruistic and selfish behaviors. One of the central impetuses to sociobiological thought has been to explain the evolution of apparently altruistic behaviors. From the sociobiological perspective, environments interact with organisms to select adaptive behaviors. Although sociobiologists differ in their acceptance of the notion that humans are capable of "pure" altruism, there is a great degree of consensus about the notion that because both prosocial and selfish behaviors are adaptive in the human species, humans have inherited dispositions toward both types of behavior. The observations of babies reported by Bridgeman and the cross-cultural research reported by the Graves is consistent with the notion that infants are both altruistic and selfish, prosocial and antisocial by nature or, more exactly, that infants inherit the capacity to behave either prosocially and antisocially depending on the context.

Although sociobiologists feature the significance of genetically based dispositions, it is quite clear that culture plays a significant role in determining which dispositions are evoked, when, and in what form. Original sin theories emphasize the conflict between biology and culture. The thrust of the research reviewed here, however, is to feature the complementarity between genetic and environmental factors. Individuals inherit dispositions to reciprocate, and cultures preach reciprocity. The underlying reason is fundamentally the same—reciprocity is adaptive, both biologically and culturally.

The chapters in Section II supply an overview of the means through which children become enculturated or "socialized." Two quite different models of socialization are featured. On the one hand, evidence is presented that children can be induced to behave prosocially from the outside—through rewards and punishments, exhortation, and modeling. In this view, the task of socializing agents is to train children to behave in a socially acceptable manner—perhaps, in Hobbes's words, to "curb the recurrent barbarian invasion" from each new generation. On the other hand, studies show that children possess a natural tendency to understand and structure their social worlds; thus, in effect, they socialize themselves. The development of role-taking ability, moral development, the development of the ability to understand conventions pave the way for the formation of increasingly organized and adaptive networks of social relations. The extent of the human proclivity to understand behavior and perfect systems of interaction is aptly demonstrated in the philosophical thought of Puka in Chapter 8. Indeed, children can be viewed as rather naive philosophers, each implicitly working on his or her theory of altruism and morality.

Presented in this volume is a wealth of data and a host of ideas. I have commented on some of them, but have developed only a few of the many possibilities. In a sense, the central goal of the volume becomes assessible only after the last word has been read. The opportunities for analysis and synthesis, comparison and contrast, are virtually limitless. The authors of the chapters have put together packages of ideas. It is up to the reader to arrange and rearrange their contents in the ways that he or she finds most meaningful.

# Subject Index

## A

Action units, 249
Activity level, 152–154, 159
Adolescence, 273, 292
Affection, 75, 78, 86
Affective perspective-taking, *see* Perspective-taking
Affiliative behavior, 157
Agape, *see* Love
Age
  and caretaking experience, 224
  and exhortation, 126–127
  and nurturant behavior, 232–233
  and prosocial behavior, 166
Age-grading, *see* Same-age groupings
Aggression, 52, 74, 91, 152–154, 276, 282, 286
  moralistic, *see* Moralistic aggression
Aggressive dominance, 233
Agonistic mands, 228, 232, 236, 240
Altruism, 5, 27, 91, 95, 110, 140, 163–165, 214, 249, 253, 276
  acquisition of, 5
  coercive, *see* Altruism, forced
  definition of, 61, 163–164
  in dolphins and whales, 53–57

familial, 13
forced, 65, 189
frequency of, 43
hard-core, 15, 64, 65
kin-directed, 43, 47
and liking, 46
motivation for, 5, 187–188
reciprocal, *see* Reciprocal altruism
reparative, 47
self-sacrificial, *see* Self-sacrifice
soft-core, 15, 65
sources of, 185–186
strong, 15, 16, 17, 65
weak, 15, 65
Altruistic acts, defined, 43
Altruistic trait, 12, 15
Ants, 16, 17, 20, 32, 37
Approval, desire for, 145, 159, 225
Area Agencies on Aging (AAA), 320
Aronson, E., 285, 342, 343
Assertiveness, 152–154, 159
Assistance, 53–54
Attachment, 2, 280, 313
Attending, 322
Attribution theory, 30, 64
Augustine, 36, 67
Authoritativeness, 281

Free-rider problem, 13, 22
Freud, S., 90–91, 107, 110
Friendliness, 2, 75
Friendly behavior, 322–325, 334
Friendship, 46, 155–157, 180

# G

Games
    cooperative, 79–80, 86, 89
    of infants, 79–80, 86, 87
    structure of, 79–80
    theory of, 5, 21–23
Geffner, R., 285
Gender constancy, 223
Gender differences, *see* Prosocial behavior, gender differences in
Generosity, 125, 127, 140–141, 157, 168, 254–260, 268, 276, *see also* Sharing
Genetic assimilation, 24
Gestures, 76–77, *see also* Nonverbal behavior
Good, concept of, 185, 198, 200, 214–216
Governmental power, 192–193
Gratitude, 5, 46–47
Graves, N. and T., 266–269, 341, 347, 348
Group orientation, 246, 247, 260
Group selection, 12, 13, 21
Guilt, 5, 47, 91, 107, 313

# H

Haldane, J. B. S., 12, 21
Hay, D., 205, 207
Helpers at the nest, 52–53
Helping, 2, 3, 4, 5, 83–85, 97, 100, 108, 116, 128–133, 141, 157, 166, 178–181, 206, 274, 282, 284, 300
    forms of, 53–54
    by friends, 315
    by infants, 83–85, 88, 206
    moral obligation for, 164–168, 181
    by older persons, 327–337
    predictors of, 313–314
    suppression of, 256
Heroism, 190–191
Hewlett Foundation, 273, 274, 292
Home health agency, 311, 320–327
Hospitality, 258
Household tasks, 3, 83–85, 88, 89, 207, 237–238, 252–254, 259, 266, 267, 290
Human life, value of, 190

Hunter–gatherers, 45
Hypocrisy, 30, 36

# I

Ignoring, 324
Imitation, 4, 33, 89, 98, 99, 231
Immorality, 192
Inclusive fitness, 12, 13, 19, 20, 26, 29–32, 36, 53
Incongruities, 115–116, 118–120, 208
Individualism, 245, 246, 253, 259, 261
Individual selection, 12, 13
Induction, 123, 300–302
Inductive statements, 3, 123–133, 210
Industrialized societies, 3, 243, 246, 267
Infants and nurturance, 231, 239
Inference, 208
In-group membership, 33–35, 36, 66
Initiation of interactions, 80–81
Insects, 12–14, 16–21, 27, 32, 62, 65, *see also* specific insects
Institute on Aging, 309, 321
Institutionalization, 311–312, 314, 315, 318
Instrumental tasks, 312–313
Instrumentality, 108
Integrity, 332
Intelligence, 55, 63, 332
Intentionality, *see* Purposefulness of behavior
Interaction with young children, 230–231
Interdependence, 251, 260
Interrupting, 322–325
Intersubjectivity, 108
Intervention strategies, 117–120
Intuition, 239
Isaacs, S., 106

# J

Jackdaws, 16
Jays, 14, 16
Jigsaw classes, *see* Cooperative learning
Justice, 4, 5, 47, 172, 174, 177, 187, 214–215, *see also* Fairness
    and morality, 189–195, 214–215
    motivations for, 187

# K

Kagan, J., 277, 280, 283–284
Kant, I., 188, 189

Stewart, B., 343–345
Stimulation, 225, 232
Stranger, response to, 75
Stress, 314, 318
Structured demes, 11, 12, 14, 17, 26, 37, 65
Subsistence economies, 3, 244, 246, 248
Superstitious belief, 25
Support, 53–54, 206, 225
Supportive statements, 322–325
Support systems, 310–327
   formal, 320–327
   informal, 310–320, 321
Sympathy, 5, 46–47, 97, 100, 206

**T**

Task performance, 223
Teachers, 280
   ratings by, 4, 149–151, 211, 212
Teaching
   by adults, 33
   opportunities, 128–132
Teleology, 192–194, 198, 214–215
Television, 281, 288–289
Termites, 16, 17, 19, 32, 37
Thematic apperception tests, 147
Tit-for-tat strategy, 28, 57–60
Title I (Old Age Assistance), 320
Tolstoy, L., 36, 67
Trait groups, 12, 14–15
Transgressions, 169–177
Trial-and-error learning, 22–24
Trivers, R., 23, 27, 62–64, 267, 341–342, 348
Turiel, E., 95, 105, 114

**U**

Ultrasociality, 5, 11–41, 67
   definition of, 16
   and social insects, 17–21

Underwomaning, 252, 260, 266
Utilitarianism, 188–189, 191, 193–195, 199, 214, 214, 245

**V**

Values, 140, 142, 191, 192, 201–202, 212, 245
Verbal activity level, 104, 108, 207
Verbal behavior, 99–100, 122–133, 207
Verbalization of need, 128–132
Visiting patterns to older persons, 325–327
Vocalization, 75, 89
Volunteering help, 322, 330–333
Vulnerability to predation, 54, 56–57

**W**

Wasps, 14, 16, 19, 37
Welfare, 4, 168, 177–178, 180, 185
Whales, 5, 53–57, 60, 63
White, B., 281
Whiting, B., 227, 266, 267, 283, 286, 343
Whiting, J., 283, 286
Wilson, D. S., 14–15, 17, 26–27, 65
Wilson, E. O., 15, 16, 275–276
Winning, 256
Wisdom, 186
Wolves, 16
Woolman, M., 279
Work of children, 226, 237–238, 252, 259
Wrongness of behavior, 170–178, 180, 212

**Y**

Young, J. Z., 276

# DEVELOPMENTAL PSYCHOLOGY SERIES

*Continued from page ii*